The New International Money Game

Also by Robert Z. Aliber

MONETARY REFORM AND WORLD INFLATION

NATIONAL MONETARY POLICIES AND THE INTERNATIONAL FINANCIAL SYSTEM (editor)

CORPORATE PROFITS AND EXCHANGE RISK

THE MULTINATIONAL PARADIGM

YOUR MONEY AND YOUR LIFE

MONEY, BANKING, AND ECONOMIC ACTIVITY (co-author)

MANIAS, PANICS, AND CRASHES (co-author)

The New International Money Game

Seventh Edition

Robert Z. Aliber
*Professor of International Economics and Finance Emeritus at the
Booth Graduate School of Business of the University of Chicago*

palgrave
macmillan

First published 2011 by
PALGRAVE MACMILLAN

Palgrave Macmillan in the UK is an imprint of Macmillan Publishers Limited,
registered in England, company number 785998, of Houndmills, Basingstoke,
Hampshire RG21 6XS.

Palgrave Macmillan in the US is a division of St Martin's Press LLC,
175 Fifth Avenue, New York, NY 10010.

Palgrave Macmillan is the global academic imprint of the above companies
and has companies and representatives throughout the world.

Palgrave® and Macmillan® are registered trademarks in the United States,
the United Kingdom, Europe and other countries.

ISBN 978–0–230–01894–5 hardback
ISBN 978–0–230–01897–6 paperback

This book is printed on paper suitable for recycling and made from fully
managed and sustained forest sources. Logging, pulping and manufacturing
processes are expected to conform to the environmental regulations of the
country of origin.

A catalogue record for this book is available from the British Library.

A catalog record for this book is available from the Library of Congress.

10   9   8   7   6   5   4   3   2   1
20   19   18   17   16   15   14   13   12   11

Printed and bound in Great Britain by
CPI Antony Rowe, Chippenham and Eastbourne

Contents

List of Figure, Tables, and Boxes

Figure

Tables

Boxes

Preface and Acknowledgments

Several individuals have been important in the writing of this book. Martin Kessler first suggested that serious economic concepts could be discussed in a relatively light manner. Martin was a superb editor and a marvelous friend, and he is greatly missed. Fran Miller cheerfully typed the N drafts of the first edition. Without her encouraging feedback, the project would have stalled.

Robert Z. Aliber

List of Abbreviations and Acronyms

ABS	asset-backed securities
ADB	Asian Development Bank
AIG	American International Group
ARMs	adjustable interest rate mortgages
ATM	automatic teller machine
BBC	British Broadcasting Corporation
BIS	Bank for International Settlements
CAP	common agricultural policy
CDO	collateralized debt obligations
CDS	credit default swaps
CIF	cargo insurance and freight
CIR	Committee of Independent Republics
CMO	collateralized mortgage obligations
CPE	centrally planned economy
CPI	consumer price index
CXT	common external tariff
DFI	direct foreign investment (also FDI)
EBRD	European Bank for Reconstruction and Development
EC	European Community
ECB	European Central Bank
ECSC	European Coal and Steel Community
EEC	European Economic Community
EMS	European Monetary System
EMU	(European) Economic and Monetary Union
ENEL	National Corporation for Electric Energy (Italy)
ENI	National Hydrocarbon Corporation (Italy)
ERM	European Exchange Rate Mechanism
EU	European Union
ExImBank	US Export-Import Bank
FDIC	Federal Deposit Insurance Corporation
FOB	free on board
FRY	Former Republic of Yugoslavia
GATT	General Agreement on Trade and Tariffs
GE	General Electric
G-7	Group of Seven countries
G-20	Group of Twenty countries
IADB	Inter-American Development Bank
IBFs	International Banking Facilities
IBRD	International Bank for Reconstruction and Development (World Bank)

IMF	International Monetary Fund
IRI	National Institute for Industrial Reconstruction (Italy)
ITO	International Trade Organization
LIBOR	London Inter-Bank Offer Rate
LIFFE	London International Financial Futures Exchange
LTCM	Long Term Capital Management
MBA	Mexico, Brazil, Argentina
Mercosur	Mercado Comun del Sur (Common Market of the South)
MITI	Ministry for International Trade and Industry (Japan)
MOF	Ministry of Finance (Japan)
NAFTA	North American Free Trade Agreement
NTB	non-tariff barrier
NYSE	New York Stock Exchange
OECD	Organisation for Economic Co-operation and Development
OPEC	Organization of Petroleum Exporting Countries
OTC	over-the-counter (market)
P/E	price/earnings ratio
PMI	private mortgage insurance
PIC	petroleum importing country
PIN	personal identification number
RDF	Radio diffusion Française (France)
R&D	research and development
S&L	savings and loan
SAR	Special Administrative Region (of China)
SDR	Special Drawing Right
STO	State Trading Organization
TVA	Tennessee Valley Authority
UNCTAD	United Nations Committee on Trade and Development
USSR	Union of Soviet Socialist Republics
WTO	World Trade Organization
ZPG	zero population growth

Introduction

International finance is frequently viewed as an esoteric subject, understood by only a few speculators in the euro and the Swiss franc and the Japanese yen, and a handful of central bankers. In part, the mystery results from the specialized use of everyday language – 'gliding parities' and 'sliding bands,' 'support limits' and 'counter-speculation,' 'SDRs,' and 'derivatives,' 'zero coupon bonds,' and 'cross-rates' and 'tax havens' and 'transfer pricing.' Most of the words are straightforward, but both the meanings and the significance are elusive. The reader is deterred because of the effort required to learn a specialized language.

Once the jargon barrier is surmounted, a second problem appears – 'recognized experts' frequently disagree about the most appropriate causal explanation for the same event. Is the US dollar 'strong' in the currency market because US imports have declined as the United States entered a recession, or because interest rates on US dollar securities are high or because the US inflation rate has declined below 2 percent or because the US Government has developed a fiscal surplus? Is the US dollar price of gold low because the Russians are selling gold, or because the Chinese have reduced their gold purchases or because the world inflation rate has declined below 2 percent? When the US trade deficit increased to more than $800 billion in 2006, the experts disagreed whether the increase in the deficit was caused by the increase in US oil import payments or by the decline in the US competitive edge in manufacturing or because of an increase in the foreign purchases of US dollar securities or because the Chinese are reluctant to allow their currency to appreciate significantly in response to the surge in their trade surplus.

The 'experts' in both Washington and Beijing disagree on the causal relationship between Chinese purchases of US dollar securities and the US trade deficit.

And even when the experts agree on their analysis, their recommendations about the most appropriate policies to adjust large imbalances often differ. The experts can't agree on whether the US national interest is better served by continued reliance on the floating currency arrangement adopted in the early 1970s or by returning to a system of adjustable parities similar to the one that prevailed in the 1950s and the 1960s. Indeed, the experts can't agree on the US national interest in international financial relationships. Some experts in the 1960s proposed that the United States take the initiative in raising the US dollar price of gold to $70

1

an ounce or even to $100 an ounce. Most experts disagreed. Subsequently, market forces led to a surge in the US dollar price of gold. The experts observe – correctly – that national inflation rates were much lower when currencies were pegged to gold in the nineteenth century; these experts prefer low inflation rates and yet very few favor a return to the gold standard. A few experts want to abandon national currencies in favor of a worldwide money, while others want to eliminate the use of the US dollar as an international money, although few have advanced proposals that would achieve this result. Disagreements among experts about the most appropriate policy solutions leave readers puzzled and skeptical about the value of expert advice.

The New International Money Game seeks to break the language barrier. Technical issues are presented in a straightforward manner with minimal use of obscure terms. Metaphor is used to clarify concepts. Explanations are provided for why experts may disagree. No policy advice is offered – instead, the reader is offered the assumptions that are central to major policy issues.

The seven editions of this book span more than 35 years. International financial relationships have changed dramatically during this period, especially the approach toward the organization of the currency market and the monetary roles of gold. In the 1970s the idea that the Germans and the French would be successful in adopting a common currency would have seemed preposterous to many observers.

The first edition was completed in the early 1970s as the Bretton Woods system of adjustable parities for currencies – established in the mid-1940s to avoid a repetition of the 'beggar-thy-neighbor' policies of the 1930s – was breaking down. Foreign exchange crises seemed increasingly frequent since the mid-1960s. There was increasing concern about a shortage of gold and of international reserve assets. The US inflation rate had begun to increase in the late 1960s and to levels above those in some European countries. The stability of the US dollar as the centerpiece of international financial relationships was being questioned.

The second edition was completed in the mid-1970s as the international economy was moving from an inflationary boom to a recession that was more severe than any other in the previous 25 years. The decreases and increases in the price of the US dollar in terms of the German mark and the Japanese yen were much larger than anticipated by the proponents of floating exchange rates in the 1960s. The spin at the time was that the traders in the currency market required more time to adjust to the new floating exchange rate arrangement. Once they had this time, the proponents said that changes in currency values would more or less track differences in national inflation rates. A number of banks failed and others incurred significant losses as a result of changes in currency values

The oil-producing countries earned several hundred billion dollars a year in the mid-1970s as a result of the surge in the oil price. The major international banks seemed threatened by the statements that individual oil exporting countries might withdraw their deposits unless the top executives of the banks became more sympathetic to the interests of these countries.

The key concern at the time of the third edition that appeared in the late 1970s was whether the United States would be able to reduce its inflation rate, which was then approaching 15 percent a year. Investors rushed to buy gold and silver and other hard assets and collectibles including rare books and antiques in the search for hedges against the decline in wealth as the price level increased. The US dollar price of gold nearly reached $1000 in January 1980. The German mark and the Japanese yen were appreciating sharply. The central banks in Europe and Japan increased their purchases of US dollars to limit the appreciation of their currencies. The Federal Reserve adopted a sharply contractive monetary policy in the autumn of 1999 to reduce US inflation and to dampen the tendencies toward a stronger German mark and a stronger Japanese yen.

One impact of the much higher interest rates on US dollar securities was that foreign currencies began to depreciate. Another was that the US inflation rate declined sharply – and the oil price fell. The US housing and auto industries were depressed. Magazine articles highlighted the 'Superdollar.' US imports increased rapidly relative to US exports, and the United States developed a trade deficit. The US unemployment rate exceeded 10 percent.

The financial tsunami hit in July 1982 when Mexico announced that it did not have the money to pay the interest on its $90 billion of US dollar indebtedness. Suddenly the market value of the $800 billion owed by the governments and the government-owned firms in the developing countries declined sharply. Few investors were willing to pay 60 cents or 70 cents of good money for $1.00 of a Mexican loan or $1.00 of a Polish loan or $1.00 of an Argentinean loan. Some of these loans traded at 20–30 cents on the US dollar. The shock that triggered this crisis – a decline in the price of oil from $36 a barrel to $29 a barrel – led to the collapse of a small bank located in a shopping center in Oklahoma known as Penn Square. The value of the $1 billion of oil loans that had been acquired by Continental Illinois Bank in Chicago – the largest bank between the East Coast and the West Coast – was immediately questioned. Depositors – particularly other large banks and large firms – withdrew $10 billion from Continental Illinois, the first run on a major bank since the Great Depression. The solvency of hundreds of US thrift institutions, particularly savings and loan associations, was threatened as interest rates increased and real estate prices declined. Investors learned that 'a real estate loan in Houston is an oil loan in drag.' Eventually the US Government paid $140 billion to ensure that the owners of deposits in government-insured depositories were made whole.

By the mid-1980s a major US economic recovery was underway. The US inflation rate ranged between 3 and 4 percent – and this rate was declining as the unemployment rate was declining. The dark clouds had moved elsewhere – the annual US fiscal deficit was about as large as the total US Government spending had been a decade earlier. The US trade deficit continued to increase, and the smell of protectionism was stronger than in any period since the early 1930s.

The remarkable US economic expansion that began in 1982 ended in 1989; 20 million more Americans were at work in 1989 than in 1981. However, the US Treasury debt had increased from $1000 billion to $3000 billion over the same period. President Reagan had a conservative spiel, and reduced taxes, and yet adopted a Keynesian pump-priming policy of large fiscal deficits. One of the rationales was that large fiscal deficits would lead to pressures to reduce government spending and the role of the government in the economy.

The United States, once the world's largest creditor country, evolved into the world's largest debtor, a development without any historical precedent. One remarkable feature of this change was that the US Treasury did not borrow in a foreign currency. Moreover, US firms continued to invest abroad; few borrowed in a foreign currency to finance their investments in the United States. The change in the US net international investment position resulted because foreigners – especially Germans and Japanese – became large buyers of US dollar securities and US real assets, including the Rockefeller Center, the Pebble Beach Golf Course in California, the Steamboat Springs ski area in Colorado, and firms including Firestone Tire, Columbia Pictures, Columbia Records, and MGM-Universal.

The US recession of the early 1990s was triggered by the sharp collapse of real estate values, which was especially severe on the East Coast and in the coastal areas of California. Prices of office buildings in New York, Chicago, and Los Angeles and many other large US cities declined by 30–40 percent. Real estate developers went bankrupt. The lenders to these real estate developers, including many of the largest US banks, incurred losses in the tens of billions of dollars. The prices of the stocks of these lenders declined sharply. More US banks failed than at any time since the Great Depression. American business firms went through a remarkable period of restructuring, downsizing, and outsourcing, and this was especially true of firms that once had been the pacesetters in their industries – IBM, General Motors, Eastman Kodak, and Sears.

The collapse of commercial real estate values was a worldwide phenomenon – prices of office buildings in Toronto, Tokyo, London, Paris, and Frankfurt were declining. Economic events in Japan appeared to follow those in the United States – with a lag of 18–24 months. By mid-1992 the stock price indexes in Tokyo had declined to slightly more than one-third of their December 1989 value. Economic activity in Japan slowed, and Japanese exports increased rapidly while the country's imports fell sharply.

One of the remarkable developments since the early 1970s has been the most far-reaching financial revolution since the development of paper money. The number of new financial instruments has surged – futures contracts in currencies, options on futures contracts, foreign currency swaps, interest rate swaps, zero coupon bonds, collateralized mortgage obligations; and the list goes on and on. Home mortgages, credit card loans, student loans with similar attributes are packaged together and placed in a trust, and the trust then issues claims on the income streams in a process known as securitization. The flip is that interest rate coupons attached to traditional bonds are separated from the corpus and each of the coupons becomes a zero coupon bond. The rapid increase in the number of new instruments is traceable to the information revolution and the sharp decline in the costs of storing, manipulating, and transmitting financial data.

Exchanges for trading futures contracts and options on futures contracts have been established in more than 20 countries. Because more and more financial transactions have occurred in unregulated markets, regulations have been liberalized to reduce the handicap imposed on firms that transact in regulated markets.

One consequence of the decline in the costs of economic distance is that New York, London, Zurich, Frankfurt, Tokyo, Hong Kong, and Singapore have moved much closer to each other. Securities denominated in the euro, the Swiss franc, and the Japanese yen are viewed as closer substitutes for US dollar securities. The buzzword is globalization. Hundreds of mutual funds invest in the emerging markets. Because foreign securities are closer substitutes for US dollar securities, the opportunities to reduce the risk of a portfolio by geographic diversification are more difficult.

Another major development since the earlier editions is the dramatic change in the political landscape. The Berlin Wall is down and the two Germanys are reunified. The Union of Soviet Socialist Republics is passé and transformed into 15 'independent' countries. Poland, Hungary, and their neighbors in what had been Eastern Europe have moved toward much greater reliance on the market – in some cases under the guidance of the same sharp-elbowed fellows that ran the command economies; these countries have moved geographically into Central Europe. (Eastern Europe is probably getting too crowded, with a host of new countries including Estonia, Latvia, Lithuania, and Belarus). Yugoslavia has fractured into seven countries – Slovenia, Croatia, Serbia, FYR Macedonia, Bosnia and Herzegovina, and Montenegro and Kosovo. Czechoslovakia has splintered into the Czech Republic and Slovakia.

The German mark, the French franc, the Italian lira, and the currencies of eight of their neighbors have merged into a common currency, the euro. Initially, 11 of the 15 members of the European Union adopted the euro, and many if not most of the new entrants also are likely to adopt the euro.

China has achieved growth rates that have averaged nearly 10 percent a year for 30 years – a remarkable achievement; China now is one of the three or four major international economic powers. The ratio of China's trade surplus to its GDP has been much larger than that of any other country that has achieved sustained economic growth for an extended period. China's holdings of international reserve assets are larger than those of any other country.

The seventh edition of this book provides one more opportunity to reflect on international monetary developments since the end of the Second World War. The period breaks into two, with the dividing point in 1971; the previous 20 plus years was one of pegged currencies and declines in the reliance on direct controls on international payments and persistent and large and eventually larger US payments deficits – even though the United States had trade surpluses during every year. The subsequent period has been identified with floating exchange rates, although central banks have intervened extensively to limit the changes in the values of their currencies and especially the appreciations.

The move away from a pegged currency system was inevitable once the US inflation rate began to exceed 5 percent a year; a pegged currency arrangement is not feasible if inflation rates are more than 3 or 4 percent a year. The 'date of no return' for the move away from the adjustable parity arrangement occurred early in 1969, soon after Richard Nixon became US President. If the US Government had been able to induce Japan and Germany to revalue their currencies, the payments imbalances in 1970 and 1971 would have been much smaller, and the money supplies in Germany and Japan would have increased less rapidly. The result would have been a less severe world inflation, and lesser instability in the subsequent decades.

The counterfactual story is that once currencies had adjusted to the differences in national inflation rates, Germany, Japan, and other countries might once again have pegged their currencies to the US dollar while the United States would once again set a parity for the US dollar in gold at a level that would have enabled various central banks to add to their holdings of gold without purchasing the metal from the US Treasury.

The years since the early 1970s have been the most turbulent in monetary history. Increases in the US price level and in the price levels in most other industrial countries were much larger than had ever occurred in peacetime. Fifteen or so years after the move away from parities, central banks adopted 'inflation targeting' or 'price level targeting' as anchors for their monetary policies – in some ways a flexible version of having a parity for the currency.

The range in the variability of currency values has been four to five times larger than the range that would have been predicted on the basis of the difference in national inflation rates. There have been four waves of financial crises; the first involved Mexico, Brazil, Argentina, and ten or so other developing countries in the early 1980s. The second wave centered on Japan in the early 1990s, when most of the financial institutions failed because of the sharp decline in property prices and stock prices. About the same time, the banks in Norway, Finland, and Sweden failed as property prices and stock prices declined sharply. The Asian financial crisis was the third in this series; Thailand, Malaysia, Indonesia, and South Korea were involved – as were Russia, Mexico, Brazil, and Argentina. The United States, Britain, Ireland, Spain, and Iceland were in the fourth wave; property prices have declined sharply in these countries, usually by 30 percent or more.

Each of these waves of crises has followed a wave of credit bubbles; during each of these bubbles the indebtedness of a readily identified group of three, four, or more borrowers increased by 20–30 percent a year for three or more years. Thus the prelude to the developing country debt crisis of the early 1980s was that bank loans to the governments and government-owned firms in Mexico and the other developing countries increased by 30 percent a year for nearly 10 years. The prelude to the financial crisis in Japan in the 1990s was the rapid increase in bank loans for the purchase of real estate in the second half of the 1980s; there was a sharp increase in bank loans for real estate in three of the Nordic countries at about the same time. The prelude to the Asian financial crisis was a surge in the flow of money from the industrial countries to the emerging market countries; the motive for the flow was that the investment bankers had discovered a new 'asset class, emerging market equities.' The prelude to the financial crisis that began in the United States, Britain, Ireland, Spain, and Iceland in 2007 was a surge in bank loans for real estate.

The likelihood is high that the countries involved in each of these waves of bubbles were impacted by the same type of shock – and the initial presumption is that these shocks were external to most of these countries. Moreover, the likelihood that the second wave of bubbles was independent of the first seems low, and similarly the likelihood that the third wave was independent of the second also seems low.

The Asian financial crisis that began in July 1997 with the sharp depreciation of the Thai baht led to great concern about the stability of global financial arrangements. In the mid-1990s Thailand, Malaysia, and their neighbors had been achieving rapid rates of economic growth, captured by the term 'Four Dragons,' more or less the next generation sequel to the 'Four Tigers' – the city states of Hong Kong and Singapore, and Taiwan and South Korea. The World Bank published *The East Asian Miracle: Economic Growth and Public Policy*. The chatter was that post-millennium years would become known as the 'Pacific Century.' Perhaps. But the advent of this century was likely to be delayed by the bankruptcy of many of the firms and most of the banks in these countries.

The debacle in Thailand and South Korea and their neighbors in the last several years of the 1990s is similar to the sharp decline in real estate prices and stock prices in Japan in the first several years of the 1990s. In both cases bank credit for real estate purchases and investment had increased at a rapid rate – at a rate that was much too high to be sustainable.

The depreciation of the currencies of the countries in Southeast Asia that began in the second half of the 1990s led to a sharp change in their external payments position; there was a rapid shift from trade deficits to trade surpluses. The counterpart of this development was that the US trade deficit increased by almost the same amount as the change in the trade balances of Thailand and its neighbors. The increase in the US trade deficit corresponded to the increase in the flow of foreign money to the United States. Most of this money contributed to the surge in US stock prices.

The turbulence in the currency markets and the asset markets since the mid-1970s reflects that variability in cross-border flows of money. The increase in the flow of money to a country has the immediate impact of inducing an appreciation of its currency – unless the currency is pegged. In addition, the increase in the demand for securities available in the country will lead to increases in their prices. In turn, the increases in prices induce adjustments within the country so that its trade deficit increases by an amount that corresponds to the increases in the inflow of foreign funds.

1
A System Is How the Pieces Fit

The years since the early 1970s have been the most tumultuous in monetary history. The world price level in 2008 was more than five times higher than in 1970; never before have price levels increased so rapidly in so many countries. The US dollar price of gold at the end of 2008 was more than 25 times higher than the US$35 parity in 1970 – and this price had been 25 percent higher in the summer of 2008 than at the end of the year. A barrel of oil nearly reached $150 in June 2008, more than 50 times higher than at the end of 1970; the oil price had quintupled between 2003 and 2008 and then declined to below $50 toward the end of the year.

The US financial system had shattered. The two large government-sponsored lenders, Fannie Mae and Freddie Mac, that together carried the credit risk associated with more than 50 percent of US home mortgages, were placed in a US 'conservatorship' because they were effectively bankrupt; the individuals and firms that owned both the common stock and the preferred stock in these firms lost all their money. AIG, the largest insurance company in the world, required a massive loan from the US Government. The US investment banking industry collapsed; two of the five largest firms disappeared, one by bankruptcy and the other by a forced merger, while two of the other large investment banking firms sold themselves to large commercial banks. Many of the 20 largest US commercial banks were forced to take capital from the US Treasury.

The British banking system also was in turmoil. Northern Rock, the largest mortgage lender in the country, was taken over by the government. The British Treasury became a two-thirds owner of the Royal Bank of Scotland and a large owner of Lloyds. Similarly, banks in Ireland, Iceland, and even Switzerland received large capital investments from their governments.

This global financial crisis led to a recession in most of the large industrial countries. Japan imported a recession because of a decline in the foreign demand for its autos and electronics and other manufactures. Similarly, Taiwan, South Korea, and Singapore experienced sharp declines in their exports. The growth rate in China declined sharply, and 20 million migrant workers became unemployed.

The global financial crisis that began in the summer of 2007 is the fourth since the early 1980s. The first involved the inability of Mexico, Brazil, Argentina, and ten or so other developing countries to make the payments on their US dollar-denominated debt in a timely way. Their currencies depreciated sharply and many of the borrowers and banks in these countries became bankrupt; some large US banks that had made extensive loans to these borrowers would have failed if the regulatory authorities had not connived in the fiction that these loans were performing. The second financial crisis was in Japan in the 1990s, when most of the commercial banks and investment banks and insurance companies failed. At about the same time, many of the banks in Finland, Norway, and Sweden failed. The third crisis began in the second half of 1997 when the Thai baht depreciated sharply, which triggered the depreciation of the Malaysian ringgit, the Indonesian rupiah, the Philippine peso, the South Korean won and eventually the Russian ruble in the summer of the 1998, the Brazilian real in January 1999, and the Argentinean peso 2 years later. Once again many of the domestic banks in these countries failed when the currencies depreciated.

Each of these financial crises followed the implosion of a credit bubble, which had involved the rapid growth in the indebtedness of a particular group of borrowers, often at annual rates of 20–30 percent for 3 or 4 or more years. During the 1970s the major international banks increased their loans to the governments and government-owned firms in Mexico and other developing countries at the annual rate of 30 percent; the external indebtedness of these countries increased from $120 billion at the end of 1972 to $800 billion 10 years later. During the 1980s and especially during the second half of that decade the real estate loans of the banks headquartered in Tokyo and Osaka increased at the rate of 30 percent a year. Industrial firms invested in real estate because the rates of return from ownership of property were so much higher than the rates of return on investment in manufacturing. The prelude to the Asian financial crisis of the second half of the 1990s was a large inflow of money from mutual funds and pension funds, which led to increases in stock prices and real estate prices. The global financial crisis that began in 2007 followed the sharp increase in real estate prices in the previous 4 or 5 years.

These financial crises have occurred in waves, which generally have involved four or five or more countries usually at about the same time, although the debacles in some of the non-Asian countries in the late 1990s followed the collapse of the Thai baht by more than a year. Similarly, the credit bubbles that preceded these crises also occurred in waves that involved four or five or more countries at the same time. That so many countries were involved in these bubbles and crisis at about the same time suggests that they have had a common origin.

The changes in the values of national currencies in the foreign exchange market since the early 1970s have been much larger than ever before, even after adjusting for differences in national inflation rates. The US dollar price of the euro varied within a range of 80 percent between 1999 and 2008 even though the annual inflation rates in the United States and Europe usually differed by less than 1 percentage point. At the end of June 2008, the US dollar price of the euro approached $1.58, higher than at any previous time – but by September the US dollar price declined to less than $1.30. The US dollar price of the British pound was above $2.00 in June 2008; by the end of the year the price had declined below $1.50.

Despite the turmoil in the currency markets and the security markets, national income and wealth surged at least until the second half of 2008. Tens of million of people have moved from poverty to the middle class in China, Brazil, South Korea, Mexico, and other emerging market countries as their economies have become more fully integrated with global markets.

In 1980 the United States was the world's largest international creditor country; its net foreign assets were larger than the combined net foreign assets of all other creditor countries. By 2000, the United States had evolved into the world's largest debtor country, and its net foreign liabilities were larger than the combined net foreign liabilities of all other debtor countries. This dramatic change is the US international investment position has no precedent in the experience of any other country. Moreover, this change did not occur because US goods and services were too expensive; the paradox is the combination of a US trade deficit that has reached 6 percent of US GDP and yet a value for the US dollar that is so low that Europeans and Latin Americans have traveled to New York and other US cities for their Christmas shopping. Tourists find Disneyland in California and Disneyworld in Florida significantly less expensive than their counterparts in Europe and Asia.

US net international indebtedness has been increasing twice as rapidly as US GDP. Mexico and Thailand and numerous other countries also experienced rapid increases in their indebtedness relative to their GDPs in the 1990s; when the inflow of foreign money declined abruptly, their currencies depreciated sharply and most experienced financial crises.

The sharp increase in US stock prices in the late 1990s was a bubble; the market value of US stocks doubled in the 3 years after December 1996 when the Chairman of the Federal Reserve commented on 'irrational exuberance.' Stock prices in Europe increased almost as rapidly as in the United States. The implosion of this bubble in stock prices was followed by a recession but not by a financial crisis.

The likelihood that the surges in national price levels, the large changes in currency values, the waves of asset bubbles, and the massive failures in banking systems are independent and unrelated events is low. A model is needed to link the large variations in the values of national currencies and the episodic surges in the prices of real estate and of stocks in different countries.

Scientists in every field search for models that describe how the basic components of their universe fit together. The pervasive view in astronomy until the fourteenth century was that Venus and Mars rotated around the Earth. Galileo and Copernicus used the data obtained from new and more powerful telescopes to propose a revolutionary model that had the Earth, Venus, Mars, and the other planets rotate in a more or less flat plane around the Sun. Their model integrated the Sun, the planets and their moons, comets and asteroids and also placed the solar system within the constellation of stars.

Einstein integrated the speed of light, matter, and energy. Biologists seek to relate the understanding of the most minute and basic components of life, including genes and chromosomes. Climatologists view patterns of wind, rainfall, temperature, and ocean currents in a comprehensive model.

Those who seek to become the Copernicus of the international financial arrangements must integrate the relationships among the monetary systems of the United States, Britain, Japan, Germany, and France and their neighbors that use the euro, Switzerland and more than 150 other countries each with its own money. The models must highlight the relationships among the changes in the values of the US dollar, the British pound, the Japanese yen, the euro, the Swiss franc, and other currencies with the changes in the rates of growth of money in each country and with the changes in the prices of domestic goods and of real assets and of securities denominated in each currency.

The relationships among the planets in the models developed by Copernicus and Galileo have not changed in the last five centuries; Mars will never replace Venus as the planet closest to the Earth. In contrast, those who deal with international monetary issues recognize that the financial arrangements are in flux; the British pound was the dominant international currency during the nineteenth century before it was displaced by the US dollar at the outset of the First World War. While the US dollar has remained the dominant currency, the supremacy of the US dollar has been challenged by the shift in the US international financial position to the largest international debtor. Gold was at the center of international monetary arrangements in 1900, but at the periphery of these arrangements in 2000.

Similarly, the relationships among both the levels and rates of growth of the GDPs of individual countries change; Japan was at the top of the GDP growth rate hit parade in the 1950s and the 1960s while China was in number one position on this hit parade in the 1980s and the 1990s. Countries often experience relatively high rates of growth during the first two or three decades after they begin to industrialize; subsequently their growth rates slow. Britain was the first country to industrialize during the middle decades of the nineteenth century; Germany and the United States then followed in the last several decades of that century.

Fitting the pieces: central bank monetary policies

From time to time, the descriptive title for international financial arrangements has changed. The 'gold standard' was the applicable name during much of the nineteenth century and until the First World War; its dominant feature was that the central bank in each of the participating countries had a fixed price for gold in terms of its own currency. In the 1920s there was a modest change in the name to the 'gold exchange standard'; its distinguishing feature was that some central banks acquired securities denominated in the British pound and in the US dollar as part of their international reserve assets. From the end of the Second World War to the early 1970s 'the Bretton Woods system' was the descriptor (derived from the village in New Hampshire where the treaty that established the International Monetary Fund (IMF) was signed); one of its key attributes – that currency values would be fixed or at least not allowed to vary significantly – was derived from the gold standard. Its innovative feature was that changes in currency values would be discrete and in accord with the provisions of the IMF Treaty. This system of adjustable parities became obsolete in the early 1970s; the thrust of the successor arrangement of floating exchange rates was that currency values would change in response to market forces, much like the prices in the markets for stocks, bonds, and commodities. One initial name for the new arrangements was the 'Post-Bretton Woods system.' Many central banks have intervened extensively to limit changes – and especially increases – in the price of their currencies and the term 'Bretton Woods II' has been applied to these arrangements.

Virtually every country except the relatively small ones has its own national money, produced by its national central bank. Iceland, with a population of 300,000, has an independent central bank and its own currency. Panama and Luxembourg have much larger populations than Iceland but do not have a national currency; Panama has used the US dollar as its money for more than 100 years and Luxembourg used the Belgian franc as its money before the adoption of the euro.

Central banks – the Bank of England, the Bank of France, the Federal Reserve, the Bank of Japan, and the Swiss National Bank – were established to enhance financial stability by providing an 'elastic supply of currency.' Each central bank initially had a fixed price for its currency in terms of gold, which was part of a 'marketing plan' to induce individuals to acquire its currency notes. During the last several decades of the nineteenth century the British, French, German, and American monetary systems were linked by flows of gold from one country to others. The theory was that the money supply and the price level in a country would increase in response to the inflow of gold; conversely, the money supply and the price level would decline in response to an outflow of gold. When a national currency was pegged to gold, it was also pegged to every other currency that was also pegged to gold.

Each central bank was supposed to insulate its national economy from the financial problems of individual banks by reducing the likelihood that depositors might rush to get their money from one or several banks at the same time, because of their concern that if the bank closed, they would lose part or all of their money. Since the banks would not have enough money to meet the demands of many depositors at the same time, these rushes for money sometimes caused the result they anticipated.

During the First World War governments borrowed from their banks to get much of the money needed to finance military expenditures. After the war governments imposed additional objectives on their central banks; one was to achieve a low inflation rate and another, at least in some countries, was to achieve a high level of employment.

Since the early 1970s central banks have not been committed to maintain a fixed price for their currencies; instead, many have given greater priority to domestic objectives in managing the growth of their money supplies. One consequence – at least for a while – was greater divergence in national inflation rates.

The unique development at the end of the twentieth century was that 11 of the then 15 member countries of the European Union (EU) adopted the euro – essentially a supranational currency – as the successor to the German mark, the French franc, the Italian lira, and the currencies of eight other countries. The European Central Bank (ECB) is owned by the national central banks and develops a common monetary policy for its members. Britain and several other members of the EU have retained their national currencies, although Greece subsequently adopted the euro. Most of the countries that are scheduled to join the EU appear likely to adopt the euro, eventually if not immediately.

Fitting the pieces: the market in national currencies

International transactions for the purchase of goods, services, and securities differ from domestic transactions in one unique way – either the buyers or the sellers must transact in a foreign money. When Americans buy new Mercedes and new Volkswagens, they pay US dollars to the dealers, who in turn pay the US subsidiaries of Mercedes and of Volkswagen. These subsidiaries then take most of these dollars to the currency market to buy the euro so they can pay their head offices in Germany.

One of the two basic approaches toward organizing the currency market is that each central bank buys and sells its currency to limit the changes in its price, usually within a narrow or modest range; this practice follows from the gold standard arrangements. The other basic approach is that the price of each national currency increases and decreases in response to changes in demand and supply, much like the prices of pork bellies and of government bonds and of copper and of stocks. The intermediate approach is that central banks buy and sell their currencies to limit changes in their prices – and to achieve some other national objectives.

For most of the 200 years from the advent of the United States as a newly independent country until the early 1970s, the US dollar price of the British pound was pegged because the British pound had a parity for gold of 87 shillings 6 pence per ounce while US dollar had a parity of $20.67 per ounce. The ratio of the two gold parities was $4.86 = 1 British pound after an adjustment for the small difference in the gold content of British coins and of US coins. The US dollar price of the British pound was not pegged between 1797 and 1821, during and immediately after the Napoleonic Wars. Nor was the US dollar price of the British pound pegged during and after the US Civil War – from 1861 until 1879. The move away from pegged values for currencies reflects the fact that wars have been associated with higher inflation rates and larger differences in national inflation rates.

A system of pegged currency values requires that central banks buy and sell their own currencies to limit the changes in their prices. The securities that central banks acquire after they have sold their currencies in the foreign exchange market are grouped as international reserve assets.

Some central banks began to acquire securities denominated in the British pound and securities denominated in the US dollar at the end of the nineteenth century because they wanted the interest income on these securities. Nevertheless, central bank holdings of gold were the largest component of international reserve assets until the 1960s. Then securities denominated in the US dollar became the largest component. In the 1960s and the 1970s central banks acquired securities denominated in the German mark and in the Japanese yen as international reserve assets, although securities denominated in the US dollar still account for two-thirds of international reserve assets; securities denominated in the euro are the second largest component.

During the nineteenth century, the stability of international financial arrangements resulted from the self-interest of individual countries. In contrast, during the twentieth century national governments signed treaties, agreements, accords, and communiqués that contained commitments about how they would manage their currencies.

One pattern about changes in currency values since the early 1970s is evident from the comparison of changes in the Japanese yen price of the US dollar with the changes in the Swiss franc price of the US dollar. At the end of 1970, the Japanese yen had a parity of 360 while the Swiss franc had a parity of 4.30; the 'cross rate' was 84 Japanese yen for each Swiss franc. At the end of 2008 the Japanese yen price of the US dollar was 111 while the Swiss franc price of the US dollar was 1.11; the Japanese yen price of the Swiss franc was 100. The declines in the price of the US dollar in terms of both the Swiss franc and the Japanese yen have been much larger than the changes in the Japanese yen price of the Swiss franc. The inference is that many of the shocks that have led to changes in the value of the US dollar have centered on the United States.

Inflation rates in the twentieth century were much higher than in the nineteenth century. The American and British price levels at the end of the nineteenth century were not significantly different from those at the end of the eighteenth century, although there had been extended episodes of sharp increases and then decreases of price levels within the century. In contrast, the US price level at the end of the twentieth century was nearly 20 times higher than at the beginning, and the British price level was more than 25 times higher.

Increases in national price levels in the twentieth century occurred in three major episodes; the first was during and immediately after the First World War and the second was during and after the Second World War. The third surge in national price levels occurred in the 1970s and differed from the earlier episodes both because the price increases were larger and because they occurred during peacetime.

During the nineteenth century governments accepted changes in their domestic price levels as a way to maintain parities for their currencies in terms of gold. In contrast, during most of the twentieth century governments – especially the governments of large countries – were reluctant to accept a significant external constraint on the choice of their domestic economic policies.

Financial crises were more severe in the last several decades of the twentieth century than in the earlier period, although the period between the First World War and the Second was also marked by major crises.

The waxing and waning of financial hegemony

Copernicus believed that the orbits of the planets were determined by gravitational pulls and would not change; similarly, he was not concerned that the relative size of the various planets might change. In contrast, one of the dominant features of international financial arrangements is that the economic standing of individual countries and of their currencies changes.

Britain was the dominant economic power during the nineteenth century and London was the primary international banking and financial center; Britain also was the largest international creditor country. The British pound was the dominant currency; import prices and export prices were quoted in terms of the pound and world trade was financed by credits denominated in the pound. US railroad firms went to London to borrow money to finance their expansion.

The United States supplanted Britain as the dominant economic power during the First World War; US GDP was three times larger than the British GDP. For the next 30 or 40 years – until the 1960s – the United States became an even more ascendant economic power, in part because of the dislocations to production and trade in both Europe and Asia associated with the Second World War. US industrial capacity surged, while wartime damage reduced productive capacity in Britain, Germany, France, and Japan.

At the end of the 1940s it seemed as if the United States would remain the dominant economic power 'until the end of time.' US industrial supremacy seemed unchallenged and unchallengeable. The US dollar was the dominant currency, in part because of US industrial leadership and in part because the US commitment to a low inflation rate seemed stronger than that of any other large country.

During the 1950s and the 1960s the United States developed a persistent payments deficit; US holdings of gold declined by more than half and foreign holdings of US dollar securities surged. Despite the decline in US gold holdings, the US international financial position seemed impregnable, in part because the United States was the world's largest net international creditor country.

In 1971, an event that seemed unthinkable 10 years earlier occurred: the US Treasury stopped selling gold at $35, and the price of gold began to increase; by the end of the decade the price had nearly reached $1000. The US dollar depreciated extensively relative to the German mark and the Swiss franc and the Japanese yen through most of the 1970s.

In 1980 the United States began to develop a persistent annual trade deficit and the US net international creditor position began to decline and by the late 1980s the United States had evolved into an international debtor; the United States became the world's largest international debtor in 2000.

The transformation of the US net international investment position from the world's largest creditor to the world's largest debtor occurred because foreign investors and central banks wanted to increase their holdings of US dollar securities. The invisible hand was at work, and the United States developed the trade deficit that was the mirror of the trade surpluses of Japan, China, and many other developing countries.

The plan of the book

The chapters in this book are arranged in two major groups. The first group – Chapters 2 through 13 – focus on macro international topics, including changes in the monetary roles of gold, the costs and benefits of floating exchange rates and of pegged exchange rates, the waves of credit and asset bubbles since the 1970s, and the evolution of the United States from the world's largest creditor country to the world's largest debtor. The second group – Chapters 14 through 24 – has a micro focus and centers on specific topics, including the nature and impacts and causes of globalization, the impacts of differences in national tax rates on the competitive position of firms producing in different countries, and the changes in the structure of the international banking industry. The impacts of the Organization of Petroleum Exporting Countries (OPEC), the cartel of the oil-producing countries, on the supply of petroleum in the long run are analyzed.

The first chapter in Part I (Chapter 3) summarizes the changes in the monetary role of gold in the last 300 years. The changes in international financial arrangements are summarized in Chapter 4. The changes in organization of the foreign exchange market are described in Chapter 5, and the attention is given to why the range of movement in the price of national currencies in the foreign exchange market has been so large relative to the difference in national inflation rates. The unique international roles of the US dollar are reviewed in Chapter 6. The thrust of Chapter 7 is the growth of the offshore banking market, identified by the mismatch between the currency in which a transaction is denominated and the currency of the country where the transaction occurs. The causes of the several inflations of the twentieth century are examined in Chapter 8. The relationships among the various asset price bubbles since the 1980s are reviewed in Chapter 9. The causes of the financial crises are analyzed in Chapter 10. The explanations for the change in the US international investment position from the world's largest creditor to the world's largest debtor are evaluated in Chapter 11. The thrust of Chapter 12 is the factors that determine the rate of growth of national money supplies. One of the major concerns since the breakdown of the Bretton Woods system of adjustable parities has been monetary reform; a major question is how to maintain an open trading system in an increasingly fractious world.

The first chapter in Part II (Chapter 14) analyzes the globalization of markets over the centuries and then provides an overview of subsequent chapters. The thrust of Chapter 15 is on the impacts of national taxation and regulatory regimes on the international competitiveness of firms that produce in different countries. The question addressed in Chapter 16 centers on the impact of the financial crisis on the competitiveness of US banks relative to banks headquartered in various foreign countries. The impact of the production-limiting arrangements by OPEC on the Malthusian specter that the world petroleum supplies will be exhausted is analyzed in Chapter 17. Whether national markets for bonds and stocks are segmented or integrated is evaluated in Chapter 18. The focus of Chapter 19 is the revolution in finance and the surge in the number of new financial instruments – futures and options and swaps and credit default swaps. Whether there is a pattern in the ownership of multinational firms is discussed in Chapter 20. The economic success of Japan in the 1960s, 1970s, and 1980s is summarized in Chapter 21. The transformation of China from a command economy to a market economy is reviewed in Chapter 22. Russia's evolution from a Marxist command economy to a market economy is reviewed in Chapter 23. The final chapter considers the likelihood these international monetary and financial problems will become less severe.

2
The Name of the Game Is Money – But the Disputes Are about Where the Jobs Are

International finance

International finance is a game with two sets of players: one set includes the politicians and bureaucrats and the central bankers in different countries and the other set includes the chief financial officers and treasurers of giant, large, medium-large, medium, medium-small, and small firms and banks and hedge funds, and other financial institutions. The government officials want to win elections and secure a niche in the histories of their countries for enhancing economic well-being and financial stability. The cliché is 'good jobs at good wages.' A few aspire to get their portraits on the national currency. And to do so, they want to manage their economies to provide more and better-paying jobs and greater financial security for their voters. These officials want to avoid sharp increases in inflation rates and sharp declines in the prices of their currencies.

The chief financial officers and corporate treasurers want to profit from – or at least avoid losses from – changes in currency values, changes that are inevitable in a world with more than 150 national monies. The traders in the large international banks and in the hedge funds want a lot of variability in the prices of individual currencies; the larger the variability, the greater the scope for trading profits.

Changes in the price of the US dollar

Consider the changes in the Japanese yen price of the US dollar in the last 50 years. Throughout the 1950s and the 1960s the Japanese currency had a 'fixed price' of 360 yen per US dollar, which had been set in the late 1940s when Japan was still occupied by US military forces. The productive power of the Japanese economy then was far below that of the early 1940s as a result of destruction of factories and business relationships during the war and the loss of what had been several colonies. In the early 1970s, the Bank of Japan stopped pegging the yen – largely at the insistence of the US Government – and the currency appreciated to 175 yen per dollar by the end of the decade. In contrast, in the early 1980s the yen declined sharply; in the second half of the 1980s the yen again appreciated, and by 1997 had reached 80 yen per dollar – briefly. For much of the period between

1995 and 2008 the yen traded in the range of 110–150 yen per dollar, although at the end of 2008 the yen had again appreciated to 90 yen per dollar.

As the yen appreciated the managers of most Japanese firms and many Japanese politicians were concerned that exports from Japan would be less profitable and decline, while imports would increase because they would be less expensive and they would pose more of a competitive threat to Japanese firms. The Bank of Japan often bought US dollars to limit the appreciation of the yen in the effort to support the competitive position of Japanese firms in global markets.

When the euro first appeared in January 1999 as the successor to the German mark, the French franc, and the currencies of nine other countries, the US dollar price of the euro was $1.19. Then the euro depreciated for years to $0.84. Subsequently the euro appreciated and – despite a few jiggles – reached $1.58 by the end of June 2008 before declining to $1.40 at the end of 2008.

A lot of money could be made – and was made – by forecasting the changes in the Japanese yen price of the US dollar and the changes in the US dollar price of the euro. Much money was lost by failure to anticipate these changes. Changes in the Japanese yen price of the US dollar were associated with changes in the Japanese trade surplus; as the yen depreciated, Japanese exports would increase relative to its imports. US producers of a wide range of products – textiles, steel, autos, and electronics – complained, especially in Washington, that the Japanese followed unfair trading and currency management practices, and were much more eager to sell to Americans than to buy from them. The view in much of corporate America was that the Japanese Government pursued policies that maintained an artificially low price for the yen, which was a boon for Japanese exporters and costly to US firms that produced similar products.

The inevitability of changes in the values of individual currencies reflects the differences among countries in their inflation rates and structural factors, including rates of population growth and rates of economic growth. As a result, payments by the residents of one country to those of all other countries as a group may differ from their receipts from foreign residents.

Every economic unit has a 'budget constraint,' and must keep its payments more or less matched with its receipts; this constraint holds for individuals, families, firms, and governments as well as for regions within a country. West Virginia has a budget constraint and even New York City has one – although New Yorkers learned that lesson slowly in the late 1970s when residents of other cities and states balked at financing the city's budget deficit. Similarly, every country has a budget constraint; its payments to foreigners cannot exceed its receipts from foreigners for an extended period.

Either governments will adopt measures so that these payments and receipts are more or less equal at the prevailing currency values or these values will change to bring payments and receipts into balance. Often it seems easier for changes in currency values to bring payments and receipts into balance rather than to change monetary policy and fiscal policy to bring payments into balance with receipts.

At the global level, an array of shocks – changes in inflation rates, surges in the oil price, national savings rates, rates of growth of GDP, productivity gains in export industries, import prices, and the rates of return on securities denominated in the domestic currency – causes payments to foreigners to differ from receipts from them at the prevailing currency values.

Within a domestic economy, there is only one currency; hence adjustments to these shocks cannot occur through changes in currency values. Instead, adjustments occur in the relationships among prices and wages and rates of growth of household income in different regions and through changes in unemployment rates. Now that more than 12 countries have adopted the euro as their money, changes in currency values can no longer occur among them – unless a country leaves the European Union. The shocks across countries usually have been much, much larger than the shocks among the regions within a country, with the result that the adjustments also are likely to be larger. Still, some of the large shocks to countries have been caused by changes in currency values.

The value of the currency, jobs, and inflation

The answer to 'Is it better to be rich or to be poor?' seems straightforward; it is always better to be rich because the rich have all the opportunities that the poor have and many more. The answer to 'Is it better to have a high value or a low value for our country's currency?' is more complex.

The higher the value of a country's currency, the greater its purchasing power in terms of foreign goods and services and securities. But the higher the value of the currency, the weaker the competitive position of domestically produced goods in foreign markets and the stronger the competitive position of foreign goods in the domestic market.

The debate about the appropriate value for a country's currency is between consumers who benefit from a high value for the currency and producers who benefit from a low value. Some countries, especially those in Asia – initially Japan and Taiwan, then South Korea, and most recently China – have followed export-led growth policies. Each of these countries maintained a low value for its currency; each wanted to increase the number of people employed in firms producing manufactured goods that could be sold abroad. Each wanted to increase its share of the world market for these goods, which meant that each needed relatively low prices for these goods. The increase in market share captured by the firms in one of these countries was inevitably at the expense of the market share of firms in other countries, almost always those that had industrialized in earlier decades.

Within each country an increase in the value of the currency means that consumers are better off because imports are cheaper while the producers – at least those in the tradable goods industries – are worse off because profits and employment are depressed by the higher level of imports.

The management of currency values

The government of each country decides whether to peg its currency to some other currency (much as currencies had been pegged to gold at the end of the nineteenth century) or whether to allow market forces to determine the value of the currency. A currency floats by default unless a central bank has a parity and adopts measures to limit the deviations of its currency from this parity.

There are numerous variants on these two basic options – if the central bank pegs its currency, it is likely to allow its currency to float within a modest range around the parity. Even in the absence of a parity or peg, a central bank may buy and sell its currency to limit the range of its daily, weekly, and monthly changes – and many sell their currencies to limit the decline in competitiveness that would follow from appreciation.

Currencies were pegged during most of the nineteenth century and until the First World War; the major extended period of floating exchange rates began in the early 1970s. When currencies were pegged, a major question involved the measures that governments would take to reduce payments deficits or, less frequently, payments surpluses – would the adjustment involve market-induced changes in relative prices and relative incomes or would monetary or fiscal policies be changed to reduce these imbalances? A related question was whether the countries with the payments deficits or those with the payments surpluses would take the initiatives toward reducing payments imbalances that were deemed too large.

The authorities in each country generally agreed that if the adjustment to an extended payments imbalance were to involve a change in the parity of a currency, it was preferable that a foreign country take the initiative in effecting this change. The authorities in the countries with the payments surpluses believed that their counterparts in the countries with the payments deficits should take the initiative because they had mismanaged their economies and allowed their price levels to increase. In contrast, the authorities in the countries with the payments deficits believed that the countries with the surpluses were acquiring international reserve assets at too rapid a rate, and thus induced payments deficits in their trading partners.

Bankers – especially foreign exchange traders in the large international banks, multinational firms, and in hedge funds – seek gains from changes in the prices of currencies; the larger the changes in these prices, the larger their trading revenues and profits. The revenues and profits of the banks from foreign exchange trading are much higher when currencies are floating than when they are pegged. (Consider the extreme case – when countries peg their currencies with a very narrow range of movement around their parities, the trading revenues are very small. When Germany and France and their neighbors adopted the euro several thousand individuals that traded their currencies against each other moved to trade some other financial instrument.)

Parities and shocks

The cryptic history of the last 200 years is that during much of the nineteenth century and until the First World War each currency had a fixed price in terms of gold. Inflation rates in different countries were similar. Once the war began, the convertibility of most currencies into gold was suspended as governments used their banking systems as a source of finance. During the war, inflation rates differed sharply. Most countries found it impossible to return to their prewar parities after the end of the war because their price levels had increased so much more than the US price level.

Most countries again had parities for their currencies from the second half of the 1940s to the early 1970s as a membership commitment to the International Monetary Fund (IMF); each member was obligated to prevent its currency from deviating from its parity, initially by more than one-quarter of 1 percent and then by more than 1 percent. Since the early 1970 most currencies have been floating, sort of, or at least not pegged, although most central banks have intervened extensively to limit the appreciation of their currencies.

The rationale for the establishment of the IMF during the 1940s was the view that much of the financial turmoil in the 1920s and the 1930s resulted from sharp movements in currency values. During the 1950s and especially during the 1960s central bankers were reluctant to change the parities for their currencies even after it had become obvious to many market participants that changes were necessary. One reason – perhaps the dominant reason for the delays – was the belief that the domestic political costs of changing a parity would be high, both when a country devalued and when it revalued its currency.

Thus in the late 1960s and the early 1970s it seemed obvious to many Americans and to a few Japanese that the yen was undervalued – Japan had a very large trade surplus in part because the value for the yen that had been set in the late 1940s when the country's productive capacity was very modest provided a substantial competitive advantage to Japanese firms in foreign markets. The view in Washington was that the Japanese should revalue the yen, perhaps from 360 yen to 300 yen so Japan's imports would increase more rapidly and its exports would grow more slowly. The view in Tokyo was that the Americans should devalue the dollar to offset the adverse impact of the increase in the US price level on the international competitive position of US firms. If the Japanese revalued the yen, Japanese autos would cost more in the United States. These autos would also cost more if the Americans took the initiative and devalued the dollar. In both cases US imports from Japan would increase less rapidly and fewer US workers in autos, steel, and textiles would lose their jobs.

Eventually, the US Government took the initiative and forced a revaluation of the Japanese yen in August 1971 – an event recorded in Japanese monetary history as Nixon Shockku II (Nixon Shockku I was the US opening to China).

Three times in years (1961, 1969, and 1971) the German mark price of the US dollar was reduced, in part because the German Government wanted to dampen inflationary pressures at home and in part to reduce the likelihood that substantial numbers of American troops would be withdrawn from Europe to reduce the US payments deficit. In the 1960s, French President Charles de Gaulle bought $2 billion of gold from the US Treasury in an attempt to force the US Government to increase the US dollar price of gold. De Gaulle believed that an increase in the US dollar price of gold would benefit those of his domestic supporters that owned gold and restore the prestige of France and its record of monetary stability and also demonstrate that the US dollar was a weak currency and the United States an untrustworthy ally.

The increase in the US dollar price of gold that General de Gaulle sought occurred after an extended delay; the first increase occurred in December 1971 when the US dollar price of gold was raised to $38 an ounce (effectively a devaluation of the US dollar by 12 percent) and the second in February 1973 when the US dollar price was increased to $42. These increases were window-dressing, since the US Treasury would not buy or sell gold at these prices.

Private investors ignored the changes in the US Treasury's gold parity, and bid the price to nearly $200 in 1974 and then to almost $1000 in January 1980. De Gaulle appeared prescient. Throughout the 1970s, the 1980s, and the 1990s, the US Treasury continued to value its 250 million ounces of gold at $42 an ounce, even though the market price was much higher; in the 1990s the gold price was in the range of $280–$400 and in the first half of 2008 the price increased to over $1000.

Pegged currencies and floating currencies

In February 1973, the United States, Germany, Japan, and the other major industrial countries abandoned the Bretton Woods system of adjustable parities, and allowed their currencies to float. During the nineteenth century Britain suspended the convertibility of the pound into gold during the Napoleonic Wars and the Americans suspended convertibility at the beginning of the Civil War. Suspension of convertibility was associated with a significant increase in the domestic price level as the governments borrowed from the banks to get the money to fight a war. These currencies floated as long as the commitment to convert the domestic money into gold at a fixed price remained suspended. The British pound was again pegged to gold several years after the end of the Napoleonic Wars while the US dollar was pegged to gold 14 years after the end of the Civil War.

The unique aspect of the move to the floating exchange rate arrangement in the early 1970s was that this change occurred when the major industrial countries were not at war. Since the early 1970s the prices of the US dollar in terms of the German mark and then after 1999 the euro, the Canadian dollar, the British pound, and the Japanese yen have varied within a wide range. From time to time central banks have intervened to limit changes in the value of their currencies, often to limit the appreciation because of the decline in the competitiveness of domestic goods that would otherwise occur.

Paradoxically, central bank purchases of the US dollar have been much more extensive when currencies have been floating than when they were pegged. Moreover, many countries had much larger imbalances as measured by the ratios of their trade deficits and their trade surpluses to their GDPs.

Devaluations and revaluations

Business fortunes are made on the ability to forecast changes in the prices of national currencies. George Soros earned more than $1 billion from the depreciation of the British pound and the Italian lira in the autumn of 1992 when the European Monetary System (EMS) broke up. In contrast, political futures became frayed as a result of these changes. Under a pegged rate system, the monetary authorities in each country 'fixed' the price of the national currency in terms of some other currency, usually the US dollar. A few currencies including the US dollar had parities in terms of gold. The direction of the change in a country's parity was almost always predictable: if a country had a payments deficit quarter after quarter and its holdings of international reserve assets were decreasing, the safe prediction was that any change in the parity would be a devaluation. Similarly, if a country had had payments surpluses and its holdings of international reserve assets were increasing, the safe prediction was that any possible change in its currency would be a revaluation. The timing of these changes and their amounts were less readily predictable.

For a while it seemed as if there were 'periodic cycles' in the changes of the parities of several currencies. The British pound was devalued in 1914, 1931, 1949, and 1967, almost as if there was an 18-year 'cycle.' But this 'cycle' was interrupted by the sharp depreciation of the pound in 1975 and 1976. Still, the British pound hit a low against the US dollar in 1985. The French franc had generally been devalued every 10 years – in 1919 (the devaluation that might have come in 1929 was delayed until 1936), 1939, 1949, 1959, and 1969. In 1979 the French franc, along with the other European currencies, began to depreciate rapidly relative to the US dollar.

Devaluations and revaluations of national currencies were more frequent in the late 1960s and early 1970s than in the 1950s. Currency crises occurred in November 1967 (British pound), May 1968 (French franc), September 1969 (German mark), June 1970 (Canadian dollar), May 1971 (German mark, Dutch guilder, and Swiss franc), August 1971 (Japanese yen, British pound, and French franc), and June 1972 (British pound and Italian lira). The increase in the frequency of these changes was closely associated with greater divergence in national inflation rates, and especially with the increase in the US inflation rate in the second half of the 1960s.

The changes in the price of the US dollar in terms of the German mark and several other European currencies and the Japanese yen are shown in Table 2.1. These currencies have tended to appreciate and depreciate at the same time relative to the US dollar. The range of movement in the price of the US dollar in terms of the German mark and the Japanese yen has been large – and much larger than would have been forecast on the basis of the contemporary difference between the US inflation rate and the counterpart rates in Germany and in Japan. The mark and the yen appreciated sharply in the late 1970s, depreciated rapidly in the first half of the 1980s, and then appreciated in the second half of the 1980s. Both the mark and the yen depreciated in the mid-1990s. Since 2001 the euro and the Japanese yen have appreciated.

Relations among countries and the standing of their political leaders are affected both by the changes in the price of their currencies and by the measures adopted to reduce payments surpluses and payments deficits. During the 1960s

Table 2.1   The price of the US dollar, 1970–2008

	SF	JY	BP	DM
1970	4.31	358	2.39	3.65
1971	3.92	315	2.55	3.27
1972	3.77	302	2.35	3.20
1973	3.24	280	2.32	2.70
1974	2.54	301	2.35	2.41
1975	2.62	305	2.02	2.62
1976	2.44	293	1.70	2.36
1977	2.00	240	1.91	2.11
1978	1.62	195	2.03	1.83
1979	1.58	240	2.22	1.73
1980	1.76	203	2.39	1.96
1981	1.79	220	1.91	2.26
1982	1.99	235	1.61	2.38
1983	2.18	232	1.45	2.72
1984	2.59	251	1.16	3.15
1985	2.08	201	1.45	1.94
1986	1.62	159	1.48	1.58
1987	1.28	124	1.87	1.78
1988	1.50	126	1.81	1.78
1989	1.55	144	1.61	1.69
1990	1.29	134	1.93	1.49
1991	1.36	125	1.87	1.52
1992	1.46	125	1.51	1.61
1993	1.48	112	1.48	1.73
1994	1.31	99	1.56	1.55
1995	1.15	103	1.55	1.44
1996	1.35	116	1.69	1.56
1997	1.46	130	1.65	1.79
1998	1.38	116	1.66	1.67
1999	1.59	102	1.62	.99
2000	1.64	115	1.49	1.07
2001	1.68	132	1.45	1.13
2002	1.39	119	1.61	.95
2003	1.24	107	1.79	.79
2004	1.13	104	1.93	.80
2005	1.31	118	1.72	.85
2006	1.22	119	1.96	.76
2007	1.17	114	2.00	.68
2008	1.09	109	1.83	.68

Note: SF = Swiss franc, JY = Japanese yen, DM = German mark, BP = British pound;
Units per US dollar except for British Pound which is US Dollars Per Pound – End of
Period Averages.
Source: International Financial Statistics.

Germany had large payments surpluses and the United States had even larger payments deficits. The US Government kept leaning on the German Government to adopt measures to reduce the country's payments surpluses, including various payments to offset some of the costs of keeping American troops in Germany; these pressures eventually forced the downfall of Ludwig Erhard as Prime Minister. The 10 percent surcharge on US imports adopted by the US Government in August 1971, followed by the 17 percent revaluation of the yen, advanced the date of Prime Minister Sato's resignation in Japan.

Throughout the 1960s US Government officials were extremely reluctant to recognize that an increase in the US dollar price of gold was inevitable. The monetary authorities in Britain and France forced this increase in 1971 by suggesting that they would buy more gold from the US Treasury – which would have led to a decline in its gold holdings below $10 billion. An increase in the US dollar price of gold was more than a US problem. Gold-producing countries such as South Africa and the Soviet Union would benefit from an increase since the value of their gold production would be higher and eventually they might produce more gold. The countries that owned large amounts of gold such as France, Switzerland, Italy, and Germany would gain since the market value of the gold owned by their central banks would be higher. The United States also would benefit because the market value of the US Treasury's gold holdings, then much larger than those of any other country, would increase.

The finance minister in virtually every country is concerned with changes in the price of the national currency because of the implications for the profits of the domestic firms that produce export- and import-competing goods and the employment in the firms that produce these goods. In the late 1970s, European governments complained that the price of the US dollar was too low and that US exporters had an unfair competitive advantage in international markets. In the early 1980s, these finance ministers complained that interest rates on US dollar securities were too high, which greatly handicapped their ability to follow policies that might offset their high unemployment rates. (They didn't complain about the exceptionally high profits their exporters were earning on their US sales when the US dollar was strong.) Part of the job of being a finance minister in Europe involves determining which US policies warrant complaints.

Similarly, whether the Japanese yen price of the US dollar should be higher involves not only the United States and Japan but also Germany and South Korea and other countries that produce goods competitive with those produced in Japan. Toyota's profits vary inversely with the price of the yen; when the yen is weak, Toyota, Nissan, Honda et al. have a large competitive advantage in foreign markets. As the yen becomes stronger, the export competitiveness of these firms declines. The Japanese auto makers will experience a decline in their profit rate if they fail to raise the selling prices of their autos in foreign markets (indeed, some may incur losses); however, if they raise their selling prices to maintain their profit rates, the volume of their sales and their market share will decline.

Between 2004 and 2007 US attention about 'unfair' practices was directed at China as its global trade surplus and its bilateral trade surplus with the United States surged – and as employment in US manufacturing declined. Increasingly, Wal-Mart was viewed as an outlet for goods produced in China. Much of Chinese manufacturing involved the assembly by unskilled labor of high-value components imported from Japan and South Korea. The US Treasury leaned on the

Chinese Government to revalue the yuan or to allow it to float. In 2006 the Chinese Government began to manage a gradual appreciation of the yuan.

Exporting national problems

Changes in currency values redistribute jobs and profits among firms and workers in different countries. The immediate consequence of a strengthening of the Japanese yen and the euro was to reduce profits in Japanese and German export industries and to increase profits and permit more rapid wage increases in competing US industries. In the late 1980s and early 1990s, the profitability of Mercedes Benz, BMW, and Porsche from their North American sales declined because of the appreciation of the German mark. Both Mercedes and BMW established plants in the United States because production costs were lower than in Germany.

Exporting national problems is a classic form of international behavior. Foreign votes are not counted in domestic elections. The political costs of domestic measures that might solve an unemployment problem, an inflation problem, or a 'depressed industry' problem frequently are higher than the political costs of exporting the problem. Yet if one country exports its unemployment problem, some other countries are likely to experience a loss of manufacturing jobs. In the Great Depression of the 1930s, nations exported their unemployment with 'beggar-thy-neighbor' policies – tariffs were raised to reduce imports and currencies were devalued to increase exports. Few countries were – or are – eager or willing to import unemployment.

In the 1990s, countries once again appeared to be adopting policies that might qualify as 'beggar-thy-neighbor.' The annual Japanese trade surpluses then were more than 3 percent of its GDP, which helped maintain employment in Japanese manufacturing firms when domestic demand growth was extremely sluggish. Between 2005 and 2008 China developed a massive trade surplus, which was larger than Japan's both in absolute value and in relation to its GDP. Many other countries want large trade surpluses to compensate for sluggish growth of domestic demand.

Obviously not every country can run a large trade surplus at the same time; to the extent that one country achieves a larger trade surplus, then another country will incur the counterpart larger trade deficit. Since 2000 many countries have had trade surpluses and the United States has had the counterpart trade deficit.

The politics and technology of money

The costs of communication have declined sharply in the last 30 years as a result of remarkable advances in computing power and telecommunications. The costs of economic distance have declined dramatically and national markets for goods and securities are much more closely linked. Tokyo and London have moved much closer to New York in economic terms. At the end of the twentieth century several dozen global financial firms had significant trading activities in these three major financial centers as well as in regional centers such as Frankfurt and Singapore.

The politics of international money is decentralized. Each country has its national interests and its economic objectives. Each national central bank wants to control the rate at which its money supply grows so as to achieve its inflation target and its employment and growth objectives. Because the objectives and economic structures of countries differ, some countries prefer higher rates of money supply growth than others. Germany and Switzerland, for example, are at the top of the hit parade of countries that want a low inflation rate. Other countries place higher priority on a low level of unemployment.

International monetary arrangements must accommodate these divergences in the priority attached to a low inflation rate and a high level of employment. International institutions including the IMF in Washington, the Bank for International Settlements (BIS) in Basle, Switzerland, and the Organisation for Economic Cooperation and Development (OECD) in Paris provide frameworks for coordinating national policies. Finance ministers meet twice a year at the IMF. Presidents and Prime Ministers of the Group of Seven Countries (G-7, née G-3 and now G-8) meet twice a year to discuss the coordination of their policies – or at least to talk about how they might coordinate policies if they were to coordinate them. And small groups of finance officials meet to discuss problems of common interest – which almost always means the size of the trade imbalances and the values of different currencies.

The forms of international financial coordination are varied. Central banks borrow national currencies from each other when their holdings of foreign currencies decline, and from time to time they intervene jointly in the currency market. Some modest steps have been taken to develop substitutes for gold in central bank holdings of international reserve assets. Such coordination, while useful as a counter to the decentralized decisions of national governments, is rarely an effective substitute for centralized decision-making.

In December 1991 the member countries of the then European Community committed themselves to develop a common currency by the late 1990s, in what has become known as the Maastricht Agreement. These countries agreed to a set of criteria to facilitate this move; each agreed to reduce its inflation rate below 3 percent, to reduce the ratio of its fiscal deficit to its GDP to no more than 3 percent, and to hold the ratio of government debt to national income below 60 percent. Soon after most of the Europeans began to learn of the costs of accepting this commitment when interest rates in Germany climbed to very high levels as the Bundesbank adopted a contractive monetary policy to reduce the inflation that followed from the reunification of West Germany and East Germany. Britain, France, and the other European countries imported these high interest rates from Frankfurt because their currencies were pegged to the German mark; indeed, their interest rates were modestly higher than those in Frankfurt because investors were concerned that their currencies might depreciate relative to the mark. Since they did not have the economic stimulus of a large fiscal deficit like the one in Germany associated with bringing living standards in the East to the level of those in the West, their inflation rates were below the German rate. As a result, real interest rates in these countries were higher than those in Germany. Germany's neighbors in the European Union (EU) imported recessions. In September 1992, Britain and Italy stopped pegging their currencies within the EMS; they were then able to reduce their interest rates significantly. Spain and Portugal and the Scandinavian countries followed their lead.

Still, the train to a common currency moved on schedule and 11 of the 15 countries in the EU adopted the euro in January 1999. Two other members of the EU have adopted the euro since then. In effect the central banks in these countries have become branches of the new European Central Bank (ECB). The adoption of a common currency has eliminated uncertainty about changes in currency values on payments within this group of countries. The underlying concern is that unemployment in one country (or several countries) may increase to high levels, and the political authorities may be feeble in their responses because they have no control over monetary policy and their use of fiscal policy to expand demand is constrained by their treaty commitments to limit their fiscal deficits.

The move to a common European currency has meant that some governments in Europe have had to raise taxes relative to expenditures. Unemployment rates in France and some other countries have been above 10 percent. President Chirac of France called an election, and the Socialists won – on the basis of promises of less severe policies. But the contractive fiscal policies were continued.

The challenge of the newly industrializing countries

One of the great stylized facts is that economic growth is associated with industrialization. Labor moves from farms and villages to factories and cities. Often the departure of labor from farms has a negligible impact on agricultural output, since there may have been too many laborers on the land relative to its productive capacity. Initially the factories produce basic manufactured commodities, often textiles and clothing and bicycles and kitchen utensils.

The owners of the factories begin to search for foreign markets, in part because prices abroad may be higher than in the domestic market. They begin to challenge the market share of foreign firms. They are likely to have the advantage of lower wage rates; they may also have the advantage of a low value for their currency.

Japan used its advantages of relatively low wages and a low value for the yen to increase its exports of manufactured goods in the 1950s and the 1960s. At the outset Japanese firms benefited from a large domestic market which enabled them to obtain economies of scale. Once their unit costs had declined, they were in a position to use this advantage to increase their share of foreign markets. Since the names of the Japanese firms were not at first known to consumers in foreign countries, they often gained market share by selling at lower prices and in the discount stores in the low-income neighborhoods where consumers were extremely price conscious.

Japanese industrialization involved moving up the quality chain and producing higher value-added goods, in part because as household incomes increased, consumers wanted better products. The quality and variety of Japanese exports increased. Initially the Japanese used the dollars they earned from their exports to buy more primary products. The pattern was that Japanese exports were competitive with US-produced goods in the US market and with British-produced goods in the British markets. The job losses associated with increased imports from Japan were visibly evident – but it was difficult to see the job gains associated with the increased exports to Japan.

South Korea and China mimicked the Japanese experience. South Korea lacks natural resources, and the success of its firms in foreign markets resulted from low wages and a low value for the currency and the desire to capture market share from the Japanese.

The new international money game

One concept associated with the gold standard was the 'rules of the game' – the practices that central banks would follow so they could maintain parities for their currencies. Rules seek to ensure that conflicts among authorities in different countries are resolved in accord with established procedures. When rules constrain national policies, countries sometimes ignore the rules and search for a legal justification later, as did President Nixon when the US Treasury closed its gold window in August 1971. During the 1970s, the rules and procedures governing currency market interventional practices of central banks eroded and practices were increasingly ad hoc. Exchange crises were less frequent, yet the conflicts between finance ministers in different countries about currency values – and about trade imbalances – became more severe.

Corporate treasurers and individual investors play against this background of changing values for national currencies in the foreign exchange market. They borrow money in the countries in which interest rates are low and invest the money in countries where interest rates are high. They borrow currencies that they expect to fall in value, and acquire securities denominated in currencies they anticipate will appreciate. Sharp foreign exchange traders and corporate treasurers earned millions of dollars – and German marks and Swiss francs – for their companies in the late 1960s and early 1970s by correctly anticipating changes in currency parities. Hedge funds earned billions in 1992 from selling the British pound and the Italian lira in anticipation that these currencies would depreciate. Investors made billions of dollars from their bet that the Mexican peso would be devalued in 1994.

Not all corporate treasurers, however, participated in these profits. In the 1960s, some of them believed the statements of the authorities that parities would not be changed, invested accordingly, and lost their jobs – and others deserved to. Corporate treasurers are paid big bucks and lots of pounds and euros – for doing 'smart finance.' During the mid-1970s, some firms reported losses in the tens of millions of dollars because of changes in currency values. In 1992 several Japanese oil firms reported losses of more than $1 billion as a result of their (misguided) currency transactions. The corporate treasurers of international firms are paid to know how to profit from differences in interest rates in various countries and from changes in currency values, and from the misfortunes of finance ministers.

Many foreign exchange traders developed great confidence in their ability to predict changes in currency values during the adjustable parities period. They continued to speculate when currencies began to float. Some profited. Some did not – Banque du Bruxelles reported losses of $60 million; Franklin National, $42 million; Herstatt, $70 million. These were the last large losses ever reported by Franklin and Herstatt, for both firms then went bankrupt.

Bankers and corporate treasurers learn and adapt – or they are replaced by those that learn and adapt. By the 1980s the large international banks were reporting annual profits of several hundreds of millions of dollars from trading national monies. These banks reported profits on their currency transactions when the US dollar was appreciating, and they reported profits when the US dollar was depreciating. A key question became the source of these profits – since the currency market is a zero-sum game, if the banks as a group consistently secure profits on their currency transactions, then it must be at the expense of some other groups.

In addition to predicting changes in currency values the international money game involves firms and individuals circumventing their national regulations. Indian peasants hoard gold because they believe the precious metal is a better store of value than the rupee. Shoppers in Warsaw hold US dollars and the euro as stores of value; indeed, the prices of apartments in Warsaw, Moscow, Istanbul, and Tel Aviv are quoted in the US dollar, and the sellers often will accept payment only in the US dollar and the euro. The US dollar holdings of Russians are almost as large as their holdings of rubles. American banks have established branches in London and Nassau and the Cayman Islands to avoid the regulations of US monetary authorities.

Interdependence of business and currency values

One view about the money game – a view reinforced by the daily newspaper columns – is that changes in currency values and international business competition are independent of each other. A competing view – the view of this book – is that these events are related, and that patterns of international trade and investment are affected by changes in currency values. Changes in currency values in turn result from changes in investor views about inflation rates and especially changes in anticipated inflation rates and the international capital flows undertaken in response to changes in these views.

In the 1950s and even more in the 1960s, US firms were on a global march (much as they had been in the 1920s) and rapidly expanded their sales abroad and their ownership of productive facilities in many foreign countries. US companies competed aggressively in Canada, Europe, and Latin America, buying some of their host-country competitors and forcing others into insolvency. Machines Bull, the last independent French-owned computer firm, could not survive in the competitive international league because the world price level for computers, set by IBM, was too low relative to French production costs. Nor could Rolls-Royce continue to compete in jet aircraft engines, for the prices set by its US competitors – General Electric and the Pratt and Whitney division of United Technologies – were too low relative to British production costs.

Rolls went bankrupt and then was restructured. British Leyland, the largest auto firm in Britain, was forced into bankruptcy because British costs were rising more rapidly than the world price of automobiles.

In the late 1970s and even more in the late 1980s, Japanese firms expanded their foreign investments. The Japanese auto firms were extremely vigorous competitors; within a span of 15 years they had upgraded the size, styling, and quality of their product lines. Japanese consumer electronics firms dominated the global industry and especially the production of quality components; the pace of new product development was exceptional.

The Asian Tigers – Taiwan, south Korea, Hong Kong, and Singapore – have experienced rapid growth, much like Japan. Then the dragons – Thailand, Malaysia, Indonesia, and, to a lesser extent, the Philippines, achieved high rates of growth. China realized growth rates of more than 10 percent a year beginning in the late 1970s, and the growth rate was significantly higher for the seacoast provinces.

These remarkable economic achievements led to the view that a Pacific Century was dawning, and that the US role as the dominant economic power in the twentieth century would be displaced. But the bloom about Japan faded in the early 1990s as stock prices and real estate prices fell sharply. By the mid-1990s the Japanese banks were retrenching, and reducing both their foreign loans and their foreign offices.

The drama of international money reflects the contrast between the politics and the technology of money. Each of the securities in the world – currency notes, bank deposits, government bonds, and mortgages – is denominated in one national currency or another; each currency – the US dollar, the euro, the Japanese yen, and the British pound – is a brand name, more or less like the brand names on automobiles, cigarettes, toothpastes, detergents, and cornflakes. The advantages of a national money are rarely questioned. Some of these advantages may seem obvious. A national money – like a national airline, a steel mill, and, at one time, a branch of the Playboy Club – brings prestige. Control of the production of a national money brings profit. Kings and presidents finance wars in Algeria and Vietnam and Iraq and build monuments to themselves with newly produced money.

Control over the production of money frequently means that the supply of money increases more rapidly than the demand, which leads to declines in its purchasing power. Inflation is an indirect or backdoor form of taxation: the US price level in 2007 was nearly four times higher than the US price level in 1970. The purchasing power of a 1970 dollar was 20 cents in 2007, and the negative rate of return was about 6 percent a year. Debtors benefited greatly from the decline in the purchasing power of money, especially in the 1970s – and the biggest debtor was the US Treasury. Taxation through the printing press and inflation is easier and less messy than raising tax rates; inflation tax is hidden, at least for a while. Sovereigns manipulate monetary policy because they want to secure full employment, speed growth and development, fight wars, or accomplish some other worthy objective that will win the approval of their constituents.

Central bankers and finance ministers may not be able to make their country's economic policies effective unless they can isolate their national market for money and credit from the international market. The US military draft of the 1960s provides an analogy: if too many potential draftees moved to Canada or Sweden or failed to register, the draft would not have been effective. Similarly, if too many holders of US dollar securities or British pound securities anticipate the actions of the authorities and move their money abroad, their governments' policies will be frustrated.

Over the last several decades the links among national monies have become even stronger as a result of changes in technology and the sharp reduction in the costs of transportation and communication across national borders. As these costs diminish, the effectiveness of national monopolies in the production of money declines. As knowledge about foreign investment opportunities grows and the cost of taking advantage of these opportunities declines, differences in national monetary systems become increasingly important.

In a world of isolated countries, kings had monopoly power over their subjects' monies; there was no other place for these subjects to send their wealth and no other currency in which they might hold their funds to escape the sovereign's taxes. The politics of money was largely national. But the monopoly power of kings and presidents has been declining, and the constituents of various governments are adjusting to this new world more rapidly than the governments. Governments frequently need international agreements to revise established institutions, and negotiating these agreements takes years.

Today, because of low-cost transportation and instantaneous communication, the several national markets for monies, bonds, deposits, and shares denominated in the various currencies are – in fact – parts of one international market. At any given moment, the price of IBM shares in Amsterdam and the price of IBM shares in London – and in the other foreign centers where IBM shares are traded – differ only by pennies from the price in New York. A particular group of traders known as 'arbitragers' buy these shares in the centers where they are cheap and sell them where they are dear to profit from the difference, thus keeping prices in line. The technology of money is international.

Part I

International Monetary Arrangements, Money, and Politics

3
Gold – How Much Is a 'Barbarous Relic' Worth?

President John F. Kennedy once observed that the US balance-of-payments problem was the second most worrisome issue he had to deal with; the first was avoiding a nuclear war. His concern was that the US Government might have to increase the US dollar price of gold, which would be costly internationally because it would break the commitment that the US gold parity of $35 was fixed forever and costly domestically because it would be interpreted as an indicator of profligate government spending policies. Yet when President Richard Nixon closed the US Treasury's gold window in August 1971 and suspended gold sales and then agreed to increase the US parity to $38 several months later and then to $42 about a year later, the international response was mild and the adverse domestic political fallout was trivial.

Nixon's decision to increase the US dollar price of gold was ironic. In his 1960 bid for the presidency, Nixon had suggested that the US dollar would be devalued if Kennedy were elected President. Nixon was right – Kennedy was elected President and the US dollar was devalued! Kennedy's estimates of the domestic and foreign political costs of devaluation proved much too high – and he greatly underestimated the domestic and the foreign policy costs to the United States of adhering to a US dollar price of gold that was too low.

Gold's role in monetary affairs often has been subject to ironic twists. John Maynard Keynes called gold a 'barbarous relic.' Charles de Gaulle said only gold could be the cornerstone of a new international monetary system. Both may have been correct.

The morphing of commodity gold into money

Gold has had an important role as a store of value and as a means of payment for many centuries. Societies at great distances from each other and with no apparent connection with each other – Peru, China, and Turkey – used gold for ornamentation and as a store of value. Currently a cliché for a valuable reputation is 'as good as gold.' The term 'gold standard' is one of highest repute. Gold prizes are awarded to first-place winners in the Olympic competitions.

The evolution of gold from a commodity into a money predates written history. A money has three essential characteristics – it stores value, it can be used in payments at low cost, and it is a unit of account – a measuring rod or a yardstick. Virtually every commodity is a store of value; yard sales and garage sales are efforts to convert used clothes and household goods – which have 'stored value' – into a more liquid asset, money. Impressionist paintings and antiques and postage stamp collections store value. If a commodity is to evolve into money, the costs associated with its use in payments must be low relative to the value of the payments. A commodity can be used as a unit of account only if it is of uniform quality or homogenous, so that units of the same size or weight are readily interchangeable – virtually perfect substitutes for each other.

Why was a money desirable? How did gold develop a monetary role? And why did gold satisfy the need for money better than virtually every other commodity?

Without money, goods were exchanged through barter, which was time-consuming. First, an individual that wanted to buy a good had to find someone that would be willing to buy a good that the individual had for sale. Then the buyer and the seller had to agree on a price for the exchange of the two goods – how many cows had the same value as a particular horse? Moreover, the values of the goods offered by both parties to the transaction had to approximate each other.

Eventually some individuals realized that the use of an intermediate good in payments would reduce the costs of transactions, provided that the intermediate good was homogenous, readily divisible into small units and would maintain its purchasing power. The sellers of different goods could state their prices in terms of a standard unit of the intermediate good measured by weight – this is the unit-of-account function. The sellers of various commodities could exchange these items for units of the intermediate good, and thus they would not need to spend time searching for goods to buy that had values approximating those of the items they wanted to sell. As long as the intermediate good was divisible into small units, the number of units of the intermediate good used in payment could be easily matched to the value of the payment.

One attribute that made gold an attractive intermediate good was that it was homogeneous – one ounce of gold was virtually identical with another ounce, regardless of where the gold had been mined. A second attribute was that gold was readily divisible into small units. Gold could be minted into large coins of high value and into smaller coins of lower value (although the smallest unit of gold that could be readily coined was too valuable to use for payments of small value). Moreover, gold had a high value relative to its weight, so the costs of transporting gold in payments were low – much lower than the costs of using any other commodity in payments. The costs of storing gold were lower than the costs of storing other commodities because of its high value-to-weight ratio. Gold was durable; it did not 'wear out.'

The high costs of mining ensured that the supply of gold would not increase rapidly – which meant that the price of a market basket of goods was likely to be more stable in terms of gold than in terms of those commodities whose supplies might increase more rapidly. Hence gold was a better store value than virtually every other commodity.

Silver was the dominant commodity money until the sixteenth century. Silver has some of the attributes of gold, including its durability and homogeneity, but it has a somewhat lower value-to-weight ratio – which reflects that silver has been significantly more abundant than gold. Using silver to make payments was more costly than using gold because of its lower value-to-weight ratio. Silver coins have proved more useful than gold coins for payments of low value.

Both gold coins and silver coins were used in different regions of the world at the same time. The sellers of many goods quoted prices in terms of both gold coin and silver coin – unless the price of gold in terms of silver had been fixed, either by a mint or a bank. A fixed price between gold coins and silver coins did not simply happen: government policies were necessary to fix or peg the price of gold in terms of silver. In the middle of the nineteenth century, the US Government set the price ratio of 15:1 (15 ounces of silver had the same US dollar value as one ounce of gold). But this ratio proved unsatisfactory because discoveries of these precious metals led to a more rapid increase in the supply of silver than in the supply of gold. Gold was becoming more valuable because it was becoming scarcer. Individuals began to hoard gold, which led to pressures to increase its price in terms of silver.

Because governments found it impossible to set a price of gold in terms of silver that would persist without leading to the hoarding of gold, the use of both gold and silver as money at the same time was discarded. Gold eventually dominated silver as the paramount commodity money.

Fiat currency and the money-back guarantee

The monetary history of the last 300 years is that fiat or paper monies have displaced gold because they were less costly to use in payments, especially in payments of very large amounts. Moreover, the production of a paper money is immensely profitable, because the purchasing power of a $1000 currency note and even a $100 currency note is many times greater than the costs of the expensive paper and the printing. Initially, the firms that wanted to produce paper money could receive a charter from their governments only if they accepted the commitment to convert the paper money into gold at the discretion of the owner of the paper money, which was designed to forestall excess production of the notes; this convertibility requirement was like a 'money-back guarantee' for the holders of the paper money.

Individuals and firms that held the paper money incurred the risk that its purchasing power might decline either because too much paper money had been produced (the same factor that led to a decline in the value of silver) or because the producers of the paper money could not fulfill their promise of a money-back guarantee.

The potential cost of the convertibility requirement was that if individuals became concerned that a bank that had produced a paper money might be in financial difficulties, they would rush to convert the paper money into gold. The bank then would need to sell assets to obtain gold and the prices of these assets would decline with the result that the financial difficulty that the holders of the paper money initially had anticipated would occur – almost a self-fulfilling event. Moreover, the decline in the prices of these assets would jeopardize the financial strength of other banks that owned similar assets.

The history of banking involves the development of institutional arrangements to reduce the likelihood that an individual bank or a group of banks would fail because of 'runs' – a sudden rush by depositors to convert the currency notes they owned into some other money that they believed would be a superior store of value in highly uncertain times.

Central banks were established as 'lenders of last resort' to provide a superior currency so the banks would not need to sell any of their loans or other securities to get the currency to pay the depositors that were apprehensive the bank might fail.

The convertibility requirement – the money-back guarantee – was a two-edged sword, because it constrained central banks from adopting policies that might help them cope with immediate financial problems, especially their government's need for money. During wars governments suspended the convertibility requirement so they could obtain money from the banks to pay their armies.

The decline in the monetary role of gold

One element in the monetary history of the first half of the twentieth century was the efforts by the governments of different countries to reduce the constraints on money supply growth imposed by the need to convert the national money into gold – or some other national money – on demand. As long as the producers of paper money were subject to the convertibility requirement, the monopoly power was 'limited'; eliminating this requirement enhanced the ability of governments to produce more money.

In September 1931 the Bank of England stopped buying and selling gold; the British authorities wanted the freedom to pursue a more expansive monetary policy to cope with a high level of unemployment. In 1933 the US Government required all US residents to sell their gold to the US Treasury as a way to protect American banks from the need to convert their deposit liabilities into gold; otherwise many more banks would have failed.

Gold's role as a domestic money declined in the twentieth century, both because individuals and firms found it less costly to use paper money in payments and because governments suspended the convertibility requirement to enhance their monopoly power. The flip side of the decline in the role of gold as money is that the purchasing power of paper monies has declined relative to the purchasing power of gold – the result that the money-back guarantee had been designed to forestall (which was why the money-back guarantee was abandoned). The US price level has increased by a factor of four since the US Treasury closed its gold window in 1971; the world price level is five times higher.

Some individuals hold gold as a store of value – either as a hedge against inflation or as a precaution against a political crisis that might reduce the acceptability of paper monies. Some investors buy gold to profit from anticipated increases in its price – and some sell gold that they have borrowed to profit from decreases in its price.

Similarly, gold's role as an international money has declined; central banks rarely use gold as a means of payment. Payments imbalances among countries are financed primarily by transfers of deposits denominated in the US dollar and in the euro.

The suspension of gold transactions by the US Treasury in 1971 was a response to a shortage that had persisted for most of the previous 50 years – and to the rapid increase in the production of paper monies that began during the First World War. National price levels increased sharply and the world price level in the early 1920s was nearly twice as high as before the war. Britain and several of the other European countries that had suspended the convertibility of their currencies into gold hoped that they would be able to return to their parities soon after the end of the war. Because national price levels had nearly doubled, central bankers were concerned that a gold shortage would develop because the mining companies would be squeezed between a sharp increase in their production costs and a selling price that was the same as in 1900. Moreover, the private demand for gold would be larger because the prices of silver and of other metals that were competitive with gold had increased relative to the price of gold. Finally, the central banks in newly independent countries in Central Europe would acquire gold as international reserve assets – as 'backing' for their currencies which would reduce the gold available for other countries. Government officials were fearful that the shortage of gold would lead to downward pressure on national price levels and complicate or delay the economic recovery. Several conferences sponsored by the League of Nations recommended that central banks hold securities denominated in the British pound and in the US dollar rather than gold as an international reserve assets.

The US dollar price of gold was increased to $35 in 1934 to stimulate the US economic recovery from the Great Depression; the belief was that the US consumer price level would increase and reverse the 30 percent decline that had occurred in the previous 3 years. Several years later, France and Italy and the Netherlands increased the price of gold by about the same percentage amount.

The increase in the monetary price of gold by about 70 percent in the 1930s led to a 'gold glut' because the amount of gold produced each year greatly exceeded the amount demanded by private parties. Excess gold flowed to monetary authorities and especially to the US Treasury, which experienced a 'Golden Avalanche': US gold holdings increased from $7 billion in 1934 to $20 billion in 1939.

The Second World War led to increases in the national price levels, although at less rapid rates than during the First World War. The gold glut soon disappeared and once again the mining companies were squeezed between higher production costs and an unchanged selling price. Private demand for gold increased anew, since gold was becoming progressively cheaper in terms of silver and other commodities.

US gold holdings peaked at $24 billion in 1949 and declined by $5 billion in the 1950s. Initially, the sale of gold to foreign central banks was viewed as a desirable way to provide the financial basis for the growth in world trade. By the early 1960s the concern about a gold shortage first became acute. US gold holdings declined by $8 billion in the 1960s, and there was growing recognition that the central bank demand for gold was larger than the available supply from new production.

Box 3.1 $35 an Ounce and 3.1416 Are Not the Same Kind of Numbers

The choice of $35 as the new parity for the US dollar in January 1934 was a historical accident; the new parity might have been $30 or $40. President Roosevelt had been convinced that the way to stimulate the US economy was to increase the US dollar price of gold by a significant amount, perhaps by 100 percent. Gold production would increase in response to the higher price. More gold would be sold to the US monetary authorities; the US money supply would increase, which in turn would lead to increases in the consumer price level. As a result, business firms would no longer incur losses because of declines in the value of their inventories, fewer firms would go bankrupt, and banks would no longer be threatened with insolvency by the decline in the values of their loans.

To increase the US dollar price of gold, a subsidiary of the US Government-owned Reconstruction Finance Corporation bought gold in New York, which caused the US dollar price to increase above the British pound price of gold in London at the prevailing US dollar price of the British pound. Arbitragers had an incentive to buy gold in London that they could ship to the United States for sale to the US Treasury. But first they had to buy the British pound, which led to an increase in the US dollar price of the British pound, and thus weakened the competitive position of British firms in the US market and in other foreign markets. The British Government objected to these purchases because a lower value for the US dollar would lead to a decline in British exports. The US authorities stabilized the US dollar price of gold when the free market price was near $35. Had the British objection been delayed until the market price was $40, the new US gold parity would have been significantly higher.

The first sharp indicator of an impending gold shortage appeared in 1960 when the market price of gold spiked to nearly $40 in the London market. The practice was that the Bank of England sold gold to keep the US dollar price in London from rising above $35; the Bank of England would buy gold from the US Treasury to replenish its holdings. Some officials at the Bank of England were not confident that they would be able to buy gold from the US Treasury to replenish the Bank's holdings and the Bank stopped selling gold, which led to the price surge. Eventually, the Bank of England sold gold to the private parties and the price fell to $35.

If the US Treasury had not sold gold to foreign central banks at $35, the increase in the demand for gold would have led to increases in its price. One approach to resolving the shortage – a view that was implicit in how the gold standard was supposed to have worked – entailed declines in price levels in many countries, which would have led to increases in gold production as mining costs fell and a reduction in the private demand for gold as the price of silver declined. (The world price level had declined by 30 percent between the late 1860s and the early 1890s.) A competing approach – the traditional response to any shortage – involved an increase in the US dollar price of gold to $70 or perhaps $100 and comparable percentage increases in the price of gold in most other currencies, much like the increases that had occurred in the 1930s. Gold production would have been stimulated and private demand would have declined. A third approach involved developing new paper monies that would be an effective substitute for gold.

The US Government and the European governments were not willing to adopt the financial policies that would have led to declines in their national price levels, because of the high costs in terms of unemployment, business bankruptcies, and lost elections. The US Government was strongly against any increase in the US dollar price of gold because of the adverse political consequences. US gold regulations were changed to prohibit American citizens from buying or holding gold outside the United States.

One of the criticisms of the proposal that the monetary price of gold be increased was that the credibility of other US commitments would diminish; another was that the domestic political fallout would be unfavorable to the party in power, and a third that both South Africa and the Soviet Union would secure large windfalls and both had unattractive political regimes. Moreover, speculators would be rewarded.

In 1965 the private demand for gold first exceeded new production; central banks sold $50 million of gold to prevent the price from increasing above $35. Uncertainties about the stability of the parity for the British pound led to a surge in private demand for gold; in 1967 central banks sold $1.6 billion of gold to prevent the price from increasing, and in the first 10 weeks of 1968 sales to private parties reached $700 million.

Central banks were alarmed lest the experience of the 1930s be repeated: they were concerned that once the British pound was devalued, investors would conclude that other currencies soon would be devalued – that once again the 'dominoes would fall.' The investors believed that, at a minimum, the US dollar price of gold would be doubled; the potential profit from an increase in the US dollar price was high. Private parties bought more than $3 billion of gold from central banks between 1965 and 1968; most of this demand was supplied, indirectly, from the US Treasury.

In March 1968 the US and the European monetary authorities agreed to separate the private gold market from the 'market' in which central banks bought and sold gold with each other. Under this two-tier arrangement, non-monetary gold and monetary gold became 'separate commodities'; the link between the private market for gold and the official market was severed. Most newly produced gold would be sold in the private market to satisfy industrial, artistic, and hoarding demands; the price in the private market might rise above – or fall below – $35. Central banks would trade gold with each other at $35.

The adoption of the two-tier gold system led to the question whether South Africa could sell its $1 billion annual gold production to private parties or to the central banks. The Government of South Africa wanted to maximize its revenues from gold sales; it wanted to sell between one-half and two-thirds of its newly produced gold in the private market, at prices of perhaps $38 or $40 or higher, and the rest to central banks at $35. The European central banks liked the South African proposal, since it would add to their gold holdings.

The US authorities, in contrast, wanted South Africa to sell all its gold in the private market in the belief or hope that the price would decline, perhaps to $30 or $32, which would shake central banks' confidence in the monetary future of gold.

Eventually, a compromise was reached. South Africa would be permitted to sell limited amounts of gold at $35 to central banks. But this compromise became irrelevant almost as soon as it was concluded, for the increase in private demand for gold meant that nearly all of South Africa's output could be sold at $40 – and even higher prices.

Once the price of gold in the private market began to exceed the official price, a second problem became apparent – central banks were reluctant to buy and sell gold with each other at the $35 parity if the market price was higher. The irony – the unintended consequence – was that the increase in the market price of gold reduced the liquidity of central bank gold holdings.

Changes in the purchasing power of gold

The US dollar price of gold since the early 1970s is shown in Table 3.1. The increase in the US dollar price above $35 was relatively small in the several years after the adoption of the two-tier arrangement in 1968. In 1973 and 1974, the US dollar price climbed to nearly $200 and then declined to just over $100 in 1976. Then the price began to increase again, initially modestly, then sharply, and eventually reached nearly $1000 in January 1980. The US dollar price then declined, and a trough value occurred in the late 1990s. In March 2008 the US dollar price reached $1040, and at the end of 2008 the price was $800.

These changes in the US dollar price have led to large changes both in the purchasing power of gold on different dates and in the rate of return on gold as an investment asset during various holding periods.

The 'Law of One Price' holds in the market for gold so its price in terms of the euro (and earlier in terms of the German mark and the French franc) can be readily

Table 3.1 US dollar price of gold in London

	End of period				
	1960s	1970s	1980s	1990s	2000s
0	35.60	37.37	589.50	385.00	274.45
1	35.15	43.63	397.50	353.60	276.50
2	35.07	64.80	456.90	333.25	342.75
3	35.08	112.25	381.50	390.65	417.25
4	35.12	186.50	308.30	383.25	438.00
5	35.12	140.25	327.00	386.75	513.00
6	35.19	134.75	390.90	369.25	635.70
7	35.20	164.95	484.10	290.20	696.70
8	41.90	226.00	410.25	287.80	872.10
9	35.20	512.00	401.00	290.25	1150.00

Source: International Financial Statistics.

calculated as the product of the US dollar price of gold and of the US dollar price of the euro.

Changes in the US dollar price of gold reflect changes in the anticipated US inflation rate and changes in the US dollar price of the euro as well as structural forces including changes in annual production and central bank sales of gold. When the anticipated US inflation rate increased in the second half of the 1970s, the US dollar price of gold increased; at the same time the US dollar price of the German mark and the Swiss franc increased, and hence the increase in the price of gold in terms of these European currencies was smaller than the increase in the US dollar price of gold. Conversely, when the anticipated US inflation rate declined in the first half of the 1980s, the US dollar price of gold declined (even though the US inflation rate remained high), the US dollar price of the German mark and the Swiss franc declined, and the price of gold in terms of the European currencies declined and by a smaller amount than the decline in the US dollar price of gold.

The second most important factor in explaining the changes in the US dollar price of gold has been the change in the US dollar price of the German mark and the Swiss franc; when these European currencies depreciated, the US dollar price of gold decreased and when these European currencies appreciated, the US dollar price of gold increased. The strong correlation between the changes in the US dollar price of gold and the US dollar price of the European currencies reflects that the market price of gold is more nearly set in Europe than in the United States.

Structural shocks including increases in the demand for gold by private parties for industrial uses and ornamentation lead to similar percentage changes in the US dollar price of gold and the price of gold in terms of these European currencies. Central bank sales of gold, initially by the Bank of Canada and then by the Netherlands Central Bank and subsequently by most other central banks in Europe, are another structural shock. (Central banks have entered into several agreements that have set upper limits to their annual gold sales.)

Similarly, forward sales of gold by the mining companies are a structural shock that lead to comparable percentage changes in the US dollar price of gold and the price of gold in terms of the European currencies (the mining companies borrowed gold from central banks). These sales increased the supply of gold and led to declines in both the US dollar price of gold and the price of gold in terms of the European currencies. Subsequently, when the mining companies repaid their gold loans and reduced their short forward positions, their sales were smaller than their production, and the price of gold increased in terms of both the US dollar and the European currencies.

Box 3.2   Changes in the Purchasing Power of Gold

One of the oldest clichés in monetary economics is that 'gold is a good inflation hedge.' The meaning is clear – if the commodity price level increases, the price of gold will increase, so an ounce of gold will maintain its purchasing power in terms of a market basket of goods.

Gold has a remarkable track record as a store of value. Consider the purchasing power of gold in terms of a market basket of British goods and a market basket of US goods between 1800 and 1900, and between 1900 and 2000.

In 1900 the purchasing power of a unit of gold over a market basket of US goods was similar to its purchasing power in 1800 – the US dollar price of gold was the same in both years and the US price level in 1900 was not significantly different from the price level in 1800.

The purchasing power of gold varied extensively between 1900 and 2000 and initially declined between 1900 and 1930 as the US and foreign price levels increased. Then the purchasing power increased in the next few years, initially as price levels declined, and then sharply once the US gold parity was increased to $35 in 1934. Then the purchasing power declined again as price levels increased until the 1970s. The purchasing power of gold surged in the 1970s as the market price increased.

The US consumer price level in 2000 was nearly 20 times higher than in 1900 and the US dollar price of gold was about 15 times higher. If an adjustment is made to reflect that the US dollar price of gold was exceptionally low relative to trend in 2000 since the US dollar price of the euro also was low relative to trend, the purchasing power of gold at the end of the twentieth century was not very different from its purchasing power at the beginning of the century.

The prices of American, British, and Swiss market baskets of consumer goods are shown in Table 3.2 for three different base years – 1900, 1935, and 1965.

Table 3.2 The purchasing power of gold, 1900–2008

	1900–34	1935–64	1965–2005	2006–2008
Market Baskets				
American	100 106	100 44	100 205	100 92
	(0.0016)	(−0.0260)	(0.0266)	(−0.0017)
British	100 103	100 51	100 151	100 82
	(0.0008)	(−0.0222)	(0.0095)	(−0.0016)
Swiss	100 63	100 63	100 106	100 43
	(−0.0131)	(−0.0153)	(−0.0010)	(−0.0092)

Sources: *The Economist*, International Financial Statistics, Swiss National Bank.

The increase in the purchasing power of gold from 100 in 1900 to 106 reflects that the increase in the US parity from $20.67 to $35.00 was modestly larger than the increase in the US consumer price level from 1900 to 1934. The values in the brackets in each of the holding periods show the average annual deviation from a constant real gold price – if the purchasing power of gold were constant, this value would be zero. The value in the brackets in the north-east cell of (−0.0017) means that the purchasing power of gold declined at an annual average rate of slightly less than two-tenths of 1 percent from 1900 to 2005.

Over extended periods, the composition of goods in the market baskets changes as new goods and services become available and displace older goods; consider the impact of the introduction of computers on the demand for typewriters and the impacts of the introduction of typewriters on the demand for pens. Moreover, the quality of many goods – indeed probably a majority of goods – has improved. Virtually all the measures of the changes in the prices of the market basket fail to capture what are effectively reductions in the prices of goods that result from improvements in their quality.

The rate of return on gold as an investment varies directly with its purchasing power; the larger the increase in its purchasing power, the higher the rate of return. Assume initially that the US dollar price of gold varies continuously by the same percentage amount as the US dollar price of the market basket of consumer goods; if the US dollar price of the market basket then increases by 10 percent in a specified holding period, the US dollar price of gold also increases by 10 percent. Then the real rate of return from holding gold is zero. (Many individuals associate a non-monetary return from holding gold, much as individuals enjoy owning paintings and sculpture.) During the accelerating inflation of the 1970s, the US dollar price of gold increased much more rapidly than the US price level – and as a result the real rate of return was positive. When the anticipated US inflation rate was revised downward in the early 1980s, the US dollar price of gold declined, and the real rate of return on gold was negative even though the US price level continued to increase.

Box 3.2   Continued

Contrast the rates of return on an investment in gold in the 1970s and in the 1980s and the 1990s. In the 1970s the US price level increased by a factor of two; the US dollar price of gold increased by a factor of 20, and the real rate of return on gold was very high. In the 1980s, in contrast, the US price level increased by 50 percent; the US dollar price of gold fell by one-third, and the real rate of return was negative. Similarly, the real rate of return on gold in the 1990s was negative.

What should be done with a monetary relic?

In the 1950s and the 1960s the US authorities wanted to avoid the political costs associated with an increase in the US dollar price of gold. They failed in their effort to maintain the $35 parity, they overestimated the political costs associated with an increase in the US dollar price of gold, and underestimated the economic costs of adhering to this parity. Moreover they underestimated the benefits to the United States of a higher price of gold. Their commitment to the $35 parity resulted from a cost–benefit calculation, and in retrospect the US authorities got it wrong, perhaps because they placed too high a weight on the political costs of an increase in US dollar price and too low a weight on the economic benefits.

One exercise in counterfactual history involves projecting the train of events if the US Government had increased the US dollar price of gold to $70 at the beginning of the 1960s or perhaps to $100 at the end of that decade. The increase in both the market price and the subsequent increase in gold production would have meant that the major countries in Western Europe would have satisfied a larger share of their demand for international reserve assets by purchasing newly produced gold; US gold sales would have been smaller. Similarly, the US trade deficits since the early 1980s would have been smaller since gold would have accounted for a larger proportion of the increase in central bank holdings of international reserve assets.

One inference from the sales of gold by various central banks since the mid-1990s is that the banks believe that gold is not likely to be as useful as an international reserve asset as securities denominated in the US dollar and in the euro. Should these central banks seek an agreement that would provide a set of guidelines for the use of gold as an international reserve asset or should they sell more of their gold?

Now that the political costs of an increase in the US gold parity have been incurred (and almost certainly long forgotten) and market forces have led to a significant increase in its price so that its purchasing power is similar to that in 1800 and 1900, the benefits and costs of retaining gold as a monetary asset or of demonetizing gold can be evaluated.

In 1950, gold was the largest component of international reserve assets. More recently, central bank gold holdings have accounted for 12 percent of international reserve assets, with gold valued at the market price of $800 at the end of 2008. The higher the market price, the larger the share of gold in the portfolios of international reserve assets.

Central banks still hold most of the gold that they held in the early 1970s. Central bank gold holdings are about ten times larger than annual production, and so the pace of central bank sales has been small relative to their holdings. Larger annual sales of gold could have a large impact on the market price. That some central banks continue to hold gold may seem irrational, for gold earns no interest in contrast to other international reserve assets; the real rate of return on these other reserve assets is in the range of 2–3 percent a year. One explanation often given for this preference is tradition; central banks began to hold gold during the nineteenth century, and their preferences remain unchanged. But this explanation is not convincing. Sales by various central banks suggest that they believe that gold is not likely to be useful in the settlement of international payments imbalances and that the market price will decline. Since central banks will continue to hold international reserve assets, the question is why some want to reduce their holdings of gold.

Three basic scenarios for the monetary role of gold can be sketched. Each scenario has implications for the countries that are large producers of gold; obviously these countries want a high price. Each scenario has implications for countries that hold significant amounts of gold. US Treasury's gold holdings are larger than the combined holdings of the next five largest holders. Just as the producers of gold are better off with a high price, so are the countries that own lots of gold.

Each country could develop its own benefits and costs calculation for each scenario. Each scenario has implications for financial stability and international monetary arrangements.

One scenario – the default scenario – is 'more of the same'; central banks would continue to sell gold, perhaps in accord with an agreement that limits the amount of sales to reduce the likelihood of a disruptive impact on the market. No central bank would be obliged to sell its gold.

A second scenario is that informal arrangements might develop so that central banks could buy and sell gold with each other, either at the market price or at a price based on the market price. A central bank that wanted to increase its gold holdings would buy the metal while those that believe their gold holdings are too large would be sellers. One extension would be that a central bank that wanted to reduce its gold holdings would have the right to ask other central banks to buy part or all of the gold that it wants to sell, perhaps at a price based on the market price; the direct transaction between the two central banks would mean that the central bank sales would not directly affect the market price.

A major rationale for this type of arrangement is that a central bank would have a more diversified portfolio of international reserve assets than if it only owned securities denominated in the US dollar, the euro, and perhaps some other currencies; these banks would have concluded that the advantages of a more diversified portfolio would dominate the cost of the lower real rate of return on gold. A rationale from the viewpoint of central banks as a group is that inclusion of gold as an international reserve asset is a partial 'solution' to the global imbalances problem that is at the core of the analysis in Chapter 11 – the desire of many countries to add to their holdings of international reserve assets while few countries want to have the counterpart payments deficits.

A third scenario – and a more ambitious one – is that several central banks might establish new parities for their currencies in terms of gold as part of an arrangement to limit the range of movement in the prices of their currencies. Initially the price at which each central bank would buy gold would be lower relative to its parity and similarly the price at which it would sell gold would be higher relative to its parity than in the nineteenth century. The spread between these two prices would determine the range of movement in the price of gold in the private market. Moreover, the central banks would specify the conditions under which they would sell gold to other central banks.

One of the major questions for this type of arrangement would be the choice of the parities.

The central banks that had established parities for their currencies would have to decide whether to sell gold to private parties and to the central banks that had not established parities for their currencies in terms of gold. The advantages of continuing to hold gold as an international reserve asset should be distinguished from the more ambitious proposal of returning to a gold standard arrangement similar to that of the nineteenth century.

Political implications of alternative monetary roles for gold

When Keynes called gold a 'barbarous relic,' he meant that mining gold to produce an international money was unnecessarily expensive. Producing $6 billion of gold uses labor and machinery that might produce $6 billion of other goods. If the IMF or some other international institution produces $6 billion of 'paper gold,' the costs are minimal – the time of some government negotiators and a few clerks to record which central banks owe how much money to whom. And the labor and machinery otherwise used to mine gold for monetary purposes could then be diverted to producing dams, schools, and hospitals.

The cost of producing $6 billion or $8 billion of gold falls on those countries which prefer to hold gold in their reserves when they might otherwise hold IMF-produced money or US dollar securities or euro securities, since these countries must earn the gold by exporting goods and services, in effect to the gold mining countries. The countries with a strong demand for gold would acquire most of the newly produced gold and would also bear most of these costs.

What about the political consequences of changing the gold price? At one time, it was feared that raising the gold price would give substantial windfall gains to the Soviet Union and South Africa; and that would be bad, the argument went, because the former was part of the Sino–Soviet communist conspiracy and the latter practiced apartheid. Much has happened since the first edition of this book.

The Sino–Soviet conspiracy to take over the world has disappeared; the Soviet Union has fragmented into a confederation of republics. Apartheid is dead in South Africa and the country has moved to majority rule. If the market price of gold is $800 an ounce, South Africa's gold production would account for 15 percent of its GNP and 50 percent of its exports. The South African mines are becoming depleted, although this might partially be the response to the lack of investment because of the concern that gold would be demonetized and that the gold price would decline.

If gold is demonetized, then the credibility of the commitments to satisfy the world's demand for international money by producing paper gold would be low. Raising the gold price would also be more nearly consistent with the structure of the IMF and its Articles of Agreement than would gold demonetization – but the IMF is almost certainly against a larger role for gold because it implies a smaller role for the Fund as a supplier of international reserve assets. Gold demonetization would impose substantial losses on those now holding gold, whereas retaining gold by increasing the monetary price imposes losses on no one, although those central banks that hold US dollars and other reserve assets might be upset because they would not share in the revaluation gains.

The move toward increasing the gold price might occur after currencies were again pegged or even before. If currencies were again pegged, the United States would again need to concern itself with its payments position and the large amount of US dollar securities owned by foreign central banks; if these central banks rushed to convert some of their holdings of dollars into gold, the US Treasury's gold holdings would be quickly depleted.

Would these scenarios work, would either be preferable to the current policy of drift?

Demonetization would 'work' because the US authorities would no longer have to worry about a US payments deficit, since foreign official institutions can no longer require the US Treasury to sell gold. And the gold price increase would work because the annual increase in the gold supply could be large enough to enable other countries to satisfy their demand for international money without forcing the United States to incur payments deficits and sell gold. Indeed, because of the increase in the value of the annual gold production, every country might add to its gold holdings at the same time.

Reliance on gold is a more costly way to meet the demand for international money than some of the alternatives. The problem, however, is not with gold, but rather with the attitudes and preferences of central banks around the world – and their experience with the credibility of commitments made by their counterparts in foreign governments. The European preference for gold may seem archaic. But it is the preference of central banks – and they pay the costs of retaining gold in the system.

Ultimately, the role of gold in international monetary arrangements is, as de Gaulle knew, a US choice. The United States must decide whether international financial arrangements will function more smoothly and US interests will be better served if central banks continue to hold gold in their portfolios of international reserve assets. For at least four decades, US authorities focused on trying to wean the European central banks away from their preference for gold; the effort was not notably successful. At some stage, US officials may still seek to build a system around these preferences.

In monetary affairs, the authorities cannot afford to be ambiguous; to do so would point toward profit opportunities open to private investors. So they can never hint that they will change a parity, shift from pegged to floating rates, or favor a change in the monetary gold price. When the timing seems appropriate, however, they can suddenly reverse their policies.

4
The Gnomes of Zurich Play in the Largest Market in the World

The global market in currencies

The 'Gnomes of Zurich' is a tag for traders that seek profits from 'bringing down national currencies.' Their gains would be at the public expense; the view was that the Gnomes caused currency values to differ from both those that the local political leaders thought appropriate and those that were consistent with the 'economic fundamentals' – whatever that means. The term became fashionable in the late 1960s when the British pound was overvalued; the transactions of the Gnomes advanced the date of the devaluation that was inevitable and that the British authorities were attempting to forestall.

The Gnomes have a heavy workload, since the market in currencies is larger than any other market. On a busy day, the volume of trading of currencies is $40 billion – since there are 250 trading days in a year, the yearly volume is $100,000 billion – more than three times world GDP, and 40–50 times the volume of international trade in goods, services, and long-term securities. The extraordinary volume of trading in currencies reflects that 90–95 percent of the transactions are between traders in two large international commercial banks, including those in the branches of the same bank in different financial centers such as London and New York. The remaining 5–10 percent of the transactions are between traders in one of these banks and the treasurers of large and small firms that import and export or with hedge funds or with those who buy and sell foreign securities and assets.

The US money center banks – eight in the early 1970s when the first edition of this book appeared, now four: Citibank, JP Morgan Chase, Bank of America, and Wells Fargo Wachovia – reported increasingly large revenues and profits on their foreign exchange transactions in the 1980s and the 1990s. It's a safe bet that the trading revenues and trading profits of some of the other large international banks – Deutsche Bank, Nomura – including those in Europe and Asia also have increased, since the banks follow similar trading strategies.

Currency transactions occur in the major financial centers in each country – in London, New York, Tokyo, Frankfurt, Zurich, Hong Kong, Singapore, and Sydney. The US dollar is used in at least 90 of these transactions because of its unique role as a 'vehicle currency'; most international trade transactions are denominated in the US dollar. When Mexican and Canadian importers buy US goods, the purchase contracts almost always specify payment in the US dollar; similarly, when Mexican and Canadian exporters sell in the United States, their sales contracts almost always specify that they will receive the US dollar in payment. Mexican importers must buy the US dollar while Mexican exporters must sell the US dollar; both are likely to undertake these transactions with banks in Mexico City – although they might do so with a branch of a US bank or with the branch of a Spanish bank. Similarly, Canadian importers buy the US dollar while Canadian exporters sell the US dollar; both are likely to do so with banks in Toronto – although they might transact in New York if the rates are more favorable.

When the Japanese importers of Mercedes wish to pay euros to the Mercedes factory in Stuttgart, the importers' banks in Tokyo first buy the US dollar (more precisely, a demand deposit denominated in the US dollar) with the Japanese yen (more precisely, with a demand deposit denominated in the Japanese yen) and then buy euros with the US dollar. This pattern reflects that the dollar is the principal foreign currency owned by banks in Tokyo; these banks hold only token amounts of other foreign currencies. Similar statements could be made about the composition of the currency holdings of the banks that operate in Toronto and in São Paulo and in Bangkok.

Moreover most central banks buy the US dollar when they sell their currencies to limit the increase in their value, just as and similarly they sell the US dollar when they buy their currencies to limit the decline in their value. About two-thirds of the securities in their portfolios of international reserve assets are denominated in the US dollar.

The market in national currencies is primarily an over-the-counter market; traders communicate with each other by telephone or computer. (There are futures markets in foreign currencies in Chicago and London; arbitragers link the prices of the currencies in these futures markets with the prices of the same currencies in the interbank, over-the-counter market.)

The markets in currencies in London, New York, Zurich, Tokyo, and the financial centers in other counties are branches of an integrated global market in currencies; the traders in these different geographic locations are linked by phone and by computer. At any moment the US dollar price of the British pound in New York and the US dollar price of the British pound in London are virtually identical; the difference between these two prices would be no larger than two or three one-hundredths of 1 percent on a 'standard transaction' of several million dollars. If the price spread were larger, a trader would buy the British pound in the center in which it was relatively cheap and sell the pound in the center in which it was more expensive and profit from this modest difference in the prices.

The volume of currency transactions in London is much larger than in any other city; the volume in New York is a distant second. London has a unique role, partly because the trading hours in London overlap with those on the European continent and partly because the London market is a European extension of the

New York market; the US dollar is traded much more often in London than any other currency, including the British pound.

Spot exchange contracts, forward exchange contracts, and swaps

Most foreign exchange transactions involve the purchase and sale of bank deposits denominated in different currencies. John Bull buys US dollars to make a payment in New York; he acquires a bank deposit denominated in the US dollar and pays with a bank deposit denominated in the British pound. A small volume of transactions involve the exchange of currency notes and traveler's checks by tourists who trade either with the office of a bank or with a firm that specializes in buying and selling currency notes and traveler's checks – especially in the evening and weekend hours when the banks are closed.

The basic types of currency trades – spot transactions, forward transactions, and swaps – are grouped by the dates when the parties exchange deposits. John Bull may enter into a 'spot exchange transaction'; in this case the exchange of deposits occurs two business days after he enters into a contract with his bank. For example, if John Bull enters into the contract on Monday, the exchange of deposits occurs on Wednesday.

John Bull might enter into a 'forward exchange transaction'; he agrees to exchange deposits in 1 month or 2 or 3 or even at a more distant date after he enters into the contract. (These standard maturities correspond with the payment dates on international trade transactions.) John Bull knows the amount of US dollars that he will receive in 3 months for his sales of Scotch whiskey to a distributor in New York, and he buys the British pound in a 3-month forward contract – the same day that he anticipates being paid for the sale of the whiskey. Because the exchange of deposits occurs at various dates in the future and time is money, the prices on forward contracts that mature in 1 month and in 3 months generally differ from each other and from those on spot exchange contracts.

John Bull might enter into a 'swap transaction'; now the exchange of deposits occurs on two different dates. (One feature of both spot and forward contracts is that the exchange of deposits occurs on the same date.) He might agree to pay British pounds to his bank in 1 month and to receive British pounds in 2 months.

Gnomes prefer to buy a currency in the forward market because they do not have to make an immediate large cash payment. But Gnomes can buy the British pound in the forward market only if some non-Gnomes sell the British pound forward. If, for example, the Gnomes believe that the British pound will appreciate they will buy the British pound in the forward market (which means they will sell the US dollar in the forward market). Many participants in the exchange market would be reluctant to sell the British pound in the forward market if they thought that the pound would appreciate.

Some investors – arbitragers – however, may sell the British pound in the forward market only after they buy the British pound in the spot market; in this way they protect themselves against a loss from an appreciation of the British pound. Thus, the arbitragers might buy the British pound in the spot market at US$1.95

per pound and at the same time sell the British pound in the forward market at US$1.98. Regardless of changes in the US dollar price of the pound, they would profit from the difference between the US dollar price of the pound in the spot exchange market and its price in the forward exchange market.

While the Gnomes seek to profit from anticipated changes in the currency values, arbitragers (who by definition are reluctant to bear the risk associated with changes in currency values) profit from the differences in the price of a currency in the spot exchange market and the price in the forward exchange market – but only if these two prices on an annualized percentage basis differ from the spread in interest rates on most nearly comparable securities denominated in the same pair of currencies.

Consider the relationship between the US dollar price of the British pound in the spot exchange market, the US dollar price of the pound in the forward exchange market on 1 month, 3 month, and 6 month forward contracts, and the anticipated US dollar price of the British pound in 1 month, 3 months, and 6 months. The US dollar prices of the British pound in the spot exchange market and the forward exchange market are printed in hundreds of daily newspapers; these prices are instantaneously available on Bloomberg's and Reuters' electronic screens. The US dollar prices of the British pound for various future dates are not known – they are anticipated, someone's forecasts about the future.

A hundred gurus provide forecasts of currency values for various future dates and for changes in these values; some charge for the service and others make the information available without charge although they usually expect to be compensated in some indirect way. Moreover, virtually every market participant including the proprietary traders at the major international banks develops their own estimates of the US dollar price of the British pound for various future dates.

Whenever an exchange market participant believes that the value for the currency in the forward exchange market differs significantly from the anticipated values on the dates that the forward exchange contract matures, they may undertake a transaction to profit from the differential. Their transactions often lead to a change in the value for the currency in the forward market and induce a deviation between the value of the currency in the forward and in the spot exchange markets and the differential in interest rates on foreign securities and most nearly comparable domestic securities. Arbitragers then observe there is a profit opportunity and they will simultaneously buy a currency in the spot exchange market and sell it in the forward market; their transactions cause the value of the currency in the spot exchange market to track the changes in value of the currency in the forward exchange market.

Time for a quick summary. Forward exchange rates are closely linked to anticipated spot exchange rates by thousands of market participants that seek to profit from any significant difference between these prices. Hence when a shock or 'new news' leads to a change in the anticipated values for a currency at various future dates, the forward exchange rates are likely to change to reflect the changes in the anticipated spot exchange rates. Spot exchange rates are immediately linked to the forward exchange rates by arbitrage.

Changes in spot exchange rates thus may reflect changes in the anticipated spot exchange rates for various future dates because of 'new news', and they may reflect change in the interest rates that links the spot exchange rates to the forward exchange rates.

Winners and losers in the currency market

The key participants in currency markets are the large international banks, who participate to provide services to their customers and also for their own accounts – to profit from changes in the values of currencies. Often the information that they gather about changes in the pattern of payments from their transactions with their commercial customers helps them develop their trading strategies. Firms involved in international trade necessarily participate in the market, and use the services provided by the large international banks. Some hedge funds participate in the market to profit from changes in currency values.

These hedge funds and the large international banks are not charitable institutions; they are motivated by the desire for profits. The currency market is a zero-sum game; if the hedge funds and the major international banks secure profits from their trades, the money must come from some other market participants. Surprisingly, no one reports these losses. (When currencies are pegged, the central banks may report trading losses; thus the Bank of England reported losses when the British pound was devalued in November 1967 and again when the pound left the Exchange Rate Mechanism in 1992.)

Four major groups participate in the foreign exchange market – the central banks, the major international commercial banks, the large multinational firms and the smaller firms that are involved in international trade and other transactions, and the firms that participate in the market in the search for profits from changes in currency values.

When currencies were pegged under the Bretton Woods Treaty, each central bank limited the deviations in the price of its currency from its parity by a modest amount – initially by one-quarter of 1 percent, then by 1 percent, and then by a bit more than 2 percent. In effect, currencies 'floated' within the band between the price at which a central bank would buy its currency and the modestly higher price at which it would sell its currency. Once parities became obsolete, central banks bought and sold their currencies to dampen the daily and weekly changes in the price of the US dollar in terms of their own currencies; many intervened extensively to limit the appreciation of their currencies.

Large multinational firms, smaller importing and exporting firms, tourists, national governments, international agencies, international airlines and shipping firms, and hotel chains buy and sell currencies as a necessary counterpart of their international transactions. Most of these firms and groups view their currency transactions as a nuisance, one more cost to be incurred when involved in an international transaction. A few firms have established departments that seek to profit from changes in currency values.

Some of the large international banks employ three groups of traders – 'market makers,' 'day traders,' and 'proprietary traders.' The market makers simultaneously provide two price quotes – a price at which they are prepared to buy a 'standard amount' of the US dollar and a modestly higher price at which they are prepared to sell this same amount – these price quotes are valid for a few seconds. These traders do not know whether the customer is more likely to be a buyer or a seller of the US dollar.

In contrast, the day traders within a bank may enter into 50 or more purchases during a day; they buy the currencies that are increasing in price and sell them after they have made a small profit. Their mantra is 'the trend is my friend.' Profits once earned are 'banked'; they are not likely to increase the size of a position because it has been profitable. They repeat the process again and again. At the end of the day, these day traders close their positions and go home.

In contrast, 'proprietary traders' within the bank have 'strong views' about the probable changes in the prices of one or several currencies in the near future; they hold their positions for a few days or a week or two.

Some individuals have skills that are better suited for one type of trading activity than another. The banks view each trader as a 'profit center' – the traders that do not produce profits are encouraged to seek new careers.

The trading profits of the large banks are exceptionally large relative to the capital committed to the activity. The source of these profits is the transactions with the firms that are involved with international trade.

To Float or Not to Float, That's the Question

One of the perennial debates in international finance is whether central banks should limit the movement in the prices of their currencies to a very narrow range or whether instead only market forces should determine these prices. The motivation for the rules in the IMF treaty that its member countries should limit the variability in the value of their currencies was that the experience with floating exchange rates in the 1920s and the 1930s was an unhappy one and for several different reasons. One was that uncertainty about the value of currencies deterred international trade and investment. Another was that speculative transactions had been destabilizing, both by increasing the range of movement in the prices of currencies and by causing currencies to depreciate more sharply than would otherwise have been the case (perhaps in response to the transactions of the day traders). A third was that if currencies were not pegged, then central banks in a few countries would intervene in the foreign exchange market to move the value of their currencies to enhance domestic income and employment; these central banks would follow what later became known as 'beggar-thy-neighbor' policies.

Two complementary developments in the 1950s and in the 1960s challenged the case for pegged exchange rates. One was that exchange crises were increasingly frequent, and especially in the second half of the 1960s because national governments were sluggish in changing the parities for their currencies. Because of these delays, the parity might increasingly differ from the values projected from the differences in the national inflation rates, perhaps by 10 or 15 or even 20 percent. Firms and investors changed the currency denomination of their assets and their liabilities to profit from the anticipated changes in currency values – and their transactions generally were low risk and profitable, because the direction of the changes in the parities was 'known' even if the timing and the amount of the changes were uncertain.

The proponents of floating exchange rates challenged these empirical assertions about movements in currency values. Their basic presumption was that the market in currencies is not different from other markets, like those in pork bellies and petroleum and stocks, and that market forces would be more effective in determining the value of individual currencies than government bureaucrats. Some of those who favored a floating exchange rate arrangement wanted to eliminate the external constraint on the choice of a central bank's monetary policy; they believed that each central bank should manage the growth of its domestic money supply at a steady rate, and not be deflected because of the concern that its currency would depreciate or because of the need to buy a foreign currency to prevent its own currency from appreciating.

Box 4.1   10 Facts Your Mother Never Knew about the Foreign Exchange Market

1. The foreign exchange market is the largest market in the world. On a busy day, the volume of transactions may reach $400 billion, 50 times the volume on the New York Stock Exchange.
2. Most foreign exchange transactions (90–95 percent) involve only banks: interbank transactions are undertaken to adjust their positions in currencies in order to offset the imbalances caused by purchases and sales with nonbank customers.
3. Large international banks act as market makers in the major currencies: they hold inventories of these currencies and are ready to buy and sell large amounts at stated prices. In other currencies, in contrast, banks operate as brokers and avoid the price risk.
4. The exchange market is the most efficient market in the world, at least as judged by the very low level of transaction costs. Assume you use US$1 million to buy the Canadian dollar. You immediately realize that you have made a mistake, and sell the Canadian dollars to buy the US dollar. You would end up with less than US$1 million by the amount of two commissions – equal to the bid–ask spread. How much less?*
5. The foreign exchange market never (well, hardly ever) closes. When it is 3 PM Tuesday in Tokyo, it is 2 PM in Hong Kong; when it is 3 PM in Hong Kong, it is 1 PM in Singapore. When it is 3 PM in Singapore, it is noon in Bahrain; when it is 3 PM in Bahrain, it is 1 PM in Beirut. When it is 3 PM in Beirut, it is 1 PM in London; when it is 3 PM in London, it is 10 AM in

---

Box 4.1   Continued

New York; when it is 3 PM in New York, it is noon in San Francisco; when it is 3 PM Tuesday in San Francisco, it is 9 PM Wednesday in Sydney. The center of trading moves with the sun around the world.

6. About 99.44 percent of all trades involve the US dollar. If a Swiss importer wants to pay his Japanese supplier, the bank calculates the Japanese yen price of the Swiss franc as the product of the Swiss franc price of the US dollar and the Japanese yen price of the US dollar.
7. The largest volume of foreign exchange trading occurs in London.
8. Most customer transactions in foreign exchange involve forward transactions – the corporate client makes a commitment to buy or sell a foreign currency at a specified future date at a price agreed today.
9. Since 1973, about 20 firms have been established to sell forecasts on currency movements. One inference is that these firms can make more money selling forecasts than trading on these forecasts.
10. A good foreign exchange trader can earn $1 million a year – and lose $1 million in a day.

*The cost is 230 Canadian dollars. The comparable estimates for other currencies will be larger.

One of the major advantages that proponents of floating in support of the proposal that currencies be allowed to float have is that, if currencies were not pegged, then currency values would change to reflect the differences in national inflation rates. They asserted that changes in currency values would be continuous and gradual rather than abrupt like the devaluation of a currency under the Bretton Woods arrangements; moreover, periods of overvaluation and undervaluation would be less frequent and the deviations of the market prices from those inferred from differences in national inflation rates would be smaller. One cliché of these proponents was that it was simpler to adjust the value of the currency to the difference in national price levels than to adjust national price levels to the fixed values for currencies. Thus foreign exchange crises would be less frequent and less severe because of the continuous changes in currency values.

The proponents of floating exchange rates responded to the criticism that speculation would be destabilizing with the assertion that destabilizing speculation would be unprofitable because the speculators would buy high and sell low, and they suggested that speculators would help currency values move more quickly to the anticipated values, and that forward exchange rates would be accurate forecasts of spot exchange rates on the dates that the forward exchange contracts matured.

The move from the Bretton Woods system of adjustable parities was facilitated by the arguments advanced by these proponents of floating currency values; however, this move became inevitable as a result of the sharp increase in inflation rates in different countries, and especially the reluctance of the Germans to accept an inflation rate as high as the one that was acceptable to the Americans. The Germans abhorred increases in their price level because of deep-seated memories of the hyperinflation of the early 1920s and then again after the Second World War. The Swiss also disliked inflation because they placed a very high value on financial stability.

Now there are more than 30 years of data on movements in currency values that can be used to evaluate these propositions.

These statements are in two groups. One set of statements involves the pattern of movements in currency values. A second set of statements involves the behavior of central banks, both as they manage monetary policy and when they intervene in the currency market.

Changes in the price of the US dollar

Consider the changes in the US dollar price of the British pound and the euro, and the changes in the price of the US dollar in terms of the Swiss franc, the Japanese yen, and other currencies.

The changes in the price of these various foreign currencies were very modest in the 1950–70 period because central banks – the Bank of England, the Bank of Japan, the Swiss National Bank, and the Bundesbank – bought and sold their currencies to limit deviations from their parities. Most countries devalued their currencies whenever they changed their parities; Germany was one of a very few that revalued its currency. The US dollar price of the British pound declined by 17 percent in November 1967 when the pound was devalued from $2.80 to $2.40. The US dollar price of the French franc declined by 10 percent in 1959 and again by 10 percent in 1969. The US dollar price of the Japanese yen in 1970 was the same as in 1950.

Since the move away from parities at the beginning of the 1970s the range of movement in the price of the US dollar in terms of these various currencies has been vary large – much larger than when currencies were pegged. Moreover, the deviation of the market values of these currencies from the values that would have been predicted based on the differences in national inflation rates has been many times larger than when currencies were pegged.

Two types of movements in currency values are evident in Table 2.1. The pattern in the changes in the price of the US dollar in terms of these different foreign currencies is similar. These currencies appreciated in the 1970s, generally until 1978 or 1979, and then depreciated until 1985, and then appreciated until 1992, and then depreciated until 2001, and then appreciated about the same time. The similarity in the changes in the prices of these currencies in terms of the US dollar suggests that the movements in currency values are primarily motivated by US events – or by events associated with the United States. The range of movement in the price of the US dollar was large.

The pattern in the changes in the price of the US dollar in terms of the Mexican peso, the Brazilian real, the Thai baht, and the currencies of other developing countries differs significantly from the pattern among the industrial countries;

now country-specific events are relatively more important. Consider the changes in the Mexican peso price of the US dollar between 1990 and 2000. Mexico had experienced a turbulent decade in the 1980s following the collapse of the dual shocks of the surge in interest rates on its US dollar debt and the collapse of the oil price. The incoming Mexican administration of President Salinas in 1989 stabilized the economy and was assisted by the funding of the overhang of bank loans that were in default. (See Chapter 8 for an extended description of the developments in the peso market in the early 1990s.) The flow of foreign funds to Mexico increased as the country's economic prospects became more promising; Mexico privatized several hundred government-owned enterprises and the Salinas administration liberalized many government regulations as it prepared the country to become a member of the North Atlantic Free Trade Area. The Bank of Mexico adopted a very contractive monetary policy to reduce the inflation rate. Large amounts of US and other foreign money flowed to Mexico. The Mexican peso became increasingly overvalued, and the Mexican trade and current account deficit soared. Mexico's external indebtedness increased to 60 percent of its GDP. The flow of foreign funds to Mexico contributed to the boom in the economy, since the increase in asset prices led to increases in household wealth and in both consumption spending and investment spending.

Some contemporary observers believed that the peso had become overvalued by 15 or 20 percent by 1994, which was the year of a presidential election – and a year of increasing political turmoil. The flow of foreign funds to Mexico diminished, and the Bank of Mexico found it increasingly difficult to maintain the value of the peso – and then its ability to continue to support the peso became exhausted. The Mexican peso depreciated at a rapid rate and went from being modestly overvalued to being extensively undervalued; the peso lost more than half of its value. Mexico's current account balance changed from a deficit of 6 percent of its GDP to a surplus of 4 percent. Interest rates on peso securities soared, and business failures surged. The sharp increase in the undervaluation of the peso had a much more severe impact on the Mexican economy than on the US economy, in part because the United States is Mexico's largest trading partner while Mexico is the fifth largest US trading partner. Moreover, the foreign sector in Mexico was much larger relative to its domestic economy than the US foreign sector is to the US domestic economy. The Mexican economy is about one-twentieth the size of the US economy.

Now consider changes in the US dollar price of the euro – in January 1999 on the date that the euro replaced the German mark, the French franc, the Italian lira, and the other legacy currencies, the exchange rate was US$1.19 = 1 euro. The US dollar price of the euro then declined to US$0.84 = 1 euro; the low price for the euro occurred in 2001. Then over the next 6 years the US dollar price of the euro increased to nearly $1.50.

During these years the inflation rates in the United States and in Germany and France and the other countries that participated in the euro were similar, and the rates did not differ by more than 1 percent a year. Thus when the US dollar price of the euro declined US goods became increasingly overvalued in global markets and when the US dollar price of the euro increased US goods became increasingly undervalued. The range of movement from peak overvaluation to peak undervaluation was 50 percent.

The debate about exchange market arrangements – pegged vs. floating one more time

Consider again the advantages claimed by the proponents of floating exchange rates in the 1950s and the 1960s. Perhaps the dominant advantage was that changes in currency values would more fully correspond with the differentials in national inflation rates, so that the scope of overvaluation and undervaluation of currencies would be smaller than when currencies were pegged. The data suggest that swings between overvaluation and undervaluation have been larger – much larger – when currencies have been floating than when they were pegged.

Since the price of a currency in the spot exchange market is its price in the forward exchange market discounted to the present by the interest rate differential, the changes in the US dollar price of the British pound and of the euro result from changes in the anticipated spot prices. Hence changes in currency values have been very large because changes in anticipated currency values have been large, and especially when there are large changes in the anticipated inflation rates.

A second reason that the changes in the currency values have been so large is that investors have increased or reduced their demand for assets denominated in a currency. For example, in 1998 and 1999 investors wished to buy more US stocks because of the surge in their prices. (Similarly, in 1988 and 1989 investors wished to buy more Japanese stocks because their prices were increasing at a rapid rate. This behavior is typical of cross-border transactions in stocks and in other securities.) Before they could buy US stocks, they first had to buy the US dollar, which then appreciated so that the United States would develop a larger current account deficit that was the counterpart of the increase in its capital account surplus. The larger the foreign purchases of US dollar securities the larger the appreciation of the US dollar. Hence in this case the dollar would necessarily 'overshoot' the value suggested by the difference in inflation rates.

When the bubble in US stocks was pricked and their prices began to decline in the spring of 2000, investors reduced their purchases of US stocks; by itself the decline in their purchases of the US dollar would have led to a depreciation of the US dollar. To the extent that they sold the US stocks and then moved their money away from the United States, the decline in the foreign exchange value of the US dollar was even greater.

Hence the first claim of the proponents of floating exchange rates – namely that changes in currency values would be more gradual and that changes in these values would more or less correspond to the differences in national inflation rates – has been belied by the data. Deviations between observed currency values and the values inferred from differences in national inflation rates have been much greater than when currencies were pegged, perhaps three or four times as large. A majority of the large changes in the foreign exchange value of currencies has resulted from the variability in cross-border capital flows.

A second claim of the proponents of floating exchange rates is that changes in currency values would be gradual. While it is the case that these changes have not been as abrupt as when currencies were devalued, the changes have been much larger. The devaluation of the Mexican peso in 1994–95 and the devaluation of the Thai baht and other Asian currencies in 1997 were very abrupt.

Remember the quip of the proponents of floating that it was preferable to allow the currency to adjust to the economy than to force the economy to adjust to the parity. Because movements in currency values have been so much larger than those suggested by the differences in inflation rates, the economies have had to adjust to the increasingly large overvaluations and undervaluations that have resulted from the large variability in capital flows from one period to the next.

One of the arguments in the case against pegged currencies is that if central banks were no longer obliged to intervene to support their currencies in the foreign exchange market, they would have greater monetary independence – they could manage the rate of money supply growth to achieve their domestic objective. The irony is that changes in currency values have been so much larger than those suggested by the inflation differential that central banks have not had the freedom that they were promised.

The financial crises when currencies have been floating have been qualitatively different – and much more severe – than when they were pegged. Many of the sudden large depreciations when currencies were floating have been associated with domestic financial crises and the failure of many corporate firms and financial institutions, in part because of the large increase in the domestic currency equivalents of their liabilities denominated in foreign currencies.

The proponents of floating exchange rates denied the criticism that speculation in the foreign exchange market would be destabilizing with the assertion that the destabilizing speculation would not occur because it would be unprofitable. The large international banks that employ foreign exchange traders are not charitable institutions. They pay their traders well, and they anticipate that their traders will produce profits; otherwise the traders are encouraged to move to some other firm. The day traders in the banks make money they run with the trend. The proprietary traders in the banks make money. Many of the hedge funds make money or they stop trading.

The foreign exchange trading revenues of a large international bank are highly correlated with the scope of the movements in currency values; the larger the movements in currency values, the higher its trading revenues. The foreign exchange trading revenues of each of these banks is highly correlated with the trading revenues of other large international banks – its competitors. Moreover, the profits of each of these banks from trading foreign exchange are highly correlated with its trading revenues; the inference is that trading has high fixed costs and low variable costs, so that a large part of any increase in revenues 'falls through to the bottom line.'

On occasion the source of revenues for proprietary traders and day traders is from the central banks that are 'leaning against the wind' and intervening to dampen the movement in the price of their currencies in the foreign exchange market. Most of the foreign exchange trading revenues of the large international banks and the hedge funds are from the firms that import and export and from the other participants in the market who need to deal in foreign exchange. The profits earned by the banks are a 'tax' on the transactions of the firms involved in international trade and investment.

Which way after floating?

The choice about the exchange rate arrangements will depend in part on the power of the arguments, the vested interests, and the political arguments. The data since the early 1970s suggests that movements in currency values are a major source of shocks, and that the costs to the national economies from adjusting to large swings in currency values are several times larger than the costs to the economy of adjusting to modest overvaluations and undervaluations when currencies are pegged. Those analysts and observers who prefer gradual movements in currency values should prefer an arrangement of parities.

The large international banks have a strong vested interest in the retention of a floating exchange rate arrangement because of the exceptionally high level of trading profits relative to the capital invested.

The United States and other mature industrial countries have a strong vested interest in an exchange rate arrangement that limits the ability of newly industrializing countries to run even larger trade surpluses.

The historical experience suggests that floating rates are inevitable in an era of double-digit inflation and worldwide recession. Reliance on a floating exchange rate arrangement may also be inevitable when international financial and political relationships are being restructured. The record also suggests that countries will move back toward some form of pegged rates once the monetary environment is more stable. Individual countries and groups of countries will decide when the time is appropriate to peg their currencies – unless there is a concerted move to return to a pegged exchange rate relationship. Such a move might follow an international conference or agreement which recognizes that a move toward pegged rates is desirable; alternatively, individual countries might unilaterally peg their currencies to that of a major trading partner.

The adoption of the euro as a common currency for 11 members of the European Union (EU) at the beginning of 1999 is one model of an approach toward reducing the uncertainty associated with movements in currency values, although in part the move was motivated by the desire to enhance the single integrated market. The EU followed the European Economic Community (EEC) that had followed the European Coal and Steel Community (ECSC). Subsequently, economic integration was expanded by the elimination of tariffs on internal trade, and the adoption of a common external tariff (CXT), and a common agricultural policy (CAP). Membership has expanded to most of the countries in Western Europe and

Central Europe; there were efforts to standardize a number of different policies and practices.

A few members of the EU decided not to adopt the euro as their currency because each believed that its economy was subject to somewhat unique shocks. Norway is subject to large shocks from changes in the price of oil. Britain is subject to shocks from changes in the demand for the securities denominated in the pound as an international reserve asset. Some of these countries viewed the adoption of a common currency as one more step on the road to greater political integration.

Ultimately, a new agreement might be reached to peg currency values. Such an agreement would differ from the Bretton Woods system in several important ways. The support limits are likely to be wider, probably even wider than the 2.25 percent limits of the Smithsonian Agreement. The rules concerning parity changes would place greater emphasis on the need to change rates that are inappropriate. And the rules are likely to be more permissive, so that some countries might permit their currencies to float while others might peg their currencies.

Just as it is predictable that there will be a move back to pegged currency values, so it is inevitable that this agreement, too, will eventually become outdated and will be shelved with the gold standard and the Bretton Woods system in the monetary counterpart of the Smithsonian Institution. Monetary agreements are matters of convenience which last for a decade or two; as the economic conditions which made the agreement feasible change, the agreement becomes obsolete.

5
The Greatest Monetary Agreement in History

The Smithsonian Institution in Washington, DC is the repository for some of America's most treasured artifacts. Lindbergh's Spirit of St Louis hangs from the rafters. The Hope Diamond is there. So are George Washington's uniforms and the largest blue whale ever caught.

In December 1971 the US Secretary of the Treasury met with finance ministers from Britain, Canada, Japan, Germany, and a few other industrial countries at the Smithsonian and agreed to a new set of values for the European currencies and the Japanese yen in terms of the US dollar. President Nixon called the Smithsonian Agreement 'The Greatest Monetary Agreement in History.' The remarkable accomplishment was that more currency values were simultaneously realigned in a multinational framework than ever before. The agreement revived the Bretton Woods Treaty, which had been torpedoed by the US decisions a few months earlier to close the US Treasury's gold window and to apply a 10 percent import surcharge on US dutiable imports.

By midsummer 1972 the Bank of England ceased pegging the pound, which almost immediately depreciated by 10 percent. Then, in mid-February 1973, Germany stopped pegging the mark, and the currency appreciated sharply. Most other industrial countries also ceased pegging their currencies. The move to a floating exchange rate arrangement occurred by default because a large number of central banks stopped pegging their currencies at about the same time.

The 'Greatest Monetary Agreement in History' lasted for a year and a month – more or less. In effect, the breakdown of the Smithsonian Agreement meant that the existing machinery for resolving disputes about trade imbalances and currency values could be sent to the monetary counterpart of the Smithsonian Institution to take its place as another artifact. The International Monetary Fund (IMF) which had been established to manage the system of adjustable parities was immediately obsolete – and several thousand well-paid international civil servants scrambled to find another raison d'être for their incomes as well-paid international civil servants.

In December 1991 the Prime Ministers of the member countries of the European Community (EC) met at Maastricht – the capital of a small province in the south of the Netherlands – and agreed to establish a new European currency by the end of the 1990s. In the 1980s each of these countries had pegged its currency to those of other members to facilitate trade and investment among themselves by reducing uncertainty about currency values. In the late 1980s changes in the parities among their currencies were less and less frequent, so the commitment to move to a common currency by the late 1990s seemed like an extension of earlier commitments to maintain parities for currencies.

In September 1992 Finland – not a member of the European Union (EU) – devalued the markka by more than 30 percent in response to a sharp decline in its exports to what had been the Soviet Union. Investors – speculators – then began to sell the Swedish krona in anticipation that Sweden's competitive position would weaken as Finland's competitive position improved, since both Finland and Sweden exported timber and newsprint. Investors began to sell the British pound, the Italian lira, and the Spanish peseta in anticipation that these currencies would also be devalued. By the end of 1992, more than half of the currencies of the members of the EC had been devalued or allowed to float. The Maastricht Agreement seemed barely alive – still it survived and subsequently Germany and France and their neighbors returned to the timetable for the adoption of a common currency.

Both the Smithsonian and the Maastricht Agreements were efforts to reduce uncertainty about currency values. The premise of both agreements was that international trade and investment would be enhanced if traders and investors had greater confidence about currency values. The political leaders in some of the countries that had participated in the Maastricht Agreement had a more ambitious agenda, for they believed that a common currency was a necessary complement to a 'single integrated market' and that both were necessary steps in the move toward greater economic and political integration.

The gold standard – rules and myths

The gold standard of the nineteenth century was an 'open membership club'; any country which agreed to buy and sell gold at a fixed price – its mint parity – in terms of its own currency could join. The gold standard was not based on a formal international agreement or treaty; instead, each participating country believed that its own economic well-being would be enhanced if it pegged its currency to gold, since uncertainty about the value of its currency would be smaller and governments and firms based outside Britain would be able to borrow on more favorable terms in London, the world's principal financial center.

Britain was the first country to establish a parity for its currency in terms of gold; in 1697 the Royal Mint set at parity for the pound of £3 17s 10d. The First Act of the First US Congress in 1793 was to establish a parity for the US dollar of $20.67. Once Britain and the United States had established parities between their currencies and gold, the exchange rate between their currencies was set by the ratio of their mint parities, adjusted for any difference in the gold content of the coins of each country. For example, the US dollar price of the British pound was $20.67 divided by £3 17s 10d, or $4.86 per pound after adjustment for the somewhat greater gold content of US coins than of British coins.

The key feature of the gold standard was that each participating central bank was committed to buy gold from private individuals at its mint parity and to sell gold at its parity. In fact the central bank's purchase price for gold was slightly below its parity and its selling price slightly above its parity; the difference between the parity and these two prices (sometimes known as 'the gold points') compensated the central bank for its transactions costs when it bought and sold gold. If British exporters acquired gold in payment from their foreign customers, they could sell the gold to the Bank of England, which would pay with newly produced money. The British money supply and the Bank of England's gold holdings would increase as part of the same transaction. Conversely, the domestic money supply would decline when British importers bought gold from the Bank of England that they would use to pay their foreign suppliers.

The attraction of the gold standard – the reason a return to this type of arrangement appeared so attractive to Jack Kemp, formerly a quarter-back for the Buffalo Bills and later a candidate for the Republican presidential nomination in 1996 and again in 2000, and to Ron Paul, a candidate for the Republican presidential nomination in 2008 – is that consumer price levels had been remarkably stable in the long run – if not in the short run as long as countries adhered to the parities for their currencies in terms of gold. The US consumer price level in 1900 was two-thirds as high as in 1800 – although there had been increases and decreases in the price level during the intervening decades. The US consumer price level increased modestly in the 1850s, and then nearly doubled during the Civil War – but the US Government had suspended convertibility of the US dollar into gold at the beginning of the war. After the war the price level decreased slowly. During various financial crises associated with the failures of large numbers of banks – 1847, 1873, 1884, 1890, 1893, and 1907 – the price level fell but usually by less than 3 or 4 percent a year.

Under the gold standard market forces – a set of invisible hands – automatically and simultaneously answered two important questions: how rapidly should the domestic money supply increase in each country, and how rapidly should the supply of monetary gold increase for all countries as a group? The 'rules of the game' of the gold standard provided that the money supply in a country increased when it had a payments surplus, which was measured by the inflow of gold. Conversely, when a country had a payments deficit, both its gold holdings and its money supply declined. The exchange rate arrangements and monetary policies were compatible; there was never any risk that the domestic money supply would increase so rapidly that the central bank's holdings of gold might be exhausted because of a surge in imports.

The adjustment process to restore a satisfactory payments balance centered on increases in the price levels in the countries that experienced increases in their gold holdings and money supplies and decreases in the prices levels in the countries that experienced declines in their gold holdings and money supplies. Residents of both groups of countries would buy fewer goods in the countries where the price levels were increasing and more goods in the countries where the price levels were declining. These changes in the amounts demanded of goods produced in the two countries would lead to a reduction in payments imbalances and in gold flows.

As long as gold flows continued, price levels would increase in the countries that were buying gold and decline in the countries that were selling gold. The change in the relationship between national price levels would continue until gold flows diminished to a level deemed sustainable for an indefinite future.

Market forces also determined how rapidly the combined gold holdings of central banks, commercial banks, and private individuals would increase. The amount of gold produced during any period depended on the relationship between the central banks' buying prices and the costs incurred by the mining firms in discovering and producing gold. As long as the mining firms continued to produce, the gold holdings of every central bank might increase during the same year, but at different rates. After the discovery of gold in California in the 1850s, and again at the end of the nineteenth century following gold discoveries in the Canadian Yukon, Alaska, and South Africa, the more rapid growth in gold holdings led to increases in domestic money supplies and to worldwide increases in consumer price levels – but at low annual rates.

When the supply of gold increased more rapidly than the demand, price levels would increase. Mining costs would increase as price levels increased and the producers would be squeezed between increasing costs and fixed selling prices, which were the mint parities. Gold holdings would increase less rapidly – and national money supplies also would increase less rapidly.

When the demand for money increased more rapidly than the supply, central bank gold holdings would decline and price levels would decline, mining costs would decrease, and the mining firms then would find it profitable to produce more gold. Money supplies would increase more rapidly, and the decline in the consumer price levels would be dampened.

The appeal of the gold standard was that changes in the amounts of gold produced and changes in the consumer price levels were components of a stable, self-correcting system. The automatic, anonymous, and consistent attributes of the gold standard attracted numerous supporters because of the limits to the growth of national monies.

The gold standard in practice

The gold standard in practice was not as elegant as the descriptive textbook model suggests. Changes in the gold supply often reflected the chance of new discoveries and innovations in refining processes rather than changes in the consumer price level and mining costs. Still, whenever a shock led to changes in monetary gold holdings, the self-correcting properties of the model came into play. These properties were attenuated because changes in the money supplies in individual countries did not follow the lock step, mechanical linkages that the model suggested.

Moreover, during the wars of the nineteenth century the money supply growth was managed to finance government expenditures. But the suspension of the convertibility requirement when countries went to war was not a valid criticism of how the gold standard worked. The combination of price level stability and rapid economic growth convinced many analysts of the merits of the gold standard arrangement.

Several developments associated with the First World War reduced the relevance of the gold standard model. Nationalism was a powerful force in Britain and in France as well as in Germany and Central Europe. Central banks then managed their monetary policies to help finance their national war efforts. The cohesiveness of international monetary arrangements became fragmented even as the costs of economic distance were declining.

Prices levels increased in every country in response to more rapid rates of money supply growth, but much more rapidly in some countries than in others. US and British price levels in the early 1920s were about twice as high as in 1910 while the French price level was about four times as high. Higher price levels meant increased demands for both money and gold and, because of higher production costs, a lower level of gold production.

There were persistent fears of an incipient gold shortage in the 1920s. Few countries were willing to accept the substantial reductions in their national price levels that would have been needed if they were to return to their prewar gold parities – and no one contemplated that central banks would pay higher prices for gold than the prices they paid before the war. Yet if the demand for international money was to be satisfied either the price of gold in terms of national currencies would have to be increased or substitutes for gold would have to be developed.

The First World War led to a sharp increase in US economic power in both absolute and relative terms, in part because the regional economies of the nation were more closely tied together. The United States, moreover, escaped both the material destruction and the postwar financial turmoil that befell virtually all of the countries in Europe. After the First World War, the US economy was about as large as the combined economies of the ten next largest countries – a much more dominant position in the world economy than Britain had ever enjoyed.

Monetary arrangements in the 1920s and the 1930s

Policy makers in the 1920s wanted to return to the gold standard and they wanted to peg their currencies to gold at the parities that prevailed before the war. They were concerned about a shortage of gold because higher costs would lead to a decline in annual production, while demand would be larger because some of the newly established central banks in Europe would want to acquire gold. Finally, the commodity demand for gold would be higher since the price of gold would be lower relative to the price of silver – whose price had increased with the general price level.

The thrust of the gold exchange standard was to maintain the features of the gold standard while reducing the demand for gold. Central banks would hold securities denominated in the British pound, the US dollar, and other currencies as part of their international reserve assets – a practice that had begun before the war. Individuals and firms would be encouraged to economize on their holdings of gold.

The monetary problems in the decades following the First World War revolved around three themes: nationalism, the shortage of international money, and shifts in economic power toward the United States. International trade declined sharply in the 1930s primarily as result of the increase in import tariffs and other trade barriers, which in turn followed from the failure to adjust international financial arrangements – both the parities of the currencies of individual countries and the mechanisms for producing international reserve assets – to the divergent increases in national price levels.

During the early 1920s the British pound, the French franc, the German mark, and virtually every other European currency floated and most of them depreciated sharply in terms of both gold and the US dollar. The floating exchange rate arrangement was viewed as temporary, because most governments wanted to again peg their currencies at their prewar gold parities. But this objective could be achieved only if their domestic price levels declined substantially – or if there was a significant increase in the US price level. Few countries were willing to adopt policies to reduce their price levels so that a return to the 1913 parities would be feasible, and the United States was unwilling to increase the US price level to facilitate the necessary adjustment.

By the mid-1920s, most European currencies were again pegged to gold. The British pound, the Swiss franc, and a few other currencies – those of countries that were neutral during the war – were again pegged at their 1913 parities. Many more currencies had been devalued extensively in terms of both gold and the dollar – for example, the French franc, which had been worth $0.183 in 1913, sold for $0.039 in 1926.

This system of pegged rates held together for several years. But there were too many inconsistencies among the pieces for the arrangement to remain viable. The British pound was overvalued, perhaps by 15 or 20 percent; the British price level had not declined sufficiently so that Britain would again have a trade surplus. In contrast, the French franc was undervalued as a result of the decline in its value as a result of several speculative attacks in 1924 and in 1926.

In the late 1920s, Argentina, Chile, and other primary-product producing countries experienced sharp declines in their export earnings as the prices of farm products fell sharply; these countries stopped pegging their currencies as their gold holdings became depleted. Then in May 1931, Austria ceased pegging the schilling to gold because the high interest rates adopted to attract funds from other countries caused so many bankruptcies that the largest commercial bank in Vienna failed. In July 1931, Germany stopped pegging the mark and for very much the same reason: maintaining the parity required that its central bank keep interest rates so high that there was massive unemployment. Then in September 1931, the Bank of England stopped pegging the pound, and the currency depreciated sharply.

In March 1933, immediately after Franklin D. Roosevelt took office as President, the US Government ceased pegging the dollar to gold at the $20.67 parity as one measure to limit the run on the banks and to reduce the likelihood that additional banks might fail. The US dollar floated in the foreign exchange market until early 1934 when a new parity at $35 was established. Then in 1936 the price of gold was increased in terms of the French franc, the Swiss franc, the Italian lira, and the Dutch guilder. Within a 6-year period, the price of gold in terms of nearly every currency had been increased by about 70 percent. The alignment of currency values at the end of the 1930s was not very different from the alignment at the end of the 1920s.

This sequence of currency devaluations in the 1930s by the industrial countries – Britain, the United States, France, the Netherlands, and Switzerland – resembled falling dominoes. Each country devalued its currency because the interest rates necessary to maintain its established parity led to high levels of domestic unemployment. Each country was concerned that a more expansive monetary policy that might lead to higher levels of employment would have led to large gold outflows.

Some countries sought to stimulate domestic employment by increasing tariffs and adopting other measures to reduce imports. Each country wanted to import jobs by reducing the price of its goods in foreign markets and raising the price of foreign goods in its domestic market. But no country wanted to export jobs when there was substantial domestic unemployment. The world economic system disintegrated behind higher trade barriers; the volume of imports declined sharply.

The Bretton Woods Agreement

The fragmentation of monetary and trading arrangements in the 1930s demonstrated the need for an institutional framework that would enable countries to follow policies that would enable them to achieve their domestic employment objectives. During the Second World War, the United States and Britain took the initiative to develop an international treaty that would reduce the likelihood that countries would adopt protectionist policies.

One of the two major components of this treaty (informally called the Bretton Woods Agreement after the New Hampshire mountain resort where the final negotiations took place in July 1944) – the Articles of Agreement of the International Monetary Fund – was a set of rules or constraints directed at the behavior of its member countries when they intervened in the currency market. These rules required that each member country state a parity for its currency in terms of the US dollar or gold and limited the country's ability to change this parity. The thrust of the rules was that unnecessary changes in the parities for individual currencies should be avoided, while changes in parities should take place in an orderly manner. The rationale for the rules – based on an interpretation of the 1930s experience – was that once a country was no longer committed to a parity for its currency, its central bank might manage the value of its currency to increase domestic employment – at the costs of jobs in its trading partners.

The second major component of the treaty was the establishment of a pool of member countries' currencies – the US dollar, the British pound, and the French franc – as well as the currencies of every other member country. The IMF then could become a 'lender of last resort' much like a national central bank; the IMF could lend these currencies to a member country to enable it to finance a payments deficit and especially a deficit that appeared attributable to cyclical factors including a decline in export prices. Access to these currencies was expected to reduce the likelihood that a country with a payments deficit would devalue its currency.

The rules about procedures for changing parities and the pool of national currencies were parts of a package; it was believed that a member country would be more likely to accept the constraints on changing its parity if it were assured that it could borrow foreign currencies to finance a payments deficits.

Stress on the IMF arrangements

One of the major shortcomings of the IMF Agreement was that there was no mechanism to induce countries to change their parities when they became inappropriate, which proved especially relevant for countries with persistent and large balance-of-payments surpluses. A second was that there was no mechanism to ensure that the supply of international reserve assets would increase to match the increases in demand.

The emphasis of national monetary policies on domestic objectives and the reluctance of countries to alter their parities subjected the Bretton Woods system to increasing stress, especially in the second half of the 1960s. Changes in currency parities became inevitable, in part because many central banks followed monetary policies appropriate for their domestic objectives. The national authorities were reluctant to recognize the implications of their monetary policies for their currency parities: they retained the exchange market arrangements of the gold standard even though they were unwilling to accept the increases and decreases in the national price levels that enabled countries to maintain the parities for their currencies. The IMF rules sought to minimize unnecessary changes in the currency parities but, in fact, changes in parities proved too infrequent and especially too long-delayed: the adjustable parities of the IMF system were 'sticky' or 'frozen.'

During the 1950s and 1960s, the supply of international money increased less rapidly than the demand. The analogy with the 1920s is strong – in both periods, the shortage of international money was aggravated by sharp increases in national price levels during and after a war, which led to increases in the demand for international money and for gold. The increase in the central bank demand for gold was greater than the increase in monetary gold stocks. As a result, individual central banks could satisfy their demand for gold only by buying gold from other countries. Between 1950 and 1970, US gold holdings declined from \$23 billion to \$11 billion in response to sales to foreign central banks and especially to those in Europe.

One alternative to an increase in central bank holdings of gold was increased holdings of short-term securities denominated in the US dollar, the British pound, and other major currencies – essentially the gold exchange standard. A country could add to its holdings of liquid US dollar securities if it achieved a payments surplus – but the purchase of US dollar securities by countries in Western Europe and Japan meant that the United States would incur payments deficits. Foreign holdings of US dollar securities increased from $8 billion in 1950 to $47 billion in 1970.

US payments deficits in the 1950s and 1960s

During the late 1950s and throughout the 1960s the US authorities adopted a series of measures to reduce the US payments deficit. Foreign recipients of US Government aid were obliged to spend the money on US goods, even though foreign goods were cheaper. US Government agencies were directed to buy their goods from domestic sources unless the prices of similar foreign goods were lower, first by 6 percent, then by 12 percent, and then by 50 percent; the US Army began to ship Milwaukee beer to Munich. Purchases of foreign securities by US residents were taxed, initially at a rate of 1 percent, then 2 percent. Purchases of foreign securities by US firms and financial institutions were subjected to 'voluntary' controls in 1965, which became mandatory in 1968. Measures were adopted to increase US receipts from foreigners – for example, US airlines offered special low fares to foreign tourists visiting the United States. Germany and several other countries were induced to buy more military equipment in the United States.

These measures effectively devalued the US dollar by the 'back door,' because taxes and other barriers to US purchases of foreign goods and securities raised their prices to US residents. Individually these measures reduced US payments abroad for particular types of purchases. Yet the annual US payments deficit remained about as large. Numerous explanations were offered for the persistent US payments deficit, including increased US imports of Scotch whisky, French brandy, and German beer; increases in US military expenditures in Western Europe and Southeast Asia; and decreases in US exports of automobiles and steel. An alternative explanation is that, as a group, other countries wanted to increase their holdings of international money at an annual rate of $2 billion to $3 billion a year – and so the US payments balance passively adjusted to supply the increase in these holdings. Whenever the payments surpluses of other countries were too low relative to their targets, they adopted measures to increase receipts or reduce payments. Thus the measures taken by the United States to reduce the US payments deficits were neutralized by offsetting measures adopted by other countries to maintain their payments surpluses (Figure 5.1).

Thus US imports and US exports adjusted so that the United States would have a payments deficit that was the mirror image of the payments surpluses that other countries as a group sought to achieve. Hence until the late 1960s the US payments deficit was 'imported,' and a result of the persistent strong foreign demand for US dollar securities and for gold. The logic is that if Germany and Japan and France

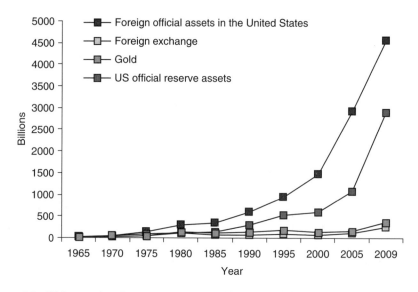

Figure 5.1   US international monetary position, 1965–2005, billion US dollars
Source: International Financial Statistics.

and Italy and other countries wanted to add to their holdings of gold and US dollar securities, they were obliged to keep the prices of their goods low relative to the price of US goods so they would achieve payments surpluses. At the time it was impossible to find a country that believed that its payments surplus was too large. The bankers and the politicians in these foreign countries were reluctant to acknowledge that the US payments deficit had evolved to provide consistency for the payments balances of all other countries as a group.

The United States could supply dollar securities to meet the demands of other countries without limit; there was a virtually inexhaustible supply of US Treasury securities and deposits in US banks. (Whether the US national interest or the system's interests would be served by the continued sale of these bills and deposits is a different question.) The US ability to supply gold to foreign central banks was limited; each sale of $1 billion of gold by the US Treasury to foreign central banks reduced its gold holdings by $1 billion. The US Government's dilemma was that it was unable to distinguish, in the design of its balance-of-payments policies, between those foreign countries that would add to their holdings of US dollar securities and those countries that wanted to add to their gold holdings.

For most of the 1950s and the 1960s (probably until 1967 or even 1968), foreign holdings of dollars increased and the US Treasury's gold holdings declined, not because US goods were too expensive or foreign goods were too cheap, but because foreign central banks wanted to increase their holdings of international reserve assets. The United States was the principal source of international money. But the

United States could not sell US dollars and gold to foreign central banks without incurring a payments deficit.

Policy responses to the persistent payments imbalances

The implication of the worldwide gold shortage was that central banks were buying and selling gold at a price that was too low relative to the costs of gold production. One solution for this gold shortage was an increase in the price of gold in terms of all currencies. Gold production would be stimulated; more gold would be mined each year and the value of gold output would increase even more rapidly as a result of the combination of a higher gold price and larger annual production. The private demand for gold would decline as gold became more expensive relative to all other commodities and securities and a larger share of the newly produced gold would be acquired by central banks. In this way, the central banks in Europe would be able to satisfy their demand for gold without buying gold from the US Treasury. Instead, they could purchase it from South Africa, the Soviet Union, and other gold-producing countries. At some price – $50 or $70 or $100 – every country would be able to satisfy its demand for gold without requiring any gold sales by the US Treasury.

If instead the monetary price of gold were to remain unchanged, then the gold shortage would disappear only if the demand for gold declined. One way to reduce the demand would be to reduce the purchases of US dollars by foreign central banks, which would lead to a reduction in their demand for gold.

The US authorities adopted several measures to reduce the purchases of gold by foreign governments and central banks. US Treasury secretaries cajoled their foreign counterparts not to buy gold. The level of US troops in Europe was tied to Germany's commitment not to buy more gold. The US Treasury developed new securities denominated in the German mark, the Swiss franc, and other foreign currencies in the hope that foreign central banks would find these securities a more effective substitute for gold.

By 1965 the US Government began to recognize that a more compelling explanation for the persistent US payments deficit was the desire of other countries to add to their holdings of gold and US dollar securities. Thus the US payments deficit was systemic and reflected a shortcoming of international financial arrangements rather than a particular US problem. Devising new institutional arrangements that would enable foreign governments and central banks to satisfy their demand for international money without forcing the United States to incur payments deficits year after year was complex. The countries with the payment surpluses were not convinced that the persistent annual US payments deficit was a problem of the system; rather, they believed that these deficits reflected the mismanagement of US monetary and fiscal policies. Moreover, some countries – France, the Netherlands, Belgium, Switzerland, and, to a lesser extent, Italy and Germany – preferred to hold gold as an international reserve asset. They favored a worldwide increase in the price of gold.

'Paper gold' and special drawing rights

The US Government wanted the IMF to produce a security that would satisfy the demands of other countries for international money. This security, colloquially termed 'paper gold,' would have the monetary attributes of gold but not its physical attributes – it would not glitter nor would it be dense. Political negotiations would determine the amount of paper gold that would be produced each year. European governments – especially the French – were reluctant to accept the US initiative until the US payments deficit declined sharply, but the conundrum was that this deficit could not be reduced significantly until the foreign demand for international money declined.

The US view eventually prevailed, and an international treaty was signed providing for the production of a new international money, known as Special Drawing Rights (SDRs) within the IMF framework. About the equivalent of US$10 billion of SDR was produced between 1970 and 1972.

Perhaps the SDR arrangement would have been successful in resolving the system's needs for an increasing supply of international money in the absence of any major shocks. But the Vietnam War and the increase in US and foreign inflation rates meant that the SDR arrangement became irrelevant even before it became operational.

The monetary impacts of the Vietnam War

The irony of the late 1960s was that just as the Europeans came to accept the view that their demand for payments surpluses might be connected with and, perhaps, even be the cause of the persistent US payments deficit, the cause of the US payments deficit changed; this deficit increased to $6 billion in 1969, about twice that in 1968. The overseas spending of US military forces had increased sharply – and more importantly, the US price level was increasing at a more rapid rate. As US incomes and US prices rose, so did the US demand for imports. For the first time Germany and several other countries concluded that their payments surpluses were too large – which meant that the US payments deficit could no longer be explained by the demand of other countries for payments surpluses and international reserve assets.

The United States wanted other countries to take initiatives to restore the payments balance. Whenever the international money holdings of one or two countries increase at a faster rate than they wish – a not unlikely event in a world of more than 100 currencies – these countries have a currency problem, which they can resolve either by revaluing their currencies or by taking other measures to increase their international payments relative to their international receipts. From time to time in the 1960s, Germany and perhaps Switzerland were in this position; so were Canada and Japan in 1969. When one or two countries have excessively large payments surpluses, it does not follow that the United States should limit its payments to all countries as a group as it did throughout most of the 1960s. But when many countries have excessively large payments surpluses at the same time, there is a much stronger case for the US Government to take initiatives to reduce its payments deficit.

Changes in currency values

The European governments were in a delicate position. They wanted the United States to reduce its payments deficit. They might threaten to buy gold from the US Treasury using the funds acquired from the sale of some of their US dollar securities; many central banks had initially acquired these securities in the belief that the US Treasury would sell gold to them at $35. A few countries might buy small amounts of gold – $10 million or $25 million at a time – from the US Treasury. But the US dollar effectively was inconvertible into gold for Germany, France, Italy, and Japan. The European threat to convert dollars into gold was no longer credible, for then the US Treasury might stop selling gold.

From 1969 through the summer of 1971, it was increasingly obvious that the alignment of currency parities would be changed; the underlying question was whether the United States or the European countries and Japan would take the initiative in altering the alignment. Germany revalued the mark in October 1969. Canada stopped pegging its currency in June 1970. Through late 1970 and the beginning of 1971, speculative pressure against the US dollar became more intense. What remained unclear was which country or countries would take the initiative in changing the alignment of parities, and when this change would occur.

In May 1971 Germany and the Netherlands permitted their currencies to float. Switzerland revalued its franc by 5 percent, and Austria revalued the schilling by the same amount. But investors were not assuaged, and continued to move billions and billions from dollar securities to securities denominated in the German mark, the British pound, the Swiss franc, and the Japanese yen.

The devaluation of the US dollar

The crisis about the misalignment of currency values came to a head in August 1971. The leading US congressional authority on international finance suggested that the US dollar price of gold be raised slightly – that the US dollar should be devalued. Speculative pressure greatly intensified; the flow of funds from the United States to major foreign financial centers accelerated. Finally, on August 15, President Nixon announced that the US Treasury would suspend gold sales. (Once it became obvious that the $35 parity would not remain viable until November 1972, it was in President Nixon's domestic political interest to advance the suspension of US gold sales as far as possible before the 1972 election.)

The Nixon administration was not convinced that closing the US Treasury's gold window would automatically lead to changes in the alignment of currency values. Most foreign countries were reluctant to revalue their currencies because of the adverse impacts on jobs and profits in the firms that produced exports. The US Government also adopted a surcharge of 10 percent on all imports subject to tariffs to raise the price of these goods to American consumers – and to reduce US purchases of these goods. US Government officials made it clear that this import surcharge would remain in effect until currency parities were realigned, discriminatory trade barriers against US imports were reduced, and Europe and Japan agreed to begin negotiations toward a 'new international monetary system.' The Europeans and Japanese stopped pegging their currencies to the US dollar, and these currencies then appreciated.

Much of the monetary history of the 1970s is traceable to the delay in not changing the alignment of parities in 1968 or 1969 – when the US inflation rate began to accelerate. Because of this delay, the United States incurred a cumulative payments deficit of $40 billion in 1969, 1970, and 1971; the counterpart was that other countries as a group had a $40 billion payments surplus – which led to a very rapid expansion in their money supplies.

Much of history has a 'what if' quality. If the US Government had increased the US dollar price of gold to $70 or even $100 in 1961 or 1962, the US payments deficits during most of the 1960s would have been smaller and probably much smaller. Similarly, if the US Government had taken the initiative in altering the alignment of currency values in 1969 or 1970, the payments imbalances and the expansion of the money supplies in the countries with the payments surpluses would have been much smaller. If the realignment of currencies had occurred earlier, the 1970s would have been much less inflationary.

Monetary artifacts and the Smithsonian Agreement

The suspension of US gold sales was inevitable; the 10 percent surcharge was not. The surcharge was levied when most countries were in a recession – and, as in the 1930s, these countries found it attractive to import jobs by increasing their exports. But they could do this only by maintaining undervalued currencies. In the first test in 20 years of its ability to prevent 'beggar-thy-neighbor' policies, the Bretton Woods system failed.

Two tangled questions complicated the realignment of currency values in the second half of 1971. One was whether European and Japanese currencies should be revalued around the US dollar while the US dollar remained pegged to gold at $35, or whether the US dollar price of gold should be increased. The second question concerned the amount of the revaluations of individual foreign currencies relative to the US dollar. The first question involved political issues, the second, economic issues.

The political aspect was especially clear in the context of US–French relations. President Nixon's standing with US voters would decline if the US dollar were devalued in terms of gold, while President Pompidou would gain support with his Gaullist followers if it appeared that the US dollar had been dethroned as the center of international monetary arrangements. An increase of 10 or 15 percent in the US dollar price of gold and other currencies would have only a modest impact on gold output, but such an increase would win points for Pompidou with his supporters.

The economic issues involved the effect of changes in the alignment of currency values on the competitive position of firms with factories in different countries. Germany would be reluctant to set a higher value for the mark until Japan had set a higher value for the yen. The Germans wanted to be sure that the yen would be revalued by a larger amount than the mark, so that German producers would be in a more favorable position relative to their Japanese competitors in world export markets. And the French would not set a new value for the franc until the rate for the mark had been set.

In mid-December 1971, agreement was reached on a realignment of currency values: the United States would increase the US dollar price of gold by 8 percent to $38 and the other countries would realign their currency parities about the dollar. The Japanese yen was revalued by 17 percent from its May 1971 parity, the German mark by 14 percent.

Thus the Smithsonian Agreement – 'The Greatest Monetary Agreement in History' – may have resolved the imbalances resulting from the US inflation associated with the Vietnam War, but it did not solve the gold shortage problem or the inconsistencies between national monetary policies and the currency arrangements. While it was agreed that a new monetary system was needed, there was no agreement on the key features of such a system.

A new monetary arrangement must accommodate itself to economic realities 'on the ground.' Most countries prefer a pegged exchange rate arrangement to floating exchange rates to reduce the uncertainty associated with international trade and investment. Some large countries may prefer to allow their currencies to float because they do not want their choice of the most appropriate rate of money supply growth to be constrained by the need to maintain a parity. More and more countries gave greater priority to independent monetary policies; countries then adjusted to external disturbances by altering controls to increase or reduce net international payments. There was a widespread belief that the international role of the US dollar would diminish – a euphemism for attempting to reduce US economic influence. And somehow the new system would have to be built through multilateral negotiations and agreement.

In June 1972 a speculative attack on the British pound forced the British authorities to stop supporting the currency, which immediately depreciated to its pre-Smithsonian parity. Speculation against the US dollar increased in early 1973; in less than a day, the Bundesbank bought $6 billion to maintain its parity. The German monetary authorities were concerned that they were losing control over the increase in their money supply and they stopped pegging the mark. Other countries followed the German lead.

A new Smithsonian-style accord was virtually out of the question. While the national monetary authorities might again commit themselves to a new set of currency parities, few investors would believe that these parities were credible – that the national monetary authorities would incur the costs to ensure that these parities would be viable.

The changes in the price of the US dollar in terms of European currencies and the Japanese yen from the early 1970s were much sharper than had been anticipated. The Bundesbank, the Bank of Japan, and other central banks intervened extensively in the foreign exchange market to limit the variations in the values of their currencies. One of the ironies was that central bank purchases of US dollar securities were much more extensive when currencies were floating than when they were pegged. Despite this extensive intervention, the price of the dollar in terms of the German mark, the Swiss franc, and the Japanese yen varied by as much as 50 percent.

The EMU is not a bird – but the euro is money

One feature of the second half of the twentieth century was a series of agreements among Germany, France, Italy, and other European countries leading to increased integration of their economies – a response to the reduction in the costs of economic distance. First there was the European Coal and Steel Community (ECSC) followed by the European Economic Community (EEC), which involved a common agricultural policy (CAP), a common tariff on external trade (CXT), and the elimination of tariffs and other barriers on internal trade among its member countries. Over the years the number of member countries has increased to 25 as numerous countries in what had been Central Europe including Slovenia and Slovakia, the Czech Republic and Poland and Hungary have joined. More and more initiatives have been adopted to integrate national markets in goods and services, including making professional qualifications in one country acceptable in others.

The values of most European currencies increased and decreased together in the 1970s and the 1980s and the 1990s because of two factors. One is that many of the shocks that have led to changes in these values originated in the United States, including changes in the US inflation rate and changes in interest rates on US dollar securities. The second is that an increasing share of the trade of most European countries was with other European countries.

The change in the name to the EU suggests the increase in ambitions for integration. The motives for integration both within and among countries for integration differ and at times overlap. The French and the Dutch want to wrap Germany into a web of economic and military and other relationships to reduce the likelihood that German armies again march west. Those in the smaller countries have often concluded that their economies are too small for their domestic markets to be competitive, and that their consumers would be better off if their domestic firms competed in a larger setting.

The French view a larger integrated Europe as a much more effective counterweight to the United States in the management of international economic affairs. The Airbus has proved – after many years and billions of marks and francs of subsidy – a remarkable challenger to Boeing's dominance of the world market for large commercial aircraft. The Maastricht Agreement was established to prepare the way for the move to a European currency; the Bank of France, the Bank of Italy, the Bundesbank, and the central banks in the other participating countries would in effect become branches of the new European Central Bank, much as the

Federal Reserve Bank of Boston and the Federal Reserve Bank of San Francisco are branches of the Federal Reserve System in Washington.

The future of monetary agreements

Monetary agreements have two general features. One is a set of commitments about limiting changes in the price of the national currencies. The second is a set of commitments about lending money to foreign central banks.

Both of these commitments limit the freedom of action in the future. Countries accept constraints on their future actions because they believe that they will benefit form the constraints that the other participating countries have accepted. In some cases countries – especially smaller countries – accept constraints because they feel they are under duress from the larger countries.

The Bretton Woods Treaty, the Smithsonian Agreement, and the Maastrict Treaty involved efforts to limit changes in currency values. The second feature is that these agreements do not last forever; the Bretton Woods system came into being in the mid-1940s and was consigned to the Smithsonian in 1971.

The floating exchange rate arrangement was necessary because of the divergence in national inflation rates; the move was facilitated by a powerful set of arguments about the advantages of not having parities for currencies. The data on currency movements since the early 1970s belie these arguments – changes in currency values have been abrupt, and the scope of undervaluations and overvaluations has been much larger than when currencies were pegged. The quip of the proponents of floating was that it was preferable to adjust the currency value to the economy rather than to adjust the economy to the currency value – but because of the large overvaluations and undervaluations, the economies are being forced to adjust to large changes in currency values – and this forced adjustment is much larger than when currencies were pegged.

One of the major motivations for the US initiative toward establishing the IMF in the 1940s was that, in the absence of a commitment to parities, many countries might adopt a 'beggar-thy-neighbor' approach toward the management of currency values. The Fund agreement would prevent countries from devaluing by too large an amount, and it could be used to force countries to revalue.

Trade imbalances have been much larger since the move away from parities, and the US trade deficit has soared. The implication is that there will be another monetary agreement to limit the variability of the Japanese yen and the euro and the Chinese yuan in terms of the US dollar.

6
Radio Luxembourg and the Eurodollar Market Are Both Offshore Stations

Radio Luxembourg developed in the late 1940s as a commercial broadcasting station that would supply its programs to more than 100 million potential listeners in two markets, Britain and France. At the time neither the British Government nor the French Government permitted commercial broadcasting. Broadcasting was a government monopoly and the programs in each country reflected what the producers – the bureaucrats at the British Broadcasting Corporation (BBC) and at Radio Diffusion Française (RDF) – felt their listening publics should have. Perhaps these government officials had correctly gauged their public's wants and needs. Perhaps, but unlikely. If they had, they would not have needed monopoly power to limit the public's choice of programs.

Radio Luxembourg found a market niche by producing consumer-oriented programs as a way to sell commercials – a profitable activity. Although the radio signals were produced in Luxembourg, they were 'consumed' in Britain and in France; neither country was willing to raise 'tariffs' or other barriers to the import of foreign broadcasts. (At the time only the Russians and the Albanians 'jammed' airwaves.) Transport costs for radio waves were low. Radio Luxembourg prospered. Predictably, numerous competitive stations were established. Radio Caroline, for example, parked its transmission facilities on a tugboat just outside the 3-mile limit of British jurisdiction.

Offshore stations and externalized activities

Radio Luxembourg is a classic example of an externalized activity – a good or service produced in one legal jurisdiction is consumed in another. The sale of alcohol and tobacco products at duty-free airport shops is another example; buyers do not pay a tax on their purchases since the products will be consumed abroad. Buyers do not pay transport costs nor do they pay import duties (hence duty-free). Washington, DC is 'a duty-free shop' because taxes on purchases of alcohol are much lower than those on purchases of comparable products in Maryland and Virginia. Residents of both states buy their booze in Washington. The importation of these untaxed products into Maryland and Virginia is illegal, but is not significantly regulated; once or twice a year the revenue agents from these states nab someone for 'illegal imports' in the hope that the newspaper headlines will deter others.

An externalized activity occurs because two different governments regulate the same transactions or activities in different ways. Production occurs in jurisdictions with low taxes or minimal regulation to satisfy the demands of individuals resident in jurisdictions with higher taxes or more severe regulation. For example, Americans travel to Mexico and to Canada to buy specific pharmaceuticals that are not available in the United States. New Hampshire does not have a sales tax, and the residents of Maine, Massachusetts, and Vermont who live near the Granite State shop there to avoid the sales taxes in their home states.

Differential regulation is necessary for an externalized activity, but these activities occur only if both the costs of transporting the goods or services from the production area to the consumption area and the barriers to these movements together are smaller than the differences in the costs of regulation.

The external currency market, née the Eurodollar market

Today the largest external transactions involve the production of bank deposits denominated in the US dollar in London, Frankfurt, Zurich, and other financial centers outside the United States and the production of bank deposits denominated in the British pound in Frankfurt and Zurich and other financial centers outside Britain. The generic term for this market is the 'external currency market'; the popular terms are the 'Eurodollar' or 'Eurocurrency' market. The unique feature of this market is that a banking office in a particular city produces a deposit denominated in a currency other than that of the country in which the office is located. Thus a deposit denominated in a currency other than the British pound and produced in London is a Eurodollar deposit – even if the deposit is denominated in the Swiss franc or the Japanese yen.

A bank that produces an external currency deposit is a Eurobank. A bank in London becomes a Eurobank whenever it sells a deposit denominated in the US dollar or the Swiss franc – or indeed in any currency other than the British pound. Similarly, a bank in Zurich is a Eurobank if it sells a deposit denominated in a currency other than the Swiss franc. A Eurobank need not be located in Europe. Singapore is a thriving center for the Asian branch of the Eurodollar market, while Panama City performs the same function in Latin America. Virtually all Eurobanks are branch offices of a major international bank.

Box 6.1   What Banks Produce

Ask 100 friends two similar questions – what do automobile firms like General Motors and Mercedes and Toyota produce and what do banks like JP Morgan Chase, HSBC, and Deutsche Bank produce? You're likely to find virtually identical answers to the first question and many different answers to the

---

Box 6.1 Continued

second. Each of these automobile firms buys steel, glass, rubber, aluminum, plastics, cloth, and other raw materials as well as some finished components like windshield wiper blades and brake pads; these basic items are the inputs to their production processes. Each of these firms then bends and presses the metal into somewhat different shapes and produces its own brands of cars. The material inputs of each of the automobile companies are virtually identical – except of course for the designs – with those of the other companies. The name of each firm is on the autos that it produces – its output. Each automobile firm is distinguished from all the other firms by the uniqueness of its output. (Of course some critics might say 'they're all alike' but clearly that statement is not descriptively correct.)

Now apply this description of the automobile industry to the commercial banking industry. JP MorganChase and Deutsche Bank buy loans and other types of securities from governments and business firms and households; the inputs of each bank are virtually identical with those of the other banks, although the composition of their portfolios of securities may differ. The output of each bank is its deposits, which carry the name of the bank; a dollar deposit produced by JP MorganChase is not a perfect substitute for a dollar deposit produced by Deutsche Bank. Each bank's brand name is on its deposits, which are its output – at least its principal output.

The source of the potential confusion is that each bank pays interest on its output – the item that it appears to be selling, and that seems strange, sort of upside-down. The interest rates that a bank pays on its deposits depend on the interest rates that it earns on its loans and the costs of managing its business; these costs are like a wedge between the interest rates that it earns and the interest rates that it pays on its deposits. The higher these costs, the larger the spreads between the interest rates that the bank earns on its loans and securities and the interest rates it pays on its deposits.

One of the costs that banks incur is that of government regulation, including reserve requirements and deposit insurance premiums. The higher these costs, the lower the interest rates that the bank can pay on its deposits relative to the interest rates that it earns on its loans and other securities.

Eurobanking is only one activity of a commercial bank. The banks in London that sell US dollar deposits also sell British pound deposits. Altogether, there are more than 500 Eurobanks; the Eurocurrency transactions for these firms are a sideline to their activities as domestic banks. The reputation and credit-rating of each of these firms as a domestic bank determine how competitive it is when it sells deposits denominated in the US dollar, the euro, and the Swiss franc; the lower the credit rating of each bank, the higher the interest rates that it must pay to induce investors to buy its deposits.

Some of the leading Eurobanks are branches of Citibank in different national centers such as London, Frankfurt, Zurich, and Singapore, others are branches of Bank of America, and still others branches of JP MorganChase and of Deutsche Bank. Participation in the offshore money market is the primary activity of most of the London branches of US banks. In the absence of the ability to sell US dollar deposits in London, relatively few US banks would maintain branches there.

That a banking office in London buys loans and sells deposits denominated in the US dollar and the euro and the Swiss franc and the Japanese yen may seem counterintuitive, since it seems more natural that a banking office should sell deposits denominated in the currency of the country where the office is located. That banks in each country sell deposits and buy loans denominated in the domestic currency is a traditional practice rather than – as in most countries – a legal necessity. A bank can sell a deposit denominated in any currency; the key question is whether individuals and firms would buy the deposits in these different currencies at the maximum interest rates that the bank would offer to pay, or whether they would conclude that these interest rates are too low.

Banks outside the United States sell US dollar deposits because investors in many foreign countries want to buy deposits denominated in the US dollar. The US dollar is a unit of account – one of the yardsticks of the world of money – a measure comparable to the gallon or the meter. The 'real' meter – the piece of metal about 39+ inches long, which is one ten-millionth of the distance between the equator and the North Pole – remains in the International Bureau of Weights and Measures near Paris. The French cannot prevent the Americans or the Japanese from using the meter to measure distance. Similarly, the US Government cannot prevent banks in London and in Zurich and in other financial centers from selling deposits denominated in the US dollar, since these banks are outside US legal jurisdiction. Thus there are London dollar deposits and Zurich dollar deposits, and perhaps one day there will be Shanghai dollar deposits. The adjective is important, for US dollar deposits in London are subject to British regulation, and US dollar deposits in Zurich are subject to Swiss regulation.

The British authorities have no incentive to regulate US dollar transactions in London (other than as a favor to the US authorities); if they did, the costs incurred by the banks that sell these deposits would increase, which would mean that the maximum interest rates the banks would pay on these deposits would decline. Then investors might transfer their money to Zurich or to Luxembourg or to some other financial center in search of higher interest rates on US dollar deposits.

Banking readily satisfies the requirements for an externalized activity. The costs of moving money from one country to another are extremely low. One hundred million dollars, or a billion dollars, can be moved across the Atlantic at the cost of a phone call or some other electronic signal.

The major factor that explains the growth of the market in offshore deposits is the avoidance of the costs attached to the production of domestic deposits denominated in the same currency. The scope of bank regulations differs widely among countries; regulation of banks in the United States, for example, has been more extensive than the regulation of banks in Britain. In most countries, moreover, a deposit denominated in a foreign currency is less extensively regulated than a deposit denominated in the domestic currency. US dollar deposits in London are not subject to the reserve requirements and interest rate ceilings that are applied to US dollar deposits in New York. These required reserves are held as non-interest-bearing deposits at the Federal Reserve. (The cliché is that 'reserve requirements are a tax on deposits', when a bank increases the reserves that it holds at the central bank, its interest-earning assets decline and hence its interest income falls. The result is that the maximum interest rates that it can profitably pay on its deposits also decline.) Similarly, Eurobanks are not required to pay deposit insurance premiums as are US domestic banks. Moreover, in London and Zurich, and other major centers for external currency transactions, the interest rate ceilings and the regulations that are applied to deposits denominated in the domestic currency are not applied to deposits denominated in a foreign currency.

Thus borrowing and depositing activities are externalized in the Eurodollar market – investors shift funds from regulated US dollar deposits in New York and Chicago to the less extensively regulated foreign centers including London and Zurich, primarily for higher interest rates on their deposits. Eurobanks can pay higher interest rates because they incur lower regulatory costs.

US, Japanese, and German banks set up branches in London and Zurich to 'intermediate' – to bring borrowers and lenders together – because they can circumvent government regulations on the geographic expansion of branches domestically. The theorem is that 'If the costs of avoiding the regulation are less than the costs of the regulation, the regulation will be avoided.'

Where Eurodollars come from

At the end of 2008 bank deposits denominated in external currencies totaled nearly $45,000 billion compared with $1 billion in 1961. About 70 percent of offshore deposits are denominated in the US dollar and about 20 percent are denominated in the euro. The proportion of US dollar-denominated deposits to total external deposits has declined modestly. Offshore deposits have grown at an average annual rate of 30 percent, much more rapidly than domestic deposits; the growth was especially rapid in the late 1960s and the early 1970s when interest rates on US dollar securities were increasing.

London is the principal financial center for Eurodollar transactions. The volume of foreign currency deposits in the United States is small because US regulations make such transactions financially unattractive to Americans since the deposits are subject to reserve requirements.

For a long time a mystery was attached to Eurodollars; no one could figure out their source. Consider the following analogy – an individual with a deposit in a bank on the west side of Fifth Avenue in New York City (hereafter the West Side bank) transfers funds to a bank on the east side of Fifth Avenue (hereafter the East Side bank). The deposits produced by the East Side bank have increased – and for a brief period, the deposits of the East Side bank at the West Side bank also have increased.

The only difference with a Eurodollar deposit is that the bank producing the deposit is in London rather than on the east side of Fifth Avenue. If Uncle Sam shifts $100,000 from a US dollar deposit in New York to the London branch of the same bank, the London branch produces (or sells) an offshore deposit denominated in the US dollar. Uncle Sam now owns a US dollar deposit produced by a bank in London rather than by a bank in New York. The London branch deposits this check in its account in a bank in New York. The total deposits of the banks in the United States are unchanged; however, individual investors hold smaller deposits in the United States, and larger deposits in London and a US bank branch in London has a larger deposit in New York. The volume of US dollar deposits in London has increased and total US dollar deposits have increased on a worldwide basis.

In the domestic economy, the capacity of banks as a group to expand their deposits is limited by the central bank which determines both the reserve base of the banking system (the supply of high-powered money) and reserve requirements. In the external currency market, in contrast, there are no reserve requirements – and there is no independent reserve base. A bank sells additional deposits whenever the interest rates it offers to pay are sufficiently high to attract investors.

The absence of reserve requirements on offshore deposits does not mean that there is the potential for an infinite expansion of deposits and credit. The growth of offshore deposits is limited by the willingness of investors to acquire such deposits in competition with domestic deposits, which involves a comparison between the risk and return on offshore deposits and the risk and return on domestic deposits. The markets in US dollar deposits in London and in Zurich are an extension of the domestic US dollar banking system into less extensively regulated offshore jurisdictions.

US banks were eager to set up branches in London in the 1960s and the 1970s because they wanted to become larger and the establishment of a branch in London often was easier than the establishment of a branch in a US state other than the one in which the bank was based because domestic regulations severely constrained the establishment of branches in other states. In the 1970s a bank headquartered in Illinois found it easier to set up an office in London than to set up a branch across the street, because Illinois state law prohibited banks headquartered in the state from establishing a branch within Illinois. Moreover, if a US bank did not establish branches in London or some other foreign center, it might lose US dollar deposits to foreign banks and to their US domestic competitors who had branches in London and in Zurich.

If interest rates on US dollar deposits in London are higher than the interest rates on US dollar deposits in New York, Chicago, and Los Angeles, why do investors continue to hold US dollar deposits in these US cities? One answer is the owners of US dollar deposits are not knowledgeable about the higher yields available on US dollar deposits in London. This answer is no longer plausible although it might have been so in the 1960s or even the 1970s. Another answer is that US dollar deposits in London are subject to risks not encountered on domestic deposits, and these risks – the generic term is political risk – might prevent or deter the movement of funds from London. For example, the British authorities might restrict banks in London from fulfilling their commitments on foreign currency deposits; they might be told that depositors could withdraw deposits only if they satisfied conditions X, Y, and Z. Or they might require the external deposits be sold to the Bank of England in exchange for a deposit denominated in the British pound. Some investors might be concerned that US authorities would penalize the repatriation of dollar funds from an offshore bank. The probability of one of these events is very low. And yet the additional interest income on offshore deposits relative to domestic deposits also is small.

The growth of money market funds in the United States is the domestic counterpart of the growth of the offshore deposits. Those who own these funds can write checks on these accounts (usually the checks must be larger than $100) and at the same time, earn interest on their deposit balances.

External currency transactions go back at least to the seventeenth century, when one sovereign would counterfeit the gold coins of another. One popular explanation for the growth of the offshore deposit market in the 1950s is that, during the Cold War, the Russians wanted to hold US dollar deposits because the US dollar was the most useful currency for financing their international transactions. But the Russians were reluctant to hold these deposits in New York because of the concern that the US authorities might 'freeze' their money; the Russians believed that the political risk of a London dollar deposit was lower than the political risk of a New York dollar deposit.

The rapid growth of offshore deposits in the 1960s and the 1970s resulted from three factors: the sharp increase in interest rates on US dollar deposits, which made it increasingly profitable to escape Washington's regulations, the expansion of multinational firms, and the desire of banks headquartered in the United States and most other industrial countries to become larger.

Depositors contemplating a shift of funds to the external market must decide whether to acquire an offshore deposit in London or in Frankfurt or in Zurich or in some other center. Depositors choose among centers on the basis of their estimates of political risk. Moscow and São Paulo seem risky – the heavy hand of bureaucratic regulation is too evident. Even though some investors might acquire Moscow dollar deposits if the proffered interest rate were high, the banks that might produce these deposits might not have the investment opportunities so that it would be profitable to pay these high interest rates.

Links among offshore deposits denominated in different currencies

External deposits denominated in the US dollar, the British pound, the euro, the Swiss franc, and other currencies are closely linked by interest arbitrage. A bank in London offers to sell deposits denominated in any of 8 or 10 currencies; in general, the bank offers a different interest rate on each of these currencies. For example, a bank in London might sell a deposit denominated in the Swiss franc. The bank then might buy a Swiss franc loan or a Swiss franc security; alternatively the bank might sell the Swiss franc funds for US dollars in the spot exchange market and buy a loan denominated in the US dollar. To protect itself against the loss that it would incur if the Swiss franc appreciated, the bank would buy the Swiss franc in the forward exchange market at the same time that it sold the Swiss franc in the spot exchange market. Hence the bank would incur a 'cost' if the Swiss franc were more expensive in the forward exchange market than in the spot exchange market. Because of this cost, the interest rates that the bank would offer on deposits denominated in various currencies differ by the costs of hedging the currency exposure – the interest equivalent of the difference between the forward exchange rate and the spot exchange rate.

The external currency market links the national money markets. Funds flow continuously between the domestic and external markets in response to changes both in interest rate differentials and in investor estimates of the risk of offshore deposits. By increasing the links between national money markets, the growth of the offshore dollar market has reduced the scope for independence of individual national central banks.

A house of cards?

Central bankers and bank regulators lie awake at night worrying about the wheelers and dealers trafficking in their currencies in jurisdictions outside their direct control. US dollar deposits in London seem outside US control because they are in London, and outside British concern because they are denominated in the US dollar. The authorities are worried that much of the growth in Eurodollars has resulted in an expansion of credit, arranged in an inverted pyramid, which might collapse. Thus, each transfer of $1 million from New York to bank A in London may lead to a large increase in Eurodollar deposits, for bank B in London might borrow dollars from investor A to lend to bank C, and so on. The borrower from one Eurobank may deposit the proceeds in another Eurobank – or buy goods, services, or securities from a seller that deposits the proceeds in a Eurobank. As a result, total London dollar deposits might increase by much more than the initial transfer of US dollar deposits from New York to London.

Central bankers worry that a shock to the base of the pyramid could have a disastrous impact, bringing the credit pyramid down with a crash – and wrecking their own careers. The metaphor is a 'house of cards.' The concern increases when the authorities remember that Eurobanks are not required to hold reserves.

Assume that bank A decides to ask bank B to repay its loan. Where will B find the money? Perhaps from bank C. Ultimately, some bank in the system must reduce loans to nonbank borrowers to get the cash to repay maturing loans. If the borrowers cannot repay, then bank C may not have the cash to repay bank B. And if bank B can't collect from bank C, then bank B may not be able to repay bank A.

In 1974, the pyramid began to shake when two banks, Herstatt in Frankfurt and Franklin National in New York City, closed because of their losses in currency speculation. Both banks had borrowed extensively from Eurobanks. The fear was that some of these Eurobanks would be unable to repay their depositors; then a run on the Eurobanking system would begin, and Eurobanks would have to call in their loans to get the funds to repay their depositors.

The worry is needless; a collapse of the offshore system is no more likely than the collapse of the domestic banking system. All Eurobanks are branches of US, Swiss, German, and other major banks, and as long as the domestic offices remain open, the offshore branches cannot close. A central bank almost certainly would provide funds to forestall the closure of an offshore branch of a domestic bank. Nevertheless, central banks might delay their assistance, since they might feel less than completely responsible for the survival of banks whose raison d'être has been the avoidance of regulation.

The authorities are also concerned that access to the Eurodollar market enables borrowers, lenders, and intermediaries to circumvent domestic monetary control, thus reducing the effectiveness of bank regulation and creating inequities between banks that participate in the market and the banks that do not. Some day a clever entrepreneur might establish a Eurobank on a tugboat 5 or 10 miles from New York City in the Atlantic Ocean, which would be the monetary equivalent of Radio Caroline. US residents would shift funds to the Tugboat Bank because it would offer higher interest rates on its deposits than those available on deposits in New York and in Chicago. The Tugboat Bank would be in a favored competitive position since it would be beyond the scope of US regulation.

Increasingly and inevitably, the long arm of regulation must reach out to Eurobanks and to external currency transactions. The Bank of England controls the foreign currency activities of banks within its legal jurisdictions, but in a relaxed way. US authorities apply a reserve regulation to funds received by US banks from their foreign branches. These controls have usually been applied only to commercial banks, for only these entities are within the functional jurisdiction of the central banks. Since regulations reduce the profitability of Eurobanking in London and Zurich, the inevitable next step is that the offshore banking activity would move to less extensively regulated jurisdictions.

Just as Radio Luxembourg can satisfy its customers because of official reluctance to disrupt its signals, Eurobanks can flourish in Luxembourg and Nassau as long as depositors and borrowers are free to do business there. The Eurobanks will prosper as long as US authorities permit the offshore branches of US banks to operate with lower reserve requirements than those applied to the domestic offices of these banks. If the US authorities were to begin to increase reserve requirements on the offshore branches of US banks, and reduce them on domestic deposits, the offshore offices of US banks would be in a disadvantageous competitive position relative to non-US banks.

The belated US policy response to the growth of offshore deposits has been to enable banks in the United States to establish International Banking Facilities (IBFs) – deposits in these banking facilities in New York, Chicago, and Los Angeles are not subject to reserve requirements. Thus far only foreigners are eligible to acquire such deposits – the irony is that foreigners can get higher interest rates on US dollar deposits in these international banking facilities in the major US cities than US residents can. The US authorities are discriminating against US taxpayers!

One day, perhaps, countries will unify their regulations both for radio broadcasting and for commercial banking. Radio Luxembourg will fade away, and the Eurobanks will diminish as a group and many will completely disappear. That day, however, does not seem imminent. The central bank authorities have had the choice of harmonizing their regulations to reduce the incentives for Eurocurrency transactions or of attempting to regulate these transactions. They have done both. As long, however, as the combined costs of various bank regulations are higher than the costs of circumventing regulations, the regulations will be circumvented. Reductions in the costs of communication mean that the cost of circumventing regulation will decline relative to the costs of regulation. The volume of regulated transactions will gradually decline.

7
The Dollar and Coca-Cola Are Both Brand Names

The money-producing industry is like the soda pop industry; a large number of firms make a similar product. Soda pop is colored water with a bit of carbon gas and a sweetener. One brand of pop is a good substitute for another; Coke and Pepsi compete vigorously for the same customers. Coke and Pepsi and Dr. Pepper and the other pop-producing firms strive to make their products attractive; each has attractively designed small, medium, and large bottles as well as cans of several different sizes. Once a product is successful, variants or extensions are developed – Coke begat Diet Coke, then Caffeine-Free Coke, then Diet Caffeine-Free, and then Classic Coke.

Coca-Cola has been so successful in its marketing strategy that a gallon of Coke – caramel-colored fizzy water – sells for more than $2, or at one time much more than the pretax price of a gallon of gasoline. High pretax profits have attracted competitive imitators who frequently choose a similar name and try to penetrate the market position of the brand leaders. Coke's great success led to Pepsi. The market leaders strive to distinguish themselves from their competitors; they protect their brand names by copyright.

Brands of money

Each national central bank produces its own brand of money; the leading brands include the US dollar, the euro, the Japanese yen, the British pound, and the Swiss franc. Each of these national monies serves an identical set of functions – as a medium of payment, a store of value, and a unit of account – in a different political jurisdiction. No two national monies are identical. Some are slightly different from most of the others, many very different from most of the others. The US dollar and the Canadian dollar are good but not perfect substitutes for each other; it is difficult to make payments with US dollar currency notes in London, Ontario, and it is even harder to make payments with Canadian dollar currency notes in Tampa, Florida. Similarly, the South Korean won is an imperfect substitute for the Japanese yen.

Some national monies have proven much better than others as a store of value; their purchasing power has declined by a smaller amount in terms of a comparable market basket of goods. The Swiss franc has a remarkable track record as a store of value over several hundred years, more impressive than that of the US dollar and of the British pound. Similarly, the Dutch guilder performed admirably as a store of value before the Dutch adopted the euro.

The analogy between the soda pop industry and the money industry may seem invalid within the United States, for while the supermarkets in New York and Los Angeles carry numerous brands of pop, most banks carry only the US dollar brand of money. Nearly all transactions in the United States are settled by payments in the US dollar. But some US firms and some US residents hold large amounts of money in London, the Bahamas, Zurich, and elsewhere for business convenience, or to avoid US monetary and fiscal regulations. (See Chapter 6 on the Eurodollar market.) More importantly, foreign central banks, foreign firms, and foreign residents continue to buy US dollar securities because of the brand leadership of the US dollar.

During the 1950s and the 1960s, the US dollar was the leading brand in the money industry. Immediately after the Second World War, US currency notes circulated extensively in Europe; the US dollar was viewed as a better store of value than most European currencies. In Latin America, Europe, and Asia, many firms and individuals hold a substantial portion of their financial wealth in the form of US dollar deposits and US dollar securities. Some business firms in Europe and Asia with substantial international business interests kept their books in dollars – even though their workers are paid in the local currency.

Real property – homes – in some countries that have experienced significant inflation and especially hyperinflations are priced in the US dollar and the sellers require payment in the US dollar.

Some central banks have changed the brand name of their own product to the 'dollar' to increase its attractiveness; this name change is sometimes accompanied by changes in packaging. When Australia, Jamaica, and Malaysia changed from the traditional British system of pounds, shillings, and pence to a decimal-based system, they rebranded their standard currency unit the dollar, a tribute to the preeminent standing of the US dollar. But there is only one US dollar; the other central banks tried to establish a kinship relation with the leading market position of the US producer.

Another favored brand of money, one that appeals to a specialized and small segment of the market (such as the Ferrari in automobiles or Glenlivet in Scotch whisky), is the Swiss franc. In the 1970s and the 1980s the German mark became increasingly attractive because of Germany's success in achieving a low inflation rate and the appreciation of the mark.

Central banks, like the firms that produce soda pop, sell their products. The production of commemorative postage stamps provides a good analogy to the production of money. The costs of production of postage stamps are very low relative to the face value of the stamps; the major expense is developing both attractive designs and papers that are costly to imitate. The producers of these bits of colored engraved paper want the public to hold more and more of their stamps; they much prefer to have these stamps pasted into collectors' books than onto letters. Liechtenstein would go broke if most of the postage stamps it sells were used to mail letters. Similarly the central banks want their publics to hold more of their currency note.

Similarly, the producers of traveler's checks – in effect a form of privately produced money – profit handsomely from their sale, for the money received when individuals buy these non-interest-bearing checks is used to buy interest-earning securities. Traveler's checks are close substitutes for currency and are almost equally profitable. More and more banks and travel companies have begun to produce traveler's checks with their own names, hoping to share some of the profits of the market leaders in the industry.

The public 'pays' for the money produced by the central bank by supplying goods and services to the government. Americans acquire these dollar currency notes produced by the Federal Reserve by selling goods, services, and securities to the Fed's owner, the US Government. The larger the public's demand for US dollar currency notes, the larger the volume of goods and services that the US Government can acquire without having to raise taxes on incomes or on imports or on other transactions. (The US Treasury sells its bonds to Federal Reserve in exchange for the currency notes; the US Treasury pays interest to the Federal Reserve on these bonds, and the Fed's profits are transferred to the US Treasury.)

Just as Coca-Cola wants the public to buy more of its soda pop, each central bank wants the public to buy and hold more of its money. The greater the demand the more readily the product – the national money – can be sold, and the smaller the need to raise taxes or to sell interest-bearing bonds to pay for the government's expenditures.

Each central bank has a marketing strategy to strengthen the demand for its particular brand of money. Packaging is one element in the marketing strategy – two or three colors are used in printing the money. In the United States, most of the currency notes carry the portraits of presidents (although Alexander Hamilton, the first US Secretary of the Treasury, is on the $10 bill and Benjamin Franklin is on the $100 bill); in Britain, the reigning king or queen is on the notes. Austria used to have Beethoven and Mozart on its currency notes before the adoption of the euro.

Russians mistrusted the ruble and their banks during the turbulent 1990s – their holdings of US dollar currency notes were as large as their holdings of ruble currency notes. Russians were estimated to hold more than $40 billion of US currency notes, mostly in the form of $100 bills, more than combined holdings of the residents of New York City and of Washington. In 1997 the US Treasury introduced a new $100 currency note that would be more difficult to counterfeit; Treasury officials were worried that if Russians got stung with counterfeit US currency notes, they would be much more reluctant to buy these notes. If the Russians had not bought these US notes, the US Treasury would have had to sell $40 billion more of interest-bearing bonds; if the interest rate on these bonds had been 6 percent, the US Treasury's annual interest payments would have been $2.4 billion higher.

The packaging arrangements in the soda pop industry are a component of pricing policy: the more attractive the package, the higher the price. Brand-name products sell at substantially higher prices than virtually identical unbranded generic goods; often the brand-name product has a more attractive package. In some cases, the firm sells a 'way of life' or a self-image rather than a product; some Americans pay $45 for prestige vodkas (vodka is odorless, colorless, and tasteless, so it is hard to distinguish the leading brands from the generics in a blind-taste test). In much the same way, the packaging arrangements in the money-producing industry are designed to enhance the attractiveness of the brand so interest rates on securities denominated in the brand are lower than those on other brands.

Finance ministers and treasury secretaries want low interest rates to minimize their government's borrowing costs. In Britain, holders of certain treasury securities can participate in a special lottery; the interest rates on these securities are below those on traditional bonds. The lottery prizes cost the government less than the savings in interest payments. Similarly, holders of some US Treasury securities receive special tax advantages that are intended to reduce the interest rates necessary to attract investors to buy these bonds.[1] From the US Treasury's point of view, the cost in terms of foregone tax revenues is smaller than the reduction in interest payments. Some countries link the interest rates on domestic securities to the price of gold or to the value of the US dollar to increase the attractiveness of these securities. All such devices are marketing innovations designed to create investor interest in a particular money brand – the government's counterpart of commemorative postage stamps and baseball cards.

Overproduction occurs in the money industry just as in the soda pop industry. In the soda pop industry, any firm that increases its output rapidly may have to cut the price or else the cans and the bottles will pile up in the warehouses and on the supermarket shelves. When more money is produced than is demanded, the price level increases, and individuals may shift from domestic money to foreign brands of money as well as to 'hard assets' that they believe will be more rewarding as stores of value. Central banks can produce more money, but individuals cannot be forced to hold more money than they wish.

Market position of national currency brands

Finance ministers often take direct measures to enhance investor demand for the national brand of money. Most governments stipulate that only the national money is legal tender within their boundaries; tax collectors refuse to accept payment in foreign monies. Finance ministers continually 'talk up' the national brand by wrapping their policies in the flag. When the voluntary approach proves inadequate, compulsory measures may be used, and purchases of monies and securities denominated in foreign currencies may be taxed or licensed or strictly forbidden.

The contrast between the number of brand names in money – and the number of brand names in automobiles and jet aircraft – is strong. Most countries, except some very small ones and 15 or so members of the European Union (EU), have their own currency brand, even though few of these countries produce

---

[1] This technique conforms to Michael Aliber's First Theorem: 'When you buy the baseball cards, you get the gum free.'

automobiles and fewer still produce aircraft. Scandinavian Airlines and Mexicana Airlines buy jet aircraft produced by Boeing and Airbus because they are less expensive – almost certainly much less expensive – than domestically produced jets would be. Their national airlines – which compete with United, American, Delta, BA, Lufthansa, Air France, and other airlines in the search for customers and for profits – would be extremely reluctant to incur the higher costs of domestically produced aircraft, for they would have a cost disadvantage when competing for passengers in the world market.

One reason nearly every country insists on producing its own money is that there seems to be no cost to having a national money – at least, the costs are not obvious. But for most countries, the decision to have a national money means that the interest rates on loans and securities denominated in the national money are higher than they would be if its currency were merged with that of a major country. If Canada, for example, were to give up its own money and adopt the US brand, interest rates for borrowers in Canada would be identical with interest rates on US dollar loans – and for most of the last 50 years the interest rates in Canada have been higher than interest rates in the United States (although since 2004 interest rates on Canadian dollar securities have been below those on the most nearly comparable US dollar securities). Having a national currency has meant that borrowers in Canada have been at a cost disadvantage in the international marketplace because they have had a higher cost of capital. When Italy adopted the euro, the interest rates on Italian Government bonds declined by several percentage points.

Indeed, during the 1970s and the 1980s many Canadian firms as well as the provincial governments like those in British Columbia and Quebec came to New York and issued US dollar-denominated securities to reduce their interest payments below those they would have paid if they borrowed in Canada. Most of these borrowers incurred a foreign currency exposure but they had calculated that the reduction in their interest costs would be larger than their exchange loss if the Canadian dollar depreciated. To the extent that the higher interest rates charged Canadian borrowers are a result of having a national money, there is a real – but hidden – cost to Canada, for some investment projects which might be undertaken if interest rates were lower are never launched, and as a result Canadian GDP increases less rapidly than it would in the counterfactual case.

Most governments retain their national monies despite the costs; relatively few have abandoned their national brands, with the notable exception that Germany, France, Italy, Spain, and their neighbors have adopted the euro. One reason that some countries retain their national currency is that they want the prestige. Moreover, a country can have a monetary policy only if it has its own money (although the EU countries that have adopted the euro share in the management of the policies of the European Central Bank (ECB) – although it's debatable whether smaller countries like Ireland, Austria, and Portugal or even larger countries including Italy and Spain have much influence on the monetary policy decisions made in Frankfurt). And kings and presidents want their constituents to be proud of their heritage: the prouder they are, the less reluctant they will be, in theory, to pay taxes.

Each government profits from having its own money because the cost of producing the money – printing the bank notes or issuing the deposits – is much less than the purchasing power of the money in terms of goods and services. (Remember the profit the US Treasury made because of the strong demand in Russia for the $100 greenbacks.) These profits are an indirect form of taxation. Indeed, issuing money is often a less costly way of taxing the public, especially if the government apparatus for collecting taxes is inadequate, or corrupt, or cumbersome. Being able to produce money enables government leaders to circumvent parliamentary opposition to higher tax rates.

In market economies, the prices of financial securities – or the prices of most of them – vary continuously in response to changes in the supply and demand. Prices adjust to induce individuals to buy the securities. If prices are sufficiently low, buyers can be found even for such risky securities as the bonds of the Penn Central Railroad in 1976 and the Argentinean Bonds of 2000. Within a country, investors continually shuffle the ownership of short-term securities, long-term securities, growth stocks, and public utility stocks as their evaluations of the future change and as the prices of these securities change. Similarly investors continually compare the attractiveness of monies with different brand names.

Each financial security – bank notes, demand deposits, government bonds, and corporate bonds – must have a brand name – every contract provides for repayment in terms of a specific national currency. The buyers of securities can choose among 12 kinds of dollars, eight kinds of francs, a variety of pesos (Spanish, Mexican, Argentinian, and Uruguayan), several different crowns or kronor and several different yuan (the Chinese yuan, the South Korean won, and the Japanese yen), the real, the baht, the ringgit, and numerous other national currency brands. Investors must calculate whether the currency brands that are most attractive currently will remain so. Possible changes in the market position of the various brand names – and hence in the value of each currency – are closely examined.

In the 1980s, interest rates on securities denominated in Danish kroner were higher than interest rates on comparable securities denominated in Swedish kronor because investors were concerned that the Danish currency might depreciate; they wanted the additional interest income to offset the possible loss from holding securities denominated in a currency that might depreciate. If investors had complete confidence in the predictability of changes in currency values, then they investors would shift funds between Danish securities and Swedish securities until the difference between interest rates on the most nearly comparable pairs of securities denominated in each of these currencies reflected the anticipated change in the Danish kroner price of the Swedish krona. If these investors anticipated that the Danish currency would depreciate by 1 percent a year, they would buy Swedish securities and sell Danish securities until interest rates on Danish securities were at least 1 percent a year higher than on comparable Swedish securities. In all likelihood, if the Swedish securities were preferred, then the interest rates on Danish securities would exceed those on comparable Swedish securities by somewhat more than 1 percent a year.

Currency brands can be ranked like songs on a hit parade, with the standings based on the interest rates on securities that are similar except for currency of denomination. Investor preferences for currency and checking account money – securities which usually carry no explicit market yield – can be inferred from their preferences for long-term, interest-bearing securities denominated in the same currencies. For example, if the interest rates on long-term US dollar securities are below those on long-term British pound securities, then the US dollar stands above the British pound on the currency hit parade. Investors would hold securities denominated in the British pound only if interest rates on these securities were sufficiently high to compensate for the anticipated depreciation of the British pound. Higher interest rates are necessary to induce individuals to buy money and other securities denominated in the pound – that is, to adjust for overproduction of the British pound. An increase in interest rates on securities denominated in a currency is the international money market's counterpart to price-cutting in the soda pop market.

Some investors seemingly ignore the brand name problem when buying securities, as do many borrowers when they issue new liabilities. Most investors deal in securities denominated in the national brand, the currency of the country in which they live. Similarly, most individuals vote for the same party in election after election. Candidates for political office pitch their campaigns to the 10–20 percent of the electorate whose changing preferences swing the election results.

Brand loyalty is – or once was – strong in cigarettes and beer. Producers within various industries – tobacco, alcohol, automobiles, laundry soaps, toothpastes, money, and politics – market their products toward swing buyers and swing voters. Convenience, ignorance, uncertainty about currency values, and exchange controls explain the preference for the domestic brand of money. Still, an increasing number of investors calculate – or at least attempt to calculate – the advantages of acquiring securities denominated in one of several foreign currencies. Residents of small countries are more likely to compare foreign securities with domestic securities than residents of larger countries, in part because there are fewer opportunities to diversify in the smaller countries. Dutch and Swiss investors, for example, are much more aware of securities denominated in foreign currencies than US investors are; many US dollar securities are listed on the stock exchanges in Amsterdam and in Zurich.

Through most of the nineteenth century and until the First World War, the British pound was at the top of the currency hit parade, and London was the world's principal financial center. Interest rates on securities denominated in the British pound were lower than interest rates on most nearly comparable securities denominated in virtually every other currency. Firms and governments headquartered in the United States, Argentina, and Canada found it cheaper to borrow by denominating their loans in the British pound because the interest rates were significantly below those on securities denominated in their domestic money; they had concluded that the anticipated reduction in interest payments more than compensated for taking on a foreign currency exposure and the risk of a revaluation loss if their currencies depreciated relative to the pound.

The US dollar displaced the British pound at the top of the currency hit parade as a result of the economic and financial events associated with the First World War. Britain had adopted exchange controls to prevent foreign borrowers from selling new securities in London. Moreover, during the war the British price level increased by much more than the US price level and interest rates on British pound securities had increased above interest rates on comparable US dollar securities – but not by enough to comfort investors. The US dollar was the only major currency that remained pegged to gold during the First World War (Table 7.1). US financial markets offered investors a wide range of securities, and the United States evolved into a much more dominant role in the international economy. The US dollar became much more important as a store of value, a means of payment, and a unit of account for non-Americans. Furthermore, the prices of most international commodities including gold and petroleum were quoted in terms of the US dollar.

Table 7.1 Interest rates nominal and real, 1970–2005 (percent)

	1970	1975	1980	1985	1990	1995	2000	2005
United States								
Interest rate	6.44	5.82	11.62	7.49	7.51	5.5	5.8	3.2
Inflation rate	5.90	9.10	13.50	4.00	4.80	2.8	3.4	3.4
Real interest rate	0.54	−3.28	−1.88	3.49	2.71	2.7	2.4	−0.2
Germany								
Interest rate	8.60	5.40	7.85	5.04	8.13	4.4	4.3	2.0
Inflation rate	3.40	5.90	5.40	2.20	2.70	1.7	1.5	2.0
Real interest rate	5.20	−0.50	2.45	2.84	5.43	2.7	2.8	0.0
Japan								
Interest rate	8.28	10.67	10.95	6.46	7.24	1.2	0.1	0.0
Inflation rate	7.70	11.80	7.80	2.00	3.10	−0.1	−0.7	−0.3
Real interest rate	0.58	−1.13	3.15	4.46	4.14	1.1	−0.6	−0.3
Great Britain								
Interest rate	7.62	6.08	15.11	11.55	14.09	6.3	5.9	4.6
Inflation rate	6.40	24.20	18.00	6.10	9.50	3.4	2.9	2.8
Real interest rate	0.62	−18.12	−2.89	5.45	4.59	2.9	3.0	1.8
France								
Interest rate	8.98	7.84	12.20	7.79	10.18	6.6	4.2	2.0
Inflation rate	5.80	11.70	13.50	5.80	3.40	1.8	1.7	1.8
Real interest rate	3.13	−3.86	−1.30	1.99	6.78	4.8	2.5	0.2
Switzerland								
Interest rate	6.75	2.75	2.29	3.75	8.33	2.8	2.9	0.7
Inflation rate	3.60	6.70	4.00	3.40	5.40	1.8	1.5	1.2
Real interest rate	3.15	−3.95	1.71	.35	2.93	1.0	1.4	−0.5
Canada								
Interest rate	5.99	7.40	12.79	9.43	12.81	6.9	5.5	2.7
Inflation rate	3.40	10.30	10.20	4.00	4.86	2.2	2.8	2.2
Real interest rate	2.59	−2.90	2.79	5.43	7.95	4.7	2.7	0.5

Source: International Financial Statistics.

Central banks in Europe and elsewhere acquired more US dollar securities as part of their holdings of international reserve assets.

Securities denominated in the US dollar were at the top of the brand name hit parade from 1915 until the mid-1970s. The currencies of the countries that had experienced greater inflation and had depreciated had lower rankings on the hit parade, evidenced by the higher interest rates on securities denominated in these currencies. Thus, interest rates on securities denominated in the British pound, the Canadian dollar, the Japanese yen, and the German mark were higher than interest rates on securities denominated in the US dollar. Borrowers in many foreign countries denominated their loans in the US dollar to reduce their net interest costs.

The Swiss franc has a special place on the currency hit parade; interest rates on securities denominated in the franc have been lower than those on securities denominated in the US dollar for an extended period. Switzerland is attractive to investors for a variety of reasons – one is political stability and another is financial stability and a third is its record in achieving price-level stability, which is superior to that of any other country. The Swiss franc has been a very strong currency and has appreciated relative to all other currencies including the US dollar, especially since the early 1970s. The tax rates on interest income on Swiss franc securities have been low. Moreover, the Swiss have provided a laundry for money of 'dubious origin.' The Swiss are well paid for this service, since those who buy the services earn low interest rate. And the Swiss sell a lot of financial services to foreign residents.

The US dollar became a workhorse currency during the second half of the twentieth century; most central banks used the US dollar when they intervened in the exchange market to support their currencies. Holdings of US dollar securities have been the largest component of central bank reserves since 1970. International firms and investors have used the US dollar as a vehicle currency: more international trade transactions are denominated in the dollar than in any other currency. Most international commodities are priced in the US dollar.

These multiple financial roles for the US dollar resulted from a combination of factors. One was the dominant size of the United States in the world economy; for several decades the US economy was as large as the combined economies of the countries in Western Europe. Economic changes in the United States have a substantial impact on economic events abroad. Changes in the US money supply have a major impact on changes in the world money supply, and changes in interest rates on US dollar securities have a major impact on interest rates on securities denominated in foreign currencies. Changes in the US price level have had major impacts on the price levels in other countries, much more so than is suggested by the US share of world GNP. Moreover, for the first two-thirds of the twentieth century the US had a superior record for financial stability and an inflation rate lower than the rates in virtually every other country. Finally, the United States was viewed as a 'safe haven' – militarily and politically secure.

Because of the central importance of the United States in the global economy, the US dollar is frequently the numeraire currency, or the unit of account on transactions that do not involve Americans. Thus international airline fares often have been quoted in terms of the US dollar; the price of a London–New York ticket in London is the product of the US dollar price of the ticket and the US dollar price of the British pound.

These roles suggest that the world is on a dollar standard, much as the world was once on the gold standard. The meaning of the term 'gold standard' is unambiguous – central banks stated parities for their currencies in terms of gold, gold was the largest component of the international reserve assets held by several central banks, and changes in the money supply in each country resulted from gold inflows and outflows. The term dollar standard is more ambiguous. One meaning is that the rest of the world holds US dollar securities for a variety of purposes. The large amounts of US dollar securities owned by non-Americans highlight the US role as the dominant producer of international money. The United States exports dollar securities to satisfy the needs of foreigners, just as Germany exports Volkswagens, Ecuador exports bananas, and South Africa exports gold. As long as investors retain confidence in the brand name of the US dollar, the use of the term 'deficit' to describe intended and voluntary increases in the US dollar holdings of foreigners is somewhat misleading.

Whither the US dollar on the currency hit parade?

The displacement of the British pound from the top of the currency hit parade leads to the question whether the US dollar might also lose its top position. The displacement of the British pound resulted from a complex of factors: Britain had become a relatively smaller economy, its use of exchange controls during the war reduced the willingness of foreign investors to acquire securities denominated in the pound, and the increases in the price level in Britain had been significantly higher than in United States. Moreover, there was increased uncertainty about the value of the pound in the currency market.

One of the major attractions of the US dollar in the 1950s and most of the 1960s was that the US inflation rate was below the rates in every other large country – at least until the late 1960s. Further, the US financial markets had depth, breadth, and resiliency so that changes in the prices of assets in response to purchases and sales of large amounts were much smaller than they would have been if a comparably sized transaction had occurred in any other market. Exchange controls did not limit the movement of foreign money into and from the United States – although such controls were applied to US residents after 1965 in the effort to reduce the US payments deficit. The marked change in international financial arrangements since the early 1980s is the shift in the US international investment position to the world's largest debtor country. Although this change has occurred in large part because of the attractiveness of US dollar securities to foreigners, the United States has developed a trade deficit that has been too large to be sustainable for an extended period. (See Chapter 11 for an extended discussion of global imbalances.)

Many foreign currencies – the Swiss franc, the euro, the British pound, the Japanese yen, the Singaporean dollar, and the Brazilian real – have appreciated relative to the US dollar. The appreciation of some of these currencies may be cyclical and have resulted from relatively large export earnings, especially for countries that export basic commodities. The appreciation of the Swiss franc, the euro, and the Japanese yen reflects that these countries have had inflation rates below the US rate.

Does the depreciation of the US dollar in the late 1970s and again in the late 1980s and then after 2000 mean it is 'Afternoon on the Potomac' for the US currency? Interest rates on securities denominated in the Japanese yen and the euro have been lower than interest rates on securities denominated in the US dollar. Interest rates on securities denominated in the US dollar, the German mark, the Japanese yen, and every other currency increased substantially in the 1970s and were much higher in the 1980s than in most previous decades. The purchases of US dollar securities by foreign private parties suggest that they have been attracted by the various attributes associated with these securities. The increase in the US dollar securities acquired by foreign central banks has limited or prevented an appreciation of their currencies; nevertheless, they might have acquired securities denominated in some other currency.

The Dutch guilder was at the top of the currency hit parade before it was displaced by the British pound. The three countries whose currencies have been at the top of the hit parade for the last 400 years – first the Dutch, then the British, and then the Americans – have had attractive financial markets, relative price stability and an economy open to international trade and investment, and had been the dominant international economic power of their time. Today no foreign country appears to challenge the United States in terms of these criteria. Despite the attractive Swiss record for political stability and a low inflation rate, Switzerland is too small and lacks adequate financial markets of the depth and scope to be the dominant international currency. Japan is too peripheral and its economy is still too closed to foreigners. Germany's long-run record for monetary stability and political stability is poor; its remarkable performance in the 1960s and 1970s follows two hyperinflations earlier in the century. No country other than the United States appears to combine economic size and a record for financial stability. But if the US inflation rate increases significantly investors will explore alternatives to the US dollar as a store of value.

The newspaper chatter highlights the roles of New York, London, Frankfurt, and Tokyo as the major financial centers. Tokyo is much the junior member of this group; its major advantages are a massive pool of savings available for foreign investment and low interest rates since the implosion of its asset price bubble in the early 1990s. But Tokyo has significant disadvantages – for a long time, regulations limited the participation of foreigners in Japan's financial markets. And its financial markets lack the depth, breadth, and resiliency that now characterize the US market. Moreover, the likelihood that Japan would allow its payments position to evolve so that foreigners would become net buyers of Japanese securities seems low, for the implication is that Japan would then have to have trade and current account deficits, which would occur only if the value of the yen increased significantly.

In some ways London is the mirror image of Tokyo. The pool of domestic savings is trivially small. There is a strong tradition of a 'hands-off' approach to the regulation of the financial transactions, especially when the transactions involve currencies other than the British pound. Indeed, London's primary role is as an offshore financial center – more transactions in London are denominated in the US dollar than in the British pound. London's principal advantage over New York is its 5-hour 'head start' and the fact that its working hours largely overlap with those in Europe. If by some magic London and New York were open during the same hours, London's role would shrink, and probably dramatically. London's primary role is as a center that enables Europeans to trade US dollar securities when the markets in New York are closed.

Until 1968 or 1969, the international payment imbalances could more easily be explained in terms of the demand of foreign central banks for international money and the undervaluation of several currencies – primarily the mark – rather than in terms of an overvalued US dollar. The statement that the US dollar was overvalued was wrong in the early and mid-1960s. The statement became correct in the late 1960s as the increase in the US inflation rate led to an increase in the US payments deficit larger than the one that could be explained by the secular demand of foreign central banks for US dollar securities. The surge in the US dollar holdings of foreign central banks in the early 1970s led to great concern about the stability of international monetary arrangements. Several questions arose. One involved determining how much of the annual purchases of international reserve assets by foreign central banks was larger than their desired holdings, and undertaken to prevent their currencies from appreciating. The related question was how much of their annual purchases of US dollar securities was undertaken to limit the appreciation of their currencies.

The increase in foreign holdings of US dollar assets in the 1970s was larger than the increase in the 1960s. Until the various currencies began to float in 1973, part of the increase in foreign dollar holdings reflected the weakness of the US dollar; foreign monetary authorities were reluctant to revalue their currencies. In the late 1970s, when the US inflation rate was accelerating, foreign monetary authorities acquired dollar securities to limit the appreciation of their currencies. The paradox is that they apparently acquired assets denominated in a currency deemed weak – to limit the rate at which it would become weaker. But in the early 1980s, the combination of higher interest rates on US dollar securities and a decline in the anticipated US inflation rate led to a surge in the value of the US dollar. The result was the 'Superdollar.' Foreign holdings of US dollar securities assets increased rapidly; the US dollar was greatly overvalued, evident in the large US trade deficits. The paradox was that foreigners were large buyers of US dollar securities when the dollar was weak, and yet they were larger buyers of US dollar securities when the dollar was strong.

The paradox is that the change in the international investment position of the United States from the world's largest creditor to the world's largest debtor has resulted from the strong foreign demand for US dollar securities. The theme of Chapter 11 is that the US trade balance adjusted to provide consistency for the trade balances of all other countries as a group. Various foreign countries wanted trade surpluses and the United States obliged by providing the counterpart trade deficits. Nevertheless, the US trade deficits of 2005, 2006, 2007, and 2008 are too large to be sustained and an adjustment is inevitable – and the likelihood is high that part of that adjustment will involve a depreciation of the US dollar.

The central question now is whether the euro might displace the US dollar as the dominant international currency. The economic size of the EU is comparable to that of the United States but the financial markets in Europe lack the depth and resiliency of the US market.

One of the major advantages of the US dollar that is so attractive to investors is the liquidity of US financial markets – their depth, breadth, resiliency, and transparency. A transaction of hundreds of millions of dollars in US Government securities has a trivial impact on the price. In contrast, there is no European counterpart to US dollar securities, since there is as yet no EU security that is 'backed' by the ability of its government to collect taxes.

The position of the US dollar on the hit parade has been enhanced by US success in reducing its inflation rate, by changes in the foreign exchange value of the US dollar, and by changes in the monetary role of gold. In the early 1980s, the US dollar appreciated sharply in response to contractive US monetary policies. If the US inflation rate continues to remain below 2 percent, then the likelihood of any significant trend movement in the value of the US dollar will be low, and the US dollar will remain at or near the top of the hit parade.

The future attractiveness of the US dollar will be directly affected by decisions about the future role of gold. A decision that gold would again be a reserve asset would remove the uncertainty about its future role. The US international monetary position would be stronger, since US gold holdings would increase greatly in relation to foreign holdings of US dollar securities. The US Treasury would be able to sell gold in exchange for any excess dollar holdings of foreign monetary authorities. And for some time thereafter, the United States would no longer need to produce international money in large amounts to satisfy the demands of other countries.

One lesson that can be learned from experience is that decisive action may be preferable to continued piddling with minor changes in financial arrangements. The British paid an extremely high price for attempting to avoid or delay inevitable changes in the parity for the pound. Throughout the 1960s, US authorities followed a similar strategy of trying to avoid what proved inevitable – initially a change in the monetary price of gold, then a change in the exchange rate structure. Fortunately, the US authorities are no longer hung up on the need to hold the dollar to a fixed value. But they have no clear view of the unique role of the dollar in international financial arrangements.

The real factors – the size and wealth of the US economy – suggest that the dollar will continue at the top of the hit parade. The monetary factors are uncertain, however. Economic mismanagement in the future could tarnish the dollar's attractiveness to investors.

8
They Invented Money So They Could Have Inflation

A hundred years ago, a mile was a mile, a dollar was a dollar, and a liter of water weighed a kilo. The 2010 kilo is identical to the 1910 kilo. The 2010 dollar is only a pale shadow of the 1910 dollar and of the 1810 dollar. All the national monies in 2010 measure less than they did in 1910.

A hundred years from now, the mile and the kilo will be unchanged as units of distance and weight (although the mile probably will be an obsolete measure as more of the Anglo-Saxon world adopts the metric system). It is equally certain that the US dollar will have a smaller value, and so will the Swiss franc and the Japanese yen. While the measurement of the value of money is less scientific than the measurement of the speed of light or the distance to the moon, the error in the measurement is not in question – the orbit of the earth around the sun also varies. Rather, the question is why money is one of the few or perhaps the only unit of account which shrinks in value – gradually at some times and rapidly at others. True, there have been periods when the purchasing power of money over the traditional market basket of goods and services increased – but probably less than 5 percent of recent annual changes in the price level have involved increases in the purchasing power of a money. The only significant declines in the prices in the twentieth century were after the First World War and again in the Great Depression.

Inflation is linked with increases in the money supply, and money supply growth within a country is managed by its central bank. Many central banks were established in the nineteenth century to reduce the likelihood and severity of financial crises, which had been relatively frequent; one of their original mandates was to maintain the fixed price or parity of the domestic currency in terms of gold. (The US Federal Reserve system was established in 1913; because the US dollar had been pegged to gold during the previous 100 years, the Bank of England was the de facto central bank for the United States.) Another mandate was to enhance the stability of the banking system by reducing the frequency and severity of 'runs on the banks.'

During the gold standard period, secular changes in the national price levels were trivial. The US price level in 1900 was not significantly different from its value in 1800, although the price level increased in some periods and then declined, especially during and after the Civil War. Similarly, the British price level in 1900 was not significantly different from the one in 1800. Again there had been periods when the price level increased followed by periods when the price level declined; the decreases offset the earlier increases. An invisible hand – or hands – seemed to manage the changes in the money supply so the price levels remained stable in the long run. The declines in the national price levels often followed a financial crisis, and the failure of an exceptionally large number of banks. The average annual change in the US price level in the nineteenth century was much less than 1 percent, and there were relatively few years when the annual increase or decrease was greater than 2 percent. The US wholesale price index declined by about 30 percent between the late 1860s and the 1890s as the opening of new lands – the American West, Canada, Australia, and the Argentine – led to declines in food prices, which then were a more important component of the price indexes; still the decline averaged less than 1 percent a year.

The changes in national price levels in the twentieth century were markedly different. The US price level in 2000 was nearly 20 times higher than in 1900, while the British price level was nearly 25 times higher.

Progress?

Inflation in the twentieth century

From time to time, the monetary authorities in various countries acknowledge the debasing tendencies of their predecessors – they knock three zeros off the monetary units, usually after the denomination of the currency notes has become too large and after the token coins have been melted because they were more valuable as commodities. In 1959, General de Gaulle adopted the 'heavy franc': 100 old francs would buy one new franc. In 1983, Argentina adopted a new peso, equal to 1000 old pesos, and the Argentineans repeated the exercise in 1985 when 1000 pesos were set equal to 1 austral. Then in 1989 three zeros were removed. The Brazilians knocked three zeros off the cruzerio in 1993; the new money became known as the cruzerio real. The Russians dropped three zeros from the ruble at the beginning of 1998. The Turks trumped them all and knocked six zeros off their currency in 2005.

Traditionally, shrinkage in the value of money was associated with wartime finance; a government 'printed money' so it would have the cash to pay the army and buy guns. From the government's point of view, inflation was preferable to defeat. The first inflationary episode during the twentieth century was during and after the First World War; the US consumer price level nearly doubled between 1915 and 1920 – the annual rate of increase averaged 15 percent, about as high as during the Civil War. The second inflationary episode occurred during and after the Second World War: from 1940 to 1948, the inflation rate averaged 7 percent. Ceilings during the Second World War limited the increase in prices, and much of the increase during that decade occurred when ceilings were lifted after the end of the war. Between 1950 and 1952, during the Korean War, the US inflation rate averaged 5 percent for 2 years. From the beginning of the major US involvement in Vietnam in 1965 to the climax in 1970, the annual increase in the US consumer price index (CPI) averaged 4 percent although the US inflation rate peaked at nearly 7 percent in 1970.

The progressive decline in the annual rate of price increase over these four wartime episodes suggests that the US Government slowly became more successful in putting wars on a pay-as-you-go basis.

The third inflationary episode during the twentieth century was in the 1970s, a decade not associated with war. The US price level more than doubled, and the annual inflation rate peaked at 13 percent in 1980.

The surge in the US, British, and world price levels in the 1970s shattered confidence in the ability of governments to control inflation. A new term, 'double-digit inflation,' hit the newspaper headlines. The US price level was increasing nearly as rapidly in peacetime as it had in most previous wartime periods. By almost any peacetime standard, inflation during the 4-year interval 1972–75 was unprecedented: the US consumer price level increased by 36 percent, or nearly 10 percent a year, more rapidly than during the Second World War.

Where does inflation come from?

When inflation occurs, there often is extensive disagreement about its source, in part because arguments based on association become confused with arguments based on causation. Many events occur at about the same time in the worlds of business and money. Distinctions must be made between causes and definitions, between causes and associations, and between causes and consequences. To say that inflation is caused by rising prices is like saying that death is caused by heart failure; while all deaths are associated with the stoppage of heart movement, heart failure has not put cancer, strokes, and auto accidents out of business. A definition is not a statement about causation. Brain stoppage measures death, just as rising price levels measure inflation; the questions that need to be answered are why the brain stops functioning and why the price levels increase.

A frequent pairing of two events sometimes leads to a 'scientific truth' or rule, as if causation could be inferred from association. An exception to a general tendency leads to the statement, 'This is the exception that proves the rule' – a statement that should read, 'This is the exception that proves the rule *wrong*.' It is a fact that the money supply increases with great statistical regularity toward the end of the year, but it would be risky to suggest that increases in the money supply cause Christmas. Casual observation suggests that fire trucks are frequently found near fires, but only a fool would suggest that fire trucks cause fires or that the fires caused the fire trucks.

Inflation can occur only in a world with money; in a barter world, relative prices change but changes in the absolute price level are not meaningful since there is no unit of account for measuring changes in the prices of a market basket of goods over periods as short as a month and as long as a century.

Inflation measures an increase in the general price level or what is the same thing, a decline in the purchasing power of money; the prices of most goods and services increase, although not necessarily at the same rate since relative prices change more or less continuously. The price levels in Europe increased by 2–3 percent a year in the sixteenth century in response to the flow of gold from Mexico and Peru to Spain and its trading partners. In the nineteenth century there were episodic increases in the price levels, often in response to new gold discoveries, but the price levels rarely increased by more than 2 percent a year except during wars. And then price levels declined so that the price levels at the end of the century were not significantly different from those at the beginning.

Box 8.1   Hyperinflation

In some cases inflation has morphed into hyperinflation, when the price level increases at the rate of 300 percent a year. Inflation tends to accelerate when rates increase above 20 or 25 percent a year, because government finances then become more precarious, since individuals and firms find it financially rewarding to delay payment of their taxes; the longer the delay, the smaller the real burden of the tax payments. Governments may raise interest rates on overdue tax payments, but often the increases in interest rates lag behind the increase in the inflation rate so taxpayers still find it worthwhile to delay their tax payments.

If inflation doesn't occur without money, hyperinflation doesn't occur without a lot of money – more precisely, without an acceleration of the rate of money supply growth. The trigger for a surge in prices may be a sharp decline in the volume of goods available relative to the outstanding money supply; thus many cases of hyperinflation has occurred after wars, and especially in countries that have been defeated or occupied. Usually the geographic territory of the defeated governments has shrunk and their real GDPs are much lower relative to the outstanding money supply. Several of the newly independent countries in what had been parts of the Austro–Hungarian Empire experienced hyperinflation soon after the end of the First World War, while Germany experienced hyperinflation in 1923. Germany suffered hyperinflation again after the Second World War, as did Japan. In the 1990s Russia and some of the countries in what had been Eastern Europe experienced hyperinflation in their transition from command economies to market economies.

As price levels increase, the demand for money decreases, and individuals and firms economize on their money holdings because they want to avoid the losses in wealth associated with increases in prices. The mirror of the decline in the demand for money is an increase in the demand for goods, so the price level rises more rapidly than the money supply. As the price level becomes higher, individuals want to hold relatively more currency notes with high denominations. The amount of high quality paper available for currency notes becomes smaller. Some governments have redenominated currency notes; an individual could take ten notes each with a face value of 10,000 units to a bank, which would stamp one of these notes with a face value of 100,000 units in exchange for nine of the notes with a face value of 10,000, which would be returned to the government.

Zimbabwe's hyperinflation began in 2004, a result of government policies that crippled a successful commercial agriculture. Land was redistributed and often by coercion at the local level; various government ministers somehow became the owners of or at least the residents in some of these properties. Agricultural production and farm exports declined sharply, and the government's tax base eroded.

The government printed more money to pay its bills. Prices rose. The government responded by placing ceilings on prices. Storekeepers were squeezed by the higher prices that they had to pay for the goods and their inability to raise their selling prices because of the ceilings. Goods disappeared from the stores and then the government agency conceded that it was impossible to measure the inflation rate because there were not enough goods in the shops.

At the end of March 2008, the *New York Times* reported that the inflation rate was 100,000 percent – 'A soft drink costs 30 million Zimbabwean dollars, a chicken 200 million, a tank of gas 1.8 billion.'

One adjustment in response to the accelerating increase in the price level is that money has lost some of its usefulness and there is a return to barter – individuals will no longer sell goods for the domestic money. Another adjustment is that an increasing share of the monetary transactions involves a foreign money. All hyperinflation comes to an end; the axiom is that when the government concludes the costs of hyperinflation exceed the benefits it receives, then it will make the adjustments necessary to increase tax receipts relative to expenditures. Often hyperinflation ends when a new government comes to power with the promise to return to monetary stability.

In the long run, inflation will not occur without an increase in the money supply. But an increase in the commodity price level may occur in response to shortages of individual commodities and increases in their prices, even if the money supply growth rate remains unchanged. A failure in the corn crop almost certainly will lead to an increase in the price of corn, for the higher price of corn 'rations' the smaller supply among competing buyers. The theory is that if individuals spend a larger share of their income on corn, they will have less money to spend on other products, and the prices of these other products should decline, with the result that the consumer price level will tend to remain unchanged. Still, increases in the prices of a few products may induce households to become increasingly sensitive to the prospect of a more rapid increase in the price level – and they may go on a spending spree and reduce their holdings of money to avoid declines in their wealth. Nevertheless, these factors lead to one-shot (or perhaps two-shot) increases in the price level rather than continuing increases.

The question about the 1970s is not what was happening in 1973 and 1974, and again in 1979 and 1980, but rather what happened in these years that had not happened before. A second question is why the rates of increase in the price levels differed so sharply among countries in the 1970s. A third question involves the relation between the severity of the inflation and the severity of the recession that follows.

While inflation has been around as long as money, there remain sharp disagreements about its causes. Even if analysts agree that inflation is caused by too rapid a growth in the money supply, they may about disagree about whether the increase in the money supply is the cause of the increase in the price level (a demand-pull story), or whether instead the increase in the money supply is a response to some autonomous factors that have led to increases in the prices of particular goods – a cost-push story. In the second case the money supply may have been increased to prevent or limit the increase in unemployment induced by the sharp increases in the prices of particular commodities.

Assume for example that there is a sharp increase in the price of petroleum, perhaps because wars or some other form of political strife have led to a decline in oil supplies. The demand for petroleum products is price-inelastic, especially in the short run. If individuals spend more money on petroleum products, they will have less money to spend on other goods and services, and fewer of these goods and services will be demanded – supposedly the prices of these other goods and services may decline. If the prices of these other goods and services are sticky in the downward direction, some of the factors that produce these goods and services become unemployed.

Now the central bank faces a dilemma; should it increase the rate of money supply growth to reduce the unemployment rate, or should it wait until market forces reduce the prices of other goods and services?

The inflation tax

The traditional association between wars and inflation is that governments relied on the 'printing press' to get the money to fight the war. The implication is that governments were reluctant to raise taxes by the amount necessary to pay for the increase in their expenditures. In addition to increases in the supply of currency, governments borrowed from the banking system – from central banks and from commercial banks. Once the price level began to increase, those who owned currency notes, bank deposits, and other 'fixed price' assets were subject to 'inflation tax' – which was the reciprocal of the increase in the price level and a measure of the decline in the purchasing power of their money holdings.

Assume that in 2000 Uncle Sam discovered $1 million in currency notes that his grandfather had placed under the mattress in 1900. The purchasing power of these notes is 5 percent of their purchasing power in 1900; inflation tax averaged a bit more than 3 percent a year. Compound interest compounds.

The beneficiaries of inflation tax are those that produced the currency notes, since they have to provide fewer goods and services in exchange for these notes.

Inflation tax is paid by those who own currency and other fixed price assets – bank deposits, and government and corporate bonds. The purchasing power of the interest payments attached to these assets declines; similarly, the purchasing power of the principal of these deposits and bonds declines.

Inflation tax differs from most other taxes, in that it is 'voluntary' – no one is obliged to pay the tax. Why would anyone pay inflation tax? Some individuals and firms are taken by surprise, they almost always underestimate inflation rate, and hence the amount of tax that they will pay. Moreover, using money for payments is efficient, and hence there is a large implicit convenience yield attached to holding money which dominates inflation tax, at least as long as the inflation rate is low – nevertheless, households and business firms may reduce the amounts of money they hold. (The alternative is to return to a barter world, which requires a set of skills long forgotten – but barter reappears in hyperinflationary periods.) The third is that the nominal interest rates attached to bank deposits may increase and inflation tax on deposits (but not on currency notes) is somewhat smaller than the annual increase in the consumer price level.

One standard feature is that during inflation 'real money balances,' measured as the ratio of the money supply to GDP, decline. Individuals and firms reduce their money holdings relative to their incomes to reduce the inflation tax that they are obliged to pay. The implication is that the inflation rate increases more rapidly than the amount that might be projected from the increase in the consumer price level because the demand for money – the amount of money that individuals are willing to hold – declines.

Inflation ends when the increase in government spending declines, either because government taxes have been raised relative to government expenditures so the government has a smaller need to borrow from the banking system, or because interest rates have been increased to exceptionally high levels to curtail bank lending.

The beneficiaries of the inflation tax of the 1970s were those that increased their indebtedness and were able to borrow at interest rates that were low relative to the increase in the price level – at real interest rates that were below their historic average values. The government almost always is the privileged borrower; some governments have placed ceilings on interest rates to enhance their gains from inflation tax.

Watergate economics

In the United States, the year immediately preceding presidential elections is likely to be one of expansive financial policies. The party in power wants the economy to be prosperous when voters go to the polls. If the economy is sluggish, those in power may soon be the outs. If inflation is soaring, the government may also be in trouble. The government wants to 'fine tune' the economy and increase the number of people at work and achieve a stable price level in the months prior to the election.

Assume the economy is in recession. Initially, measures taken to expand the economy are likely to lead to higher output and employment rather than to increases in prices and costs, as long as there remains substantial unutilized or underutilized productive capacity. As the economy expands, it will bump against more and more supply constraints, and prices will rise to ration those goods that are increasingly scarce. At first price increases will be selective as scarcities develop in particular goods; then the price increases will become more general as scarcities become more pervasive. Fine tuning suggests that the authorities will try to time the expansion so that the maximum employment effects are felt in the 2 or 3 months before the election; someone else can worry about subsequent price increases after the election.

In 1959 the prospects for a US recession in November 1960 seemed strong. Arthur F. Burns, formerly Chairman of the Council of Economic Advisers and an informal adviser to then Vice-President Nixon, recommended that measures be adopted to enhance spending and the growth rate of the economy to set the stage for a Nixon victory in the 1960 election. Supposedly, President Eisenhower refused to pass on the advice to William McChesney Martin, then Chairman of the Federal Reserve Board. Kennedy won the election on the promise of 'Getting the Economy Moving Again.' Nixon moved to California.

In 1969, President Nixon appointed Arthur F. Burns as a White House adviser; a year later Burns became Chairman of the Federal Reserve. After continuing a monetary crunch designed to wring inflationary excesses out of the US economy in 1970, in the spring of 1971 the Fed began to expand the rate of money supply growth. In August 1971, one element in Nixon's New Economic Policy was price and wage ceilings, which tilted the impacts of increased expenditures from increases in the price level to increases in output and employment. The US economy began to boom – industrial production, employment, worker-hours per week, and the stock market all went up.

As a recession year, 1971 was unusual. The unemployment rate peaked at about 6 percent, but the consumer price level was still increasing at an annual rate of 3 percent. In previous recessions, in contrast, the price level usually increased by no more than 1 percent when unemployment peaked.

One interpretation is that the structure of the US economy had changed: an increase in the unemployment rate to perhaps 7 or 8 percent for several years would have been necessary before the inflation rate declined to 1 percent. A second interpretation is that if monetary expansion had not begun in mid-1971, the economy would not have been booming in November 1972. Nixon's margin of votes in the 1972 election was the largest ever.

The 1972 inflation began at a time when the price level was already increasing at a rate of 3 percent a year rather than at the 1 percent rate in the recession years of the 1950s and early 1960s. In 1972 the American public had seen the purchasing power of the US dollar shrink by 30 percent in the previous 5 years – an unprecedented peacetime event. When the price level resumed its rapid increase, the public began to anticipate that the inflation rate might increase; rather than risk holding money while its value declined, the public began to reduce its money balances to avoid further losses in wealth. The public spent money more rapidly (and the price level increased more rapidly than would have been predicted from the increase in the money supply alone).

Increases in price levels were inevitable after the 1972 election when the ceilings on wages and prices would be lifted; the uncertainty was the timing. The price ceilings of phase 1, phase 2, and phase *N* in Nixon's economic policy delayed the upward movements in prices. Nixon and Burns had a tiger by the tail, and they could not afford to let go – at least not until after the election.

Upward pressures on US prices also resulted from the decline in the value of the US dollar in the currency market at the end of 1971 and again in 1973. In the late 1960s, US consumption increased more rapidly than US income because US imports were increasing relative to US exports. As long as foreign central banks were willing to add to their holdings of US dollar securities, the increase in US imports relative to US exports dampened upward pressure on the US price level. The combination of the delayed depreciation of the US dollar and price ceilings meant that the price increases which probably would have occurred in 1971 and 1972 were instead bunched in a much shorter interval in 1973. After the depreciation of the US dollar, the incomes of US consumers increased more rapidly than the supply of available goods, and price increases were inevitable. Following the depreciation of the US dollar, the prices of imported goods to Americans increased more rapidly than prices of domestic goods. Following the devaluation of the US dollar in 1973, the price of US goods to consumers in other industrial countries declined; US exports soared, and US consumers shifted to domestic from more expensive foreign goods. The reduction in the supply of goods because of the decline in the US trade deficit, together with the higher domestic price of US imports, reinforced the upward pressure on the US price level caused by the Fed's monetary expansion. The price ceilings delayed the increases in the price level, but these ceilings were removed early in 1973 – soon after the 1972 election, long before the 1976 election.

Governments rarely admit their mistakes. If their policies backfire, the problem is that unforeseen – and unforeseeable – events occurred. So the US inflation of the mid-1970s was attributed to supply shortages rather than to excess demand. Anchovies disappeared from the west coasts of Peru and Ecuador, so there was a deficiency in the world supply of protein. The Russians had a bad wheat crop, and so the world price of wheat soared. These supply shortages contributed to the increase in the price level. But the prices of most other commodities were also increasing. In the absence of a demand boom, the supply shortfalls would have had a much less severe impact on the price level. The Federal Reserve had sailed too close to the wind; these supply shortfalls would have been far less troublesome if the government had followed a less expansive monetary policy in the months prior to the 1972 election.

Watergate was an exercise in overkill: Nixon would have won the 1972 election even without any possible information that might have been gathered from Democratic national headquarters. Similarly, Nixon would have won in 1972 even without the rapid monetary expansion of 1971. The Nixon group chose not to take the risks. These costs fell on the American public, and the costs were immense.

Nixon returned to California in 1974. When Gerald Ford became President, the inflation rate was 11 percent. Ford was not reelected in 1976.

Traditionally, Democrats have placed more emphasis on jobs than the Republicans; their campaign slogan is 'get the economy moving again.' When Jimmy Carter became President in January 1977, the unemployment rate was 7.4 percent and the inflation rate was 5 percent. When he left the presidency 4 years later, the unemployment rate was the same but the inflation rate was 12 percent.

The Fed's policy in the late 1970s was to increase the rate of money supply growth in response to increases in the demand for money so that interest rates would not increase too rapidly. The result was that the money supply increased at a rate which led to increases in the consumer price level. The increase in the price level induced investors to sell bonds and so interest rates increased by an amount that was larger than was comfortable for the Federal Reserve.

Interest rates were about the same level as the inflation rate, so real interest rates were very low or negative. While nominal interest rates had been increasing in the second half of the 1970s, real interest rates had been declining.

Box 8.2   Does the Federal Reserve Cause Bank Failures?

Bank failures were commonplace in the nineteenth century. Banks closed their doors when their deposit liabilities exceeded the value of loans, mortgages, and other assets. Once the word got out that a bank might be in difficulty, depositors rushed to get their money, much more rapidly than if they were to sell a currency about to be devalued. If the bank closed, depositors might receive 30 or 40 cents on the dollar, depending on how badly the bank had been managed.

In some cases, the run on the bank caused an otherwise good bank to fail. Banks were forced to sell assets to meet their depositors' demand for money. Such sales further weakened the banks' position, for inevitably the best assets were the first to be sold because the losses that the banks would have incurred would be smaller than if they sold damaged assets. The failure of one bank had a domino effect on the stability of other banks; bankruptcy became contagious. Credit systems collapsed when the public lost confidence in the banks. Bank failures also meant that the money supply fell, and recessions often followed.

Several institutional innovations were adopted to minimize failure. The National Banking Act of 1863 provided for a Comptroller of the Currency to protect banks and their depositors by ensuring that the assets held by banks were 'good.' Yet there were substantial bank failures in 1883, 1896, and 1907. The Federal Reserve was established in 1913 to act as a lender of last resort, supplying funds – newly printed money – to banks in distress so they could pay depositors who sought to reduce or close their accounts. Nevertheless, nearly 6000 banks failed in the 1920s, 1352 in 1930, 2294 in 1931, 1456 in 1932, and 4000 in 1933. To dampen the snowball effect of deposit withdrawal, the US Government in 1933 set up the Federal Deposit Insurance Corporation (FDIC). Initially, individual deposits were insured to $10,000, then $20,000; in 1975 the ceiling was raised to $40,000, and in April 1980 to $100,000. Banks pay an insurance premium to the FDIC, which has built up reserves over the years. At the end of 2009, capital accumulated by the FDIC from these insurance premiums totaled $21 billion; the FDIC has an open credit line at the US Treasury of $500 billion.

A few US banks failed in the 1970s despite these institutional safeguards. The US National Bank in San Diego failed because its managers made high-risk loans to captive firms. The Franklin National Bank went under in 1974 because of foreign exchange losses. The Security National Bank of Long Island was closed because it had made too many nonsecured loans.

More than 3000 US banks and thrift institutions failed in the early 1980s. The eighth largest US bank, Continental Illinois, failed because of large losses on loans to developers in the oil industry as well as on loans to governments and government-owned firms in Latin America.

Virtually all the large banks in Texas failed as a result of losses, partly to firms in the oil business and to firms dependent on those in the oil business. The quip was that a 'housing loan in Houston is an oil loan in drag.'

The second largest bank failure was that of IndyMac in mid-July 2008; this California-based bank had incurred large losses on mortgage loans, and especially on subprime loans as US house prices fell following the implosion of the real estate bubble.

A key question is whether a significant number of banks could fail again, and how adequate the safeguards will be. In 1974 and 1975, newspaper reports suggested that the Treasury and the Fed were keeping a close watch on several hundred banks. Some of the business and real estate loans made by these banks went sour during the recession. And the market value of their assets was less than that of their liabilities. The losses dwarfed the accumulated reserves of the FDIC.

The Fed faced a dilemma. Its tight-money policy had caused the value of bank assets to decline and had forced the banks into technical bankruptcy. The rationale for setting up the Fed was to prevent the failure of banks. But the desire to break double-digit inflation had driven the banks to the brink of failure. To prevent bank failure, the Fed was obliged to expand the economy – to 'float off' the credit crisis. Monetary expansion could lead to inflation, which would lead to tight money, which would lead to increased bank failures. And so it goes.

Still, inflation rates in the 1980s were significantly lower than in the 1970s – the 1980s was a decade of declining inflation rates while the 1970s had been a decade of increasing inflation rates. And by the end of the 1990s the inflation rates in the United States and in France and in Britain were below 2 percent a year – more or less where they had been in the 1950s and the early 1960s.

Political leaders – at least US political leaders – frequently suggest that if things are not quite perfect at home, at least they are much worse abroad. Nixon was fond of comparing the rate of US inflation with rates in other countries – as long as the US rate was lower. One of the factors – the Fed's expansive monetary policies – which put upward pressure on US prices during the early 1970s did not directly affect other countries; the Europeans and the Japanese could not vote in the 1972 election. Moreover, if the devaluation of the US dollar was supposed to have led to a more rapid increase in the US price level, the converse – the mirror-image appreciation of the German mark, the Swiss franc, and the Japanese yen – should have dampened upward pressure on price levels in these countries. For both reasons, price levels abroad should have increased less rapidly than in the United States. But, in fact, prices in most foreign countries including those with the appreciating currencies increased more rapidly than in the United States. See Table 7.1 (p. 99).

Reaganomics

When Ronald Reagan entered the White House in January 1981, the US inflation rate was nearly 15 percent, and the US Government's debt was $1000 billion. When Reagan left the White House, the US inflation rate was 3 percent, and the debt $3000 billion. The US Treasury's debt increased by another $1000 billion during the 4 years that George Bush was President.

The decline in the US inflation rate was attributable to the tough contractive monetary adopted by the Federal Reserve in October 1979. Two months earlier, President Carter had appointed Paul Volcker, then President of the Federal Reserve Bank of New York, as Chairman of the Federal Reserve Board, and charged him to get the inflation rate down. The Fed adopted a new set of operating procedures – rather than seek to minimize changes in interest rates, the Fed would instead seek to stabilize the rate of growth of the money supply. The rate of growth of the money supply declined, and interest rates on US dollar securities soared, because the limits to the rate of money supply growth meant a significant reduction in the rate at which banks could make loans.

For the first time in more than a decade, the increase in US interest rates was larger than the increase in the US inflation rate. As a result, real interest rates – which are calculated as the nominal interest rate adjusted by the inflation rate – surged to the highest level since the Great Depression. Throughout the 1970s, real interest rates on US dollar securities had been trending down; by the late 1970s, real interest rates were negative. The surge in nominal interest rates led to an almost comparably large surge in real interest rates.

The immediate result of the sharp increase in real interest rates was that spending declined – the United States moved quickly into a recession. Investors were attracted to US dollar securities by the combination of the high interest rates on US dollar securities and the reduction in the anticipated US inflation rate. Before these investors could buy US dollar securities, they first had to buy US dollars in the foreign exchange market, which induced an appreciation of the US dollar. In turn, the stronger dollar led to a sharp increase in US imports, which reduced the US inflation rate – both because the supply of goods available to Americans increased and because US producers were less able to increase their prices.

Inflation targeting – a new religion

The period since the early 1980s has been one of gradual declines in inflation rates; the term 'The Great Moderation' has been used to describe changes in price levels. The thrust of monetary policy in many countries has been to reduce the inflation rate gradually and to avoid shocks to investors' anticipations.

The move away from the Bretton Woods system of adjustable parities meant that central banks could no longer motivate their monetary policies because they wanted to avoid the increases in their price levels that would lead to a persistent payments deficit. In effect, the elimination of the parities also meant that the monetary policy was no longer anchored to a particular objective.

One approach to managing monetary policy is that a central bank would increase its discount rate when the inflation rate increases above a certain range and reduce its discount rate when the inflation rate falls below this range. The target inflation rate is within a narrow range, perhaps of 1–2 percent. If the inflation rate is within the range, the central bank would set the interest rate so that the real rate of interest would approximate to the growth rate of the economy. If the inflation rate is above the range, then the interest rates would be set somewhat higher. Many central banks have targeted an inflation rate with the range of 1–2 percent, and others appear to be following similar policies even though they have not announced a range.

The policy raises several questions – one is why a range, and the second is why not a value of zero? Targeting a range rather than a value provides the central banks with some leeway; they do not have to lean toward a more expansive policy immediately when the inflation rate is below the lower bound of this range nor adopt a more contractive policy when the inflation rate is above this range. The inflation rate can be highly variable from 1 month to the next, and the range provides them with the ability to purse a policy for an extended period.

Why not target a range around zero, say from plus 1 percent to minus 1 percent? The fear is that if the inflation rate were to decline to 1 percent a year, nominal interest rates would fall; but since the nominal interest rates could not decline to less than zero, the lower bound to real interest rates would be plus 1 percent. The central bank may have concluded that it would be advantageous to reduce the real interest rates to less than 1 percent as a way to stimulate investment spending. (There is fear of the debt deflation trap. Note the lack of symmetry.)

As long as the primary economic objective is a low inflation rate, inflation targeting is likely to remain a successful policy. At some stage the costs of inflation targeting in terms of some other objective may be deemed too high, and an alternative approach may be followed, even without changing the name. Few governments have ever deliberately sought to achieve a high inflation rate, but nevertheless such rates have developed as a by-product of their desire to achieve some other objective.

9

Global Imbalances and the Persistent US Trade Deficit

In 1980 the United States was the world's largest international creditor country; its net foreign assets were larger than the combined net foreign assets of all other creditor countries as a group. Britain, France, the Netherlands, and Switzerland were the other large creditor countries. By 2000 the United States had become the world's largest debtor country, and its net foreign liabilities were larger than the combined net foreign liabilities of all other debtor countries as a group. Between 2000 and 2008 US net international indebtedness increased from $1600 billion to $3200 billion; the ratio of the US net international indebtedness to US GDP increased from 16 percent in 2000 to 24 percent in 2008.

This dramatic change in the net international creditor position has no parallel in the experience of any other country. At the beginning of the First World War Britain was the world's largest creditor country, and it remained a creditor, albeit a smaller one, for the next 70 years; the shrinkage of its net creditor position reflected the massive financial burdens of two costly world wars. In the last few years Britain has evolved into an international debtor, as have France and the Netherlands. Switzerland is the only country that was a significant net creditor in 1980 that remains one.

This dramatic reversal in the US international investment position was associated with a counterpart change in the US trade balance. In virtually every year from 1915 to 1980 the United States had a trade surplus and its net international creditor position increased. From 1980 on, the United States had a trade deficit; initially its net creditor position declined and subsequently its net debtor position increased.

A descriptive proposition is that the change in the net international investment position of a country from one year-end to the next reflects the value of its trade balance during that year; the net creditor position of a country increases if the country has a trade surplus and its net creditor position declines or its net debtor position increases if it has a trade deficit. No causality is implied by this arithmetic relationship; in some cases the changes in the relationship between imports and exports cause changes in a country's net creditor position and the competing possibility is that changes in cross-border capital flows directly lead to changes in the country's net creditor position that induce the corresponding appropriate value for its trade balance.

One metric that facilitates comparison among countries in the changes in their net creditor positions and their trade balances is the ratio of the absolute value of these changes to their GDPs. Japan is now the world's largest net creditor country, after having been a trivially small creditor in 1980; at the end of 2008, its net creditor position was 42 percent of its GDP. Switzerland's net foreign assets are as large as its GDP. Singapore's net creditor position is four times its GDP. China is a large net creditor because of its extremely large holding of international reserve assets.

These changes in the US net international creditor position have resulted from voluntary exchanges in both the security markets and the commodity markets. One of the major questions is whether the shocks that led to the changes in the US net creditor position originated in the United States or instead in various foreign countries; a related question is whether these shocks primarily originated in transactions in the goods market or whether instead these shocks originated in transactions in the securities market that induced the corresponding changes in the trade balance. A third question is whether the annual increases in US net international indebtedness are sustainable and, if not, whether the adjustment to sustainable values for the changes in the US net international investment position is likely to occur without a major economic or political crisis.

A life-cycle model of a country's net creditor position

The changes in the US net creditor position in the last 200 years can be viewed in a life-cycle model of the changes in the rate of economic growth in a country as it moves from an agricultural economy to an industrial economy. The stylized fact is that the rate of economic growth is rapid in the early stages of industrialization and then declines as industrialization slows. One analogy to the life-cycle model is the relation between individuals' incomes and their consumption, and hence their 'savings' as they move along the life cycle from infancy to old age. Infants, toddlers, and young children spend more than they earn, using the money obtained from gifts and loans from parents and perhaps others. Once these individuals enter the labor force, their incomes increase and often exceed their consumption, although they may increase their indebtedness for several years while acquiring durable goods – homes and automobiles. Then as incomes increase further the amounts saved each year in anticipation of retirement become larger. Most individuals again spend more than their incomes when they leave the active labor force.

Similarly, most countries spend more than they earn when they are young and at the beginning of their industrialization; they use gifts and loans from other countries to finance the excess of spending over income. Initially most countries are debtors, although obviously a country can become a debtor only if some other country is a creditor. (The Dutch were the first international creditors; see Chapter 20 on the color of the passports of multinational firms.) Both the debtor and the creditor phases of the life cycle have a young stage and subsequently a mature stage. The defining features of a young debtor country are that it has a trade deficit and that the money to pay the interest on its foreign indebtedness is obtained from its creditors in the form of new loans. The country then moves to the mature debtor stage, which is characterized by a trade surplus, which initially provides some of the money to pay the interest on its foreign indebtedness. Subsequently, as the trade surplus increases and exceeds the payment of investment income to the foreign creditors, the country acquires foreign assets at a more rapid rate and reduces its net indebtedness to foreigners.

Then the country evolves into a young creditor as its industrial growth slows; the defining features are a trade surplus and the receipt of investment income on its net foreign assets. Subsequently the country becomes a mature creditor, characterized by a trade deficit; initially the trade deficit is smaller than the receipt of net investment income from the debtors and for a while the country's creditor position increases. Subsequently, as the country's trade deficit increases and becomes larger than its receipt of investment income, the value of the net creditor position declines.

The initial change in the country's trade balance from a deficit to a surplus results from an increase in its competitiveness, most often because its currency has depreciated. The counterpart shift from the young creditor to the mature creditor results from a decline in the country's competitiveness, in part because the firms producing in the younger countries that are industrializing at a rapid rate are increasing their shares in global markets. The country may continue to have a trade deficit for an extended period – or for as long as the country can finance its trade deficit.

When George Washington took the oath of office for the first time in 1789, the newly independent United States was a debtor country because the colonial governments had borrowed from the French and the Dutch to help pay their armies during the Revolutionary War. Moreover, various properties in what had been the 13 colonies were owned by residents of other countries.

US international indebtedness increased modestly as a share of US GDP until the Civil War, when the convertibility of the US dollar into gold was suspended; the US dollar depreciated sharply and the United States developed a trade surplus. The United States remained a mature debtor until the beginning of the twentieth century.

The United States evolved into an international creditor during the First World War partly as a result of US loans to the British and the French Governments and partly because European individuals and European governments were selling foreign assets to get the money to buy guns; some of these assets were acquired by Americans. Moreover, the international competitive position of firms in the European countries declined, since firms shifted production to materials needed for their war effort and hence the exports of these countries declined sharply. The counterpart was that the US trade surplus increased rapidly, largely the mirror of the surge in the imports of the European countries.

US exports exceeded US imports during nearly every year until 1980. The transition from a young creditor to a mature creditor occurred in 1980, when the US dollar appreciated sharply and US imports surged; the annual string of US trade deficits began. In 1980 and 1981, the United States still had current account surpluses, so its net international creditor position continued to increase; the US current account surplus reflected that the net income on the international creditor position was larger than the trade deficit. In 1982 the US current account balance began negative.

The US net creditor position peaked in 1981 at 10 percent of US GDP. The United States evolved into a net international debtor in 1987 if the historic values are used for the valuation of the foreign investments of US multinational firms and the US investments of foreign multinationals; if instead these investments are valued at market prices, this crossover year is 1995.

Table 9.1   US trade deficit and US current account deficit as ratios of US GDP

	(billions of US dollars, columns (1), (2), and (3))				
	(1)	(2)	(3)	(4)	(5)
	US TB	US CAB	US GDP	(1)/(3)	(2)/(3)
1980	−24	2	2,684	0.9	−0.1
1981	−28	5	3,001	0.9	−0.2
1982	−36	−12	3,115	1.2	0.4
1983	−67	−45	3,356	1.9	1.4
1984	−113	−99	3,725	3.0	2.8
1985	−122	−126	3,974	3.1	2.8
1986	−145	−151	4,205	3.5	3.6
1987	−160	−167	4,497	3.6	3.2
1988	−127	−127	4,847	2.6	2.6
1989	−113	−106	5,198	2.2	2.0
1990	−104	−79	5,522	1.9	1.4
1991	−74	−28	5,723	1.3	0.5
1992	−96	−38	6,020	0.9	0.6
1993	−131	−74	6,343	2.1	1.2
1994	−164	−105	6,931	2.4	1.5
1995	−172	−114	7,398	2.3	1.5
1996	−189	−125	7,817	2.4	1.6
1997	−196	−140	8,304	2.4	1.7
1998	−245	−214	8,747	2.8	2.5
1999	−343	−299	9,268	3.5	3.0
2000	−450	−415	9,817	4.6	4.2
2001	−424	−389	10,128	4.3	3.8
2002	−479	−472	10,467	4.6	4.5
2003	−544	−527	10,961	4.9	4.8
2004	−662	−665	11,713	5.7	5.7
2005	−779	−792	12,456	6.3	6.4
2006	−832	−857	13,247	6.3	6.5
2007	−815	−731	13,807	5.9	5.3
2008	−800	−714	14,350	5.6	4.9

Notes: USTB = US Trade Balance; USCAB = US Current Account Balance.
Source: International Financial Statistics.

One of the axioms is that if the ratio of the US current account deficit to US GDP is identical with the rate of growth of US GDP, the ratio of US net international indebtedness to US GDP will be a constant. For example, if this ratio is 3 percent and US GDP increases at the rate of 3 percent a year, then the ratio of US international indebtedness to US GDP will not change. During most years between 1980 and 1999, US economic growth was robust and at a rate greater than the ratio of the current account deficit to US GDP, so the ratio of the US net international indebtedness to US GDP declined even as the absolute value of US net international indebtedness increased. Since 2000, however, the ratio of the US current account deficit to US GDP has been much higher than in the earlier years, and the ratio of US net international indebtedness to US GDP has been increasing. US net international indebtedness cannot continue to increase two to three times more rapidly than US GDP, or at some distant date all of the assets in the United States would be owned by foreigners. Long before that date, an adjustment will occur – and the adjustment could involve either a 'hard landing' with severe adjustments in employment and the price level or a more gradual soft landing.

Global imbalances – is the United States the cause or the victim?

At the global level the sum of net creditor positions and the sum of net debtor positions must approximate each other; this relationship is an accounting identity. An invisible hand ensures that changes in the trade balances of all countries as a group should sum to zero; if the trade surpluses of some countries increase, the trade deficits of other countries must increase by the corresponding amount. (More precisely, imports are valued CIF (cargo insurance and freight) while exports are valued FOB (free on board) so the value for imports should exceed the value of exports by transport costs and similarly the sum of changes in the trade surpluses should exceed the sum of the changes in trade deficits by an amount that corresponds to the cargo insurance and freight.) Finally, the invisible hand ensures that changes in each country's net creditor position from the end of one accounting period to the end of the next accounting period are consistent with the country's trade balance (more precisely, its current account balance) between the two accounting dates.

'Global imbalances' is a euphemism or proxy for the persistent and increasingly large US trade deficit, and the decline of the US creditor position and the increase in US international indebtedness. One set of explanations for these imbalances centers on shocks that originated in the United States; an alternative set highlights shocks that originated in various foreign countries, including Norway and the other oil producers, and in Japan and in China and other countries that have persistently large trade surpluses. The feature of the second set of shocks is that the US trade deficit developed as the counterpart of the 'demand' for trade surpluses in other countries, either directly because the authorities in these countries wanted to achieve surpluses or indirectly because they were reluctant to adopt policies that reduced the surpluses that developed because of the operation of market forces.

The inference from the life-cycle model is that the decline in the US net creditor position was associated with a US trade deficit, either because the prices of US goods were increasing more rapidly than the prices of foreign goods or because of the depreciation of various foreign currencies, certainly in real terms and perhaps in nominal terms. By itself the life-cycle model does not answer whether the change in the competitiveness of the US goods followed from autonomous developments in the goods market of the firms that trade with the United States, or alternatively whether this change resulted from changes in currency values.

One approach to analyze the source or causes of persistent imbalances is to develop two groups of explanations – one group highlights the United States as the source of the shocks, while the other group includes the explanations for the shocks that originate in foreign countries. Then each explanation can be 'tested' against the stylized facts.

Four US-centered explanations for the change in the US net creditor position can be identified; several are modestly overlapping. One is that in the early 1980s US private and public consumption surged relative to US supply and US supply capabilities; domestic US demand exceeded US productive capabilities. US imports and the US trade deficit surged in response to excess US demand.

A second US-centered explanation is that US goods were becoming less competitive in global markets because the US inflation rate was higher than comparable rates in other countries. The implication is the US dollar should have depreciated to minimize the increase in the US trade deficit. This explanation differs from the first in that the increase in the prices of US goods was not associated with excess US demand.

A third explanation – the 'Twin Deficits' story – is that the increasingly large US fiscal deficits in the early 1980s induced increases in interest rates on US dollar securities; as a result the flow of money from foreign countries to the United States increased and induced an appreciation of the US dollar – and US imports increased relative to US exports. This explanation focuses on the change in relative price levels induced by changes in currency values.

A fourth explanation highlights the decline in the US household saving rate that in turn induced an increase in interest rates on US dollar securities that attracted an increase in the flow of money from abroad. (This story differs from the Twin Deficits story in that interest rates increase because of the decline in the US saving rate rather than because of the increase in the US Government's demand for these savings.) The increase in the US trade deficit resulted from a change in relation between national price levels induced by the appreciation of the US dollar.

The implication of the first and the second of these US-centered explanations is that the US dollar initially should have depreciated, while the implication of the third and the fourth is that the US dollar appreciated.

Now consider the explanations that highlight that the shocks that have led to persistent imbalances have originated in one or several foreign countries as an increase in their 'demand' for trade surpluses. Distinguish why an individual foreign country developed a trade surplus from why this increase induced a counterpart increase in the US trade deficit rather than in the trade deficits of Argentina or Zambia, say.

In 2008 the countries that produced and exporte petroleum – a group that includes Saudi Arabia, Kuwait, Mexico, Russia, Iran, Venezuela, and Norway – had a combined trade surplus of $400 billion. Their combined trade surplus was exceptionally large relative to trend because the oil price was exceptionally high. These countries are converting physical wealth into financial wealth; their exports of oil enable them to pay for the purchases of various goods and services as well as the purchases of foreign securities. The imports of goods and services of some of these oil-exporting countries approximate their receipts from exports of oil in the medium term; these countries have relatively large populations and do not have trade surpluses when oil prices are at their trend level. (Indeed they may have trade deficits because they spent some of the money they accumulated when oil prices were exceptionally high.) In contrast, the imports of goods and services of some other oil-exporting countries – those with small populations relative to their earnings from oil exports – are smaller than export earnings, and they buy foreign securities with the money represented by their trade surpluses. They increase their financial wealth for the benefit of future generations, at a time when the country's imports of goods and services will be larger than its export earnings. The countries in this group will have trade surpluses until their oil production declines because of diminishing reserves, and these surpluses will be exceptionally large when the market price of oil is much higher than its long-run trend value.

Once an oil-producing country has developed a trade surplus, its central bank and sovereign wealth fund must decide how to invest the cash, and in particular whether to buy securities denominated in the US dollar, or securities denominated in the euro or in some other currency. Consider several corner portfolio choices for this country; if the central bank uses all its cash to buy US dollar securities, the US trade deficit would increase by an amount that would correspond to these purchases.

If, in contrast, the oil-exporting country does not buy US dollar securities, the US trade balance would remain zero despite the large US imports of oil. (Whether the oil-producing countries as a group would be able to have a payments surplus of $400 billion would depend on the willingness of the oil-importing countries to have the counterpart trade deficits.) The third assumption intermediate between these two corner choices is that the oil-exporting countries buy some US dollar securities; in this case the US dollar will have a somewhat lower value in the currency market than in the first case and a somewhat higher value than in the second case.

Some countries that have followed 'export-led growth' policies have developed trade surpluses. Each country in this group wants a low value for its currency so its exports of manufactures will be competitive in global markets and increase at a rapid rate; each seeks to capture market share from countries that have higher wage rates and higher values for their currencies. The low values for their currencies means that profits in the export industries will be high, and the firms in these industries will be able to finance most of their expansion with their profits; they implicitly believe that their growth rates will be faster if they have large and grow-ing trade surpluses. Japan, South Korea, and Singapore have been in this group. China has had a trade surplus that has been as high as 10–12 percent of its GDP. This view can explain the increase in the US trade deficit only if the countries in this group use the cash obtained from their trade surpluses to buy US dollar securities.

A third group of countries with trade surpluses have recently experienced a significant slowdown in their rates of economic growth, almost always because investment rates have declined relative to the savings rates, much as in Britain in the 1870s at the end of its railroad building boom. Japan has been in this group since the early 1990s. Germany is in this group (although there was a hiatus for 10 or so years following the reunification of East Germany and West Germany). The increase in the purchase of foreign securities leads to a depreciation of the currencies of the countries in this group, and their trade surpluses increase. The flow of savings from these countries leads to an increase in the US trade deficit only if the central banks in the countries with the larger trade surpluses increase their purchases of US dollar securities.

A fourth group consists of countries that are politically fragile or on the verge of instability. Often the rule of law is not firmly grounded in these countries and individuals are not confident that their financial wealth is secure from the arbi-trary action of high government officials or even of lower-ranking officials. These individuals move part or all of their wealth to a more secure financial center or safe haven, which reduces the values of their currencies. Russia has been in this group since the early 1990s. This explanation leads to an increase in the US trade deficit only if the investors in these countries increase their purchases of US dollar securities.

A fifth group consists of countries with currency boards, like Hong Kong and Ecuador and Estonia – and for a while in the 1990s, Argentina. The financial sys-tems of these countries are designed so that if the demand for money increases the countries develop trade surpluses and payments surpluses so the reserve base of their banking systems increases. These countries develop trade surpluses as the counterpart of the increase in their purchases of foreign securities; the US trade deficit increases only to the extent that the central banks increase their purchases of US dollar securities.

A sixth group consists of countries that are reluctant to increase their money supplies, perhaps because of concern about inflationary implications. These coun-tries have an excess supply of goods (which is the inverse or reciprocal of the excess demand for money). The excess supply of goods leads to trade surpluses; the foreign monies earned from these surpluses are sold to their central banks.

China is somewhat unique, in that rapid growth countries often have had trade deficits. China has followed an export-led growth policy and some Chinese firms – including some state-owned enterprises – have increased their holdings of foreign monies and securities because they have been concerned with domestic regulations.

The thrust of the second group of explanations is that the United States devel-oped a trade deficit because other countries wanted to have trade surpluses and they used part of the money received from these trade surpluses to buy US dollar securities. The United States was passive and played a unique international role of providing global consistency – if all other countries wanted to have trade deficits and were able to finance these deficits, the United States would oblige and develop the counterpart trade surplus, much as during both world wars. And if all other countries as a group wanted to have trade surpluses, then the United States would provide the counterpart trade deficit as long as the trade surplus countries were acquiring US dollar securities.

One implication of this view that the US role has been to provide global consistency is that the US saving rate has declined in response to the inflow of foreign saving. And another implication is that the US fiscal deficit has developed in part in response to the US trade deficit; if US imports increase relative to US exports because some foreign countries are following export-led growth policies, then the tax base in the US tradable goods sector will erode.

One test of whether the autonomous shock that led to the imbalances originated in the United States or in the countries with the trade surpluses is whether any country in this group believes that its trade surplus is too large. No country is obliged to buy US dollars in the currency market; instead, its central bank can allow its currency to appreciate. The smaller the number of countries that believe that their trade surpluses are too large, the smaller the likelihood that the autonomous shock that led to the trade imbalance originated in the United States. If other countries managed or mismanaged their policies to achieve trade surpluses, then the invisible hand ensures that the United States would develop the counterpart trade deficits if the central banks and the investors in these countries purchase US dollar securities.

The search for an explanation for the sharp change in the US international investment position should not deflect attention from changes in the international investment positions of Britain and the Netherlands and France – these countries were also net international creditors in 1980 and experienced an inflow of money; one characteristic that they share with the United States is that they have attractive financial markets, although their markets are much smaller than the one in the United States.

The inflow of foreign money is also associated with a decline in the domestic savings rate. One explanation is that the decline in the domestic saving rate has triggered economic forces that have induced the inflow of foreign money. The alternative explanation is that the inflow of money has induced the operation of the invisible hand that has led to declines in the domestic savings rates.

The sustainability of the US trade deficit

Economic systems – every type of economic system – need some mechanism or mechanisms for obtaining consistency among their components. One mechanism is the adjustment of prices of individual goods or of the general price level. If a country has a large and persistent payments surplus while it adheres to the gold standard, the adjustment mechanism is that its payments surplus leads to an increase in the money supply that in turn leads to increases in the price level; the competitiveness of goods produced within the country declines. Similarly, the induced decline in the price level in a country with a persistent payments deficit leads to a reduction in its payments deficit.

Alternatively, if one or several prices are constrained by some sort of regulation from adjusting, then the quantities must adjust. Thus in the 1950s and the 1960s the demand for gold at $35 an ounce exceeded the supply; the adjustment to the excess demand was effected by the willingness of the US Treasury to sell gold. In contrast in the late 1930s, the supply of gold at $35 an ounce exceeded the demand, and the price would have declined had the US Treasury not bought the large excess supply at $35.

In the sixteenth century, the flow of gold from the New World to Europe led to an increase in European price levels in response to a more rapid increase in the supply of money than in demand. In contrast, during the later years of the nineteenth century, say the early 1870s to the early 1890s, the world price level declined by about 30 percent – seemingly a large number, although the annual average rate was just over 1 percent a year. This period was one of remarkable prosperity: industrial production soared in much of Europe and the United States, and there was a rapid expansion of agricultural output in the 'New Lands' of Australia and Canada and South Africa and Argentina. Railroads and steamships linked farms in distant areas with the markets in the cities that were growing rapidly. The increase in the demand for money associated with exceptionally rapid economic growth exceeded the increase in the supply, and the result was that there was modest downward pressure on prices – in this case prices adjusted to the quantities.

Imbalances have developed and evolved as a result of voluntary exchanges. The countries that have developed trade surpluses believe that they are better off because of these surpluses – or they would have managed their economies to have smaller surpluses. To the extent that the US trade deficit has increased the supply of goods available to Americans, many Americans have become better off. The increase in the US trade deficit has meant that the US tradable goods; sector has shrunk both in relative terms and in absolute terms, even though the US economy has grown. Employment in US manufacturing has declined significantly, although not all of the decline can be attributed to the increase in US imports relative to US exports. Some Americans have incurred the costs associated with the shift from the production of tradable goods; often their wages are lower – or they have taken 'early retirement.' Moreover, some of the resources that were displaced from the production of tradable goods may have been unemployed for an extended period during the transition to the production of nontradable goods. The owners of the capital and of the labor displaced from the production of tradable goods have become worse off, otherwise most would have moved to the nontradable sector even before the increase in net imports prompted this move. Finally, Americans may incur some costs in future if part of the process of adjustment to a smaller US trade deficit means that resources must shift from the production of nontradable goods to the production of tradable goods.

Should there be concern about these trade imbalances and the persistent US trade deficit? The key question is whether the US trade deficit in 2008 of $825 billion, which is in the range of 5 to 6 percent of US GDP, is too large to be sustainable for an extended period. If so, can the adjustment to a sustainable value for the US trade deficit be effected without a severe or a sharp change in prices and employment?

The central proposition for each economic unit – the family, the firm, the local government, and the country – is that its net indebtedness cannot increase more rapidly than its income for an indefinite period. The US experience in the nineteenth century is that net international indebtedness can increase more rapidly than GDP for an extended period – although at the end of 80 years the ratio of US external assets to US GDP was never above 20 percent.

Since US net external indebtedness cannot increase relative to US GDP without limit, at some stage the increase in US net external indebtedness must slow to a rate commensurate with the growth of US GDP. The scope of adjustment in the US trade balance will depend on the ratio of US net external indebtedness to US GDP when this adjustment occurs.

The global trade imbalances since the mid-1990s are somewhat analogous to the persistent payments imbalances of the 1950s and the 1960s. There was then no mechanism that would have enabled the countries that wanted to add to their holding of international reserve assets to achieve their objective without inducing a US payments deficit that was too large to be sustainable. One institutional change that might have reconciled their secular demand for international reserve assets would have been the adoption of a much higher price for gold in terms of the US dollar and every other currency; gold production would have increased, the monetary value of existing gold holdings would have been higher and the commodity demand for gold would have been smaller. There would have been a gold price that would have enabled every country that wanted to increase its holdings of international reserve assets to do so without forcing the United States to incur a payments deficit. (If a country wanted to increase its holdings of US dollar securities rather than gold, then US gold holdings would have increased.)

The US Treasury closed its gold window in 1971 and forced the adoption of a system of floating currencies in the effort to reduce the US payments deficit. The US dollar depreciated extensively in real terms in the 1970s, but without a significant reduction in the US trade deficit. One of the ironies is that the increase in foreign central bank holdings of US dollar securities has been much greater when currencies have been floating than when they were pegged.

The surge in global imbalances reflects that the central banks in the countries with the trade surpluses want to increase their holdings of international reserve assets. Their demand to sustain their trade surpluses is stronger than the US demand to resist or forestall or otherwise prevent both the trend increase in the US trade deficit and the cyclical variations around this increasing trend – although in recent years the US Government has urged the Chinese Government to allow the yuan to appreciate.

Consider the characteristics of the countries that are willing to accept the increase in their trade deficits that are the counterpart of the increase in the trade surpluses of the other countries. The necessary condition is that countries are willing to accept the increase in the trade deficits and the sufficient condition is that the country is 'bankable' – that its securities are attractive to foreigners. Argentina and Zambia both may wish to have larger trade deficits, but neither country is bankable, and the securities markets in both countries are trivially small. Argentina is a deadbeat, a rich country that has a tradition of defaulting on its financial obligations. Hence a country must accept or at least be agreeable to the movement of the resources from the tradable goods industries as its trade deficit increases and the financial markets in the country must have attributes attractive to foreign investors.

The US trade deficit reflects the desires of the authorities in various foreign countries to add to their holdings of US dollar securities. These authorities also have increased their holdings of assets denominated in the euro and several other currencies; their strong preference for securities denominated in the US dollar reflects both the large US economic size and the attractive attributes of US financial markets – their depth, breath, resiliency, and transparency.

The ratio of US net external indebtedness to US GDP can stabilize at a large number of levels – 30 percent, 40 percent, 60 percent, 70 percent, or even 120 percent – even though the ratio cannot continue to increase. Once one of these 'levels' is reached, US net international indebtedness and US GDP would increase at the same rate. The higher the level of this ratio when it stabilizes, the larger US net payments of investment income to the foreign creditors, and the greater the minimum required decline in the US trade deficit.

The initial assumption of Table 9.2 is that there are seven different sustainable values for the ratio of the US net international indebtedness relative to US GDP, ranging from 40 percent to 200 percent. US GDP is assumed to be $15,000 billion, and to increase at the rate of 3 percent (the implicit assumption is that the consumer price level is not increasing). The rate of return on US net international indebtedness is assumed to be 5 percent. The sustainable increase in US

Table 9.2   Adjustment to a sustainable US external balance

1. Ratio	40%	50%	60%	70%	80%	120%	200%
2. Net debt (in billion)	$6000	$7500	$9000	$10,500	$12,000	$18,000	$30,000
3. GDP growth 3% (in billion)	$180	$225	$270	$315	$360	$540	$900
4. Net investment income (in billion)	$300	$375	$450	$525	$600	$900	$1500
5. US trade surplus (in billion)	$120	$150	$180	$210	$240	$360	$600
6. Change in US trade balance	870	900	930	960	1000	1120	1370

net international indebtedness consistent with these assumption and the different levels for the ratio of net external indebtedness relative to US GDP is shown in row 2. US net payments of investment income to foreign creditors are shown in row 3.

Assume that the value for the ratio of the US net international indebtedness to US GDP stabilizes at 50 percent; then if the US economy grows at 3 percent a year the maximum value for the US current account deficit would be $225 billion in the first year, the product of rows 2 and 3. US net payments of investment income to the foreign creditors in this year would be $375 billion, the product of rows 2 and 5 percent. The United States would need a trade surplus of $150 billion, the difference between rows 3 and 4. Given that the US trade deficit was $825 billion in 2008, US exports must increase relative to US imports by $975 billion.

That's a massive change – and the implication is that it can occur only if foreign countries as a group are willing to accept an increase in their imports relative to their exports of the same amount.

One inference from Table 9.2 is that the United States must develop a trade surplus, regardless of whether the ratio of the US net international indebtedness to US GDP stabilizes at 40 percent or at 200 percent. Indeed, the increase in the US trade surplus as US net indebtedness increases seems relatively small, although the higher the ratio, the larger the required US trade surplus.

Two of the basic assumptions embedded in Table 9.2 can be easily modified. One is the rate of growth of US GDP; the higher the growth rate, the more rapidly US indebtedness can increase, and the smaller the minimum required US trade surplus. If the US economy were to grow at 4 percent a year while the indebtedness ratio is 50 percent, the US current account deficit could be $300 billion (rather than $225 billion), and the US trade surplus then would be smaller by $75 billion. The second assumption is US net interest payments to the foreign creditors; if the net rate of return is 4 percent, the payment of net investment income would be $480 billion, or the same as the US current account deficit. In this case the US trade surplus would be zero, and the reduction in the US trade deficit would be $700 billion.

The range of the required change in US trade balance is from $870 billion to $1370 billion. The counterpart of the change in the US trade balance is that the US tradable goods sector must expand as a share of the US economy. The US tradable goods sector is about 15 percent of US GDP, or $2250 billion. Excess capacity in the US tradable goods sector is in the range of $100 billion to $150 billion; productive capacity in the tradable goods sector might increase by $200 billion a year. The required change in the US trade balance might take 4 or 5 years.

The counterpart of the increase in the size of the US tradable goods sector is that the tradable goods sectors in the countries with the trade surpluses must shrink, just as the US tradable goods sector shrank as the US trade deficit increased. Increasing US productive capacity in the tradable goods sector is likely to be more readily accomplished than shrinking the tradable goods sectors in the countries with the trade surpluses.

Soft landings and hard landings

One cliché for the adjustment to a sustainable value for the US trade balance is from aviation in the form of a 'soft-landing vs. hard-landing.' The soft-landing scenario is smooth, without significant increases in the inflation rate or the unemployment rate. In contrast a hard-landing in the aircraft implies as a minimum that several of the tires blow out and it might mean that the landing gear collapses.

A soft landing for an economy is illustrated by the Canadian experience in the early 1990s. The Canadian Government had large fiscal deficits, and interest rates on debt denominated in the Canadian dollar were high; investors moved funds into Canada to take advantage of the high interest rates, and Canada developed a trade deficit and a current account deficit. Its external debt was increasing more rapidly than its GDP. Canada was a young debtor and it obtained the funds to pay the interest to its foreign creditors from foreigners. The Canadian Government raised its tax rates relative to its expenditures, its fiscal deficit declined, interest rates on debt denominated in the Canadian dollar declined, and the flow of money from other countries declined; the Canadian dollar depreciated in the foreign exchange market, and Canada developed a trade surplus. A soft, cushioned landing.

In contrast, Mexico experienced a hard landing in 1994–95 during the transition from the Salinas presidency to the Zedillo presidency. In 1994 Mexico had a current account deficit of 7 percent of its GDP; it needed $25 billion of new foreign money each year to maintain its policy of allowing the peso to depreciate at a slow rate. The inflow of foreign money dried up suddenly as a result of several political incidents, and the Bank of Mexico was forced to stop supporting the peso in the foreign exchange market as its holdings of international reserve assets were exhausted. The Mexican peso depreciated sharply from 3.40 pesos per US dollar to 6.40 pesos, and the result was that the current account balance shifted by nearly 11 percent of GDP from a deficit of 7 percent to a surplus of 4 percent. The adjustment probably was too large since there was no need for Mexico to develop a trade surplus. This shock was simultaneously inflationary because of the surge in the peso prices of imported goods and of exported goods, and deflationary because of the surge in peso interest rates associated with the sharp increase in the inflation rate and the sharp decline in the availability of credit.

The Mexican and the Canadian examples are useful, but both are reasonably small countries; moreover much of the adjustments in both countries involved changes in their bilateral trade balance with the United States. In both cases the depreciation of the currencies led to an increase in their exports relative to their imports, and much of the counterpart adjustment involved the mirror-image increase in US imports relative to US exports. The analogies are tested because the United States is so much larger than its trading partners, and many, if not most, of these countries will be reluctant to have their imports increase significantly relative to their exports as the United States seeks to reduce its trade deficit.

The depreciation of the Mexican peso was very large. In contrast, the Canadian dollar depreciated by about 15 percent. The required reduction in the US trade balance is about 5 percent of US GDP – and an increase of 30 percent of the size of the US tradable goods sector – a massive adjustment in 5 or 6 years.

The smoothest possible adjustment scenario – one of the soft-landing scenarios – would involve an increase in the foreign demand for US goods while currency values remain unchanged. The US tradable goods sector would expand relative to the nontradable goods sector, while the tradable goods sectors in the countries with the large trade surpluses would shrink. At the same time, the savings rates in various foreign countries would decline and the increase in expenditures would be associated with an increase in the demand for US goods. This increase in the foreign demand for US goods would be gradual and correspond with the increase in the US ability to expand the production of these goods.

One variant would involve a significant decline in the price of oil and of other primary commodities; the trade surpluses of the countries that produce these commodities would decline and hence the counterpart trade deficits would decline.

The next smoothest adjustment would involve an increase in the foreign demand for US goods in response to a depreciation of the US dollar, which might occur in response to the decline in interest rates on US dollar securities, either because the US fiscal deficit declined in response to an increase in US tax rates or because the household saving rate increased.

The third scenario involves a decline in the US demand for foreign goods either because of the exhortation to 'Buy American' or because the US Government adopts import barriers on all US imports or on US imports from selected countries. In this case foreign currencies would depreciate, but by less than the effective import barriers. One assumption is that this change might be adopted gradually to reduce the likelihood that the increase in the US demand for US goods would lead to significant price increases.

One of the hard-landing scenarios is that the foreign demand for US dollar securities declines because of the apprehension that the US dollar will depreciate sharply – a self-justifying event. At the new and lower value for the US dollar, the increase in the American and foreign demand for US goods surges relative to excess productive capacity in tradable goods, and the US inflation rate increases sharply.

Consider what would happen if the US productive capacity in the tradable goods increases but some foreign countries are unwilling to accept a decline in their trade surpluses implied by the desire of the United States to reduce its trade deficit. The global supply of tradable goods would increase relative to the supply of nontradable goods.

This is a ball park estimate, and the adjustment might not occur in 1 year; indeed if all of the adjustment were to occur in 1 year, the consequences would be costly. If the adjustments were to occur over 5 or 10 years, the same sort of factors would be present. The longer the period of adjustment, the more gradual the adjustment, but the larger the overall adjustment.

The adjustment in the countries with large trade surpluses would involve shifting capital and labor from the production of tradable goods to the production of nontradable goods, similar to the adjustments within the United States as the US trade deficit has increased since the early 1980s. This adjustment would have a contractive impact on income and employment. In contrast, within the United States labor and other resources would shift from the production of nontradable goods to the production of tradable goods; this adjustment would have an expansive impact on the economy because investments would have to be made in the production of tradable goods.

10
Five Asset Price Bubbles in
30 Years – A New World Record

In December 1979 the Nikkei 225 stock price index in Japan was 8500; 10 years later the index peaked at nearly 40,000. Real estate prices in Japan in 1989 were nine times higher than in 1979. The market value of Japanese real estate was twice the market value of US real estate (even though Japan's GDP was less than half of US GDP); one quip in Tokyo was that the land around the Imperial Palace in Tokyo was more valuable than all the real estate in California.

In the 1980s Japan experienced an extraordinary asset price bubble – probably the largest ever, at least in a major industrial country. Investors – and ordinary individuals like Mrs Watanabe, the John Doe or the John Smith of Japan – were buying both real estate and stocks because their prices were increasing. The prices of real estate and of stocks were increasing because Mrs Watanabe and her friends were buying these assets. Mrs Watanabe and her friends were buying these assets because their prices were increasing. If it sounds circular, it was. The defining feature of a bubble is that recent increases in the prices of assets provide the rationale that prices will continue to increase and hence motivate continued purchases.

Consumption spending and investment spending in Japan surged as asset prices climbed; the economy experienced a massive boom. Japan had been at the top of the hit parade of economic growth rates in the 1950s and the 1960s and the 1970s, a remarkable come-back success story after devastating losses during the Second World War. (See Chapter 21 for the Japan story.) The high levels of economic growth in these three decades led to mostly steady increases in the prices of real estate and of stocks.

Asset price bubbles involve a move across a fuzzy threshold from rational exuberance associated with high rates of economic growth to irrational exuberance associated with projecting asset prices in the near future as an extrapolation from recent increases. As long as the economy is on the rational side of this threshold, the price of real estate is based on rental incomes and the price of stocks is based on corporate earnings and estimates of their rate of growth. Once the economy moved to the irrational side of the threshold, the increases in the price of real estate were divorced from the current and anticipated rental rates of return. Similarly, the projections of stock prices were no longer related to corporate earnings and their prospective rate of growth.

The 'Greater Fool Theory' was alive and well and flourishing in Tokyo in the second half of the 1980s. The buyers of real estate and of stocks recognized that their prices were exceptionally high, nevertheless they anticipated extraordinary rates of return on their purchases of these assets because they believed that other buyers soon would pay even higher prices.

One feature of a credit bubble is that the rate of growth of indebtedness of a particular group of borrowers often is in the range of 20–30 percent a year. The interest payments of the borrowers increase about as rapidly as their indebtedness, but the borrowers have an impeccable record for paying the interest on a timely basis because all of the money they need for these payments is obtained from new loans. A second feature is that the indebtedness of the borrowers increases more rapidly than their incomes. At some stage the lenders inevitably will become concerned that the borrowers' indebtedness is increasing at too rapid a rate; then the slowing of the growth of their indebtedness triggers a sudden adjustment and often significant defaults by the borrowers. A third feature is that once asset prices stop increasing, they do not plateau; instead, real estate prices decline because they are too high relative to rents, and stock prices decline because they are too high relative to corporate earnings A fourth feature is that risk is 'under-priced'; the interest rates set by the lenders prove to be too low relative to the probability of losses and the amounts of the losses that they will incur when the borrowers default.

In the last several decades of the nineteenth century, after the invention of the telegraph and the stock market ticker, those in search of short-term speculative profits from trading stocks were called 'tape watchers'; they correlated changes in the prices of a particular stock with the changes in the volume of transactions in that stock. If the stock ticker tape indicated that the volume of purchases of a particular stock and its price were both increasing, these investors bought the stock. In contrast if the volume of transactions in a stock and its price were both decreasing, they sold the stock. Their 'strategy' is captured by the cliché 'the trend is your friend.' More recently the term 'momentum traders' has been applied to those that follow this strategy.

Box 10.1   On Bubble Terminology

The term 'bubble' means that the rate of increase in the price of an asset or in the indebtedness of a borrower is too rapid to be sustained; when the increase slows, the price immediately declines because some of the recent buyers have become distress sellers since they no longer have the money to pay the interest. A 'credit bubble' involves an exceptionally rapid increase in the indebtedness of a group of borrowers, usually in the form of bank loans. An 'asset bubble' involves an exceptionally rapid increase in the prices of real estate or of stocks or in many cases of both real estate and stocks.

Box 10.1   Continued

Credit bubbles and asset price bubbles are closely related and partially overlapping; most credit bubbles lead to asset price bubbles and most asset price
bubbles result from credit bubbles. A real estate bubble always requires a rapid
increase in credit, since many buyers borrow most of the money they need for
their purchases. One credit bubble that was not associated with an increase
in asset prices centered on the rapid increase in bank loans to governments
and government-owned firms in Mexico and other developing countries in
the 1970s. Another exception is that the surge in US stock prices in the late
1990s involved a trivial amount of credit.

An extraordinary feature of the last 30 years is that there have been five 'waves'
of bubbles; each wave has involved rapid increases in credit and indebtedness
in four, five, or even more countries at the same time. In contrast, there had
been very few bubbles in the previous 200 years although the United States
had a stock price bubble and a real estate bubble in the late 1920s. The first
wave of credit bubbles involved the sharp increase in bank loans to governments
and government-owned firms in Mexico, Brazil, Argentina, and other developing
countries in the 1970s. The second wave was centered in Japan in the second
half of the 1980s, with particular spillover impacts on the real estate and stock
markets in Finland, Norway, and Sweden. The third wave included Thailand,
Malaysia, and some of their Asian neighbors in the early to mid-1990s as well
as Russia, Brazil, and Argentina. Stock prices and real estate prices in Mexico
also increased rapidly during this wave. The United States experienced a stock
price bubble the last several years of the 1990s. Moreover, between 2002 and
2007 the United States and Britain and most other Anglo-Saxon countries as
well as Ireland and Spain and Iceland had bubbles in their residential real estate
markets.

The likelihood that the bubbles in different countries during each of these waves
were unrelated seems low. Moreover, the likelihood that the bubbles in several of
the successive waves were unrelated seems low.

Box 10.2   Charlie Ponzi and the Real Estate Bubble in Albania

Carlos Ponzi was one of the most famous 'bankers' in American history, now
memorialized in the term 'Ponzi scheme.' Ponzi promised that he would pay
an annual interest rate of 45 percent on his 3-month IOUs. He claimed that
the source of the money to pay the interest came from the exceptionally high
profits he earned arbitraging international postal reply coupons. The British
pound, the French franc, the Italian lira, and other European currencies had
depreciated sharply in the early 1920s relative to their pre-First World War values. Ponzi said he bought the European currencies at the depressed prices and
then used the money to buy these coupons in various European countries,

which he then shipped to the United States to be redeemed for the US dollar at their parity values. Then Ponzi would repeat the process, and again buy the depreciated European currencies and then buy more postal reply coupons to be shipped to the United States, and so on.

Ponzi's story about arbitraging these postal coupons was smoke – flimflam. He obtained the cash to pay the interest to those who bought his IOUs on Monday from those who bought his IOUs on Tuesday; similarly he obtained the cash to pay the interest to those who bought his IOUs on Tuesday from those who bought his IOUs on Wednesday.

Most of the individuals who bought Ponzi's IOUs initially were happy to reinvest most or all of their interest income; in effect they would earn 'interest on the interest.' As long as most of those who bought his IOUs on Monday reinvested most of their interest income, Ponzi's need for cash for interest payments was modest.

The manager of a Ponzi scheme inevitably encounters a cash flow problem because an increasing number of investors want to take a larger part of their interest income in cash as their financial wealth increases. The manager then has to sell the IOUs in a wider geographic area to bring in more new money to meet the growing demand for cash. As it becomes increasingly difficult to obtain new money, the manager increases the interest rates on the IOUs but the higher interest rates intensify the cash flow problem because the amount owed to the holders of the IOUs increases even more rapidly.

The manager then seeks to forestall the inevitable collapse as the supply of greater fools becomes increasingly scarce by limiting the cash that a depositor can withdraw each day. The adoption of this rule dooms the manager since the inflow of new money ceases and all the holders of the IOUs withdraw as much cash as they can each day.

Ponzi schemes were endemic in the 1990s in Eastern Europe – in Russia, Yugoslavia, and Albania. During the earlier command economy period most of the public's financial wealth consisted of deposits in government-owned banks that offered very low interest rates. A regulatory vacuum appeared when the command economy collapsed; there were no rules to prevent individuals from selling IOUs and offering interest rates much higher than those offered by the banks. And there was a lot of money lying around waiting to be invested at the high-promised interest rates.

Albania experienced a massive Ponzi bubble managed by several army generals. The high interest rates offered by the new 'banks' induced many Albanians to sell their homes to get the cash to buy deposits; these sellers continued to live in their properties, renting them from the buyers, but they calculated that they were still much better off, since the interest income on their deposits was much higher than their rent payments. (The buyers of the homes were the operators of the new banks; even though their rental incomes were much less than the interest rate on their deposits, they concluded they were better off, since they now owned the homes and the rents led to an

---

Box 10.2   Continued

inflow of cash while part or all of the interest payments on their deposits was an entry in a deposit book.) Moreover, the overseas Albanians – individuals that lived in Italy, Berlin, New York, and Chicago – shipped millions of dollars to Albania to buy the high interest rate deposits.

There was a feel-good experience in Albania; a large number of individuals were getting rich – and very rich – and for the first time. Consumption spending soared. Investment spending increased.

It was too good to last – and it didn't.

Not all Ponzi schemes led to an asset price bubble. But virtually every credit bubble has an embedded Ponzi scheme.

'Countries don't go bankrupt' – the 1970s surge in bank loans to Mexico, Brazil, Argentina, and other developing country borrowers

Walter Wriston was the head of Citibank in the 1970s. He transformed the firm into one of the dominant global financial institutions, with branches in more than 100 countries. Citibank's loans to governments and government-owned firms in Mexico and other Latin American countries surged. Wriston's quip 'Countries don't go bankrupt' cost the shareholders of the firm several tens of billions of dollars.

One defining feature of the 1970s was the sharp increases in the prices of primary products – petroleum, copper, wheat, soybeans, coffee, rubber, and tin. These commodities are produced in Mexico and in other developing countries, and the real incomes in these countries increased sharply as the prices escalated.

Bank loans to these countries began to increase at the rate of 30 percent a year in 1972 and the external indebtedness of these countries increased at the rate of 20 percent a year for a decade. The innovation was that banks headquartered in Europe and in Japan wanted to increase their share of the market for loans to the borrowers in Latin America, which traditionally had been the turf of US banks; these banks sourced the funds for these loans in the offshore deposit market. The US banks responded by matching the reductions in interest rates on loans. The borrowers were primarily governments and government-owned firms that produced steel or electric power or managed airlines or subways. The fiscal deficits of the governments in these countries increased, partly because it was so much easier to finance these deficits from the major international banks than from their domestic taxpayers.

Most of the loans were denominated in the US dollar. The interest rates on these bank loans were floating, perhaps three-quarters of 1 percent or one-half of 1 percent over the London Inter-Bank Offer Rate (LIBOR); as the lenders' costs of funds increased, the interest rates charged the borrowers on particular loans went up by the same amount – a cost-plus interest rate arrangement. Many of the loans had an 8-year repayment period; often there was an initial grace period of a year or two before the borrowers would make the first debt service payments.

The increase in the flow of dollars from bank loans to these countries induced an appreciation of their currencies and their imports increased relative to their exports.

The surge in interest rates on US dollar securities in the autumn of 1979 led to a world recession. The prices of the primary products plummeted, and GDP growth in both the industrial countries and the developing countries declined sharply. The international banks concluded that the indebtedness of the governments and the government-owned firms was too high relative to their revenues; the lenders' willingness to make new loans declined sharply.

'The mother of all asset price bubbles' – Tokyo real estate

The asset price bubble in Japan in the second half of the 1980s was the largest ever in terms of the increase in the household wealth as a share of GDP. At the end of the 1980s real estate prices were five to six times higher than at the beginning of the decade. Since Japanese GDP had doubled in nominal terms, the ratio of the market value of real estate to the country's GDP was three times higher than at the beginning of the decade.

Three factors contributed to the massive increases in the prices of real estate and of stocks. The Japanese economy had been extensively regulated for more than three decades after the Second World War as government bureaucrats tried to speed reconstruction. The destruction of productive plant and infrastructure had been extensive during the war; moreover, the country had lost what had been considered its colonies and especially its captive sources for raw materials and foodstuffs. The Japanese Government adopted a series of 'Ten Year Plans' to encourage economic growth. One motivation in the design of the plans was the 'Never Again' syndrome; the government mandarins that managed the economy wanted to minimize Japan's dependence on other countries.

Financial regulations were extensive; the interest rates that banks paid their depositors were low, often below the inflation rate – hence the real rate of interest on bank deposits was often negative. The interest rates that banks could charge on their loans also were subject to low ceilings. The demand for credit from business firms at these low interest rates was much greater than the supply; government bureaucrats provided 'window guidance' that indicated which firms should be the first to receive loans. These regulations severely restricted the credit available for the purchase of real estate.

The decline in the real value of household financial wealth that followed from modest inflation meant that households needed high annual savings to ensure that the purchasing power of their financial wealth would increase as their incomes increased.

Property prices increased somewhat more rapidly than GDP and the real rate of return on real estate was positive. The real rate of return on stocks also was positive and reflected that corporate sales and profits were increasing somewhat more rapidly than GDP.

Two factors contributed to the surge in asset prices in the second half of the 1980s. One was that Japanese authorities were reluctant to allow the yen to appreciate; they wanted to maintain the competitive advantage that they had developed when the yen depreciated sharply in the first half of the decade. The other innovation was that financial deregulation in Japan began in the early 1980s, in part at the urging of the US Government; the Japanese Government agreed to these US initiatives because the firms in large sectors of the Japanese industrial economy had access to the credit they needed to expand. The domestic component of deregulation involved raising interest rate ceilings and reducing the administrative controls over the allocation of bank loans. Japanese banks were permitted to increase their real estate loans without constraint, which then increased three times as rapidly as their total loans.

Borrowers used the cash obtained from these loans to build new homes and apartment buildings and office buildings and to buy existing properties. Because the assembly of land into large building sites was a slow process, much of money from new loans was used to buy existing properties – at ever-higher prices.

Property prices began to increase at a more rapid rate. There were a large number of property companies in Japan; as the market value of their real estate assets increased, the market value of their shares increased. Moreover, Japanese banks owned large amounts of real estate and of stocks, and hence the increases in the prices of these assets led to large increases in the value of bank assets and bank capital – and in the prices of the stocks of Japanese banks.

Japan appeared to have discovered the economic counterpart of a 'perpetual motion machine.' The increases in the value of real estate of 20–30 percent a year encouraged many individuals to buy real estate. Firms in the automotive and steel and paper and chemical industries observed that the rates of return on real estate investments were much higher than the rates of return on investment in new plant and equipment and they used some of the money from bank loans to buy real estate and shares in other firms. Because of the continued increases in real estate prices, bank losses on their real estate loans were trivially small.

Japanese banks increased the number of their foreign branches and subsidiaries in London, New York, Frankfurt, Zurich, and other national financial centers at a rapid rate. These branches sought to increase their loans at a rapid rate, using the funds borrowed in the offshore money markets in London and in other financial centers. Their strategy was to set interest rates at a smaller mark-up over their cost of funds, so they had a pricing advantage.

At more or less the same time, the governments in Finland, Norway, and Sweden reduced their regulations that limited the ability of their domestic banks to borrow in the offshore money market. These banks borrowed US dollars from the offshore branches of the Japanese banks in London and Zurich and other offshore centers, and then bought their own currencies with the US dollar, which induced an appreciation of their currencies. Moreover, the flow of more foreign money to Finland, Norway, and Sweden led to increases in the prices of real estate and of stocks.

The increase in real estate prices and stock prices in Tokyo could have continued until the end of time or least as long as the borrowers could get cash from new loans to pay the interest on their outstanding loans. At some stage it was inevitable that the banks would reduce the rate of growth of their real estate loans as these loans became an increasingly large share of their loan portfolios. The 'end of time' occurred when the incoming Governor of the Bank of Japan in January 1990 instructed the banks to limit the growth of their real estate loans to match the growth of their total loans. Heavily indebted borrowers then no longer could obtain the money from new loans to pay the interest on their indebtedness; some were forced to sell their properties. Real estate prices soon peaked and then declined for the next 15 years. Japan experienced a deflation and the economy went into the economic doldrums for 15 years.

The asset price bubbles in Thailand et al.

Stock prices and real estate prices in Bangkok, Kuala Lumpur, Jakarta, Singapore, and Hong Kong increased sharply in the mid-1990s; in 1993, stock prices doubled in most of these countries. Real estate prices surged. Several of the major cities in China – Shanghai, Beijing, and Guanchou – experienced booms in the construction of office buildings.

The economic boom was widespread and involved each of the countries in Southeast Asia as well as Mexico and other countries in Latin America. The innovation was that the Brady bond initiative of 1989 had led to a resolution of the overhang of borrowers' indebtedness to the major international banks; there was a surge in flow of money from pension funds and mutual funds to the emerging market countries. The chatter was that the rates of return on stocks would be higher in these countries than in the United States and other industrial countries because the rates of economic growth would be so much higher.

The combination of the resolution of the overhang of bank loans and an attractive new technocratic government led to a surge in the flow of funds to Mexico, whose economy was being prepped for membership in the North American Free Trade Area. The Salinas administration had three major economic policies. One was the privatization of several hundred firms, in virtually every industry except petroleum. The second was the liberalization of many regulations that hampered business, especially the need for multiple permits. The third was macro stabilization, and especially the reduction in the annual inflation rate from about 140 percent when the new administration took power.

US, European, and Japanese multinational firms began to view Mexico as a low-wage source of supply for the high-wage US and Canadian markets, so their investments in Mexico surged. Foreign firms acquired some of the government-owned firms that were being privatized. US and global money market funds were attracted by the high real interest rates on peso securities as the Bank of Mexico followed a very contractive monetary policy to reduce the inflation rate.

The flow of funds to Mexico led to the real appreciation of the peso. Mexican imports increased rapidly relative to Mexican exports, and the trade deficit increased to 6 percent of GDP.

The chatter in the press was about the little tigers or dragons of Thailand, Malaysia, Indonesia, and the Philippines. (Taiwan, South Korea, Hong Kong, and Singapore had been the first set of tigers.) The World Bank published the book *The East Asian Miracle*. The Asian currencies appreciated (except for the Hong Kong dollar and the Chinese yuan, which were pegged to the US dollar) in nominal and in real terms and most of these countries developed increasing large trade deficits. The trade surpluses of Singapore and Taiwan declined as their currencies appreciated.

Nonbank financial lenders in Thailand and several other countries were making loans that the banks were prohibited from making by regulation. Some of these nonbank lenders were owned by the banks (a feature that was also present in Japan).

The external indebtedness of Thailand and most of its neighbors was increasing much more rapidly than their GDPs. The borrowers in these countries obtained the money to pay the interest on their external debt by increasing the amounts borrowed from foreign banks, and the inflow of money enabled the countries to finance their increasingly large trade deficits.

The boom in these Asian countries ended when the nonbank lenders in Thailand began to incur large loan losses. The willingness of foreign banks and other suppliers of credit to lend more money to these Thai borrowers diminished. When the inflow of foreign money diminished, the Thai central bank initially supported the baht in the foreign exchange market by selling some of its holdings of international reserve assets. When its holdings of international reserve assets became exhausted, the central bank stopped supporting the baht and the currency depreciated sharply.

'Irrational Exuberance' and the bubble in US stocks

When Federal Reserve Chairman Greenspan remarked about irrational exuberance in the stock market in December 1996, the Dow Jones industrial index was at 6600 and the NASDAQ index was at 1300. When these indexes peaked in the first few months of 2000, the Dow was at 11,700 and the NASDAQ index was at 5400.

It seems unlikely that Chairman Greenspan would have remarked on the level of stock prices unless he believed that they were overvalued by at least 15–20 percent. Despite the concern that stocks were pricey, the Fed did not increase its discount rate; in fact it reduced this rate by 0.25 percent on three occasions in 4 months in 1997 in response to the financial debacle in Asia. Then in the summer of 1998 the Fed reduced the discount rate at the time of financial collapse in Moscow and the implosion of the largest and the most prestigious US hedge fund – Long Term Capital Management (LTCM). In 1999 the Fed provided ample credit for the financial economy because of its concern that the monetary system might freeze in the transition to Y2K.

The surge in the US stock prices in the late 1990s is identified with the dot.com boom; the development of new technologies associated with the computer and with the world wide web. The stocks of most of the firms identified with these new technologies are traded on the over-the-counter market and the changes in prices were measured by the NASDAQ index; the stocks of four firms – Microsoft, Cisco, Intel, and Dell – accounted for more than 80 percent of the increase in the market value of NASDAQ. In contrast, the stocks of 'older firms' were traded on the New York Stock Exchange (NYSE). The percentage increase in the market value of the NASDAQ stocks was more than twice that of the stocks traded on the NYSE, but the increase in the dollar amount of the NYSE stocks was almost twice as large as the increase in the market value of the NASDAQ stocks.

The market values of stocks traded in most other industrial countries also increased in the second half of the 1990s, although not as rapidly as US stocks.

The US economy boomed in the late 1990s – both the inflation rate and the unemployment rate were trending down, and the growth rate was increasing.

The US dollar appreciated in response to an increase in the inflow of money from abroad, and the US trade deficit increased from 2 percent of US GDP in 1995 to 5 percent in 2000. Part of the surge in the flow of money to the United States resulted from the Asian financial crisis, which led to a sharp depreciation of the Asian currencies, and an increase in their exports relative to their imports of $160 billion. Money also flowed to the United States from Europe as investors sought to participate in the buoyant US stock market.

The Americans that sold US dollar securities and assets to foreigners had two basic choices about what to do with the cash they received from these sales – they could increase their consumption expenditure and they could buy securities from other Americans. If they bought securities from other Americans, the sellers of these securities then had the same problem – what to do with the cash received from the sale of securities. They did both, although most of the cash was used to buy other US securities.

If these sellers increased their consumption spending, the rate of growth of US GDP increased. If they bought securities from other Americans, the prices of these securities increased – which meant that the cost of capital to US firms declined.

The invisible hand was at work: the prices of US securities increased until the greater consumption spending and its dual, the decline in the saving rate, matched the increase in the flow of foreign money to the United States.

The ratio of US stock prices to corporate earnings increased to 41, more than twice as high as its long-run average of 18. Some of analysts on Wall Street had forecast that corporate earnings would increase at the rate of 15 percent for 5 years, or nearly three times as rapidly as US GDP; they believed that the high level of stock prices could be justified by the anticipated rate of growth of earnings.

One of the basic propositions in finance is that in the long run corporate profits increase at about the same rate as GDP. (One competing statement is that corporate profits increase less rapidly than GDP, which would mean that the profits share would diminish and eventually disappear which would be the end of the corporate sector. The alternative competing statement is that if corporate profits increase more rapidly than GDP, then eventually US corporate profits would become larger than US GDP – also an unlikely outcome.) At times corporate profits increase more rapidly than GDP and at other times less rapidly – it is as if there is a 'regression to the mean' phenomenon that drives corporate profits. Profits fall sharply in recessions and increase more rapidly than GDP in expansions.

Soon after the beginning of the millennium, the Fed began to withdraw some of the liquidity provided in anticipation of Y2K. The bubble in US stocks imploded and stock prices declined by 40 percent in the next 36 months.

The bubble in Anglo-Saxon real estate

One of the remarkable features of the first several years of the new millennium was the surge in the prices of residential real estate in the United States, Britain, Australia, and most of the other Anglo-Saxon countries as well as in Ireland and Spain and Iceland; Canada was the major Anglo-Saxon country that did not experience a comparably sharp increase in real estate prices. In 2006 US house prices were twice their level in 1997; house prices were two-thirds higher relative to household income. House prices in South Africa were more than three times higher than in the base year, while house prices in Britain, Ireland, Iceland, and Spain were about twice as high.

Most of the countries that experienced large increases in house prices also had current account deficits. Many of the countries with current account deficits had significant increases in house prices. China was one of the relatively few countries with current account surpluses that had significant increases in home prices.

US real estate prices declined briefly in the early 1980s and again in the early 1990s; in 1994 these prices then began to increase in nominal terms and in real terms. Much of the increase in US housing prices occurred between 2002 and 2006 following the adoption of a more expansive monetary policy by the Federal Reserve, which wanted to dampen the contractive impact of the decline in stock prices on business investment and household consumption spending. Interest rates were reduced steadily and systematically for 2 years, until the short-term interest rates were at 1.5 percent – less than the inflation rate.

One remarkable innovation in the US mortgage market was 'securitization,' which involved the packaging of mortgage loans with similar attributes into bundles, which then could be used as the basis for selling a 'mortgage-backed security'; the buyer of one of these securities then had a claim to the payments that would be made by those who had borrowed money to buy homes. This innovation meant that investors from around the world could invest some of their money in the US mortgage market. Previously the US mortgage market had been local; individuals that wanted to buy a home would borrow from the local bank or thrift institution.

Moreover, US mortgage bankers became remarkably innovative in the developing new debt instruments such as adjustable interest rate mortgages (ARMs), interest-only mortgages, and negative amortization mortgages, sometimes called option mortgages. During the first 3 or 5 years, the monthly payments made by the borrowers who had taken out a negative amortization mortgage were less than those they would have made if they paid all of the interest, hence the borrowers' indebtedness increased by what in effect was the unpaid interest. A second innovation in documentation was that the borrowers could choose between a well-documented mortgage at one interest rate and a slightly less well-documented loan at a modestly higher interest rate (the latter were sometime known as liars' mortgages). Moreover, individuals could purchase homes without any down payment if they purchased mortgage insurance.

Increases in US house prices were much more rapid along the Atlantic Coast and the Pacific Coast and in Nevada and Arizona; most of the increases occurred in 16 states that account for about 50 percent of US GDP. In contrast, the increase in home prices in Texas and much of the Midwest was modest. The implication is that home prices in southern Florida and southern California and the other booming areas more than doubled.

The dispersion in the increases in home prices in different US regions and in different member countries of the European Union suggests that local or regional factors have an important impact in explaining increases in home prices.

Some of the buyers – 10–25 percent – purchased homes with the intent to sell the property or to sell the purchase contract rather than to live in the units. Since prices were increasing at the rate of 15–20 percent a year while the mortgage interest rates were in the range of 5–6 percent, the rate of return that these investors were achieving was exceptionally high, especially since their cash investment in the property was modest. (These buyers wanted to minimize their cash investment in each property because they wanted to buy a large number of properties.) Moreover, these investors were happy to hold their properties off the market because the rate of return was so high.

Arbitrage also occurred between regions. Price increases in California were more rapid than in Colorado and Utah and other mountain states, and some individuals sold their California homes and bought homes in Nevada and Arizona and other less pricey areas. The increase in US home prices was the most extensive ever. For a long period the ratio of the market value of US residential real estate to US GDP approximated 100; however, from 2001 to 2006 this ratio increased to 160.

During this period the flow of foreign money to the United States increased, and the US household saving rate declined. At the national level house prices peaked in 2006, although there were significant differences among the regions; prices continued to increase in some regions even though they were declining elsewhere in the country.

Box 10.3   Iceland and Its Perfect Asset Price Bubble

Iceland is one the smallest country in the world with an independent central bank and its own currency, the kronur. The population is slightly above 300,000, and two-thirds of the people live in or near the capital, Reykjavik. The country has three basic natural resources – an abundance of cod and

---

Box 10.3   Continued

haddock, geothermal power, and hydroelectric power. Educational levels are high, the standard of living is one of the highest in the world.

Between 2002 and 2007 real estate prices doubled and stock prices increased by a factor of eight. In 2002 the combined assets of the three large banks – which had been privatized in the previous few years – were about as large as the country's GDP; by 2007 their assets were eight times its GDP.

The chatter in Reykjavik was that Iceland was becoming an international financial center. Employment in banking and financial services more than doubled. Icelandic banks acquired branches in London. Some Icelandic entrepreneurs acquired department stores in Britain.

The foreign demand for bonds denominated in the Icelandic kronur increased sharply beginning in 2002, and the currency appreciated by more than 20 percent; the ratio of the country's trade deficit to its GDP was more than 25 percent – among the highest in the world. The inflow of foreign money was large relative to the market value of the real estate and the stocks that were traded in Iceland, and the prices of these assets increased. The Icelandic banks owned stocks in the 15 or so companies that were traded on the local stock exchange, and when stock prices increased, the value of bank assets and more importantly the value of bank capital increased. Because their capital was increasing, they were able to lend more money. Some of the borrowers used the cash from these loans to buy stocks, and stock prices increased further. The value of the shares owned by the Icelandic banks increased. The capital of the banks increased further. The banks were able to increase their loans. And so it went.

Foreign money continued to flow to Iceland because the interest rates that the banks were paying was high, and the kronur had been increasing. Some of those who borrowed from the Icelandic banks used the money to buy assets in Europe. Those who borrowed from the Icelandic banks used more and more of the cash to buy assets in Europe. Some of those who borrowed from the Icelandic banks had been turned away when they tried to borrow from other lenders – but the Icelandic banks had plenty of money to lend.

The increase in home prices in the United States has been attributed both to the expansive monetary policy of the Federal Reserve and to the surge in the credit for subprime mortgages. Until 2004 subprime mortgages accounted for about 8 percent of the number of mortgages and since these mortgages are somewhat smaller than prime mortgages, for a somewhat smaller percentage of the total new mortgage credit. The continued increase in home prices led to the increase in subprime mortgages since the risk attached to these mortgages seemed low; those borrowers that had difficulty making the monthly payment on their mortgages would be able to sell their homes without difficulty and repay their indebtedness.

The increase in home prices in the United States, Britain, and numerous other countries suggests that a generic global factor was the cause of the increase in the asset price.

Linkages within each asset price bubble

When Willie Sutton, America's most famous thief, was asked why he robbed banks, he replied 'That's where the money is.' These waves of bubbles are all about the ready availability of money – a lot of money, and eventually, too much money.

The several waves of surges in real estate prices and in stock prices lead to three related questions. The first involves the linkages among the increases in prices in several different countries in each wave. The second involves the linkages between the successive waves of increases in asset prices – especially between the increases in asset prices in Japan in the second half of the 1980s, and the increases in asset prices in Thailand et al. in the early and mid-1990s. Similarly, was there a systematic relationship between the increases in asset prices in the Southeast Asian countries in the first half of the 1990s and the increases in US stock prices in the second half of the 1990s. The third focuses on the uniqueness of this 35-year period and why there have been so many waves of bubbles.

The first bubble involved the surge in the external indebtedness of Mexico and other developing countries in the 1970s. The GDPs in these countries were increasing rapidly as a result of the sharp increases in the prices of petroleum, copper, wheat, and other primary products. Moreover, the large international banks headquartered in Europe and in Japan increased their loans to these borrowers using the money they had obtained in the offshore deposit market. Finally, banks headquartered in the United States and these other countries wanted to grow – to expand their balance sheets – and it was easier to increase their assets by lending to a group of borrowers that they had previously not served. Loans to governments and government-owned firms in different developing countries were viewed as a form of portfolio diversification – and some of the lenders apparently believed that the credit risk on loans to sovereigns was trivially small. Hence the surge in bank loans to the developing countries reflected factors external to the developing countries and the coincidence of the commodity price boom and the desire of the major international banks to increase their loans and their assets.

The surge in the prices of real estate and of stocks in Japan in the second half of the 1980s resulted from the combination of the rapid increase in the central bank holdings of international reserve assets and the relaxation of credit controls on bank loans for real estate. The surge in asset prices in Tokyo impacted several of Japan's Asian neighbors through both an income transmission mechanism and a property price arbitrage mechanism. Both mechanisms were evident in Hawaii, which is to Japan as South Florida is to New York City – a favorite warm-weather destination for golf and relaxation. Japanese tourism surged in response to the economic boom in Tokyo – and because the yen was appreciating, the cost to the Japanese of their Hawaiian vacations declined. Moreover, the surge in real estate prices in Tokyo led to Japanese purchases of real estate in Hawaii – hotels and apartment buildings and homes and golf courses – because prices were so much lower than those in Tokyo and in Osaka. (Investors used their real estate in Japan as collateral for the loans that provided the money to buy properties in Hawaii.)

The boom in the Japanese economy led to an increase in purchases from factories in Taiwan and South Korea that were in the supply chains for Japanese manufacturing firms.

The third impact of the sharp increase in asset prices in Japan was on the reserve base of banks in three of the Nordic countries – Finland, Norway, and Sweden. Financial liberalization in Japan was undertaken in part to reduce upward pressure on the yen by contributing to a sharp increase in the flow of money from Japan, which would put downward pressure on the yen in the currency markets. At about the same time that the foreign branch systems of the Japanese banks were expanding, Finland, Norway, and Sweden were relaxing their exchange controls so their domestic banks could source money in offshore markets. The European branches of Japanese banks provided funds to the Finnish, Norwegian, and Swedish banks.

The currencies of the Nordic countries appreciated. The Nordic banks then lent the money to domestic borrowers who used the funds to buy real estate and stocks, which led to rapid increases in their prices. The Finns, Norwegians, and Swedes that sold these assets then had large amounts of cash, and most of the cash was used to buy similar assets from their neighbors.

The coincidence in the increases in stock prices in Thailand, Malaysia, Indonesia, and the Philippines in the early 1990s suggests a common factor. The increase in the asset prices in these countries was part of the 'discovery' of the emerging market countries both in Asia and in Latin America after the Brady bond initiative in the late 1980s had consolidated the overhang of bank loan arrears into bonds. The investment banking industry had discovered 'emerging market equities' as a new asset class, one with higher returns than those in the industrial countries.

Most of the countries that have experienced sharp increases in real estate prices after 2000 also have had capital account surpluses and its flip, current account deficits. The currencies of these countries appreciated much as the US dollar had appreciated in the last half of the 1990s; however, the US dollar depreciated even as the US capital account surplus increased. The flow of funds to these countries led to increases in their asset prices. The inflow of money to these countries enabled them to provide larger amounts of mortgage loans. The demand for mortgage credit is idiosyncratic and country specific; a major factor in the demand for mortgage credit is the growth of employment and income. The supply of mortgage credit is global as a result of the securitization; in many countries some of the mortgage lenders obtain funds from the major international investment banks. These banks will buy mortgage-backed securities denominated in the British pound, the Australian dollar, and other currencies; they will hedge the foreign exchange exposure. Hence mortgage interest rates tend to be similar across countries after adjustment for the costs of hedging the foreign exchange exposure.

Hence the fact that four, five, or more countries were more or less involved at the same time reflects that each of them experienced inflows of money from abroad, often from the same source or sources. The 'money was there.'

Cash flows and bubbles

Real estate bubbles, such as those in Japan, Thailand, Malaysia, the United States, and South Africa, always involve a rapid increase in credit from banks and other lenders that enable the borrowers to buy existing structures and to pay for construction of new homes and office buildings. The supply of credit for real estate purchases is procyclical; as real estate prices increase, banks become more eager lenders because real estate values are rising, and the net worth of the buyers is increasing more rapidly than their indebtedness. Because the supply of homes and office buildings and apartment buildings increases slowly, the increase in demand leads to a rapid increase in property prices.

As real estate prices increase, the rental rate of return on both existing properties and new construction declines below the interest rates on the loans that the recent buyers of real estate have agreed to pay. These investors are comfortable increasing their indebtedness because they anticipate that prices will increase two or three times as rapidly as the interest rate and their interest payments.

Some of these borrowers eventually develop a cash flow problem as their interest payments increase to exceed their rental incomes (the technical term is 'negative carry') – but the increase in the market value of their real estate means that their wealth is increasing and their properties are pledged as collateral for new loans. The lenders are happy because the borrowers have an impeccable record for making their debt service payments in a timely way and because the loans are well collateralized.

Bubbles in real estate in Japan and in many other countries – but not the United States – have been associated with bubbles in stocks. Often many of the firms that account for a large share of the total stock market valuation are real estate companies; the value of their assets increase as real estate prices increase. Hence investors will pay more for the stocks of these companies.

Moreover, the sellers of real estate must decide what to do with the money received when they sell their properties; their basic choices are to buy more real estate or to buy stocks. Their purchases lead to further increases in the prices of real estate and stocks.

Asset price bubbles produce economic exuberance. Business investment increases because the rate of economic growth is above trend and the cost of capital is low. Household consumption spending surges as the owners of stocks and of real estate react to the increase in their wealth by increasing their consumption, their savings rate declines. Because of the surge in economic activity, government revenues increase rapidly and often the governments develop fiscal surpluses.

Some event – a surge in interest rates, a new regulation – induces one or two lenders to become more cautious in extending new loans. Asset prices now are too high relative to rental incomes; some of the heavily indebted borrowers then are in a cash bind because their rental incomes are less than their scheduled interest payments. A few of these borrowers become distress sellers of real estate. Real estate prices then decline, and the price falls can be extremely sharp as investors rush to convert their unrealized profits to cash.

Links among successive waves of bubbles

One feature common to virtually all of the countries involved in these bubbles – with the exception of Japan in the 1980s and China in 2007 – is that they had current account deficits which increased as asset prices in the country increased. In balance of payments accounting terms, these countries developed larger capital account surpluses and larger current account deficits. The increase in the flow of money to a country was autonomous and had two direct and immediate impacts; one was that the country's currency appreciated in nominal and real terms (unless the country's currency was pegged to that of some other country) and the other was that asset prices in the country also increased.

The increase in the flow of money to a country – as reflected in the increase in its trade deficit – increases the supply of saving in a country, which by itself would be deflationary and lead to a decline in the rate of growth of its GDP. Yet each of these countries experienced an economic boom which resulted from increases in both investment spending and consumption spending. The domestic sellers of the assets and securities to foreigners used the cash to buy other assets and securities from other domestic residents. These residents had the same problem of what to do with the cash; they used most of the cash to buy other assets.

The stylized fact is that GDP has increased in virtually each of these countries that experienced an increase in its trade deficit and an appreciation of its currency. The indirect effect of the increase in the flow of money to a country is that the asset prices increased as the investors who are moving money into the country agree to pay more for these assets to induce those who own these assets to sell them.

The first wave of credit bubbles followed the surge in commodity prices, which led to sharp increases in GDPs in the commodity-producing countries. The increase in the flow of funds to these countries enabled them to have larger trade deficits, which meant that the industrial countries developed the counterpart larger trade surpluses. The interest rate shock that triggered the implosion of the bubble led to an unprecedented appreciation of the US dollar and the resulting increase in the US trade deficit was significantly larger than the decline in the trade deficits of the developing countries; other industrial countries experienced increases in their trade surpluses.

When the US dollar began to depreciate in the mid-1980s, Japan was reluctant to accept the decline in its trade surplus. The purchases of US dollar securities by the Bank of Japan dampened the appreciation of the yen, and led to rapid increases in the reserves of the Japanese banks at the central bank and in the money supply. Much of the increase in the money supply went into the asset market, in large part initially because of the regulations that limited bank credit for real estate. Many of the firms listed on the Tokyo Stock Exchange own property, and the increase in real estate prices meant that investors purchased more of their shares. The Japanese banks owned both real estate and shares, and increases in the prices of these assets meant that their capital was increasing, so they were able to increase their loans.

When the bubble in Japan imploded at the beginning of the 1990s, Japanese firms reoriented production from the domestic to foreign markets, the country's exports increased relative to its imports, and the yen appreciated. The appreciation led to fears about the 'hollowing out' of the Japanese economy and Japanese firms increased their investment in the Southeast Asian countries to take advantage of lower wage rates and lower labor costs. Before these firms could invest in Thailand and Malaysia and the neighboring countries, they had to purchase the Thai baht and the Malaysia ringgit and these currencies appreciated – within the limits provided by central bank intervention policies. Banks headquartered in Japan, the United States, and Europe increased their loans to borrowers in the Southeast Asian countries.

The flow of foreign funds to these countries led to both an appreciation of their currencies and an increase in their current account deficits. The Thais and the Malaysians and the Indonesians that sold domestic assets to the foreign investors then had the problem of what to do with their sales receipts. Most used virtually all of the money to buy domestic assets from other domestic residents; the prices of these assets increased.

The spurt of higher real estate prices and higher stock prices in Thailand and the other countries in Southeast Asia resulted from two factors – one was the surge in the flow of funds to the emerging market countries as a group after the Brady bond initiative consolidated the overhang of overdue bank loans at the end of the 1980s. There was a general surge in the purchase of securities in the emerging market countries by pension funds and mutual funds (in part motivated by the data that showed exceptional returns to global portfolios based on the spectacular increases in the prices of Japanese stocks in the 1980s.)

Before Japanese firms could invest in Thailand and the neighboring countries, they first had to buy the currencies of these countries in the foreign exchange market; these currencies appreciated. Banks headquartered in Japan as well as in the United States and Western Europe increased their branches in these countries. Non-Japanese firms followed the Japanese firms to these countries.

When the asset price bubbles in Thailand and its neighbors countries imploded, their currencies depreciated sharply, and the trade balances rapidly evolved from deficits to surpluses by $150 billion, which almost automatically led to the increase in the US trade deficit of about the same amount. The increase in the flow of foreign funds to the United States led to an increase in the value of the US dollar in the currency market and to increases in the prices of US securities. The American sellers of these securities then had to decide what to do with the money; they could buy securities from other Americans and they could buy consumption goods – and they could do both. Most of the money was used to buy other securities, which led to increases in their prices; the sellers of these securities then had the same problem of what to do with the money.

The surge in US stock prices in the late 1990s in part was a response to the increase in the flow of money from abroad. US stock prices had been increasing since 1982, and despite the sharp price declines in November 1987, stock prices at the end of 1987 were slightly higher than a year earlier. Changes in stock prices in a number of countries – Canada, France, Germany, and Britain – were strongly correlated with changes in the US stock prices. At the time the market value of US stocks was more than 50 percent of the market value of all stocks on a global basis. The increase in US stock prices was larger in percentage terms than in any other country; the increases in the prices of US stocks 'pulled up' prices of stocks in other countries as investors diversified.

Three of the waves of bubbles were associated with flows of funds to countries that led to increases in their current account deficits. The first impact of the increase in the flow of funds to a country was to induce an increase in the value of its currency in nominal terms unless the currency is pegged, the real appreciation is necessary to induce an increase in imports relative to exports so that the increase in the country's current account deficit more or less corresponds with the increase in its capital account surplus. (The real appreciation conforms with the overshooting hypothesis.)

Adjustments must occur in a country that receives capital from abroad so that the real resources associated with the increase in its trade and current account deficit are 'absorbed'; the adjustments involve some combination of an increase in the fiscal deficit, an increase in business investment, or an increase in household consumption (which means that its dual, the household saving rate, declines). The increase in asset prices in the country receiving more funds from abroad was part of the adjustment process, which was needed to effect the real transfer.

The currencies of most of the countries that experienced a credit bubble or an asset bubble appreciated in response to the inflow of money from abroad. Several countries, primarily China and Hong Kong, were exceptions because their currencies were pegged, several others including Japan, Singapore, and Taiwan were exceptions because they had current account surpluses. Still, money flowed to the countries that were experiencing bubbles because the anticipated rates of return were high as asset prices increased.

The sharp depreciation of the Thai baht in July 1997 triggered a series of devaluations that rippled through the emerging market economies and ended with the financial crisis in Argentina in 2001. The depreciation of these currencies led to marked change in their current account balances, almost always a reversal from the current account deficits to current account surpluses, or in some cases, to larger current account surpluses.

Just as the counterpart of the depreciation of the Asian currencies was the appreciation of the US dollar in 1997 and 1998, so the counterpart of the reversal of their current accounts from deficits to surpluses (or in a few cases an increase in their surpluses) was an increase in the ratio of the US current account deficit to US GDP by several percentage points. The increase in the flow of money to the United States as revealed by the increase in the US trade and current account deficit contributed to the bubble in US stock prices in 1998 and 1999, although the bubble already was underway. The US trade deficit had increased in 1995 following the collapse of the Mexican peso and the reversal of Mexican payments position from a trade deficit to a trade surplus.

The increase in the US current account deficit had as a mirror the decline in the domestic saving rate. The invisible hand operated and the primary mechanism was the increase in US stock prices which led to an increase in household wealth and a decline in the household saving rate.

The link between the decline in US stock prices that began in the late winter of 2001 and the increase in the price of residential real estate that began in 2002 centers on the Federal Reserve's adoption of a very expansive monetary policy in 2001. The decline in interest rates impacts house prices much like the decline in interest rates impacts bond prices (although the more precise statement is that the change in interest rates is the mirror and dependent on the increase in bond prices). Speculative purchases of real estate soared.

The uniqueness of the post-1970 period

One feature of most of these waves of bubbles is that they were associated with an increase in the flow of money to a country, which led to an appreciation of its currency. A second feature is that a group of borrowers were involved in Ponzi finance and obtained the money to pay the interest on their indebtedness from the borrowers in the form of new loans. In the 1970s, the indebtedness of the government and the government-owned firms in the developing countries increased at least twice as rapidly as the interest payments on their indebtedness; the pattern of cash flows was not sustainable. Similarly, the interest payments of many of those who purchased real estate in Japan in the second half of the 1980s exceeded their rental income, but they obtained the money to pay the interest on their indebtedness by increasing their indebtedness. The external indebtedness of Mexico, Thailand, and many of the other developing countries increased rapidly in the early 1990s, and the funds to pay the interest and dividends to the creditors were obtained from new loans. The general feature of the property markets in the United States and most of the other Anglo-Saxon countries was that mortgage indebtedness was increasing much more rapidly than the interest rate.

One of the paradoxes of the last several decades has been that rates of economic growth have been high despite the spasms associated with sharp changes in asset prices. The range of movement in currency values has been much greater than ever before. Moreover, the values of current account surpluses and current account deficits have been much larger than ever before; a few countries have had current account deficits that have been in the range of 6–8 percent of their GDPs. Some countries have had current account surpluses that were in the range of 4–6 percent.

The flow of money to a country was associated with a high rate of economic growth; the country's currency appreciated in nominal and in real terms, which dampened the increase in the price level – and especially the prices of tradable goods – that otherwise would be associated with the above-trend rate of growth. The favorable impact of the increase in the value of the currency on the price level might allow the expansion to continue for a somewhat longer period than if the currency had not appreciated. The increase in domestic asset prices that followed from the inflow of money contributed to the prolonged boom because of the increases in investment spending and household consumption spending.

Four of the five bubbles in this period were associated with increases in the prices of real estate and usually but not exclusively residential real estate. Real estate bubbles always depend on the rapid growth of credit since the buyers make modest down payments. The real estate bubble in Japan followed an extended period in which bank loans for real estate had been limited by government directive; once these restrictions were lifted, bank loans for real estate increased at a rapid rate. Because the assembly of land into significant sizes was time consuming, the increase in the demand for real estate had a large price effect relative to the output effect in the short run. Real estate loans were collateralized by the value of the property, and so property values increased in response to the increase in the demand for real estate and hence the banks believed that the loans were 'sound.'

Most of the Anglo-Saxon countries that had experienced real estate bubbles after 2001 also had current account deficits; foreign funds were flowing to these countries. Not every country that had a current account deficit had a real estate bubble, and not every country that experienced a significant increase in real estate prices had a current account deficit. Nevertheless, the association between the flow of money to a country evident in its current account deficit and the increase in real estate prices within the country is a strong one. The flow of money to a country led to an increase in the prices of securities and real estate in the country, and the prices of these assets continued to increase until the positive wealth effect led to a decline in domestic saving that more or less corresponded with the flow of money from abroad.

In contrast, the real estate bubble in China in 2007 like the one in Japan in the late 1980s occurred when they had trade and payments surpluses, which led to the rapid growth in central bank reserves. Banks were able to increase their loans at a rapid rate because their reserves were increasing at a rapid rate.

The bubble in the US real estate market and in the markets in most other Anglo-Saxon countries was associated with the inflow of money from abroad and in some cases increases in the inflow of money from abroad. These inflows contributed to the increase in asset prices and the economic booms, and the appreciation of the currencies in real terms as a result of the inflows dampened the upward pressure on commodity prices associated with the booms. Central bank initiatives to raise interest rates to dampen spending had the unintended impact of attracting more money from other countries and led to further appreciation of the currencies.

In many countries, including both Japan and China – although not the United States and most of the other Anglo-Saxon countries – bubbles in stocks occurred at the same time as the bubbles in real estate.

The flow of money from abroad and the real appreciation induced current account deficits that ranged from 2 to 5 and 6 percent of GDP. These countries then became dependent on the continued inflow of foreign money to maintain the values of the currencies in the foreign exchange market. When the inflow of money declined, the currencies depreciated, and a modest initial depreciation often triggered a much larger decline in the inflow because the anticipated loss from the depreciation of the currencies dominated any additional income.

One feature of this period is that the economic expansions – the number of months between recessions – have been longer than in the earlier decades. The US economy experienced two brief and modest recessions between 1982 and 2007. Traditionally an economic expansion ended when the central bank raised interest rates and reduced availability of credit, almost always to dampen inflationary pressures. The implication is that central banks may have become more reluctant to raise interest rates, either because they have become more tolerant of inflation or because the expansion can continue for a longer period before the inflation rate increases to an unacceptable level. Inflation rates peaked in 1980 and then showed a downward trend for more than 20 years; central banks may have been willing to accept higher inflation rates than in the past as long as the downward trend continued. Moreover, central banks may be somewhat more willing to accept increases in price levels that have been modestly higher than when currencies were pegged, perhaps because they felt that the costs of a gradual depreciation of the currency were significantly smaller than the costs of devaluation when currencies were pegged.

Another feature of the period is that the economic expansions often have been associated with an autonomous inflow of funds to a country and an appreciation of its currency and an increase in its trade deficit (or with an reduction in the trade surpluses of Japan, Taiwan, and Singapore). (The major exception is that the flow of funds to Japan in the 1980s was a response to the rapid increase in stock prices.) The inflow of funds continued for an extended period and contributed to the economic booms; the domestic adjustment to the autonomous increase in the inflow was some combination of an increase in the fiscal deficit, an increase in business investment, and an increase in household consumption. In the 1970s, the flow of foreign funds to Mexico and the other Latin American countries was not associated with asset price bubbles; the counterpart of the increases in trade deficits were larger fiscal deficits, and in the 1990s the counterpart were the purchases of shares in government-owned firms that were being privatized. In contrast the asset price bubbles in the Asian countries and in the United States resulted as part of the adjustment process to the increase in the inflow of money from abroad as reflected in the increases in trade deficits. The invisible hand assured that asset prices increased until the saving rate declined by the amount that more or less corresponded with the increase in the trade deficit.

The economic booms in these countries persisted for as long as the inflow of money continued – or until the central banks in the capital-importing countries adopted more contractive monetary policies to cope with the increase in the inflation rates. In all of these episodes the pattern of capital flows was non-sustainable; either the indebtedness of a sector within the economy was increasing more rapidly than its income or the indebtedness of the country was increasing more rapidly than its GDP.

When the flow of funds diminished, the currencies were likely to depreciate; even a modest depreciation might trigger a sharp decline in inflows. The first episode was in the 1970s and involved the increase in bank loans to borrowers in Mexico and other developing countries at the rate of 30 percent a year during most of the 1970s; the external indebtedness of the borrowers in these countries increased by 20 percent a year for nearly 10 years. The governments and government-owned firms that were borrowers obtained the money to pay the interest on their indebtedness from new loans. When the availability of money from new loans declined, the currencies depreciated.

The second episode occurred in Japan when many of those who borrowed to get the money to buy real estate were similarly involved in Ponzi finance; the interest payments of these borrowers were larger than their rental incomes. When money from new loans was no longer available to the borrowers, the borrowers were unable to pay the interest on a timely basis. One aspect of Mexico's experience in the 1990–94 period was similar to its 1970s experience; there was a surge in the capital inflow (although from pension funds and mutual funds and direct investors), an appreciation of the peso in real terms, and the increase of the ratio of the current account deficit to GDP to a nonsustainable level. A similar episode occurred with respect to real estate investors in Thailand and its neighbors.

The flows of capital to these countries often were a cause of the economic boom that in turn attracted more money from abroad. The 'transfer problem process' was at work; adjustments were necessary in the capital-importing countries to absorb the real resources that represented the increase in their current account deficits. The necessary adjustment within the capital-importing countries led to an increase in spending – some combination of government spending, investment spending, or consumption spending. Much of the increase involved consumption spending. The mechanism was that domestic residents that sold securities and assets to foreign investors used a large part of their receipts to buy other securities and assets from other domestic investors. This group of investors then had the same problem of what to do with their receipts. Most of the money was reinvested. Asset prices continued to increase until the domestic saving declined by an amount that corresponded to the increase in the inflow of money from abroad.

It is as if there is a pool of mobile funds that was attracted to the anticipated high rates of returns available in a country. When the bubble in Japan was expanding in the second half of the 1980s, some of this money flowed to Japan; the yen appreciated. When the bubble in Japan imploded, money flowed to Thailand and its neighbors; their currencies appreciated even as the yen was depreciating and their trade deficits increased. When the flow of money to these countries in Southeast Asia declined, their currencies depreciated sharply; the money flowed to the United States and the US trade deficit surged and the stock market bubble intensified. When the US stock market bubble was pricked, the US dollar depreciated. In this case, money continued to flow to the United States, and eventually this money contributed to the boom in US housing prices.

11

A New World Record – Four Financial Crises in 25 Years

A run on a bank – at least in an advanced industrial country – seems like an event out of the Great Depression of the 1930s. Frenetic depositors line up waiting for the bank to open because they want to be among the first to get their money; they anticipate that the bank soon will close because its money holdings will be exhausted. In September 2007, Northern Rock, the largest mortgage lender in Britain, experienced two runs, one in the wholesale commercial paper market and the other in the retail market. Northern Rock borrowed more than 40 million pounds from the Bank of England to avoid bankruptcy and then was taken over by the British Government. About the same time Countrywide Financial, the largest US mortgage lender, also experienced a run in the wholesale money market and received a capital infusion from Bank of America. Subsequently the US Treasury made a large investment in Bank of America to ensure that it had adequate capital.

The similarity of the timing of the runs on the largest mortgage lenders in the United States and Britain was not a coincidence. Countrywide and Northern Rock had the same business strategy. Both firms obtained some of the money to make long-term mortgage loans by selling their short-term IOUs in the commercial paper market; both obtained the money to repay maturing IOUs by selling new IOUs. Both firms faced insolvency when buyers of commercial paper were no longer willing to buy the new IOUs, which meant that both firms lacked the money to repay the maturing IOUs. The inability of both firms to sell their IOUs in the commercial paper market was an early warning that the house price bubbles both in the United States and in Britain were imploding and that the market value of mortgages – and of mortgage-related securities – would decline.

Since the early 1980s more than 50 national banking systems have failed – collapsed – gone kaput – tumbled into bankruptcy. Moreover, most of the banks in 20 or 30 other countries incurred such large loan losses that they would have failed if they had not already been owned by their governments. In part the large number of countries that experienced financial collapses reflects that the break-up of colonial empires has led to more independent countries. Still, the number of national banking systems that have collapsed seems large after an adjustment to standardize for the larger number of countries.

A bank fails when the value of its loans declines sharply relative to the value of its deposit liabilities, almost always because the bank miscalculated one or several risks, both their likelihood and the probable losses when the borrowers failed to repay. The loans were backed by collateral in the form of pledges of property, but at times property values declined below the amounts of the loans. The credit risk (sometimes called default risk) is that borrowers will default and repay less than they owe – or much less than they owe. Another risk is that changes in currency values will lead to an increase in the payments that some firms must make relative to their receipts; some of these firms may become bankrupt, and be unable to repay their domestic loans. Banks encounter the liquidity risk that the depositors will rush for their money and that they may have to sell assets at a loss to get the cash to repay these depositors. Banks always face the maturity risk (sometimes called the duration risk) that short-term interest rates may increase sharply relative to long-term interest rates and that their interest payments on short-term deposits may exceed the interest income on their long-term loans.

Governments have regulated financial institutions for more than 200 years, initially to protect depositors from losses and subsequently to protect the economy from the hardships that have occurred when a large number of banks have failed at the same time. In the 1930s governments began to require that the banks buy insurance to protect depositors from loss – and to reduce the likelihood that the depositors would rush for their money. In some cases governments have used taxpayer money to make depositors 'whole' after banks have failed; a government agency has provided the banks with loans at below-market interest rates – in effect a loosely disguised subsidy to the depositors.

The failure of an individual bank is not likely to be associated with a financial crisis, but the failure of a large number of banks – or even of similarly placed borrowers – qualifies as a financial crisis.

Much like an earthquake involves a sudden shift in the relation between two tectonic plates, a financial crisis involves a sudden unanticipated change in the relative price of two assets, perhaps by as much as 30 or 40 percent. The values of a large bundle of assets suddenly become highly uncertain, and hence the net worth, and the solvency of the firms that own many of these assets and securities also becomes highly uncertain. Prior to the crises, these assets and securities could be readily traded and were considered liquid; large amounts of these assets could be sold with minimal downward pressure on the price. Once the crisis developed, the securities became highly illiquid; the sale of the assets would lead to sharp reductions in their price.

Financial crises continue as long as there remains significant uncertainty about the market value of the assets and securities owned by the banks. The onset of the crises is a surprise to most market participants, even though in retrospect they can see that they crossed a threshold that was like a 'point of no return.'

The uniqueness of the period since the early 1980s is that there have been four waves of financial crises; each wave involved four or more countries, often in different geographic regions. The first wave occurred in the early 1980s and resulted from the impact of the surge in interest rates on US dollar securities at the end of 1979 on US GDP and global GDP and on the prices of crude oil and other primary products. The decline in commodity prices led to a sharp decline in the GDPs in countries that produced and exported petroleum, iron ore, wheat, copper, and other commodities; the governments and government-owned firms in these countries had greatly increased their international indebtedness in the 1970s. The major international banks headquartered in New York, Chicago, London, Tokyo, and Toronto suddenly reduced their willingness to lend to these borrowers, who then were no longer able to make their debt service payments in a timely way. Similarly, some of the firms involved in the production of oil in Texas, Oklahoma, and Louisiana defaulted on their loans. Moreover, the decline in prices of cereals meant that many small banks in Iowa, Kansas, and other grain-producing areas incurred large loan losses when farmers defaulted on their loans. At the same time, US thrift institutions were adversely affected by the surge in interest rates and especially the sharp increase in interest rates on short-term securities; these lenders typically had used the money from the sale of short-term deposits to buy long-term mortgages. Suddenly the interest rates that they were paying on short-term deposits were higher than the interest rates they were earning on their loans, and they were incurring continuing losses.

The second wave of crisis occurred in the early 1990s after the real estate bubble in Japan imploded. At about the same time, the banks in Finland, Norway, and Sweden collapsed as real estate and stock prices crashed in these countries. Real estate developers in these countries were unable to repay their loans.

The third wave was the Asian financial crisis, which began with the devaluation of the Thai baht in July 1997 that triggered the contagion effect; investors began to withdraw money from Malaysia, Indonesia, and the Philippines in the anticipation that their currencies would depreciate sharply. South Korea was caught and unable to fund maturing loans denominated in the US dollar. Eventually the crisis engulfed Russia, Brazil, and Argentina.

The fourth crisis began with the runs on Countrywide Financial and Northern Rock in the late summer of 2007 and continued into the winter and spring of 2009. One component of this crisis involved failures of banks in the United States, Britain, Ireland, Spain, and Iceland in response to the decline in real estate prices. Another component involved Poland, Hungary, Latvia, and other countries in Central Europe that had experienced significant inflows of foreign money.

Cash flows and financial crises

The prelude to each of these waves was an extended period when the cash flows to a group of borrowers or across a currency border were increasing at a rate that could not be sustained for an indefinite period; the borrowers' indebtedness was increasing much more rapidly than their incomes. In these cases the foreseeable 'end-game' was that the borrowers would eventually need a new source of money that they could use to pay part or all of the interest on their indebtedness. When the flow of cash to a country slowed, its currency would depreciate, and the decline might feedback to a much sharper decline in the inflow.

Consider the arithmetic in the pattern of cash flows between banks in New York, London, and Tokyo and the borrowers in Ruthenia as a model for the pattern of the cash flows between the international banks and the developing countries in the 1970s. If Ruthenia's indebtedness increases at the rate of 20 percent a year and the interest rate on its indebtedness is 8 percent, the flow of cash to the borrowers in Ruthenia from new loans is two and one-half times larger than the interest payments that the borrowers make on their outstanding loans. For example, assume that Ruthenia begins the year with an external indebtedness of US$100 million, its external indebtedness increases by $20 million in the first year, and its annual interest payment during the year is $8 million. The $12 million excess of the cash from new loans over the interest payment on the outstanding loans can be used to pay for imports of goods or to buy foreign securities or military equipment. The borrowers do not incur any burden in paying the interest on their foreign indebtedness as long as the inflow of money on new loans is larger than the interest payments on the outstanding loans.

As the money from new loans increases relative to the interest payments on the outstanding loans, the Ruthenian currency – the pengo – appreciates because the borrowers use some of their newly acquired US dollars to buy the pengo. The appreciation of the pengo induces an increase in Ruthenia's imports relative to its exports and its trade deficit increases.

This pattern of Ruthenian international cash flows is 'explosive' since its external indebtedness is increasing more rapidly than its GDP. Debt can increase more rapidly than GDP when this ratio is low or modest; however, the higher the ratio of external indebtedness to GDP, the more likely that some lenders would conclude that borrowers were becoming 'overextended.' Lenders then would become more cautious when making new loans, and the inflow of cash from new loans would decline relative to interest payments on the outstanding loans.

The lenders could slow the rate of growth of their loans to Ruthenia or they could raise the interest rate mark-up over their own cost of funds; in both cases Ruthenian borrowers would receive less money relative to their scheduled interest payments and the pengo would depreciate. However, the real debt servicing burden on Ruthenia would remain trivial as long as the money from new loans continued to exceed interest payments on outstanding loans.

When the cash from new loans declines below the interest payments on outstanding loans, the Ruthenian borrowers need a new source of money to pay the interest on their outstanding loans. Governments would have to increase their taxes relative to their expenditures, perhaps by as much as 4 or 5 percent, and government-owned firms would have to increase their revenues relative to their noninterest payments.

If the governments are unable to raise taxes relative to expenditures by the amount necessary so they would have the cash to pay the interest, they would default on the loans. The loan losses incurred by lenders might then impair their own capital adequacy.

Mexico and the developing country debt crisis of the early 1980s

Mexican financial history in the last several decades of the twentieth century resembled an economic yo-yo, alternating periods of extended booms followed by major busts. In the 1950s and the 1960s Mexico was a 'gold standard' country, at times characterized as the 'Thirteenth US Federal Reserve District.' The primary objective of the Bank of Mexico was to maintain the fixed price for the US dollar in terms of the Mexican peso.

The 1970s was a 'good news' decade for Mexico because its oil production increased sharply as the oil price surged. The outgoing Mexican president in 1976 promised a 'new school and a new bridge' for every village. Toward the end of his term the government's fiscal deficit increased, the inflation rate surged, and the peso was devalued from 12.5 pesos to the US dollar to 20 pesos. Mexican export earnings surged as a result of the rapid growth in oil production and sharp increases in oil prices. Together these oil market events contributed to an increase in the rate of economic growth in Mexico, which led to a sharp increase in loans to the Mexican Government and to government-owned firms from the major US, European, and Japanese banks.

In the 1970s the economic prospects of the developing countries seemed much brighter because of the anticipation that commodity prices would continue to increase, which would lead to increases in their rates of GDP growth. The surge in profits attached to the production of these basic raw materials in turn led to an increase in the investment in their production and the anticipated increases in the GDP growth rates attracted foreign funds. During the 1970s the external indebtedness of Mexico and other developing countries increased at the rate of 20 percent a year, from \$125 billion at the end of 1972 to \$800 billion at the end of 1982.

Since the external debt of Mexico and other developing countries could not increase more rapidly than their GDPs for an indefinite period, it should have been evident that the rate of growth of bank loans to these countries would decline, which would mean that the currencies of this group of countries would depreciate. This inevitable adjustment should have been foreseen by the borrowers, by the lenders, and by the international financial institutions including the International Monetary Fund (IMF). Each of these groups should have asked, 'Where will the borrowers get the money to pay the interest on a timely basis when they can no longer get this money from new bank loans?'

The inevitable adjustment from a nonsustainable rate of increase of indebtedness would involve a depreciation of the Mexican peso and the currencies of other developing countries; the depreciation could be large in percentage terms because its prospect could lead to a surge in the outflow of funds. Then the value of the loans that the major international banks had made to the governments and to the government-owned firms in Mexico and the other developing countries would decline because of uncertainty over whether the borrowers would be able and willing to pay the interest on a timely basis. The adjustment in currency values would impose large costs on the firms and banks in the debtor countries, as well on their governments. Interest rates on securities denominated in the peso and in the currencies of the other developing countries soared because of the sharp depreciation of their currencies. The domestic currency counterpart of the debts denominated in the US dollar increased in proportion to the changes in the currency values, and many firms went bankrupt in part because of the sharp increase in the domestic counterpart of their US dollar liabilities and in part because of the sharp increase in domestic interest rates. Many of the domestic banks in these countries went bankrupt because many domestic firms went bankrupt.

The governments in these countries had a massive adjustment problem; they needed to increase their tax revenues relative to their domestic expenditures so they would have enough domestic money that they could use to buy US dollars that they needed for their debt service payments. Few of the governments in the developing countries had the political will to increase their taxes relative to their expenditures so that they would have enough domestic money to make their debt service payments; instead, they increased the amounts borrowed from domestic banks to obtain the money to repay the foreign banks. Despite domestic borrowing, few of the developing country borrowers were able to make their debt service payments on their US dollar loans in a timely way; the market value of these loans declined sharply.

There were two major types of adjustment costs in the creditor countries. The losses incurred by the international banks on their loans to these developing countries were $250 billion, or a 'haircut' of more than 30 percent. These lenders continued to make 'new loans' to these borrowers but in much smaller amounts; the lenders wanted to claim that the loans were performing, and they wanted the borrowers to pay some of the interest – but the borrowers would pay the interest only if the lenders made money available from new loans. Virtually all of the money from new loans was used to pay some of the interest on the outstanding loans. If the lenders had not continued to make new loans, some of the borrowers would not have paid any interest, and the lenders would have had to recognize the losses on these loans. The second adjustment cost that the creditor countries incurred was that their exports to the developing countries declined sharply as their currencies depreciated.

The US bank regulatory authorities connived in the fiction that these loans to the developing countries were performing. Had they not done so the major banks would have had to write down the value of these loans; some banks might then have had too little capital relative to the regulatory minimums.

One of the great clichés of international finance is that 'countries don't go bankrupt'; the idea is that governments aren't subject to the credit risk since they can always borrow from their central banks. These central banks can't print a foreign money. Foreign lenders may not be repaid on their loans to the governments since they have no collateral if the borrowers fail to adhere to the terms of the loan agreements. Lenders are dependent on the governments' regard for their own credit reputations.

The surge in interest rates on US dollar securities at the end of the 1970s also led to the collapse of nearly 1000 US banks, savings banks, and savings and loan associations. One group of lenders had extended loans to firms engaged in the production of oil and other primary products including foodstuffs; these lenders were caught in the rhetoric of the 1970s that the commodity prices would climb sky-high. The banks were eager to lend to firms involved in the production of oil and to the farmers that wanted to expand their acreage at a time when land prices were increasing at a rapid rate. When the prices of oil and cereals declined sharply in the early 1980s, many of the borrowers were unable to make their debt service payments.

The second group included the US thrift institutions that traditionally made home mortgage loans. These thrifts funded their purchases of long-term mortgages with the money received from the sale of short-term deposits – these thrifts had a 'maturity mis-match.' As interest rates on short-term US dollar securities increased, the interest payments on their short-term deposit liabilities increased relative to their interest income on their long-term mortgages, and eventually increased above their interest income, and the thrifts began to incur losses and bleed capital.

These thrifts were between the proverbial 'rock and the hard place' – if they did nothing, the continued operating losses would bleed their capital as long as short-term interest rates remained higher than long-term interest rates. If instead they sold their mortgages, they would incur a large immediate loss because the sales price would be lower than the face value of their mortgages.

When the losses of the thrifts exceeded their capital, they were closed by the regulatory authorities, and the depositors were 'made whole' by the Federal Savings and Loan Insurance Corporation and the Federal Deposit Insurance Corporation; the failed thrifts usually were merged into banks and other lenders that were believed viable. Eventually the reserves built up by the government insurance agencies were exhausted – and as more thrifts failed they remained open through a policy of forbearance because the government-owned deposit insurance firms were bankrupt and did not have the cash to make the depositors whole.

The implosion of the asset price bubble in Tokyo

The second wave of financial crises began in the early 1990s and was associated with the collapse of real estate prices and stock prices in Japan. When these prices stopped increasing, it was inevitable that they would fall to the level appropriate for their earning power – or perhaps even below this level for a while.

Many Japanese firms were organized into groups – Mitsui, Mitsubishi, Sumitomo, and Yamato were among these groups, which had been known as 'zaibatsu' before the Second World War. Each group was a mutual support system. Initially a bank was at the center of each group and was partly a holding company for the operating companies in the group. These holding company arrangements were outlawed in the postwar occupation of the late 1940s, and the bank in each group was demoted to same level as the other firms. Each firm and the bank in each group owned small amounts of the shares of each of the other participants in the group in a practice known as 'cross shareholdings.'

During the bubble years, the value of the shares in the industrial firms owned by the major banks was increasing at a rapid rate, with the result that the banks' capital also was increasing at a similar rate. The increase in bank capital meant that they were able to 'grow their loans' at a rapid rate, which led to increases in real estate prices and stock prices and hence in bank capital. Neat.

Banks and other lenders to the buyers of real estate believed that their lending policies were conservative since borrowers had pledged real estate as collateral and since borrowers almost always had a sterling record for paying interest on a timely basis. The rapid increase in bank loans to finance the purchase of real estate became self-justifying because real estate prices were increasing.

At some stage it was inevitable that bank lenders would reduce the rate of growth of their real estate loans; if they did not these loans would become too large as a share of their total loans. Then some of those who bought real estate with borrowed money would no longer have enough cash to pay all of the scheduled interest to the banks. These borrowers would be in a position much like the US thrift institutions that were paying higher interest rates on their short-term deposits than they were earning on their long-term mortgages – they would incur a negative cash flow month by month or they could sell the properties, which would depress prices further.

At the end of 1989, the newly appointed Governor of the Bank of Japan told the banks to limit the growth of their real estate loans to the growth of their total loans. Stock prices in Tokyo began to decrease almost immediately, and real estate prices began to decline a few months later; stock prices fell by more than 30 percent from December 1990 to December 1991. As real estate and stock prices declined, the loans losses of the Japanese banks soared and their capital declined. The Japanese banks incurred losses on their loans to the credit cooperatives that had made real estate loans. Similarly, the banks incurred losses on their loans to industrial firms that had invested in real estate and stocks when these borrowers went bankrupt.

The bank regulators followed a policy of forbearance; the Japanese banks remained open, despite their negative capital. Even though there was no formal deposit insurance, the banks were not subject to a run; it was understood that the depositors would not incur losses if a bank was closed.

The sharp decline in the prices of real estate and of stocks meant that household wealth declined sharply; one response was that household savings increased. Business investment declined because firms had significant excess capacity as a result of the surge in investment during the bubble-boom years. A 'credit crunch' developed; the Japanese banks were reluctant to make new loans because they were unsure of the creditworthiness of the borrowers – and they did not want to make any loan that might be considered risky because of their negative capital position. Investors were reluctant to buy the shares of the Japanese banks because they were uncertain about the extent of the loan losses of the banks.

In the 1970s and the 1980s, Japan had been the most rapidly growing industrial country. In the 1990s, Japan was the one of the slowest growing industrial countries and its economy remained in the economic doldrums for 15 years. The unemployment rate surged. During some years the price level declined. Nominal interest rates were low, but because of the decline in the price level, real interest rates were higher.

The Mexican debacle of the mid-1990s and the Asian financial crises

Mexico was one of the great economic success stories of the early 1990s. Carlos Salinas with a PhD in Economics from Harvard became president at the end of 1988; many of the top administrators in his cabinet also were PhDs with extensive experience in previous administrations. Salinas sought to stabilize the Mexican economy. Soon after he became president, the Brady bond initiative funded (and reduced) the overhang of bank loans from the 1970s; the foreign banks exchanged the bank loans that were in default for a type of bond that was partly guaranteed by the US Treasury (the interest payments on these bonds was guaranteed, but not the repayment of principal).

In the late 1970s Mexico developed a limited free trade area with the United States known as 'maquilidoras,' which were factories along the US–Mexican border that provided for the duty-free importation of components that would be reexported to the United States without paying any tariff on Mexican value-added.

The Salinas administration adopted three major types of policies to prepare Mexico so that it might join the United States and Canada in the North American Free Trade Area. One was macro stabilization, and the reduction of the inflation rate from nearly 150 percent in 1988 to 15 percent in 1993; the major policy for reducing the inflation rate was a tight-money policy similar to the one adopted by the United States in 1979. A second was the privatization of more than 500 government-owned firms; the major government-owned firm that was not privatized was Pemex, the oil monopoly. Many of these firms were prepared for privatization by reducing their bloated employment and cost structures. The third was liberalization and especially the elimination of a variety of government controls that limited imports and protected the monopoly positions of Mexican firms in their home market.

This three-part program attracted US and foreign firms that wanted to integrate Mexico into their global supply chains; they planned to use low-wage Mexico as a source of supply for the high-wage US and Canadian markets. Several European and Asian automobile companies established plants in Mexico that would produce cars for the US market. US and other foreign firms purchased many of the firms that were being privatized. The high real interest rates that followed from the strong antiinflation policy of the Bank of Mexico were attractive to the global money market funds.

The Salinas administration welcomed the inflow of foreign money and foreign firms, because they would provide employment opportunities. From 1989 to 1993 the capital flow to Mexico increased, and the Mexican peso appreciated in real terms even as it was depreciating in nominal terms. Mexican imports increased more rapidly than its exports and its trade deficit increased to 7 percent of its GDP – and its net international indebtedness increased to 60 percent of its GDP. The inflow of new foreign money provided Mexico with the cash to finance its trade deficit and to pay the interest on its increasing foreign indebtedness.

The year 1994 was one of a presidential transition in Mexico; the election was in August and the newly elected president would take office in December. Political uncertainty surged: in January there was an Indian uprising in the southernmost state of Chiapas. In March the leading presidential candidate of the dominant political party was assassinated. A senior official of the Department of Justice was assassinated in September.

The increase in political uncertainty led to a sharp decline in the flow of foreign money to Mexico. The Bank of Mexico responded by using its international reserve assets to support the peso. The Mexican Treasury issued 'Tesobonos,' a new security that had a currency guarantee to attract foreign investors – essentially a US dollar-denominated obligation of the Mexican Government. The Mexican peso depreciated sharply when the Bank of Mexico stopped supporting the currency; the crisis was halted only after the US Treasury arranged an exceptionally large loan for the Mexican Government.

The Mexican peso prices of imports and of exports soared, which contributed to a surge in the inflation rate. The sharp decline in external loans led to a surge in the demand for domestic credit and interest rates on peso loans skyrocketed. Many businesses failed. The loan losses of the Mexican banks surged and these banks – which had only recently been privatized – failed.

At some stage it was inevitable that Mexico's ability to increase its external indebtedness relative to its GDP would decline. When that stage was reached, the growth of Mexican external debt would slow, and Mexico would be unlikely to have the money to pay the interest on its foreign indebtedness and to finance its trade deficit at the prevailing value of the peso. This stage might be approached gradually if the trade deficit declined modestly from one year to the next either because exports surged or because the peso depreciated.

The cash flow problem for Mexico in the early 1990s was similar to that in the late 1970s, although suppliers of the foreign funds to Mexico in the earlier decade were banks and the suppliers in the subsequent period were mutual funds and pension funds and multinational firms. In both cases the cash from the inflow of money from abroad led to an increase in foreign indebtedness at a rate that was nonsustainable.

The Asian financial crises of the late 1990s began with the sharp depreciation of the Thai baht at the beginning of July 1997. The prelude to this crisis was a surge in the flow of foreign money to Thailand and the other Asian countries in the early 1990s which led to bubble-like increases in real estate prices and stock prices. Much as in Mexico, the inflow of foreign money led to the appreciation of the currencies of the countries in the region (except for the Hong Kong dollar and the Chinese yuan which were pegged to the US dollar). Several countries developed trade deficits that were in the range of 4–6 percent of their GDPs.

The depreciation of the Thai baht in early July 1997 triggered a contagion effect, more or less the Asian equivalent of the tequila effect that followed the financial debacle in Mexico. Owners of stocks rushed to sell, and prices plummeted. Bank lenders were unwilling to extend any new loans and reluctant to renew maturing loans because they had become skeptical of the solvency and the liquidity of the borrowers.

The contagion effect was like the train of falling dominoes. South Korea got sideswiped in December 1998 even though it had not experienced a surge in capital inflows; its current account deficit was 1 percent of its GDP, much lower than the ratios in the countries in Southeast Asia. Real estate prices and stock prices had not surged. However, many of the large South Korean industrial conglomerates had borrowed extensively to finance their expansion and to increase their market shares.

Moreover, South Korea was holding a presidential election; for a few days candidates competed with each other in terms of how strongly each would resist the IMF conditions for financial assistance.

The international banks were reluctant to renew their maturing loans to the South Korean banks, and the country did not have sufficient international reserve assets to repay these loans. The South Korean won price of the US dollar increased by nearly 50 percent within several weeks, which led to large revaluation losses for many of the 'chaebol,' the family-owned conglomerates, and the South Korean banks incurred large loan losses.

Russia was a mid-1998 casualty of the Asian crises. Russia differed from the developing countries in Southeast Asia in that it had a current account surplus, a result of the relatively high prices for its raw materials. The Russian Government was privatizing a number of firms. The Russian banking system was fragile. The Russian Government incurred a large fiscal deficit, the tax base was modest as the country moved toward a market economy, and the government found it difficult to reduce expenditure because of adverse impacts on employment. Firms lacked the money to pay wages and paid in the goods they produced, which the workers might sell. The increasingly large fiscal deficit was financed by borrowing from the newly privatized Russian banks, which rapidly increased the interest rates they would pay on their IOUs. The lenders to these banks were Western banks and investors, who sold US dollars and German marks to obtain the rubles that were used to buy the Russian Government debt; at the same time, they bought the US dollars and the German marks in the forward exchange market to hedge their foreign exchange exposures.

As the outstanding debt of the Russian Government increased, in part because of the surge in its interest payments, it had to increase interest rates to sell its debt. The IMF made several large loans to assist the Russian Government even though the government's primary problem was a fiscal deficit associated with the transition to a market economy rather than a balance-of-payments deficit.

Argentina was the last domino to tumble. The country had experienced hyperinflation at the end of the 1980s. It then pegged its currency to the US dollar and adopted a currency rule that tied the growth in the peso money supply to growth in the Argentinean central bank's holdings of US dollars, much as if the country was on the nineteenth-century gold standard. Individuals and firms in Argentina could make domestic payments in Argentina in either the peso or the US dollar.

During the early 1990s, the Argentinean Government had a fiscal deficit that it financed with proceeds from the sale of government-owned firms. By the late 1990s, this source of money had diminished because there were relatively few firms still to be privatized, so the government began to issue US dollar-denominated bonds to finance its deficit. The interest rates that were offered to attract buyers for the bonds increased. The ratio of government indebtedness to the country's GDP increased to more than 100 percent. The government got the cash to pay the interest to its creditors by issuing new bonds.

This crisis – or set of crises – lasted three and a half years from the depreciation of the Thai baht in midsummer 1997 until the depreciation of the Argentinean peso at the end of January 2001. During this period, investors were waiting for the next 'shoe to drop' – the next country that would devalue its currency.

The implosion of the global housing bubble in 2007

House prices in the United States had peaked toward the end of 2006, although there were substantial differences among geographic regions; prices were continuing to increase in Charlotte, North Carolina, and Seattle even as they were declining in Florida and Arizona and Nevada. House prices in Ireland and Spain peaked slightly earlier, while prices in Britain peaked later.

The decline in prices reflected that supply had been increasing more rapidly than the demand associated with population growth, in part because speculative purchases had led to increases in demand in anticipation that the properties could be sold at a significant profit. Moreover, developers had increased the number of units in their inventories in anticipation of the growth in demand.

When house prices stopped increasing in the United States, the prices of some mortgage-related securities that were related to subprime mortgages began to decline. The generic feature of these mortgages was that they were associated with borrowers with lower credit ratings, perhaps in part because the down payment made by the home buyers was less than the traditional 20 percent. Interest rates on these mortgages were significantly higher than on prime mortgages. Defaults on these mortgages were low, in part because the homeowners that had difficulty in making their mortgage payments could sell their properties and repay the lenders. In 2005 and 2006 there was a surge in subprime mortgages; in part this was based on significant increase in the demand for these securities because of the higher interest rates.

The first tremor in the implosion of the housing finance bubble was the announcement by Bear Stearns, one of the more aggressive US investment banks, that it had lent nearly $2 billion to one of the hedge funds that it managed because of the fund's large investment losses. Several weeks later Bear announced that several of the hedge funds that it managed were being closed; their assets would be sold and the investors in the funds would receive the proceeds, which was estimated to be about 10 cents for each dollar that they had invested. Then a small bank in Germany announced that it had received a $2.5 billion capital infusion from Deutsche Bank. The President of Paribas, a leading French bank, said that limits would be placed on the amount of money that investors could withdraw from funds managed by the bank.

Some US homeowners defaulted on their mortgage loan payments as the market value of their properties declined, a practice that initially was identified with the subprime mortgages. As we have seen, borrowers for such mortgages often had low credit scores and made modest down payments, often less than 10 percent – if they had made any down payment. As long as property prices were increasing homeowners that had difficulty in making their monthly mortgage payments could sell their homes and repay the indebtedness.

Until the 1980s the US mortgage market was local, and the banks and the thrift institutions lent money to families in their neighborhoods; lenders knew their borrowers. The financial innovation in the 1980s was that mortgages were 'securitized' – hundreds of mortgages with similar features were bundled into packages, and a new asset-backed-security (ABS) or mortgage-backed security (MBS) was sold to pension funds and other investors that wanted the higher interest rates attached to mortgages. This innovation led to an 'infinite distance' between the families that wanted to borrow the money to buy homes and the firms that provided the cash for their mortgages.

US mortgage banking firms were the 'bridge' between individuals that wanted a mortgage and the investment banks; these firms were paid fees for bringing the mortgages to the investment banks. The investment banks retained the right to 'put' a mortgage back to the mortgage bankers for 12 or 18 months; they would do so if the homeowner failed to make one or several monthly payments. These mortgage bankers began to fail in the last quarter of 2006, and more than 100 of these firms had closed by the time that Bear Stearns had announced that its hedge funds were in difficulty.

The subsequent development was the creation of collateralized debt obligations (CDOs); the collateralized mortgage obligations (CMOs) were sliced into five tranches, and the risky tranches were bundled into one CDO, the next most risky tranches into another CDO, and so on. The owners of the CDOs that involved the most risky tranche would be the first to receive a decline in payments if some of the borrowers defaulted. Initially the difference between the interest rates on the most risky CDOs and the least risky CDOs was one-half to three-quarters of 1 percent.

Each time the investment banks bundled the mortgages into CMOs they earned a fee. Each time the investment banks sliced the CMOs and bundled the tranches into CDOs they earned a fee. And they received a fee for packaging the CDOs into CDO2s. The investment banks also managed the hedge funds that were the buyers of the CDOs.

A number of hedge funds 'promised' investors that they would be able to earn annual rates of return of 11–12 percent. The prime way to convert a 6 percent rate of return on a mortgage into a 12 percent rate of return on a CDO was leverage – the hedge fund would borrow $200 or $300 or $400 in the short-term commercial paper market for each $100 of investor funds, and it would pledge the CDO as collateral for the loans. The aggressive hedge funds purchased the CDOs that had bundled the riskiest tranches of the CMOs. If they had four to one leverage and the interest rate on the borrowed money was one and one-half percentage points below the interest rate on the mortgages, they could earn 11–12 percent.

The first hedge funds to encounter financial problems were those that specialized in buying subprime mortgages. As long as home prices continued to increase, the default rates on the subprime mortgages were low; borrowers who had difficulty making their monthly payments would sell their properties and repay the mortgage loan. When real estate prices stopped increasing, many of these subprime borrowers had 'upside-down mortgages' – the amount they owed on the mortgages was larger than the market value of the mortgaged properties.

Many of the subprime borrowers then defaulted on their mortgages. The consequence was that the market value of the CDOs that had the riskier tranches of these securities declined sharply. The owners of these CDOs then incurred large losses, and the owners of the CDOs that had purchased them with borrowed money incurred massive losses.

The mystery was the identity of the owners of these securities. Because no one was certain who owned these mortgages, the credit markets 'went on strike' – those with the cash were reluctant to lend to those who wanted to borrow.

The next major tremor was the virtual collapse of Countrywide Financial, the largest mortgage lender in the United States. The first indication that Countrywide had a problem was that it borrowed $11.5 billion from 40 banks; the money from these loans was used to fund mortgages that previously had been funded by selling commercial paper but the buyers for this paper had disappeared. Several weeks later the Bank of America announced that it had bought $2.4 billion of newly issued preferred stock; in effect BA became a nearly 20 percent owner of Countrywide. The implication was that BA would purchase more of the preferred stock to keep Countrywide afloat.

Another tremor was a 'run' on Northern Rock, the fourth largest financial institution in Britain and the largest mortgage lender. Northern Rock had a business strategy that suggested that it was a clone of Countrywide in that it relied on the money received from the sale of commercial paper to fund its purchases of mortgages. When Countrywide was shunted from the commercial paper market because the would-be buyers were apprehensive about the credit quality and its own viability, Northern Rock also was in a beleaguered position in the commercial paper market.

These tremors reflected a credit crunch, and the reluctance of lenders to acquire the IOUs of those financial institutions that might have acquired mortgages from high-risk borrowers. There was a great deal of 'toxic waste' in the mortgage market, and it remained so until the holders of these securities could be identified. A very large number of US mortgage bankers failed, perhaps more than 50 percent; these firms originated mortgages and then sold them to the investment banks that would bundle them as the basis for issuing an MBS however, the investment banks retained the right to 'put' the mortgage back to the mortgage bankers if the borrowers failed to make the monthly payments for the first year or two.

The crises in the mortgage market initially involved the securities that had been issued on the basis of subprime mortgages, which generally refers to the loans to the borrowers with poor credit histories who may have made a modest down payment, or whose down payment involved a second mortgage. As long as property prices were increasing, the loss rate on these mortgages was low; the homeowners who were unable to keep up with the monthly payments sold the properties and repaid the mortgage loans. When property prices stopped increasing or declined, the homeowners defaulted, and the lenders eventually acquired title to the property.

In March 2007 Bear Stearns was subject to a silent run; it found that other banks and financial firms were increasingly reluctant to enter into contracts. Bear was in a position much like Countrywide 6 months earlier; it could no longer obtain the cash that it needed to finance the inventory of securities that it owned – some of these securities were highly illiquid because their underlying value was so uncertain. The Fed helped arrange a takeover of Bear by JPMorgan Chase, in large part by agreeing to acquire up to $30 billion of the securities owned by Bear. JPMorgan Chase would incur the first $1 billion of losses on these securities, and the Fed would have to make good any subsequent losses; any gains on these securities would accrue to the Fed.

The major concern is the scope of the decline in house prices and the length of the period before prices are again at an equilibrium relationship with household incomes. As long as prices fall, the firms that own mortgages will continue to incur losses, and some of these firms are likely to be subject to runs.

The decline in prices of mortgage-related securities led to significant loan losses by the other investment banks, including. Fannie Mae and Freddie Mac, the two government-sponsored firms that owned more than 50 percent of the credit risk attached to all US mortgage.

Lehman Brothers also went bankrupt in mid-September. The credit-rating agencies downgraded the securities of American International Group (AIG), then the world's largest insurance company. AIG had been the largest seller of credit default swaps (CDSs), which were a form of insurance policy that guaranteed the owner of a CDS against loss if a borrower defaulted.

House prices have declined in Spain and in Ireland, and have begun to decline in Britain, and are likely to decline in the other countries that experienced a sharp increases in prices.

Each of these waves of financial crises followed a credit bubble, marked by the growth in the indebtedness of a group of borrowers at a relatively high rate, often in the range of 20–30 percent a year. The second, third, and fourth waves were associated with an increase in credit for purchases of real estate while the first wave was associated with increase in bank loans to governments and government-owned firms in the developing countries.

The paradox was that the rapid growth of credit was associated with economic booms, but the growth of credit at a rate much higher than the rate of growth of GDP was not sustainable for an indefinite future; at some stage it was inevitable that the indebtedness would increase at a much slower rate. In anticipation of this decline, the lenders should have asked 'Where will the borrowers get the money to pay the interest on the outstanding loans if they can no longer obtain this money from new loans?' Since most of these bubbles involved an increase in external indebtedness, a counterpart question is 'What will be the impact of a decline in the rate of growth of indebtedness on the value of the currency?'

Banks and other financial institutions fail when they misprice a risk by a large amount – when the interest rate on the loan is too low. Moreover, lenders may have believed that they had a diversified portfolio of loans; they failed to recognize or slighted that the defaults by different borrowers may not be independent events. Defaults tend to be episodic, and bunched when the economy is approaching a recession or in a recession, and often result from a decline in the availability of new credits.

The triggers for these crises defined as the event that interrupted the pattern of nonsustainable financial flows differed. The developing country debt crisis of the early 1980s was triggered by the surge in interest rates on US dollar securities as the Federal Reserve shifted to an extremely contractive monetary policy; the reduction in the flow of cash from new loans caused sharp falls in the receipts of governments relative to their payments, and sharp declines in the value of their currencies. The trigger that led to the implosion of the Japanese asset price bubble was guidance from the central bank that the Japanese banks limit – and hence sharply reduce – their new loans for real estate. The Asian crisis was triggered by the recognition that the indebtedness of some of the borrowers in Thailand was too large relative to their incomes. The implosion of the real estate bubbles in the United States and other countries was prompted by the slowdown in the foreign demand for mortgage-related securities.

Financial crises, illiquidity, and insolvency

The universal first step in the sequence of events associated in a financial crisis is that some lenders find that they – like Countrywide Financial and Northern Rock – have liquidity problems that they cannot 'roll over' maturing short-term liabilities. Mexico had this problem in 1982, and South Korea had this problem in 1997. The suppliers of short-term liquidity suddenly have become much more cautious about the solvency of the financial institutions that have relied on short-term borrowings to finance their purchases of long-term securities.

The initial, almost universal, reaction is that indebted borrowers have a liquidity problem; they lack access to the money that might be used for their debt service payments or to support their currencies. Firms and banks also may be subject to a liquidity problem if lenders are concerned that borrowers might be insolvent; few lenders are likely to increase the amount of credit they will make available to others if they have a significant concern that the borrowers will become bankrupt and unable to repay.

One of the major rationales for the establishment of central banks in the nineteenth century was to reduce the likelihood that a bank would become insolvent because the sale of assets undertaken to raise the cash necessary to satisfy the withdrawals of money by depositors would depress the prices of these assets. The effort of one bank to meet the demands of the depositors would have adverse impacts on the capital of other banks that owned similar assets. The provision of liquidity by a central bank would reduce the likelihood that a liquidity problem would escalate into a solvency problem. But the provision of liquidity cannot solve an underlying solvency problem.

Consider whether the banks that had made loans during each of these four waves of crises were insolvent because of large loan losses when the borrowers defaulted. The loan losses incurred by the major US banks in the early 1980s when Mexico and other developing countries defaulted were large and some of these banks might have failed if the bank regulators had not connived in the fiction that these loans were performing. In effect, this policy of forbearance enabled the banks to earn their way out of their problem of inadequate capital over a few years. During this period, one of the eight large US money center banks failed, and nearly 1000 thrift institutions failed.

The Government of Japan similarly followed a policy of forbearance when the bubble in Japanese real estate and stocks imploded. Ultimately the loan losses of the Japanese banks were two to three times as large as their capital. These banks had a solvency problem, but curiously they did not have a liquidity problem; there was an effective understanding that the banks would not be allowed to close with losses to depositors or to others with financial claims on the banks – other than the shareholders.

The unique feature of the period that preceded the Asian financial crisis is that the foreign suppliers of funds to Thailand and Indonesia as well as to South Korea, Russia, Brazil, Argentina, and Mexico were a mixed group that included banks, mutual funds, pension funds, and multinational firms. When the crisis occurred and these countries devalued their currencies, the domestic banks in most of these countries failed; a principal exception was Singapore and another was Hong Kong. No foreign bank appears to have encountered a liquidity problem or a solvency problem because of losses on loans to borrowers in these countries.

The implosion of the house prices in the United States, Britain, Ireland, Iceland, and other countries has led to large declines in the value of mortgage-related securities, which has led to sharp declines in the capital of the investment banks and the commercial banks both in the countries in which these securities originated and in countries where the banks had purchased these securities for the high anticipated yields. Many of these firms clearly have had a solvency problem in that the decline in their capital was so large that they found it difficult to attract capital from private investors.

The lenders had become insolvent in three of these waves of crisis. The major international banks were largely unaffected by the Asian financial crisis. The domestic banks in most of the Asian countries as well as in Mexico, Russia, and Argentina were insolvent because of the large decline in the value of their domestic loans in the crisis that followed the sharp depreciation of their currencies.

Most of the countries that borrowed from the IMF following the crisis eventually repaid their loans; similarly, Mexico repaid the monies that it had borrowed from the IMF.

South Korea differs from Thailand and the other countries in South Asia in that its current account deficit was much smaller relative to its GDP; indeed the ratio of foreign indebtedness to its GDP was declining. The large business conglomerates in South Korea were heavily indebted.

The solvency question is somewhat akin to a bankruptcy question. The accounting definition of bankruptcy is that value of the firm's assets is smaller than the value of its liabilities; the economic definition is that the present value of its payments is larger than the present value of its receipts. A firm might reduce the present value of its payments if it can induce its labor force to accept lower wages or its suppliers to accept lower prices.

Were Mexico and the other developing countries insolvent in the early 1980s or were they only illiquid? The problem of the governments in most of these countries was that if they raised taxes and reduced expenditure by the amount needed to generate a cash surplus that could be used to buy the dollars necessary to pay the interest on their external indebtedness, their domestic political support would wither and the governments would lose office. The voters in these countries had to decide whether it was worthwhile to accept the burden associated with maintaining the credit reputation of the country; they concluded that the value of the credit reputation was smaller than the costs of the measures to maintain the reputation.

Many Japanese real estate investors were insolvent when prices began to decline, and the Japanese banks were clearly insolvent. The problem in Japan was that real estate prices had increased too rapidly relative to the country's GDP, and that the explicit and implicit rents were too low relative to the scheduled interest payments. The greater availability of liquidity might have slowed the decline in the real estate prices, but the decline was inevitable.

Mexico repaid all the money borrowed in 1995; did Mexico have only a liquidity problem or did Mexico have a solvency problem? The Mexican peso had become overvalued in the early 1990s, and an adjustment in the foreign exchange value of the peso was necessary. If the Bank of Mexico had had greater access to external finance earlier in the presidential transition, the peso might have depreciated less rapidly, and hence less extensively than it did. The depreciation of the peso in real terms in effect was comparable to a decline in the real wage of Mexicans. That the Mexicans repaid all they borrowed at the new and much lower value of the peso does not mean that they would have been able to repay all they might have borrowed if they intervened and pegged the peso at a higher value.

Most of the countries that were hit by the contagion effect following the depreciation of the Thai baht repaid their IMF loans; nevertheless, their currencies had depreciated extensively in real terms.

The IMF was established as an international counterpart to a domestic central bank; the Fund would provide governments of its member countries with foreign funds so they would be able to finance payments deficits and especially those of a cyclical or temporary form. The rationale was to reduce the likelihood that countries would devalue their currencies only because they had transient payments deficits. The implication was that a payments deficit due to fundamental disequilibrium would require a devaluation of the country's currency, while a payments deficit that was not attributable to a fundamental disequilibrium might require a devaluation if the country did not have sufficient reserves and credit lines to finance what appeared to be a temporary payments deficits.

Two different risks were associated with the IMF's loans to its member countries. One – the moral hazard issue – is that countries might use the money obtained from the IMF to delay the devaluations of their currencies even though they were in fundamental disequilibrium and their currencies should be devalued. The other was that too little money would be available from the IMF and so the devaluation or depreciation of the member country currencies would be larger than the change that would have been necessary to return to fundamental equilibrium.

When currencies are not pegged, the change in the volume of cross-border flows and the change in the direction of these flows almost always lead to a sharp decline in the value of the currency in the foreign exchange market – classic 'undershooting.' The decline in the value of the currency in the short run always has been larger than the decline in the value in the longer run, in part because consumers cannot immediately shift between domestic and foreign goods when their relative prices change and similarly firms cannot immediately shift from selling in the foreign market to selling in the domestic market.

There are two aspects of the solvency and liquidity relationship at the international level that have no counterpart at the domestic level. In the domestic economy an adjustment that may be necessary for the firm to become solvent after a bankruptcy is that its labor costs must decline, and many of the workers may leave if their real wage were reduced; in the international economy the depreciation of the currency provides a countrywide reduction in the real wage. At the international level, the country may be illiquid even though the households, firms, and governments are solvent and have abundant liquidity; the illiquidity of the country reflects that funds are not available to cushion the depreciation of the currency when import prices surge or the demand for the country's exports declines.

The relatively large movements in currency values in the short run have had significant domestic consequences – the domestic currency equivalent of the liabilities denominated in a foreign currency increases in direct proportion of the change in the exchange rate. The domestic prices of imported goods increase sharply, which leads to an increase in the domestic inflation rate. Domestic interest rates surge and the market value of the assets held by the country declines; some firms and perhaps even some banks may tumble into insolvency because of the decline in the market value of financial assets.

The larger the liabilities denominated in a foreign currency of the firms and the governments in a country, the more likely the depreciation of its currency will cause some economic units to become insolvent, according to either the accounting criterion or the economic criterion. Some of these economic units could become insolvent even if the central bank had sufficient liquidity to forestall undershooting.

The Government of Mexico and governments in many of the other developing countries in the 1980s defaulted on their US dollar loans as a result of the combination of the surge in interest rates on US dollar securities and the large depreciation of their currencies.

Some observers believed that the Mexican peso was overvalued by 15 or 20 percent at the beginning of 1994. Mexico had a liquidity crisis, and the peso price of the US dollar increased by nearly 100 percent. The sharp depreciation triggered large revaluation losses. Loans from the IMF proved too small, and the US Treasury took the initiative in developing a massive loan program that enabled the Government of Mexico to forestall a much larger depreciation.

The Asian financial crisis involved massive depreciations of the Indonesian rupiah, the Thai baht, and the Malaysian ringgit; large flows of funds to these countries led to trade deficits that were in the range of 6–8 percent of their GDPs and to the implicit overvaluation of their currencies. When the flow of funds was reversed, the currencies depreciated, and they went from being overvalued to an undershooting as trade patterns were reoriented. The sharp large depreciations triggered massive insolvencies of domestic firms that had borrowed abroad to reduce their interest costs as the domestic counterpart of their foreign currency liabilities surged.

South Korea was sideswiped in this crisis primarily because of its geographical proximity; its current account deficit was much smaller as a percent of its GDP. Foreign lenders to South Korean firms were reluctant to roll over maturing debt that would have been the normal practice, and the South Korean price of the US dollar increased by 50 percent. Massive undershooting of the South Korean won greatly enhanced the competitiveness of South Korean firms even as it caused many of these firms with debt denominated in foreign currencies to become bankrupt as a result of the sharp increase in the won equivalent to their liabilities denominated in foreign currencies.

The undershooting of long-run values for these currencies is dramatic evidence that the affected countries had a shortage of liquidity and were unable or unwilling to prevent the dramatic decline in the foreign exchange value of their currencies. The IMF was established to forestall crises of this sort, and it failed to do so, either because its resources were too paltry or because its management was too timid.

Lenders mispriced the credit risk and the currency risk. Firms that borrowed in a foreign currency to reduce their net interest payments frequently increased their foreign currency exposure; a sharp depreciation of their domestic currency led to a large increase in the domestic currency equivalent of their liabilities denominated in a foreign currency. The firms that denominated liabilities in a foreign currency mispriced this risk and the banks that became lenders to these firms also mispriced this risk because they failed to recognize the impact of changes in currency values on the net worth of borrowers and the value of their loans to these borrowers.

The lenders to governments and firms headquartered in foreign countries did not recognize that many of these borrowers were involved in Ponzi finance and paid interest on their outstanding loans with cash received from new loans. The lenders do not appear to have asked 'Where will the borrowers get the cash to pay the interest if we stop advancing the cash?' The banks in Tokyo and Osaka were stung by the failure to ask the question on two different occasions; the first was in the 1970s when they lent money to governments and government-owned firms in developing countries and the second was in the 1980s when they rapidly increased their domestic real estate loans. The prelude to the Asian financial crises was a surge in the flow of foreign funds to Mexico, Thailand, Brazil, Argentina, and other emerging market countries; investors appeared to be hooked on the belief that the rates of return on investments in these countries were substantially higher than the rates of return in the industrial countries. The rapid increase in real estate prices in the United States, Britain, and most of the other Anglo-Saxon countries reflected that many buyers were interested in short-term investment profits rather than rental income.

Lenders and investors failed to recognize that the pattern of cash flows in these four waves conformed with the Ponzian model. In two of these episodes, the value of the currencies was extensively influenced by these cross-border flows of funds; a reduction in the flows would lead to a depreciation of the currencies, which was self-justifying. The sharp depreciation would lead to a domestic surge in interest rates. The borrowers were on the proverbial 'slippery slope'; in the absence of the cash from new loans, they would have to sharply reduce their payments relative to their receipts to get the cash to make the interest payments.

12
Central Bankers Read Election Returns, Not Balance Sheets

The holy grail of monetary reform

The financial crisis that began in 2007 has led to ad hoc actions to 'save the banks' in the United States, Britain, Ireland, and Iceland. The policy judgment has been that if the loan losses of the banks were much larger than their capital and they were closed with losses to the depositors, the economies would encounter massive deflationary pressures as the money supplies declined and as households and business firms became more cautious spenders. The governments felt the need to supply capital to banks to ensure that depositors would not take a 'haircut.' The provision of the capital was ad hoc, and then the policy makers realized that a new problem had developed as a result of partial government ownership of the banks.

For most of the last several decades, the finance ministers of the world have pursued the grail of monetary reform. They want to reduce the uncertainties associated with changes in currency values and they are fearful of domestic pressures for protectionism. They have met each other at the annual autumnal meetings of the International Monetary Fund (IMF) and at the interim committee meetings every spring, at the meetings of the Group of Ten and the Committee of Twenty, at the ad hoc meetings of the Organisation for Economic Co-operation and Development (OECD), at United Nations Committee on Trade and Development (UNCTAD) in New York and Geneva. The finance ministers of the member countries of the European Union (EU) have met in its Brussels headquarters and on a rotational basis in various national capitals. The presidents and prime ministers of the United States, Germany, Japan, Canada, Britain, France, and Italy have met at Vancouver, Denver, Rambouillet, Puerto Rico, London, Bonn, Tokyo, Ottawa, Versailles, and Williamsburg at annual summit meetings. There have been scores of meetings on a bilateral basis. The prize remains elusive.

Yet without reform, international trade has expanded at a rapid rate and international investment has grown – at least until the advent of the financial crisis of 2007. Many once-developing countries have achieved high rates of growth, and tens of millions of individuals have moved from poverty into the middle class. Would trade and investment and per capita income have increased at an even more rapid rate if there had been a System with a capital S, a set of rules that governed the intervention policies of the central banks in the currency market and the growth of international reserve assets?

Have floating exchange rates delivered on promises?

The first question is whether the floating currency arrangement has operated effectively, and delivered on the key promises that its proponents had made in the 1950s and the 1960s. Their general view was that if currencies were not pegged, then the changes in currency values would track the differences in national inflation rates. Thus there would be only modest (if any) change in the competitive position of firms producing in different countries as a result of deviations of currency values from those forecast from the differences in national inflation rates. Moreover, they suggested that changes in currency values would be gradual rather than abrupt, and that these changes would be depoliticized because they would not be associated with changes in the competitive positions of firms in different countries.

The surprise over the last 35 years has been that the changes in currency values have been larger – indeed, much much larger – than the changes based on differences in the national inflation rates. In the late 1970s the US inflation rate was higher than the inflation rate in Germany by 2 or 3 percentage points and yet the US dollar depreciated by more than 10 percent a year. Then, in the first half of the 1980s, the US dollar appreciated by 12 percent a year relative to the German mark, even though the US inflation rate remained higher than German rate. Another example – from 1995 to 1998 the inflation rate in Japan was several percentage points below the US inflation rate and yet in one year the yen depreciated by more than 20 percent. Between 1999 and June 2008 the difference between the inflation rates in the United States and the EU was almost always smaller than 2 percent and yet the US dollar price of the euro almost doubled.

The range of movement in currency values has been much larger than the range that would have been predicted based on differences in national inflation rates. In the long run, changes in currency values tend to be consistent with differences in national inflation rates; this long-run relationship is one of the 'established facts' of international finance. But in intervals of 2 or 3 years, there is no systematic relationship between the changes in currency values and the differences in national inflation rates. Moreover, the average annual deviation between currency values and the changes that would have been predicted on the basis of the difference in national inflation rates has been much greater when currencies have been floating than when they were pegged. The movements in the currency values have been far less smooth or gradual than the proponents of a floating exchange rate arrangement had promised.

The major advantage of the system of floating exchange rates is that the national monetary authorities have not had to contend with overvalued currencies and undervalued currencies – they could blame these deviations on anonymous market forces. Moreover, they have been less hawkish about the need to maintain an inflation rate in the range of 1–2 percent a year because of the need to adhere to a parity for their currency; any tendency toward a loss of competitiveness would lead to a slightly more rapid depreciation of their currency.

The paradox from the US point of view is that US dollar is one of the most undervalued currencies, and yet the ratio of the US trade deficit to US GDP is higher than that for almost any other country. Somehow the textbook story that a low value for the currency should lead to a trade surplus has not worked for the United States. The irony is that the United States took the initiative in the move toward a floating currency arrangement, and yet overvaluations and undervaluations have been much larger than when currencies were pegged; similarly, trade imbalances have been much larger.

Reform of the monetary system

Most of the member countries of what was the European Economic Community (EEC) reacted to the changes in currency values in intra-European in the 1970s and the 1980s with the decision to adopt a common currency. Some member countries believed that a single currency would be the appropriate monetary counterpart to a single integrated market in goods and services; others had a political rationale for a common currency.

The irony is that the institution established in the 1940s to be the guardian of international monetary stability, the IMF, has largely ignored the systemic problems of international monetary arrangements. Cynics might say that it's more fun and heroic for the managers of the Fund to deal with monetary crises in Russia and in Asia than to develop arrangements that would reduce the likelihood and severity of these crises.

The criticisms that have been directed at the Fund because of its policies toward South Korea, Indonesia, Russia, and Argentina might induce the Fund to pay more attention to the types of systemic concerns that were the rationale for its establishment. But it is also possible that the Fund has lost so much credibility because of its failure to foresee the large number of crises and devise policies that would be appropriate to forestall these inevitable responses to increasing imbalances. The Fund staff travels around the world and regularly visits each of its members to evaluate its policies. But it appears that the Fund was surprised by the sharp depreciations associated with the Asian financial crisis. The Fund failed to foresee the debacle in Iceland and that the global housing bubble would implode and trigger a recession.

Reform of international monetary arrangements could be accomplished with changes in a few key features. A system of pegged currency values could be designed to allow for more flexible responses to payments deficits and payments surpluses, while reducing uncertainty about currency values encountered by those involved in international trade and investment. A mechanism could be found to produce the appropriate amount of international money without forcing the United States to incur trade deficits and payments deficits.

The politics of international financial stability

Political factors provide an explanation for why international monetary reform is so difficult. One of the most dramatic solutions to problems raised by more than 100 national monies would be to adopt a common worldwide money. There would be then no exchange rates and hence there could not be crises associated with changes in currency values. There would be no need to coordinate the monetary policies of different central banks, for there would be only one central bank and one world monetary policy. Nor would there be any need to be concerned with the relationship between the rates of growth of national monies and of international monies, since there would not be any distinction between the two. Indeed, the advantages of a worldwide money appear so overwhelming that one wonders why national monies are retained.

Once there was a worldwide money – gold. The move away from the gold standard suggests why the idea of a worldwide money is utopian. One dominant aspect of the twentieth century has been nationalism – three big wars and large military establishments. National governments have given increased priority to domestic economic objectives, and neither the growth in the power of the state nor the greater priority to domestic objectives is an accident. During the second decade of the twentieth century monetary policy was managed to help finance the First World War. Then, during the Great Depression, national governments geared monetary policy to expand domestic employment. Monetary policy was managed during the Second World War to finance wartime expenditure. The attachment to the gold standard faded because governments wanted to manage the national money to achieve domestic objectives, and particularly high levels of employment and price level stability: that's where the votes are.

The library shelves are lined with books that are full of plans for reforming monetary arrangements and reducing their susceptibility to crises. These books are full of articles, paragraphs, sections, and subsections which spell out, in detail, when a country could change the parity for its currency and when it could not, when a country would have the right to borrow the currencies of other countries either from them or from an international institution, and when a country would be obliged to lend its currency to other countries. In reality, all of these articles, paragraphs, sections, and subsections are proxies for issues that are rarely discussed. Each national government wants to know how each proposed arrangements will affect its ability to achieve its national objectives – full employment, a stable price level, rapid growth, and control over its own destiny. The leaders in each government want to know how any plan will affect their ability to keep their constituents sufficiently happy to win the next election or forestall the next coup. When adjustments must be made, national governments want to be sure that most of the burden and costs fall on other countries. If some event occurs that adversely affects their constituents, they want to be able to show that the event, like the weather, was imported and beyond governmental control.

Many countries are concerned that an international monetary agreement might limit their freedom to set domestic policies, thus making it more difficult to satisfy their domestic constituencies. Even though Britain is a member of the EU (although not a charter member of the EEC), the British decided not to adopt the euro with Germany, France, Italy, and eight smaller members on day 1, because they were worried about employment in Birmingham and Coventry once the bureaucrats in Frankfurt set monetary policy. True, the British would have a voice in selecting these bureaucrats but they preferred that the Bank of England retain its independence rather than become a branch office of the European Central Bank (ECB). Every government would readily sign an agreement for international monetary reform if it were allowed to write the treaty, select the managers for the institution, and formulate its policies. Each would design the arrangements so as to minimize any external constraint on its choice of domestic policies. In this case, membership would impose no cost on the government generating the proposal. The inevitable costs of adjustment to changes and to shocks would fall on other countries. Naturally, the proposals of various nations would be inconsistent. What is good for France is not necessarily good for Germany – as the Germans have learned, at some considerable cost over the years to their own taxpayers.

One reason that efforts to establish new rules have not been successful is that the interests of residents of different countries frequently conflict. Some produce and export oil, many import oil; the exporters want high prices for their oil and the importers want to pay low prices. Some are interested in price level stability or at least an inflation rate no higher than 2 percent while others place much higher value on full employment. Some believe major economic decisions should be resolved by the decentralized interplay of market forces; others believe these decisions should be made in accord with a central plan – or by bureaucrats in Brussels or some other center. Whenever payments imbalances occur, there is conflict over whether the deficit countries or the surplus countries should take the initiative in making the adjustments necessary to reduce the imbalances. When currency values change sharply, the debate is over whether the countries with appreciating currencies or those with depreciating currencies should intervene to dampen the movements. Political leaders talk about the virtues of international cooperation, but domestic factors frequently take priority, especially when the next election may be only months away.

Monetary reform has a small constituency – a handful of economists and some central bankers and a few editorial writers. The impetus toward reform is likely to develop only after a major crisis.

The movement toward monetary reform might be advanced if the positions of each of the major countries on the central issues could be predicted: if their proposed arrangements for producing international money and for adjusting to large imbalances in trade and payments were known in advance. Someplace, somewhere, there may be some systematic knowledge about this question. But in the absence of such knowledge, anecdotal evidence about differing national attitudes toward inflation, bureaucracy, economic openness, and the market must suffice.

Inflation is no accident

Consider how the views of Britain and Germany can differ toward reform of the system. Since the early 1950s the British pound price of the US dollar has more than doubled, while the US dollar price of the euro has more than doubled – after recognition of the adoption of the euro as a successor to the German mark and other legacy currencies. The decline in the value of the British pound reflects that the inflation rate in Britain has been higher than in the United States, while the increase in the value of the euro reflects that the inflation rate in Germany has been lower. These differences in inflation rates are not an accident – the financial policies pursued by each country during the 1960s and 1970s and even the 1980s can be traced to its experiences in the 1920s. In the interwar period, Britain's unemployment rate reached nearly 20 percent. After the Second World War, British economic policy sought to maintain full employment, regardless of the impact of its monetary policy on the inflation rate. Germany, on the other hand, has been almost paranoid about increases in its price level, as a result of German experiences with hyperinflation in 1922–23 and 1944–48; during both episodes the German mark and securities denominated in the mark became worthless.

Countries whose prices have increased more rapidly than the average, such as Britain and Denmark, tend to have payments deficits and depreciating currencies; they also have more ambitious approaches toward international monetary rules than do countries that place higher priority on price level stability, such as Germany and Switzerland, which tend to have payments surpluses and appreciating currencies. The deficit countries want foreign loans and credits available on an automatic basis, without strings and lectures about good financial behavior; they want to avoid the need to devalue, and they hope their currencies will not depreciate. If changes in currency parities are necessary, they want the surplus countries to take the initiative. If the deficit countries must take the initiative, then they want to be able to restrict their foreign payments without subjecting themselves to the criticism or surveillance of their trading partners or of international institutions.

Countries with payments surpluses, on the other hand, do not want to commit themselves to extending large credits to the countries with the payments deficits; they fear that if they do, their payments surpluses might become even larger and they will import inflation. Nor do they want to be put in the position of having to revalue to avoid having to inflate.

Substantial payments imbalances or changes in currency values result from differences among countries in the rates at which their money supplies grow and their price levels increase. Differences among countries in rates of monetary growth are likely to reflect institutional differences in their tax systems or in their union–management relations.

Bureaucracy is a French word and a growth industry

Change is as inevitable in economic life as it is in biological life. Individuals go through a sequence of stages as they grow; the rates of increase of weight and body mass are rapid when they are young, then their weight stabilizes as they mature. Throughout the life cycle, they are subject to shocks of disease and accident, which may alter the growth process.

Economies also go through stages, although the distinction among the stages may be less clear. Moreover, the length of particular stages in the various countries may differ. Finally, economies are subject to shocks – both structural such as crop failures and surges in import prices and wars and monetary shocks in the form of sharp changes in the inflation rate and interest rates. Technological change is a shock to individuals and firms within an economy, since it may result in a decline in the demand for their products as the demand for new more cost-effective substitutes increases.

Adjustments are necessary whenever shocks occur. Few individuals welcome shocks unless they lead to an increase in their income, and an increasingly large part of governmental activity has involved dampening shocks, and ameliorating their impacts. Frequently, governments seek to reallocate the costs of a shock among taxpayers; costs and the risks of the shock are 'socialized.' Disaster relief is a tax on the general population to subsidize those who have incurred large losses because of floods, fires, or tornadoes. Unemployment compensation is a tax on the employed to subsidize the unemployed. Social security is a tax on the working population to subsidize the aged.

Countries differ sharply in the way they respond to the same shock. Most countries have a traditional economic style, evident from the different roles played by government in determining price, wage, credit, and investment decisions. In Japan (and in France, to a lesser extent) the bureaucracy plays a major role in setting the target growth rates and the investment levels of particular industries and firms. In other countries these decisions reflect market forces. Americans, for example, favor decentralized decision-making: the government should be responsible for monetary policy and fiscal policy, while households should make the consumption decisions, and business firms the investment decisions. The mix of goods and services to be produced and who is to produce them are the outcomes of millions of private-sector decisions. A few other countries, such as Germany and Switzerland and recently Britain, share the US perspective. Elsewhere governmental authorities are more fully involved in production and investment decisions.

National attitudes toward government intervention closely reflect the prestige enjoyed by the bureaucracy. In Japan and France the brightest graduates of the most elite universities compete for careers in government service; in these countries bureaucratic intervention in investment and production decisions is readily accepted. A strong central government is deemed desirable, and the bureaucrats are regarded as highly competent. In the United States, in contrast, the bureaucracy has low prestige, and pay ceilings on the salaries of bureaucrats have led to a Gresham's Law – the most capable employees leave the bureaucracy for the higher salaries available in the private sector.

The more powerful the bureaucracy, the smaller the scope for market-oriented decisions. Governmental intervention is justified on various grounds, from reducing uncertainty associated with free markets to minimizing excessive competitive waste or reducing business conflict. The bureaucracy affects decisions in several ways, for example, through its influence over the allocation of credit, through taxes, and through the issuance of building, investment, and import permits.

Managing the international economy

The views of most politicians about how the international economy should be managed are an extension of their views about how their domestic economies should be managed. Countries that place a low value on bureaucracy tend to favor an open international economy, with minimal barriers to the free flow of goods and capital internationally. They feel that currency values should be determined by market forces. Individuals and firms should be free to choose between domestic and foreign goods on the basis of price, without arbitrary restrictions at the border.

Countries with strong centralized bureaucratic controls over their domestic economies, on the other hand, tend to favor the use of bureaucratic controls to manage international payments. International monetary reform usually has a lower priority for such countries, since their bureaucrats are in a position to correct payments imbalances by tightening or easing controls on purchases of foreign exchange and on imports. Moves toward a more open economy would tend to weaken bureaucratic control and thus threaten the future of the national bureaucracies.

Initially US Government officials were more favorable to floating exchange rates than their French and Japanese counterparts. Nor is it surprising that US Government officials are more intensely concerned with the adequacy of international money than officials in other countries, for the officials in other countries are more willing to make arbitrary decisions regulating international payments at their borders.

Inevitably, government officials in countries outside the United States are concerned about costs to the national economies of two types of error: one is too small a supply of international reserve assets, the other, too large a supply. If the supply is too small, as it was in the early 1960s, other countries may still be able to earn payments surpluses by forcing the United States to incur payments deficits. If the supply is too large, as in the late 1960s, these countries import inflation, perhaps from the United States. Foreign bureaucrats believe the cost to their countries of adjusting to too small a supply of reserves is much less than the cost of adjusting to too large a supply. The US authorities, not surprisingly, come to the opposite conclusion.

The authorities in many countries might review developments in the global economy since the breakdown of the Bretton Woods system of adjustable parities and conclude that the changes in currency values have been much larger than they had anticipated. They might also have concluded that five or six credit and asset price bubbles in 30 years were exceptional, as were the three or four financial crises. The surprise is that real economic growth has remained reasonably stable despite the large changes in currency values, the asset and credit bubbles, and the extensive financial crises. One interpretation is that the large changes in financial variables are considered a modest nuisance or distraction as long as the economic growth remains stable and employment remains high.

Views about the advantages of a floating exchange rate system in many foreign countries differ from the US view, which has been that market forces determine the value of national currencies. In many foreign countries the significance of a floating exchange rate arrangement is that there are no constraints on their exchange market intervention practices – a country can peg its currency to the US dollar or to the euro or it can intervene extensively to limit or prevent its currency from appreciating.

The new mercantilists

One of the conflicts in the international economy is economic openness: are foreign residents treated on a par with domestic residents, or are they discriminated against in access to markets, jobs, investments, and tax relief? In earlier periods, nationalism was the opposite of openness, and 'mercantilism' was the term for this nationalistic behavior. Mercantilists were interested in acquiring and hoarding gold to enhance their country's power. An open international economy would threaten, almost by definition, the advocates of nationalism. Nationalism means that the economic interest of domestic producers is preferred over those of foreign competitors – that domestic residents have preferred access to markets, products, and jobs. Tariffs, quotas, and restrictions on the ownership of domestic assets by foreigners reflect nationalist pressures.

The thrust of the last half of the twentieth century has been toward greater openness – toward the reduction of barriers to the free movement of goods and capital. Tariffs and non-tariff barriers (NTBs) to the movement of goods have been reduced. Discrimination against the entry of foreign banks and financial institutions into the domestic financial markets in different countries has been reduced. Controls on international capital flows have been reduced – although there are pressures to restore such controls because of a belief that they were a major cause of the Asian financial crisis.

Countries subject to strong nationalist pressures are likely to place substantial barriers in the way of imports of foreign goods and services, as well as on the sale of domestic securities to foreigners. Japan has a strong nationalist bias. The Japanese rush toward modernization in the last third of the nineteenth century reflected the fear that foreign imperialists would begin to dismember Japan into colonies or enclaves: Japan developed its industry to resist a perceived external threat. Japanese attitudes toward trade and investment decisions continue to reflect this strong desire to maintain a cultural identify, so Japan resists foreign investments and is reluctant to liberalize its import policies; domestic residents should not be injured or inconvenienced for the sake of international harmony. Japan responded to the problem of tens of thousands of Vietnamese refugees by permitting fewer than 100 to settle permanently in Japan; in contrast, more than 100,000 settled in the United States. US automobile workers should lose their jobs so that Japanese automobile workers can produce for the US market.

Nationalization and privatization

One worldwide tendency of the last 100 years has been an increase in the government's role in production. Often, when private entrepreneurs find a particular industry increasingly unprofitable, foreign competition further reduces the number of domestic producers. Yet the government, while reluctant to subsidize private entrepreneurs, usually wants to maintain domestic production. So the activity is shifted to the public sector. Many 'private' firms in Italy are owned by one of three large holding companies: the National Institute for Industrial Reconstruction (IRI), the National Hydrocarbon Corporation (ENI), and the National Corporation for Electric Energy (ENEL), each of which has been largely owned by the government. Sometimes national ownership may be justified on grounds of national security. General de Gaulle insisted that France needed a computer industry for national security, and so part of Machines Bull, the largest French computer firm, was absorbed by the government when it would otherwise have been liquidated. Similarly, the Conservative government in Britain nationalized Rolls-Royce because immediate unemployment in areas near the company's factories would have been excessively high had the company folded.

The marked change in the last 15 or so years has been the worldwide move toward privatization. In part this move has occurred as a result of the increased openness of the world economy; government-owned firms as a rule have not been competitive because they have not had to meet a market test. The result is that countries with a large number of government-owned firms in manufacturing are reluctant to reduce barriers to external competition; such moves might jeopardize the survival of these domestic firms or raise the cost of the subsidies to the treasury.

Although other countries may seem more nationalistic than the United States, the difference is partly an illusion. The large economic size of the United States means that any direct foreign threat to the United States is small; foreign economies have a smaller impact on the level of US business activity than they do on the level of business activity in other countries. While Canada and France may worry about US domination of their economies and their national institutions, size alone protects the United States from foreign domination. Foreign ownership of firms or shares of firms located in the United States has been small. The relatively liberal US position toward foreign ownership would almost certainly change if foreigners tried to acquire a sizeable proportion of major US firms such as IBM or Intel. Shifts in US foreign economic policy in the last 10 years to more and higher import barriers – such as quotas on imports of textiles, apparel, steel, beef, and petroleum – suggest that the United States is not immune from nationalist pressures.

Reform requires a consensus

International monetary reform would be a cinch if countries were homogeneous – if each were made in the same image. But most national borders are not arbitrary; rather, they tend to segment economies with differing industrial and institutional structures and electorates with different values. Conflicts in interests are inevitable and complicate monetary reform. Moreover, the increasing priority given to national interests is a worldwide phenomenon; the pull of nationalism intensifies the growth of bureaucracy and domestic demands for monetary flexibility. In time, perhaps, the strength of these national pulls may diminish. In the meantime, efforts at monetary reform which ignore these pressures are not likely to succeed.

13
Monetary Reform – Where Do the Problems Go When Assumed To Have Been Solved?

Competing national interests

The financial crisis that began in 2007 has led to several more or less standard remarks. One is the fear of protectionism – governments tend to favor domestic residents over foreigners when the supply of good-paying jobs is much smaller than the demand. The second is the need for more regulation, especially of financial institutions. (It is not as if the financial institutions were not regulated or abundantly regulated – the question is why the regulators failed to forestall the series of financial crises and the bubbles that preceded these crises.) The third is the need for a 'new Bretton Woods.'

A paradox of the last several decades has been the glaring contrast between the problems of the system – the asset price bubbles and domestic banking crises, the crises in the currency markets, the trade disputes – and all the good advice in the editorials of the *New York Times* and *The Economist* and the *Financial Times* and the *Nihon Keizai*, in congressional testimony, in international conferences of economists and bankers, in the policy papers produced by the think-tanks in Washington and London and Tokyo, and in university lectures. Salvation was readily available. The system's problems would be solved if central banks intervened more extensively – or less extensively – in the currency market, if there were greater coordination of national monetary policies, or if national currencies were eliminated. Or if...

Each of these proposals had the support of eminent authorities. Nearly every expert has left the impression that if only his or her favorite proposal were adopted, the system's problems would soon disappear, or at least become less costly and less pressing. Since few of the proposals – other than that of floating rates – have been adopted, the experts' convictions cannot be readily tested. The wide diversity of the 'solutions' is surprising. Some proposals – to increase the monetary price of gold or demonetize gold, more extensive central bank intervention in the currency market or less extensive intervention – are contradictory; some of the 'authorities' must be wrong if others are right. Some of these proposals are advanced by those who have been the ministers of finance or chairs of their national central banks. Somehow their seminal ideas appear only when they are in the private sector – if these proposals were as attractive as their proponents suggested, why were so few adopted? Why was the adoption of a floating exchange rate arrangement a necessity rather than a move of conviction, at least on the part of most central bankers? The answer to the general question is that the politicians around the world were not convinced about the merits of any one proposal. But if not, why not? Perhaps the national political leaders were unable to understand the proposals. Perhaps vested interests in the various countries prevented their adoption. Or perhaps the proposals were ahead of their time – whatever that means.

The institutional talisman

One feature common to each of these diverse proposals was the belief that changes in the institutional framework of the international monetary arrangements would resolve the problems associated with large trade imbalances or at least reduce these imbalances to sustainable values. Old problems, however, unlike old soldiers, do not always fade away. Changes in the institutional framework may help countries reconcile some conflicts between their domestic objectives and their external objectives and between their national economic objectives and those of other countries. Just as some conflicts are inevitable within countries, some conflicts are inevitable among countries, each with its own sets of voters and constituencies. The poor want to become richer, and the rich want to protect their hard-earned wealth and their market shares. Those who are unemployed want work, and the employed want protection from those who will work for lower wages. Everyone wants to protect his established market share – which makes it difficult for the newly industrialized countries to increase their shares of the global market for commodity-like manufactured goods.

The central question becomes the design of institutional arrangements that will provide the optimal way of resolving conflicts among competing national interests. Changing the institutional arrangements for the currency market or for producing international money may make it easier to resolve some conflicts. But such arrangements, by themselves, do not eliminate the conflicts of interests; rather, they alter the institutional framework within which these conflicts appear.

A country, after all, is a group of individuals with somewhat similar aspirations and values. Some countries – including Belgium, Canada, Malaysia, and Switzerland (Yugoslavia used to be on this list before it fractured) – contain two or three diverse cultural or ethnic groups. Some countries in Africa have 20 or 30 tribes; Nigeria has three dominant ethnic groups – the Yoruba, the Hausa, and the Ebo – and many smaller tribal groups. The differences of opinion across groups within a country can be extensive. In a few cases, the country is smaller than the group; this is especially true of the English-speaking countries that share many of the same values and priorities. In most cases, the country is larger than the group, and the political leaders find it difficult to achieve a consensus.

Within each country, there are sharp conflicts of interests; political parties, elections, revolutions, and coups are about enhancing the well-being of a particular group. Differences in views and interests and values must be accommodated. If the

money means that the flexibility inherent in national monies would be lost – and the costs of excessive flexibility would be avoided or at least reduced.

Politicizing economic conflict: an international money

A frequent observation is that national monies are redundant, since the price of wine in terms of wheat is pretty much the same in each country, after conversion at the prevailing value for the currency. The argument is that since relative prices are similar across countries, no economic function is served by having separate national currencies. In fact, the observation is incorrect – or, more politely, insufficiently exact.

The cost of virtually identical Holiday Inn rooms may vary from $50 to $200, depending on whether the room is in a small town in Alabama or in New York City. The United Nations (UN) calculates that with the costs for a particular standard of living set at an average of 100 for all the capital cities of the world, the specific cost may range from a low of 50 in Manila to more than 200 in Tokyo and Paris. The costs of producing the standard Volkswagen in different countries also differ sharply even though the selling price is the same. The prices of goods and services which are less readily traded – haircuts are the standard example – may differ across countries by substantially more than the prices of tradable goods.

Those who believe that national currencies are redundant also sometimes argue that changes in currency values rates are ineffective, since relative prices do not change. Perhaps. But there is much evidence that changes in currency values are effective because they lead to changes in the relation between the prices of traded and of nontraded goods.

Many changes in currency values result from differences in national rates of inflation. It might be argued that inflation changes only absolute, not relative prices. But if that were the case, no one would be concerned with inflation, except for the minor inconveniences of having to carry more money around – and this inconvenience could be negated by printing more large-denomination notes. In fact, inflation changes relative prices, at least for a while – which is why inflation occurs. In the early stages of inflation farmers become better off and city folk less well off; borrowers do well and lenders poorly. In a deflation, and even when the rate of inflation declines, the tables are turned: the lenders gain and the borrowers lose.

The demand for separate national monies has an analogy in the need for national armies. During most years, most countries are at peace. If a country is at peace, it might seem that it has no need for military forces; indeed, its army might be disbanded. But military forces are needed when peaceful means of settling disputes between nations are not deemed satisfactory by at least one party.

So, too, a separate national currency may be needed to attain national price level and employment targets.

New problems

Proposals for a common international money as a substitute for separate national monies are attractive. Were such proposals accepted, currency crises would disappear. There would no longer be a need to debate whether a country with a payments surplus should lend international money or its own currency to countries with payments deficits, for there would be no measurable payments imbalances and no bickering over which countries should take the initiative in adjusting to payments imbalances. There would no longer be a concern with whether a currency was overvalued or undervalued: the words would no longer be relevant.

But a common international money would not eliminate the problems of the existing system; it would simply shift their location. Problems of accommodating divergent national interests would be centralized in the management of the international money-producing institution. This institution would have a set of directors who would be ultimately responsive to the political authorities of the member countries, much as some of the members of the board of the European Central Bank (ECB) are responsible to their national governments. The institution's directors would have to determine how its managers were to be selected, how rapidly the institution should produce money, and when countries might control payments to foreign areas.

The participating countries would also have to agree on the voting strength of each member country. Would the United States, China, Japan, Venezuela, the Netherlands, and Brazil each have the same number of votes, as in the General Assembly of the United Nations and most other international institutions? If not, what criteria should be used to determine the voting strength of each member country? Would the largest countries have veto power over any decisions of the institution's managers, or would they be obliged to follow their mandate? The UN principle of one country, one vote would mean that the United States, a nation of 300 million, could readily be outvoted by Trinidad, Jamaica, and other Caribbean countries whose combined populations are less than that of Chicago. The costs of adjustment to payments imbalances might be shifted to the United States. At the other extreme, if votes of each country were in proportion to its population (on the principle of one person, one vote), then China and India together would come close to having a voting majority for the world.

Clearly, some accommodation is necessary between these extremes. But what formula would be acceptable to countries with large and small populations, with high and low per capita incomes? Until this issue can be resolved, an agreement on the management of the rate of money supply growth is virtually impossible. Some countries would be more willing than others to compromise, not because the agreement fully satisfied their needs but because they would know that if the costs of abiding by the agreement were too high, they could ignore their commitments; they could adopt exchange controls or refuse to lend their currencies to other countries. Some countries are substantially more cynical than others when signing international treaties.

Almost as soon as a new international monetary authority was established, a decision would have to be made about how fast the supply of the international money should grow. Each country would have its own views: some might favor a growth rate of 5 percent a year, others a rate of 10 percent. This disagreement would reflect differences in national economic structures and priorities. Some countries grow more rapidly than others, perhaps because they have higher savings and investment rates, or because their labor forces expand more rapidly, or because they adapt better to new technologies. Labor unions are much more militant in some countries than in others; these countries may favor a more rapid growth in money supplies to permit sustained full employment. Moreover, some countries are more tolerant about inflation and would be willing to risk more rapid price increases in the belief that they might thus reduce their unemployment rates.

Thus, countries which formerly permitted their national money supplies to grow at a 15 percent annual rate probably would want the supply of common international currency to grow at a similar rate. Countries that had previously favored a slower growth for their own national money would probably also want the international money to grow at a slower rate. Japan, for example, would want a rapid rate of monetary growth, while Germany would want a slower rate. But Japan and Germany cannot each have its way if there is only one money.

Perhaps the directors from different countries could be shown that the differences among them regarding the appropriate rate of money supply growth are unimportant. If so, the rate of money supply growth could be determined by a more or less random process. Then each country could quickly adjust to the new rate, and the costs and inconvenience of forgoing the preferred rate for the community rate would be small. Perhaps. But it is unlikely.

The debates among directors from different countries about the preferred rates of money supply growth would be vigorous, just as they frequently are within individual countries. Countries with similar interests would form caucuses and vote as a club. The small countries would be concerned that their interests might be steamrollered by the large countries. Large industrial countries, on the other hand, would worry about being outvoted by coalitions of the many small countries.

Some countries might devise numerous ad hoc means to limit their international payments – even in defiance of the rules. A few might threaten to secede from the common currency union rather than accept a monetary policy deemed inappropriate to their needs. As long as there is substantial diversity among nations, a common international money and a unified monetary policy are contradictory. Those who advocate such a union either blithely ignore the real problem or else harbor secret knowledge about how diversity among nations can be readily reconciled – knowledge that is not generally available.

As long as basic structural differences in national economies remain, and countries retain sovereignty, there is little chance that a common international currency might be adopted – and even less that it would work if it were. Control over the production of national money is a large part of what sovereignty is all about. It is not an accident that member countries of the European Community (EC) were able to eliminate tariffs on internal trade, accept a common tariff on imports from outside the group, harmonize their tax policies, and yet still found it difficult to unify their currencies. Moreover, several members of the EU, including Britain and Norway, decided to retain their currencies rather than adopt the euro. That countries would give up the flexibility of a national money – and the associated domestic political advantages – to avoid the costs and the newspaper headlines of exchange crises seems unlikely. Perhaps more importantly, such a move would be questionable on the grounds that as long as national economic structures and values differ, countries as a group may gain if this diversity of interests is recognized and accommodated rather than suppressed.

In time, differences in the national interests of participating countries may diminish and be eliminated. Eventually, business cycles will be in phase across countries, and rates of productivity growth – even attitudes toward inflation and the inflation – unemployment trade-off – might be more nearly similar. The usefulness of the nation-state as a political unit will then be much lower. However, the date at which interests will become so similar that the nation-state can be shelved as an effective decision-making unit does not seem imminent.

National monies have been around for about as long as there have been nations. One implication – the most likely, if not the only one – is that national monies will disappear only as distinctions among nations lose their economic significance. This process is likely to occur on the basis of regional groupings, as countries with similar characteristics merge their currencies. The EU is one such group; other potential groups are in Southeast Asia, East Africa, Central America, and South America.

An SDR system

A move to a common worldwide currency is an extreme proposal and a strawman, and relatively few experts favor the idea. Yet the political problems associated with less ambitious reform proposals are similar to those encountered in this more extreme solution. The smaller the scope that individual countries have in setting their own monetary policies and the values for their currencies, the larger the energies they will inevitably direct to how the international monetary arrangements are managed. The politicians in each country are understandably reluctant to permit international civil servants to adopt measures whose costs they must bear: the civil servants do not compete for office.

A less ambitious approach involves adoption of one international money and the retention of national monies. The US prospect of the shortage of gold in the 1960s and the reluctance to increase the price of gold led to proposals for a new international monetary system to be built around Special Drawing Rights (SDRs) as the dominant international money; the roles of the US dollar and of gold as international reserve assets would be phased out. National monies would be retained, and each national currency would have a parity in terms of the SDR. Each country could devalue its currency in terms of the SDR if it had a large payments deficit or it could revalue its currency – perhaps even be obliged to do so – if it had a large payments surplus.

The SDR-producing institution would become an international central bank. Member countries would jointly decide how many SDRs to produce each year and how many newly produced SDRs to allocate to each country. Each country's view about these decisions would almost reflect its view of how best to advance its national interests. The rate at which the supply of SDRs would grow would not satisfy all of the participating countries, any more than all would be satisfied if there were a common international currency which increased at the rate of 3, 5, or 8 percent a year.

Proposing an SDR system, either by that name or by some other, is easier than getting it accepted, for countries are naturally concerned with the future value of the SDR. Gold was acceptable as an international money because of its underlying commodity value. Central banks owned gold in the belief that if it were demonetized their losses would be minimal, since they could sell gold in the commodity market. Similarly, US dollar assets and British pound assets were acceptable as international money because it seemed – once – that these monies could be used to buy gold from the US Treasury and the Bank of England, or at least to buy American or British goods.

Every central bank recognizes that holdings of SDRs are useful only if they can be converted into a national currency. Central banks in a few countries must worry that some other central banks might prove reluctant to sell their currencies for SDRs. US participation is essential to the success of the SDR system, for holders of SDRs would want assurance that they could convert SDRs into dollars to make payments for the purchase of US goods and US dollar securities. The United States has the world's largest market in goods and the most comprehensive set of financial markets. Participation in the SDR arrangement by Argentina and Zambia is insufficient for its success if the United States does not participate. Without US involvement, the SDR arrangement would flounder, whereas it makes little difference if Argentina and Zambia do not participate. The reason is that the supplies of goods available in those two countries are not so large that the various central banks would want to hold the Argentinean peso or the Zambian kwacha as international money.

As it is, many countries would probably prefer US dollars to SDRs as international money, for the dollar has greater 'moneyness.' Foreign central banks would hold SDRs because they could be used to buy dollars. Some countries would fear that the United States might at some future date stop selling dollars in exchange for SDRs; in that case, holdings of SDRs would become much less valuable than the dollar. Few countries would accept SDRs if they were not acceptable at the US Treasury. To minimize this concern, the United States could pledge to remain attached to the SDR standard. But this pledge could be broken. The United States could give a super-pledge; but the super-pledge could be broken, as was the US commitment, and a succession of super-commitments, to maintain the $35 gold parity. Many countries would remain reluctant to hold a substantial part of their reserve assets as SDRs, as long as they doubted the commitment of the US authorities – currently and in the indefinite future – to buy SDRs in exchange for dollars.

A paper money or paper gold proposal can succeed only if countries have confidence in the money – that is, in its future purchasing power in terms of goods. This confidence requirement is not likely to be satisfied simply because the members agree to a treaty. For any member might, when it suits its pressing national needs, walk away. And every other member recognizes this reality.

The nonpolitical market solution

A system of pegged exchange rates is much like a fair-weather friend – as long as the major countries are able to achieve reasonable price stability, the system is workable. If currencies are free to float, movements in the currency values would be modest. However, if there are substantial differences among major countries in their price-level targets, or even in the strengths of their commitments to realize these targets, floating rates are inevitable, if only because currency movements are inevitable. Investors shift funds to profit from anticipated appreciations and to avoid losses from anticipated depreciations.

Currency values as a policy instrument

The proposals for a floating currency values advanced in the 1950s and the 1960s recognized the divergent pulls of independent national monetary policies. The central bank in each country could produce the amount of money deemed appropriate for its domestic needs. In Japan the money supply could grow at 20 percent a year, in Belgium at 10 percent. Each country would choose the rate of money supply growth that it believed would enable it to achieve its principal economic objectives – high levels of employment and reasonable price stability. If errors occur (which is likely), no country would have to worry about its payments balance since market forces would ensure that the country's international payments would correspond with its international receipts even if it did not succeed in achieving price level stability. Currency values would change continuously and smoothly, without the volatile movements associated with parity changes.

Developments in the last several decades tested these claims of the proponents of floating currencies. Contrary to predictions, changes in currency values often have been volatile. Countries have worried greatly about their trade positions and about whether their currencies were appreciating or depreciating and whether these changes have been too rapid. The central banks in many countries have intervened extensively in the exchange markets. Paradoxically, the payments imbalances have been substantially larger when currencies have not been pegged than when they were pegged. Some of these imbalances were attributable to the surpluses of the Organization of Petroleum Exporting Countries (OPEC) countries (see Chapter 18) and other oil-producing countries. But the sum of the surpluses of all countries as a group was in some years more than twice as large as those of oil-exporting countries as a group. Some countries have sought to achieve a payments surplus as a basis for growth in their own money supplies; not every country has wanted to follow an independent monetary policy. Other countries have found that the depreciation of their currency is the most convenient way to stimulate exports and increase employment; their central banks have bought dollars in the foreign exchange market to limit appreciation of their currencies so as to keep their goods competitive in world markets. Indeed, for some countries, export-led growth may be the preferred way to stimulate the economy. Some countries have a mercantilist preference for exporting goods and importing international money.

The assumption made by proponents of floating currencies – that once the rate was free to move in response to market forces, central banks would no longer be interested in the level of the exchange rate – has been proved invalid since 1973. Once the value of the currency is no longer subject to international rules, many governments are likely to manage or manipulate these values as a useful instrument of policy and as a supplement to their monetary and fiscal policies.

To the extent that central banks intervene in the exchange market, most buy and sell the US dollar. For example, the Bank of Japan is happier when the yen depreciates than when it appreciates. But Germany and France would not welcome this move, since their competitive position in the US market, the Japanese market, and their own domestic markets would be threatened. They might respond by permitting the Euro to depreciate in terms of the dollar; the Japanese threat to German and French exports would be neutralized. One result would be that the US market would be flooded with Japanese, German, and French goods. US exporters, in turn, would find themselves at an increasing competitive disadvantage in foreign markets. And so the US authorities would be under domestic pressure to depreciate the dollar.

The original objective behind the IMF rules of currency parities was to prevent individual members from adopting such 'beggar-thy-neighbor' policies. During the 1960s, when most countries were relatively successful in achieving full employment, this problem appeared unimportant. But it became significant in the worldwide recession of 1970 and 1971, when countries sought to import jobs. There is considerable evidence for the proposition that whenever countries find it difficult to attain domestic targets by changes in domestic financial policies, they will manipulate their international transactions.

In 1974, many countries allowed their currencies to become undervalued; they did not take the initiative to borrow the amounts necessary to finance the increase in their net oil imports. Instead, they paid for their oil imports on a pay-as-you-go basis, which meant their currencies depreciated – in effect, they increased their exports to earn the dollars to pay for their more expensive oil imports. The lesson of the last decade is that few currencies float freely; most central banks intervene extensively. Central bankers are not about to rely exclusively on market forces to determine the foreign exchange value of their currencies; most want to hedge such forces. The temperament of central bankers – and of their constituents – makes them reluctant to accept the market's verdict about what the appropriate exchange rate is, and how rapidly it should change.

In both 1977 and 1978, the US payments deficits were so large ($30–$40 billion) that any prediction of their magnitude 4 to 5 years earlier would have been considered lunacy. The explanation was straightforward. The United States was recovering more rapidly from the world recession than its trading partners, and so the US demand for imports – and the foreign supply of exports – was increasing sharply. The dollar tended to depreciate. Yet most other industrial countries were reluctant to accept the appreciation of their currencies because of the adverse impacts on prices and employment in their export- and import-competing industries.

In 1981 and 1982, by contrast, the US dollar appreciated sharply, to the levels of the early 1970s. Whereas in the late 1970s the European complaint to Washington was that the dollar was too weak, in the early 1980s the complaint was that the dollar was too strong. From the US point of view, it began to seem that no US policies could satisfy the Europeans – although the continual complaints may have instead reflected European apprehensiveness about their economic dependence on the United States. The experience demonstrates that the floating currency arrangement failed to live up to its advertisements.

Most of the minority of economists who favor pegged rates would agree that a floating rate arrangement is workable and feasible, except perhaps in the relatively few periods when individual countries are subject to intense uncertainty about their political and economic futures. But the choice of exchange rate system is made by central bankers and government officials, not by economists. And judging by their behavior, most officials favor parities, with only a few exceptions; the experience with floating rates has been chastening. It is not an accident that the officials who favor floating rate arrangement rates are in the larger countries, while those in the smaller countries favor pegged rates.

Rules might be negotiated to prevent or limit central bank intervention under a floating rate arrangement. The problem, however, is complex – and complex international rules tend not to be workable. Like the US commitment to a $35 gold parity, adherence to such rules would cease when the national interest was deemed overriding.

Before a great deal of progress can be made in devising a new set of rules, the disturbances, including changes in monetary policy, which have led to the sharp movements in exchange rates, must be attenuated. Inflation rates will have to be reduced further, at least to the range of the 2–3 percent a year of the 1960s.

The limited scope for reform

Several themes stand out among the events following the suspension of gold transactions among central banks in the last decades.

First, central banks around the world want to stay in business; few central bankers are interested in phasing out their institutions in favor of an international central bank.

Second, most central bankers, with the exception of those in Canada and Germany, abhor the uncertainties and the vagaries of floating exchange rates, except as an interim measure; they believe floating rates have worked far less smoothly than their academic proponents predicted.

Third, recent events have reduced confidence in national government commitments which are necessary in any type of international system – an international central bank, an SDR arrangement, even floating rates.

Fourth, within many countries bureaucratic regulation of international payments is now accepted as a means of balancing international payments and receipts. Bureaucrats tend to distrust the uncertainties of the market – indeed, trusting the markets would lead the bureaucrats to the unemployment office.

These factors limit the scope of reform. The differences between ambitious and modest proposals for reform center on two variables. One is the size of payments imbalances that could occur before exchange rates changed or were changed, or before controls on international payments were altered to restore equilibrium, or at least reduce imbalances. The size of imbalances is limited by the ability of deficit countries to finance them and by the willingness of surplus countries to export goods in exchange for international money. The second variable is how the inevitable changes in exchange rates would occur: would they involve explicit changes in the rate, or would the changes be implicit, as bureaucrats tighten and loosen controls on international payments?

The unfavorable outcome, from the point of view of an integrated or open international economy, is a system with small scope for payments imbalances, with international payments balanced by variations in controls on international payments rather than by changes in the exchange rate, and with countries competing with each other to secure export and payments surpluses. One cost of this outcome would be that possible gains in economic efficiency from further integration of markets would diminish because of investors' uncertainties about how the system would evolve. A less measurable concern is that the 'beggar-thy-neighbor' trade policies would produce political discord: economic problems are too central to be segmented from political relationships.

Economic expertise cannot solve political problems

Each of the systems discussed – an exclusive international money, floating exchange rates, pegged rates, and exchange controls – involves the tug of the international market against the pull of national constituencies. Most politicians win or lose elections on domestic issues or on broad foreign policy issues, not on whether currencies float or the price of gold is raised. The first two sets of proposals involve a change in the way countries establish their policies and exchange rates; the third, in contrast, revamps the arrangements to accommodate the pressing needs of individual countries. The fourth approach is less ambitious, although it might be more successful because it acknowledges the diverse interests and preferences of individual countries.

The international money problem reflects that while communications technologies have unified the world of national monies, national economic structures and national values remain diverse. Changes in institutions may provide a more or a less favorable framework for reconciling these national differences, but they cannot eliminate the conflict posed by divergent national interests. The problem appears again and again in determining the rate of growth of international money, in setting appropriate exchange rates, and in determining the allocation and use of international money. The diversity of interests among countries is real. As long as some national monetary authorities have monopoly power, domestic political forces will compel them to exploit it. Crises result when the established 'rules of the game' limit domestic choices.

The historical record suggests that there will be a move back toward pegged exchange rates once inflation rates in the industrial countries decline and converge. This conclusion is reinforced by the extensive intervention of various central banks when currencies have been free to float.

The move toward pegged rates is likely to more nearly resemble pegging under the gold standard than under the Bretton Woods system. Individual countries will peg their currencies when movements in the exchange rates are small; pegging may be the climax of increasing intervention to limit large swings in the rates. Some countries are likely to peg sooner than others. Moreover, countries are likely to differ in the width of the support limits around their parities or central rates. After currencies are pegged, an international agreement might be negotiated formalizing the exchange market arrangements as they exist, rather than forcing sharp changes from the practices then prevailing.

Similarly, arrangements about the future international monetary role of gold will be negotiated after central banks begin to trade gold with each other at or near the market price. Rules will then be developed to formalize the practices. These practices will result from the give-and-take of trading monies and gold.

Part II
The Cost of 100 National Monies

14
Globalization 1.0 – The Silk Road to Asia and the Salt Caravans across the Sahara

Marco Polo traveled on the 'Silk Road' from Venice to China in the thirteenth century to obtain goods that could be sold in Europe. Venice was then the dominant economic power in Europe; goods from China moved on caravans to the eastern coast of the Black Sea and then were transferred to seagoing vessels for shipment to markets in Western and Northern Europe. Traders had moved along the Silk Road for nearly 3000 years before Marco Polo; his trip was a great personal adventure but not a significant discovery. Goods moved along the road from one trading center to another in a series of stages. Entrepreneurs managed the trade at these way-stations so that much of what would now be considered international trade involved a series of barter transactions at various market towns along the Silk Road.

Five thousand years ago the Egyptians acquired cedar logs in what is now Lebanon to use in the construction of temples in the Nile Delta. Some of the granite used in the construction of these monuments came from the Aswan region, 800 miles south of Cairo, and was moved on barges down the Nile. Caravans crossed the Sahara Desert carrying salt from Timbuktu on the Niger River to ports on the Northern coast of Africa. The Phoenicians traded throughout the Mediterranean. The Celtic salt trade in Central Europe developed 4000 years ago and was centered on what is now Salzburg in Austria.

Trade across long distances in prehistory – along the Silk Road, along the caravan routes in the Sahara, in Central Europe, and throughout the Mediterranean – is globalization 1.0, which is all about specialization – trade enables families and individuals to consume a broader range of goods and services than they produce themselves. Specialization occurred even in small Robinson Crusoe-like self-sufficient economies; the men were the hunters while the women gathered fruits and vegetables and nuts. The development of cities in the Tigris–Euphrates valley occurred because the farmers in the countryside produced a surplus of food that they traded for the clothes and tools produced by urban artisans. Cities could not have developed until farmers produced a surplus.

Trade was a response to the uneven geographic distribution of natural resources and of human skills. Some regions were endowed with fast-moving rivers, which led to water power, some with navigable bodies of water, others with abundant trees or with land that could be managed to yield rich crops – perhaps wine or wheat. Nature gifted the Spice Islands in what is now Indonesia with many plants whose petals and bark and roots and leaves could be shredded and used to enhance the flavor of food; the European demand for these food additives was large.

Entrepreneurs often moved the production of particular commodities and foodstuffs closer to the markets. The likelihood is high that some individuals transplanted bushes and trees from the East Indies to Europe in the effort to reduce transport costs, much as the potato and maize (corn) plants had been transplanted from North America to Europe.

Both wine and wheat can be produced in many different regions at the same time. Soils and climates in some regions are better suited to the production of wine; similarly, soils and climates in other regions are better suited to the production of wheat. Individuals in the regions better suited to the production of wine eventually recognized that it was less costly to obtain wheat through trade than through production – they would barter wine for wheat. Individuals in the regions better suited to the production of wheat concluded that the cost of obtaining wine through trade was lower than the cost of using the same land and resources to produce wine.

Trade in wine and wheat between different regions at some distance from each other incurred costs of transport, broadly the 'costs of economic distance' which included costs of obtaining information about the goods available in distant lands, the costs of transporting these goods, the costs of paying for these goods, and the costs associated with relying on distant sources of supply, which were less certain than nearby sources. One risk – and a possible cost – was that the goods would be appropriated by unfriendly agents while in transit. Individuals in both the wine-producing areas and in the wheat-producing areas continually compared the cost-saving from importing with the 'costs of economic distance'; they would import when the cost-savings were greater than the costs of economic distance.

Much trade is repetitive, although there are also many one-off transactions. Those involved in repetitive transactions developed conventions to reduce the uncertainty associated with their purchases and sales. One convention was a system of weights and measures. Another convention involved the provision of credit and the terms attached to the extension of credit, including the procedures available to the lenders if the borrowers failed to adhere to the credit agreements. Farmers borrowed during the planting season to obtain the seed, and merchants borrowed during the harvests to finance their purchases of new crops. Institutional arrangements were developed between farmers and merchants to reduce the costs of resolving disagreements. Because the movement of goods toward the markets incurred the risk that some parties would steal the property, arrangements were developed to provide 'law and order' – to protect property. The Romans developed a comprehensive road system so they could move their armies from one border to another to limit the incursions of plundering barbarians.

Columbus was a fifteenth-century Genose who sailed west in search of a route to India that would be less costly than the journey around the Cape of Good Hope at the southern tip of Africa. Henry Hudson sailed up the tidal estuary that bears his name – immediately west of Manhattan Island in New York City – in search of a water route to what is now known as the Far East. The seagoing explorers of the fifteenth and sixteenth centuries sought new routes that would lead to a reduction in transport costs across large distances; their voyages were facilitated by the development of an arrangement for the placement of masts that enabled vessels to carry larger sails and travel at higher speeds, and its counterpart was the keel that enhanced the stability of the vessels. The development of the sextant enabled ship captains to have a much better awareness of their positions. Globalization 2.0.

The history of globalization is the story of technological developments that reduced the costs of economic distance – the costs of moving wheat and wine and other commodities from the low-cost supply sources to the markets – and to move goods from these markets to the regions where the commodities were produced. These technological developments occurred in spurts. The costs of moving goods and individuals over water always has been lower than the costs of moving them over land; almost all the great cities were at the mouths of rivers – or upstream as far as the rivers were navigable. One remarkable innovation in the last several decades of the eighteenth century was the canal – essentially a man-made river – although in the fourth millennum BC the Babylonians had developed canals in what is now Iraq. The Dutch developed a canal system in the seventeenth century, partly as a by-product of land drainage arrangements. The significant innovation in the eighteenth century was the construction of a series of locks on canals that enabled boats 'to climb hills.'

Canals are extremely capital intensive; a very large investment must be made before any revenues are received. The opening of the Erie Canal ('The Wedding of the Waters') in the 1830s between Buffalo in the western part of New York State and Albany in the eastern part provided a water route between the Great Lakes and the Midwest and the Atlantic Ocean; the prices of wheat and other foods in these cities along the eastern seaboard declined dramatically. (The price of farmland in the eastern states declined, and fields which had been painstakingly cleared of rocks and trees three and four decades earlier reverted to forests.) The success of the Erie Canal led to similar investments to connect other cities on the major river estuaries along the eastern seaboard to their hinterlands. Philadelphia was near the terminus of the Delaware Canal and Washington DC was the terminus of the Chesapeake and Ohio. Call the canal period Globalization 3.0.

The development of steam power led to the rapid expansion of the railroad and railroad systems in the middle and the late decades of the nineteenth century. The earliest railroads relied on horses for power, which could pull much larger loads over iron rails than over the highways because the grades were smaller and the surface was smoother. A steam engine was much powerful than a team of horses, which meant that larger loads could be pulled at faster speeds over longer distances. The transcontinental railroad sharply reduced the duration of transport between New York and San Francisco from a 6-week ocean trip around Cape Horn to a 10-day trip, and a costs about one-tenth that of the ocean trip. The railroad systems initially were national and then were integrated at borders between countries. The railroads offered lower costs, faster speeds, and greater flexibility than the canals – and they did not freeze in cold winters. Globalization 4.0.

The Suez Canal greatly reduced the costs of moving goods and individuals between Europe and Asia and the Indian Ocean, and similarly the Panama Canal reduced the economic distance between the US East Coast and both the US West Coast and the Far East. These canals required large investments; the Suez Canal was privately financed while the US Government paid for the construction of the Panama Canal. The development of canals complemented the much more capital-intensive and larger ocean going vessels that combined steam power, the screw, and steel hulls. Together these faster vessels and the canals shortened travel times between Europe and the Mediterranean and the Indian Ocean and the Far East and between the US East and West Coasts. Globalization 5.0.

The telegraph and its underwater counterpart, the cable, brought sharp declines in the costs of communication across large distances; previously the speed of communication over land was linked to horse-relay systems like the pony-express and the speed over water by the movement of wind-driven sailing vessels. The telegraph and the cable meant that communications over long distance became instantaneous; the collapse in time was dramatic. The subsequent development of the telephone, the radio, and e-mail enriched the variety of messages that could be exchanged but the speed had been established. Now the costs of communication over long distances are only marginally higher than costs for local calls. Globalization 6.0.

The internal combustion engine led to a dramatic increase in the power-to-weight ratios of engines and facilitated the development of automobiles and trucks. Previously, horseless carriages had been powered by electricity and by steam. The autobahn and the interstate highway system and the motorways significantly reduced costs of moving goods and individuals over land, and larger vehicles were developed for the movement of goods because they were more economic. Globalization 7.0.

The development of the commercial aircraft that could span the continent led to reductions in transport costs. Aircraft have replaced ships as the primary source of transport for individuals among continents and have also displaced ships for the transport of high-value items. Globalization 8.0.

Some discoveries contributed to the integration of markets that were distant from the sources of supply even though they did not directly involve transport. The provision of citrus juices to sailors forestalled scurvy and enhanced their health and reduced their mortality rate and hence contributed to declines in the costs of transport across long distances. Similarly, new drugs that treated malaria contributed greatly to the success of efforts to build the Panama Canal. The modular 'container' – a standardized enclosed box that could be carried on trains, trucks, and oceangoing vessels – reduced transport costs sharply by lowering the costs of transshipment at the breakpoints in the transportation networks.

As markets in different areas became more fully integrated, initiatives were taken to modify institutional arrangements to reduce the costs of transactions.

The development of the railroad led to the need to standardize time in different locations so that individuals could coordinate their personal schedules with those of the trains. Initiatives have developed to reduce the costs of economic distance by standardizing weights and measures across countries; the Anglo-Saxon world is slowly going metric. National accounting systems are being standardized.

National financial systems are more fully integrated, in part because a few international banks have branches in many different countries. International payments of money are effected electronically, much as they are domestically. Tourists and business travelers can use their ATM cards in many foreign countries to draw funds from their deposit accounts and their credit lines.

Initially most international transactions involved purchases of goods and of the shipping and other services directly associated with the movement of goods. As costs of distance have declined, additional services are imported. Computer programmers in the Philippines and in India are hired by US and European firms because of their lower wage rates. Reservationists for some US airlines and hotels are in Ireland, Jamaica, and the Philippines.

Nonmarket responses to the declining cost of economic distance

Each time one of these technological developments reduced the costs of economic distance, firms and individuals found it more cost-efficient to substitute a distant source of supply for nearby sources of supply. The owners of the productive factors in the nearby source of supply could respond by lowering their selling prices and their costs – and often their wages – or of becoming unemployed or of shifting to some other productive activity. Often they use political muscle to protect their privileged positions.

Government policies toward globalization have been ambivalent. One set of policies has been adopted to enhance the gains from trade by reducing deterrents that resulted from differences in national policies and practices that were inconsequential when the costs of economic distance were much higher. The US Constitution prohibited the various states from adopting barriers to domestic trade. The Zollverein was a customs union of the German states adopted to eliminate tariffs on internal trade.

Other policies were adopted to facilitate exports and enhance the incomes of the groups that produce export goods – and to provide employment for excess agricultural labor. Tariffs were increased to enhance the incomes of domestic producers of the types of goods that might be imported; the rationale for the 'infant industry' argument is that young domestic firms must be shielded from foreign goods until they develop the experience and skills to compete effectively. The Japanese Government used tariffs and other protective devices to limit imports until the domestic firms had improved the quality of their products and reduced their costs and selling prices so they would be competitive. Government agencies were directed to buy from domestic firms. Cheap credit often was available for domestic firms.

Some governments especially in small countries developed tax policies and credit policies to poach manufacturing employment from other countries.

Governments in 'older countries' – those that were among the first to industrialize – often intervene to protect firms and workers in mature industries from the challenges of younger firms in foreign countries. A classic example is the competitive impact of Toyota, Nissan, Honda, and other Japanese automobile firms on General Motors, Ford, and Chrysler; comparable examples are available in many different industries. The US Government leaned on the Japanese Government to induce Japanese firms to limit their exports to the United States by 'voluntary export quotas.'

Trade in money and securities

Trade requires that buyers pay sellers. These payments incur various transactions costs. Reductions in the costs of payment across large distances were like reductions in transport costs, and brought markets and sources of supply closer together. Barter, the exchange of goods for goods, was costly. The next development was the exchange of goods for a commodity money – units of gold or silver; payments involved the transfer of 'warehouse receipts' – ownership titles to specific units of a commodity money. The next step in reducing payments costs involved transferring ownership of deposits in a bank from the buyers to the sellers; the message to the bank initially involved checks as a signaling mechanism and more recently has involved electronic communications.

Financial globalization involves the movement of money from savers and investors in one area to firms and governments and other borrowers in distant areas. Initially, the movement of money was closely tied to the movement of goods, often in a form of vendor financing; the sellers of the goods provide credit to the buyers to facilitate the transactions. One of the requirements for these financial transactions was that savers and lenders needed information about the likelihood that they would be repaid.

International trade across long distances is capital intensive in terms of the vehicles to carry these goods, including stagecoaches, trains, ships, buses, and aircraft, and the transport infrastructure of roads and railroads and ports and airports. The development of these facilities required institutional arrangements for the accumulation and allocation of capital. Initially – back to prehistory – capital was accumulated for religious and civic purposes, as with Egyptian pyramids and Greek temples. Capital was allocated to the construction of cities 5000 and 6000 years ago. Capital was accumulated for defense; the Great Wall of China was designed to keep marauders out. At first capital was accumulated through coercion, and involved the labor of slaves and indentured workers.

Much much later capital accumulation became voluntary. Once capital accumulation expanded beyond the family, some form of contractual arrangements were needed that summarized the terms of indebtedness, and the obligations of the borrowers to the lenders, and some mechanism to protect the lenders if the borrowers defaulted. Initially, savings were allocated near the area where they had been accumulated; investors would advance money only if there was a significant prospect that they would be repaid, and they had much more information about nearby borrowers than they had about distant borrowers. Stock markets were local and regional. The first international investments generally involved loans from bankers in one country to political leaders in other countries, including loans by the Fuggers and other Germans and Italians to the Spanish monarchs. Queen Elizabeth I sent her Chancellor of the Exchequer, Thomas Gresham, to Amsterdam in 1588 to borrow money that would be used to build a naval fleet that would defend England from the Spanish Armada – and protect the Dutch from their former imperial rulers.

One of the earliest forms of financial globalization involved the development of sources of supply in distant lands for the domestic markets – a precursor to what is now the multinational firm. In the sixteenth century political borders were imprecise, since the nation-state was not then a reality. The Dutch East Indies Company was established to acquire spices; the company was a gatherer and invested in warehouses, ports, and housing for its employees in the Spice Islands. In contrast, the London-based Hudson Bay Company was more nearly like a hunter and bought the pelts and hides and skins that had been collected by trappers in North America. In both cases the 'flag' followed 'trade' and then these foreign areas were claimed as colonies after the companies had made investments in these then-distant areas.

The British and the Dutch were the leading overseas investors in the eighteenth century; British overseas investment surged in the nineteenth century. Both countries relied on private companies to develop the infrastructure for the movement of goods. The Dutch companies had drained the low-lying lands and built canals – more or less a joint activity; while several centuries later the British built a massive railroad system. The financing of infrastructure contributed significantly to the development of capital market institutions; once the projects were complete, investors sought other investment undertakings that would provide comparably high returns.

Subsequently financial globalization often involved loans or credits to the sovereigns – to the heads of government. Initially, markets in securities were like those in goods – local and then regional and then national. The consolidation of markets was responsive to the decline in the costs of economic distance. The advantages of larger markets are greater liquidity, which meant smaller changes in asset prices in response to a given shock.

Globalization is 'discovered' each time one of the technological developments has led to a significant decline in the cost of economic distance, often in part because of the dislocations to nearby productive factors as more goods and services are imported from distant sources. The most recent innovation has been the surge in manufacturing in countries in the Western Pacific – first in Japan and in Taiwan, then in South Korea, and most recently in China and in Vietnam. Each time one of these developments sharply reduced the costs of economic distance, some observers conclude that a new era of globalization has begun. The words differ, but the music is the same. The world is shrinking, but it is not flat.

Globalization 100.0 – the end of the process – will be realized when differences in wages and prices across countries are no larger than the differences within countries. At that time, national borders will not have a significant impact on the location of production. The world will then be flat.

Financial crises and an overview of Part II

One of the major impacts of financial crises is that traditional patterns of production are disrupted as firms go bankrupt and release resources. Another is that governments become more inward looking; they seek to protect domestic producers even at the expense of domestic consumers. Moreover, government involvement in the economy increases as a supplier of financial assistance; firms that had been privately owned become publicly owned with severe impacts on economic efficiency and on government budgets – fiscal deficits balloon in part because of the investments in the failing financial institutions and in part because of declines in tax receipts. Patterns of cross-border money flows change as investors become more greatly concerned with the safety of their money and less concerned with an additional 30 or 40 basis points that they might earn on a somewhat riskier investment.

One useful model of the world economy is that of the bazaar or marketplace. Individuals and firms continually buy and sell, wheel and deal, seeking to increase their wealth and their power, esteem, and prestige. Governments seek to enhance the welfare of their domestic electorates, although often there is tension between policies designed to protect income and wealth from the negative impacts of increased imports and policies to enhance the income and wealth of those who would benefit from increased exports. Some of the chapters in Part II focus on some of the consequences of the segmentation of the world into more than 150 different currency areas; the distinctions among monetary systems more or less parallel national boundaries, with the primary exception of the supranational money for more than ten members of the European Union. New technological developments provide incentives for more trade, but policies of national governments frequently stymie these opportunities, in some cases deliberately and in others as an indirect consequence of some policy or practice. Market forces continually provide incentives for increases in trade in goods, services, and securities across national borders as the costs of economic distance decline. Some of the consequences are direct and reflect that firms headquartered in countries whose currencies are at the top of the hit parade have significant advantages in international competition because they have lower costs of capital. Similarly firms and individuals resident in low-tax jurisdictions may have an advantage relative to their counterparts in higher-tax countries. Individuals and firms that are based in countries identified with low levels of regulation have a competitive advantage in world markets. Young French entrepreneurs have moved the headquarters of their businesses to Ashford, the British terminus of the Chunnel (a hybrid of 'channel' and 'tunnel') to take advantage of the more favorable – read less oppressive – regulatory environment.

The chapters in Part II are organized in three groups. One group examines the impact of national regulations and the way that these regulations segment national markets; one form of regulation is the difference in national tax systems. Another involves the national regulation of banks. A third involves the cartel organized by the oil-exporting countries and the impacts of higher prices on the eventual exhaustion of petroleum.

The second group considers the impacts of the development of new financial instruments on the integration of national markets for bonds and for stocks. These instruments have facilitated the transfer of risks associated with the ownership of these securities. Insurance has enabled owners of certain securities to share some of the ownership risks with others.

The third set of chapters reviews the experiences of several different countries and groups of countries as they have become integrated into the global economy; the economic successes of Japan and, more recently, of China are compared. Similarly, the problems that Poland and its neighbors in what had been Eastern Europe encountered as they made the transition from command economies to market economies and the break-up of the Soviet Union and the emergence of Russia as a semi-market economy are examined.

Sharp declines in the costs of economic distance reduce the 'protection' afforded by firms in individual countries from distant competitors. Economic distance is a form of protection, like a tariff; when costs decline, the firms that lose protection often claim that the playing field has become 'uneven', even though they may have been the unwitting beneficiaries of an uneven playing field. One traditional claim is that the Japanese Government subsidized the country's exports by offering credit at below-market interest rates. In many cases the claim is that foreign firms benefit from child labor. Or that foreign firms benefit because they do not have the same costs of protecting the environment as US firms and European firms. Many of these arguments have been refocused on China's policy toward growing its exports. General Motors and Ford assert that they have health care insurance costs that their foreign competitors do not incur.

Government regulations and taxes raise the costs of domestic firms. Firms headquartered or producing in a country often claim that they are at a disadvantage in the global marketplace because they pay higher taxes than their foreign competitors. Corporate taxes, like wages and rents, are a cost, and unless the firms avoid or evade the taxes, they pay the costs and almost always raise selling prices to capture the cash from their customers to pay the taxes. Similarly business regulations – minimum wages, health and safety standards – also raise costs. Firms establish subsidiaries in low-tax jurisdictions to avoid or to reduce the costs of taxes; where possible, they shift profits to these jurisdictions by transfer pricing among their subsidiaries in different countries. In the same way, they use transfer pricing to shift profits from the countries in which they are headquartered to countries where the tax rates are lower.

Government regulations are avoided and evaded in many different countries. In some countries the chatter is about the 'underground' economy, in others of the 'black' economy or the 'moonlight' economy. Regardless of the term, the meaning is always the same – some of the taxes and business regulations are ignored, slighted, circumvented, avoided, or evaded. Before the early 1990s move to the market economy in Moscow, Warsaw, and Prague, there had been extensive black economies run by individuals with access to goods in short supply, including Levis and the disco albums of Donna Summer and Michael Jackson.

The axiom is that the more severe the regulation and the easier the regulation can be evaded or avoided, the more likely the regulation will be avoided. The implication is that governments will either reduce the scope of regulation to match the regulations in nearby foreign countries or they will have relatively little economic activity to regulate. Government expenditures must be financed, and if some taxes are avoided or evaded, then other taxes must be higher unless expenditures are reduced.

The almost universal tendency is to consider competitive advantage in an absolute way. China has a large trade surplus and has low wages; therefore China's trade surplus must be attributable to its low wages. If low wages were a sufficient explanation for a trade advantage, then the Haiti and Zaire should have large trade surpluses, since wages in both countries are significantly lower than in China. Wages in the United States are among the highest in the world, and yet US exports are larger than those in most foreign countries.

Just as currency values change so that the exports and the imports of most countries tend to approximate each other, so currency values change to offset other types of advantages. Assume that Britain abolished corporate income tax. British firms would reduce their selling prices. British exports would increase, and the British pound would appreciate. The increase in the value of the pound would offset some of the competitive advantage of the elimination of corporate tax; some British firms would lose more from the increase in the value of the British pound than they would gain from the elimination of corporate tax.

Just as the value of the country's currency would change to offset the change in corporate tax, so it would change in response to changes in other taxes and regulations. The thrust of Chapter 15 is the impact of national tax systems on the competitive positions of firms that produce in different countries.

Forty years ago, banking was an extensively regulated national industry. Banking structures differed extensively among countries. In many countries – although not in the United States or Japan – three, four, or five banks accounted for 80 or 90 percent of bank deposits. There were thousands of US banks; the largest US bank accounted for no more than 5 percent of the country's deposits. Banks benefited from a strong home or national bias; firms and individuals in each country did most of their banking business with domestic banks, largely because they had few if any other choices. The financial services industry has been revolutionized in the last few decades, and there has been a rapid expansion of branches and subsidiaries of banks across national borders. Since then bank consolidation has been extensive in the United States and in Japan and has also been ongoing in other countries, in part because of the relaxation of regulation and in part because banks in Japan and the United States have failed, and their deposits and most of their assets have been merged with those of viable banks. Moreover, the growth in the size of banks has been driven in because some regional banks have not wanted to shrink relative to the mega-banks and so they have merged. Two of the ten largest banks in the United States have foreign passports. Banking remains an extensively regulated national industry. One of the major questions involves the structure of the banking industry in the globalization 100.0 scenario, where regulatory factors would not provide a home bias to domestic firms.

The impact of rapid changes in the technology of money payments on the competitive position of commercial banks headquartered in different countries is discussed in Chapter 16. Banking is one of the most extensively regulated industries in virtually every country, and for several reasons, but primarily to protect the consumer interest – to reduce the likelihood that the banks will fail, with losses to their depositors. Regulation increases costs; the regulation of banks means that they must raise the interest rates they charge on loans or reduce the interest rates they pay on deposits. Inevitably, the banks in the countries with the most extensive regulations are at a disadvantage in the international marketplace; if the transport costs of money are high, then their cost disadvantage may have a negligible impact on their competitive position and market share. As costs of transporting money internationally decline, banks headquartered in different countries can compete over a wider market area, so the cost differentials attributable to regulation will become more important. The buyers of the commercial banks' services will seek out low-cost producers of money, even if they are abroad. The question is whether US, British, or Swiss banks are likely to have a competitive advantage as the costs of dealing with banks in distant locations decline.

The financial crisis that began in 2007 has led to significant investment of government funds in banks in the United States, Britain, Ireland, Switzerland, and the Netherlands. For a while, a claim on a bank headquartered in one of these countries will be like ownership of a government security. A safe prediction is that private capital will supplant government capital, but not necessarily at the same time in different countries.

World economic booms are almost always associated with significant increases n the price of natural resources relative to the price of industrial products, primarily because the gestation periods for increasing the supplies of petroleum and copper are much longer than the periods for increasing the supplies of manufactured goods. The industrial revolution that began in the early eighteenth century was fueled by coal and then by petroleum. Despite the surge in demand, the real price of energy has declined. The supplies of these fuels are finite and the prospect is that eventually the price will increase. When the price of petroleum surged from $25 a barrel in 2002 to $150 a barrel in 2008, the fear developed that the world's supply would soon be exhausted. Higher prices encourage the development of energy in hitherto too-costly locales, and lead to the development of alternative sources of energy and greater conservation. OPEC, the cartel of 11 oil-exporting countries, seeks to curtail supply to keep revenues high, and with two results – the increase in energy consumption associated with economic growth is dampened and the production of alternative sources of energy is encouraged. OPEC's dilemma is that the more successful it is in the short run, the more problematic its success in the long run. The focus of Chapter 17 is on the impacts of the OPEC cartel on energy prices in the long run.

Consider the question 'How many stock markets are there in the world?' One approach to the answer is to count the stock exchanges; thus in the United States there are exchanges in Boston, Chicago, Philadelphia, Denver, and San Francisco as well as the New York Stock Exchange and the ubiquitous over-the-counter (OTC) market NASDAQ. Similarly, there are five stock exchanges in Germany and two in Japan. Consolidation of trading in stocks has been going on for many years in each country; the market share of the New York Stock Exchange of global trading has been increasing. An alternative answer is that there is a world stock market, with branches in various countries. The rationale is that large numbers of investors constantly scour the markets for stocks and bonds in each country, hunting for bargains – for securities whose returns are high relative to their risks. The returns on the major securities available in different countries may differ because the securities have embedded country-specific risks. The focus of Chapter 18 is on the global market for securities.

Changes in financial instruments in the 1970s, 1980s, and 1990s were more extensive than in any period since the substitution of checks for currency notes in the payments process (or perhaps even since the move from commodity to paper monies), so these three decades can be identified with a financial revolution. One aspect of this revolution was the rapid expansion in the number of new financial instruments – there were interest rate swaps and foreign currency swaps, call options on futures contracts in foreign exchange and put options on futures contracts in foreign exchange, call options and put options on stock market index funds, and zero coupon bonds. A second aspect of this revolution was that the boundaries between commercial and investment banks and insurance companies and asset managers were shrinking; many financial institutions are evolving into 'department stores' even though some specialized 'boutiques' in each major activity will remain. The causes of this revolution and the impacts are evaluated in Chapter 19.

Most business firms want to grow. Their motivation is that if they cease to grow, or even if they grow slowly, they may age relative to their competitors; the costs of aging firms tend to increase relative to the costs of firms that continue to grow rapidly. In business, as in biology, aging is a prelude to death – but in business aging can be postponed for an extended period if the growth rate can be maintained. The firms that grow rapidly almost always 'outgrow their traditional market,' so the maintenance of their growth rates means that they will either have to develop a new set of products or services for customers in their domestic markets or else grow their sales in foreign markets. Reductions in the costs of economic distance have facilitated the growth of multinational corporations – large, diversified firms with operating subsidiaries in many different countries. Production in these subsidiaries is often integrated across national borders: each plant produces components for its domestic market and for numerous foreign markets. The marketing messages may be similar, although they will be adapted for the local markets and especially for the large national markets. In the late 1960s most multinational firms were headquartered in the United States; many Europeans and Canadians feared the eventual domination of their domestic economies by these US firms. Yet by the late 1970s, firms headquartered in Western Europe and Japan became aggressive buyers of US firms; British firms bought Howard Johnson's and Marshall Field & Co. and a German firm acquired A&P – the Great Atlantic and Pacific Tea Co. The big surprise of the 1980s was the surge in the foreign investments of Japanese firms and especially the acquisition of established US and European firms. Sony bought Columbia Records and then Columbia Pictures and Matsushita bought MGM-Universal; Bridgestone Tire bought Firestone Tire. In the early 1990s Japanese foreign investment declined sharply, and some Japanese firms began to sell some of their foreign investments. The change in the pattern of international ownership is discussed in Chapter 20.

Japan has been one of the glorious economic success stories of the 40 years before 1990. In the 1950s, national income in Japan was between one-twentieth and one-tenth of that in the United States; national income is now nearly one-half that in the United States. In the 1950s there was general skepticism as to whether Japan could become a competitive industrial economy given its handicaps of geographic isolation, the absence of domestic raw materials, discrimination toward Japanese goods in foreign markets, and its own penchant for exclusiveness. By the early 1970s, Japan was realizing trade and payments surpluses that threatened the stability of the Bretton Woods system; one analyst predicted that the Japanese economy would continue to grow at annual rates of 10–12 percent, so that before the year 2000 per capita incomes in Japan would be substantially higher than in the United States and other Western industrial countries such as Sweden and Switzerland. A large number of competing explanations have been offered for the remarkable economic performance of Japan, and these are discussed in Chapter 21. Unfortunately for both Japan and these models and these analysts, Japan has been among the slowest growing of the industrial countries since the early 1990s as the economy adjusted to the implosion of its asset price bubble.

Rapid growth in Japan has been followed with rapid growth in several of its smaller neighbors, once grouped as the 'Four Tigers' – Taiwan (sometimes called China Taipei), Hong Kong (formally a British colony that was handed over to China in mid-1997 and now is a Special Administrative Region (SAR) of China), Singapore, and South Korea. Each of these countries has benefited from close economic association with Japan; firms in these countries often assemble components imported from Japan which are then reexported to either Japan or more often to the United States. Two of these countries are almost completely Chinese, while Singapore is 85 percent Chinese. South Korea shares the Confucian ethic with the overseas Chinese. More recently, the 'Four Dragons' – Thailand, Malaysia, Indonesia, and the Philippines – were touted as the paragons of rapid growth, at least until the advent of the Asian financial crisis in 1997.

For the 30 years of Mao's rule on the Chinese mainland, economic growth was stymied by a series of misadventures – first the backyard steel mills, and eventually the Cultural Revolution (see Chapter 22). Since Mao's death in 1979, national income in China has increased at double-digit rates, a phenomenal achievement.

Part of this growth has been making up arrears. The key question involves the scope for continued rapid growth and the impacts of the slowdown.

The discussion in previous chapters assumed that the world consists of market-oriented economies which have reasonably similar per capita incomes. One exception to this view was that the Soviet Union, Poland, Hungary, and their neighbors in Eastern Europe relied on central planning, at least until the end of the 1980s. The basic economic decisions about what goods should be produced, the amounts of these goods to be produced, and the prices of these goods were determined by bureaucrats. These countries participated in the international economy – they traded extensively both with each other and with the market economies, and since private firms could not import and export for profit as in the market economies, other institutional mechanisms were necessary for arranging trade. The financial relations between the planned economies of Eastern Europe and the market-oriented Western economies, as well as the relations between the Soviet and other Eastern European countries, are discussed in Chapter 23. Business was done and bargains were struck. Imbalances in trade were settled by payments of money, frequently the US dollar. Exchange rates were inevitable, although they were not used, as in the West, as a mechanism for balancing receipts and payments. Nevertheless, the question is whether the exchange rate is a fair price. In trade among Western countries, the fair price is the free market price or the official parity. But since there were no free markets within communist countries, some other mechanism was needed to determine domestic prices, export and import prices, and the exchange rate. And some Eastern European countries believed that the prices used in their trade with the Soviet Union were not in their own best interests.

Russia and its neighbors in what was Eastern Europe are moving toward the market; the encompassing label is now 'transition economies.' Some countries, especially the smaller ones like Slovenia, have made substantial progress. But life has been difficult in Russia and the Ukraine, for they have experienced hyperinflation that has wiped out the value of the money savings and the pensions of millions of people. Integration of their national markets with the world economy has been a dislocating experience. Fortunes have been made, often by the opportunists who were at the top of heap when the rubric was that of the command economy.

Several themes run through the chapters of Part II. The costs of economic distance are declining; market areas are expanding beyond national boundaries. Differences in business frameworks that were insignificant when the costs of distance were high are now becoming more important and are likely to be a cause of friction among nations. There has been a massive move to privatization and a powerful move to reduce of tax burdens – especially tax rates on anything that moves. While pressures for harmonization and coordination will develop, counterpressures for retaining the advantages of high costs of economic distance will also rise.

15
Taxation, Regulation, and the Level Playing Field

Financial crisis leads to government creep

One way to get the trains to run on time is to straighten the tracks. Another is to use more powerful locomotives. A less costly way – indeed, the cheapest way – is to lengthen the time allowed for the journey. In the 1920s, the trip from Chicago to New York on the Twentieth Century Limited took 15 hours; passengers got refunds if the train was late, with the amounts of the refunds scaled to the length of the delays. The same journey on Amtrak now takes 19–20 hours on the Broadway Limited – and there are no refunds if the train is late. The mileage between Chicago and New York is constant. If the trains can't adjust to the timetables, then the timetables adjust to the trains.

Improvements in transport technology should almost certainly have led to a decline in the time required for most trips over the last half century. Seventy years ago, air travel between Chicago and New York took two days with an overnight in Cleveland. Today the same trip takes 90 minutes. Even with the 65-miles-per-hour speed limit, the driving time between New York and Chicago is 12 hours.

Japan has Bullet Trains between Tokyo and Osaka, while France has the Train à Grande Vitesse (TGV) between Paris and Lyon with speeds of 300 kilometers per hour. Britain has some new trains that travel at 125 miles per hour – not quite as fast as the TGV. The Chunnel – the rail tunnel under the English Channel between Britain and France – has reduced the travel time from London to Paris to two and one half hours.

The Darwinian view of economics is that the efficient survive and expand, while the inefficient shrink and die. Nevertheless, from the 1960s to the 1980s the roles of government in most countries – as measured by the government spending as a share of GDP – increased despite the general view that government was becoming less efficient in delivering goods and services and the mail. The US Immigration and Naturalization Service finds it difficult to prevent illegal entry into the United States; it is estimated that there are 12–14 million 'illegals' in the major US cities and on farms – although no one knows – mostly those who have overstayed visitors' visas. The Internal Revenue Service finds it difficult to collect all the taxes owed to the US Government – tax revenues would be 10–20 percent higher if there

219

were 100 percent compliance. There are horror stories of the John Smiths who continue to collect Social Security checks 10 years after they've passed away and the John Does who can't manage to collect their unemployment compensation checks because the system has lost their employment records. The Food Stamp Program was established to reduce government-owned surplus food stocks and at the same time to provide better nourishment for the poor; subsequently, food stamps became a second US currency and a source of fraud. When New York City integrated the data on its welfare recipients with the State of New York's data on workers' compensation, it discovered that several hundred thousand of the recipients were fully employed.

Horror stories are not unique to government; some center on the shortcomings of large organizations in the private sector. Patients occasionally get lost in hospitals; someone goes into the hospital needing a tonsillectomy and leaves without an appendix. The power companies turn off the electricity at the wrong house. Deliveries are made to the wrong apartment. There are oil spills off the California coast, and tankers run aground in the Delaware River and in Alaskan bays. Commercial airline pilots land at the wrong airports.

Yet inefficiency in the government is unique, and for several reasons – the governments in the industrial countries are usually much larger than private firms and employers, and government agencies are responsive to different political interests rather than to the profit motive. Government-owned airlines and steel mills and railroads and telephone systems generally have operated at a financial loss; the money necessary to finance these losses has almost always come from general taxation. Moreover, the money necessary to pay for the new investments of government-owned firms has come from general taxation or government-backed bond issues.

One reason that most government-owned firms have operated at a loss is that the wages of their employees have generally been higher than the wages for similar labor skills in the private sector; moreover, there are more employees and they generally have more job security and usually have more attractive medical benefits and retirement pensions. The government is a monopolist; traditionally government-owned firms haven't worried about competition, at least in their domestic activities. But there are numerous exceptions – increasingly the US Postal Service has been concerned with competition from FedEx (formerly Federal Express) and UPS (formerly the United Parcel Service) as well as from the telephone companies, fax services, and the Internet. Most government-owned airlines have had to compete with airlines owned by other governments on international routes and as well with privately owned airlines. A few governments have sold – or tried to sell – the government airlines because of the financial drag of persistent operating losses.

One reason for the apparent inefficiency in the government sector is size – and the increase in size – which is evident in Table 15.1. Government outlays as a share of GDP are smaller in the United States than in any other large industrial country: the government sector in Japan has expanded more than twice as rapidly as the government sector in the United States – maybe it's those fast trains. The

Table 15.1 General government total outlays, 1960–2007 (percent of nominal GDP)

	1960	1970	1980	1990	2000	2005	2007
United States	25.5	31.6	31.8	33.3	33.5	36.6	36.6
Japan	13.6	19.4	32.0	31.7	36.4	37.4	37.8
Germany	27.7	38.6	47.9	45.1	51.6	46.8	45.0
France	30.9	38.5	46.1	49.8	54.5	53.9	53.0
Great Britain	29.9	39.0	43.0	39.9	43.9	44.9	45.7
Canada	25.4	34.8	38.8	45.8	47.3	39.5	40.0

Source: OECD Economic Outlook.

government sector in Germany is half again as large as that in the United States. The only country that experienced a significant decline in the size of its government sector in the 1980s was Britain – and that development was reversed in the next decade.

The expansion of the role of government usually has been associated with noble purposes – providing more comprehensive health care, better housing, quality education, smoother and safer roads, and law and order and national security. Everyone wants more of these activities, for the value or at least the cost of services provided by the government has almost always been higher than the price paid for them. (Consider the mirror statement – if the prices charged for the services provided by the government were higher than their value, no one would buy any of the services.) In effect, governments specialize in 'loss leaders' – if the production activities were profitable, the odds are high that the activity would be in the private sector. Urban transport is one of these loss-making business activities.

Since government expenditure must be financed, it follows that the larger government expenditures are as a share of GDP, the higher tax revenues must be as a share of GDP. Few individuals want to pay higher taxes. Governments always can borrow to pay for these expenditures but there are limits to the share of total expenditures that can be financed by borrowing. For a few years a government may be able to borrow to get funds to pay the interest on its outstanding debt; however, as government indebtedness increases relative to the country's GDP, the interest rates that the government must pay on its outstanding debt increases. It's a safe rule of thumb that the higher the level of expenditures, the higher the level of taxes.

Very few government taxes are directly related to the value of services provided – the exceptions are the 'user taxes,' the tolls on the highways, to a modest extent gasoline taxes, and the airport departure taxes which may be somewhat related to the costs of the services. In the private sector individuals and firms set prices to cover production costs; if prices remain below costs for long, a trip to the bankruptcy court is inevitable. If, instead, prices are significantly above costs, then new firms will enter the industry, and their efforts to increase market share will lead to a decline in prices.

Taxes and the level playing field

One of the great economic clichés is that the 'playing field is not level' – that firms headquartered or based in a foreign country have an unfair advantage. Government officials in Paris often call on the cliché when French firms appear to be losing market share in global competition. Airbus complains that the euro has become too strong, and its ability to compete with Boeing has been diminished. American firms and Japanese firms and firms headquartered in many other countries use the same playbook to indicate that they are also at a competitive disadvantage in global markets. No one appears to have made newspaper headlines by claiming that they have a competitive advantage in foreign markets because of their government's policies.

One reason that the playing field is not level is that nature was not even-handed in the distribution of resources – of raw materials and arable land, and good harbors and water power. Who knows why nature placed large petroleum reserves in Saudi Arabia and the Persian Gulf when there was greater need for these reserves in the colder climate of northern New England?

The second reason that the playing field is not level is because of government regulation and taxation. The claim is that the governments in Japan (or China or x) provide loans at below-market interest rates to domestic firms or tax holidays or subsidize job training. Boeing complains that Airbus receives outrageous credit subsidies from the German and the French Governments, and Airbus complains that Boeing's development costs are indirectly subsidized by its near monopoly position as a supplier of aircraft to the US military.

Governments use tax policy and credit policy to attract firms; they want the jobs associated with their productive activity. Governments establish tax-free enterprise zones as a way to attract investment to particular regions – the west of Ireland, the south of Italy, and so on. The objective is to attract economic activity – jobs – from other countries. Cities compete with each other for jobs, states compete with each other, and countries compete with each other.

Consider Miss X, once a nubile factor of production that engaged in tax avoidance. She lived in Switzerland and worked elsewhere – Hollywood, London, Rome, and Budapest. Her 'dramatic abilities' resulted in a very very high income, nearly all from sources outside Switzerland. Because she was a Swiss resident, her income was not taxed in the United States or in Britain or in Italy. Swiss taxes on her income were much lower than US taxes would have been if she had lived in Hollywood, or than British taxes would have been if she had lived in London.

Miss X and the Swiss had struck a bargain. The Swiss 'sold' Miss X a tax-avoidance service – the right to live in a low-tax jurisdiction. Miss X 'bought' these services because she liked the higher after-tax income; better to live – at least to have a home for tax purposes – where tax rates were low than where they were high. The Swiss profited from the transaction, for the taxes paid by Miss X to the Swiss canton where she lived greatly exceeded her demand on local public services for the schooling of her children and plowing the snow in front of her mansion. In effect, Miss X was subsidizing the Swiss, and as a result other Swiss – the

Swiss Swiss rather that the Vagabond Swiss like Miss X – paid lower taxes. Had she lived in London, Swiss tax revenues would have been lower, and the Swiss would have had to raise tax rates on the Swiss Swiss to provide the same public services.

Switzerland is also a tax haven for mobile factors of production, for the tax rates in its various cantons are substantially lower than tax rates in most other developed countries. Most taxes in Switzerland are levied by the various cantons like Zug (which is near Zurich, and one of the busiest tax havens in Europe) and St Gallen rather than by the federal government in Bern.

Liechtenstein, Panama, the Bahamas, the Netherlands Antilles, and the Cayman Islands provide similar tax-avoidance services. Tax havens are established to attract income from foreign sources – by promising to tax this income lightly. Tax havens are almost all small geographically. Most – Switzerland is an exception – have modest if any defense expenditure. Expenditure on welfare also is modest. Competition among these political entities keeps their tax rates on foreign-source income very low. If the tax rate in the Cayman Islands on foreign incomes were increased most foreign-source income now taxed by the Caymans would be diverted to one of these other tax havens.

Low-tax jurisdictions

Tax havens are one example of tax avoidance. England's richest lords leave London for low-tax jurisdictions in Bermuda, the Bahamas, and the Channel Islands to avoid high British inheritance taxes. US firms and German firms issue bonds in Luxembourg because interest income there is not subject to withholding tax; buyers of the bonds want to avoid having part of their interest income taxed at source – in effect, withheld.

Most individuals, however, cannot move to low-tax jurisdictions without suffering a serious loss in income; their employment ties them to a particular city or region. Only when the possible tax savings are large relative to the costs of shifting residences do individuals move to a foreign tax jurisdiction. (Within the United States individuals, and especially the retired, move to Florida and to Arizona because of their low income tax rates and their low inheritance tax rates.)

One alternative to moving to a low-tax jurisdiction is to shift income to the haven. Some London-based professors have their royalty and consulting incomes paid to bank accounts in Zurich and in Liechtenstein. When a US firm or a British firm uses an Antillean or a Zugian tax haven, the transfer prices – the prices at which its affiliates in several countries buy and sell goods and services from each other – are frequently set to shift income to the low-tax jurisdiction. For example, a US firm exports goods to its German subsidiary, and arranges the documentation for the transaction so the goods are first sold to one of the firm's subsidiaries in Bermuda. The parent company charges the Bermudan sub an unusually low price, thereby 'income' is shifted from the United States to Bermuda. The Bermudan sub charges a higher price when it in turn sells the goods to the German subsidiary, so 'income' is shifted from Germany to Bermuda. The taxable income of the Bermudan sub of the US firm increases, while the firm's taxable incomes in both the United States and Germany decline. The goods never get to Bermuda – indeed, neither the documents nor the money go there.

Both the US and the German tax collectors know about tax havens. They scan the prices used in transactions between foreign subsidiaries and domestic offices of firms to forestall attempts to shift income to low-tax jurisdictions. They relate the stated prices on intrafirm transactions to the prices of similar goods that are sold in markets, which provide an effective benchmark for a 'fair price.' But many intrafirm transactions have no readily available commercial counterparts and no ready-reference market prices, so firms can be somewhat arbitrary in setting these prices – within reason. Similarly, firms can be somewhat arbitrary in their allocation of common overhead costs among their branches and subsidiaries in various countries; again to the extent they have discretion, they will shift an exceptionally large share of these costs to the jurisdictions with relatively high corporate tax rates.

Firms find it profitable to use tax havens despite the ever-watchful eyes of the tax collectors; sales subsidiaries would not be established in tax havens unless the anticipated savings in taxes more than compensates for the legal fees charged by high-priced lawyers (lawyers, incidentally, who frequently received their most valuable education about the ins and outs of the taxation of foreign income while working for the Internal Revenue Service or the Inland Revenue Service or the local tax collector). If the use – or abuse – of tax havens were so extensive that governments felt a serious loss from runaway income and foregone taxes, transfer pricing would be examined even more closely.

Members of the US Congress have complained that the corporate income tax payments of the US subsidiaries of foreign firms have been much too low; they note that many of these subsidiaries stopped paying taxes once they had been acquired by a foreign firm. It's possible that the subsidiaries ceased being profitable soon after the change from US ownership to foreign ownership (which raises the question of why the foreign firms acquired these US subsidiaries – but that is a different topic). And it's also possible that the new foreign owners were shifting income from the United States to Zug or to some other tax haven.

Economic impacts of different national tax rates

At one time the transfer-pricing issue became particularly intense with respect to the US subsidiaries of Japanese firms which have paid virtually no tax to the US Treasury because they said they had no US income. Most of these subsidiaries had been profitable before they had been acquired by a Japanese firm. Thus the 700 Japanese subsidiaries of US firms paid more tax to the Japanese Government than the 3700 US subsidiaries of Japanese firms paid to the US Government. In part, this difference could be explained by differences in the 'ages' of these firms – the Japanese subsidiaries of US firms generally have been significantly older than the US subsidiaries of Japanese firms; newly established foreign subsidiaries may not earn profits in their first few years of operation. The British subsidiaries of Japanese firms also have reported very low profits. Several officials of the Nissan subsidiary in Britain were jailed because of tax fraud.

Even without tax havens, differences among national tax systems might have a significant impact on the pattern of international transactions. All governments tax, but their tax structures and tax rates differ. Governments tax corporate income and they tax personal income, including interest income, dividend income, and capital gains on securities and on real estate. Governments tax real property, including houses, land, machinery, and even clothing. Governments tax transactions – retail sales, purchases, imports and exports, births and deaths.

Most governments have a virtually unlimited need for revenues; the larger revenues are, the larger expenditures can be, and large expenditures enhance domestic political support. But taxes have a cost, for they diminish political support. Each government seeks to increase its tax revenues at minimal cost in terms of the loss of political support. Ideally, governments would like to tax foreigners to get the funds to commit to expenditure that benefits domestic residents.

Not unexpectedly, tax rates on personal income and corporate income are higher in some countries than in others. Similarly, the tax base – the types of income and the types of transactions that are taxed – also differ. These differences in tax rates are frequently used to explain why some nations grow slowly and others grow rapidly, why the exports of some countries grow more rapidly than those of others, and why investors move money from some countries to others. In nearly every country, businessmen allege that they are at a disadvantage in international trade because they are taxed more heavily than their foreign competitors; they believe that they would be better off if their tax burdens were smaller. (All of us would be better off if our tax burdens were lower, but the second statement in the previous sentence doesn't necessarily follow from the first.)

Taxes, like wages, interest rates, and the cost of electricity, have an economic impact; many firms raise the prices of the goods and services they sell to get the money to pay taxes. (The alternative is to reduce the prices paid to the suppliers of goods that the firm buys and the wages paid to the firms' workers.) The key question is whether differences among countries in tax structures and tax rates have a significant economic impact on the international competitive position of firms producing in each of these countries.

Why national tax rates differ

It is axiomatic that the larger the public sector within a country, the greater the revenue needs of its government. The larger the public sector within a country, the larger the range of incomes and of transactions which are taxed, and the higher the tax rates on these incomes and transactions.

Americans have been fond of saying – especially to the Japanese – that US tax bills are higher because US forces have been 'defending' the free world. US military expenditure has ranged from 3 percent to 7 percent of US GDP; in Japan, the constitution limits such expenditure to 1 percent of its GDP. In most other industrial countries the military budget is in the range of 1–2 percent of GDP.

The government sectors are larger in Germany, Japan, and other industrial countries than in the United States, even though these countries spend a smaller share of their GDPs on defense. In general, they spend a larger share of their GDPs on social welfare, including health care and housing.

Everyone agrees that taxes should be fair. Fairness, after all, is like motherhood. The disagreement arises over what is 'fair' – over the amount of taxes to be paid by those with low incomes relative to the amount of taxes to be paid by those with higher incomes. Governments supply goods and services below their cost of production. Many of these goods and services are given away; some are sold, but at prices substantially below cost. But while particular goods and services can be sold below cost, the total supply of goods and services cannot be sold below production costs, unless a country can borrow abroad indefinitely. To the extent that some goods and services are available below cost, the prices of other goods and services must exceed their costs of production, and the subsidy to the buyers of goods produced by the first group must be financed by taxes on the buyers of the goods produced by the second. In a crude way, the net tax revenues on the second group must more or less match the subsidies to the first group. An individual can get a 'free lunch'; society as a whole cannot. Someone must pay for the goods and services produced by the government. One reason the size of the government sector has expanded is that 'everyone' – well, nearly everyone – wants that free lunch from the government; the implicit view is that someone else will pay most or all of the cost. A free lunch is cheaper than a cash lunch; attractive as the free lunch may be, however, someone has to pay for it.

The size of government is a good measure of the amount of goods and services that individuals consume collectively, which has ranged from 20 percent of GDP in some industrial societies to 60 percent in others. The cliché is that the amount of goods and services supplied by the government is a response to the demands of society. But the cliché is a cliché; some government expenditures reflect the ability of different groups – the farmers, the defense contractors, small businesses – to get support. Most of the benefits of government payments go to selected groups – farmers receive agricultural extension services and price supports, students get free school lunches, and professors receive research stipends from the National Science Foundation and the National Institutes of Health – while the costs fall broadly on taxpayers. The firms that produce military goods are – naturally – extremely fond of military expenditure. Each group sees its own interests advanced if the government spends more on the goods and services it produces; the value of these benefits will almost certainly exceed their share of costs. For as long as the production of additional government goods and services is dissociated from their costs, advantages may accrue to the government and to those members of the bureaucracy associated with the extension of new services.

Corporate tax rates

Tax collectors love to bury taxes so they are not visible to those that pay them. Corporate income tax is buried – embedded in the prices of the products sold by firms – as long as the firms are profitable. (One of the disadvantages of corporate tax is that profitable and efficient firms are penalized relative to their unprofitable and presumably less-efficient competitors.) Most buyers of virtually any good or service – an automobile, a new home, an airplane trip – would be hard pressed to indicate the amount of the tax payment associated with any of their purchases.

Corporate income tax payments are larger as a share of both national income and total tax payments in the United States than in any other industrial country. Someone might conclude from this data that US corporate income tax rates are higher than tax rates in other industrial countries. Similarly, one might conclude that since personal income taxes account for a larger share of GDP and total taxes in the United States than in these other countries, then their personal income tax rates must be higher than the personal income tax rates in the United States than in these other countries.

Neither conclusion is warranted. It's a mistake to deduce tax rates on corporate income and on personal income from the share of government receipts from each type of tax.

One reason why the ratio of corporate tax receipts to total taxes is higher in the United States than in most foreign countries is that foreign governments spend a higher proportion of their country's GDPs and they have larger revenue needs. Even if they had the same corporate tax rates, the yield of the corporate tax would be lower as a percentage of total taxes because their corporate sectors are smaller, and corporate income is a smaller share of GDP. Thus many of the public utilities like railroads, the telephone companies, and the electric power producers may be government-owned firms; another is that there are relatively more small firms that are not incorporated. Moreover, corporate profits relative to corporate sales may be lower abroad, so the corporate income tax base would be smaller even if the corporate sectors in these other industrial countries were as large as the US corporate sector.

Similarly, the tax base for personal incomes is smaller abroad; a much larger proportion of taxpayers have incomes too low to pay personal income taxes. Tax rates on personal incomes are higher in Britain than in the United States, in that tax payments are larger for each level of personal income. But since personal incomes are lower, revenues from taxes on personal income are smaller relative to both GDP and to government expenditure.

Comparison of national tax rates is a necessary first step in determining the impact of taxes on the competitive position of the firms producing in each country. The US corporate income tax rate, now 36 percent, is generally lower than the corporate tax rates in most other industrial countries. However, definitions of taxable income differ, in part because some countries permit firms to depreciate their plant and equipment more rapidly than others so their expenses are higher and their profits are lower and hence their tax payments are lower. Moreover, countries differ in the scope of investment tax credits extended to business firms; investment tax credits reduce the effective tax rates for the firms that take advantage of them. Rapid depreciation and investment tax credits reduce the effective tax rate significantly below the posted rate.

Taxes can be avoided, evaded, or paid. Avoidance is legal, although there are costs. Subsidiaries in tax havens have to be established, and lawyers are expensive. Evasion of taxes – which is illegal – incurs costs and risks; in some countries, payments to the tax collectors in their personal capacity may obviate the need for much larger payments to the collectors in their official capacity. Still, evaders are sometimes caught, fined, jailed, and in some cases ostracized.

Despite all the attention to corporate tax rates, only individuals pay taxes. Corporations may have an infinite life, but they do not feel, suffer, breed, or smile; only people do. Corporations do not 'pay' taxes– they collect funds to pay these taxes from their customers, their shareholders, their employees, and their suppliers. The burden may fall not on the corporation's owners (in the form of a decline in their after-tax incomes), but on the customers, who pay higher prices, or on the suppliers, who receive lower prices. General Motors (GM) would pay a tax at the rate of 36 percent on its corporate profits if it had any profits to tax; until 1971 GM also paid a sales tax of 7 percent on its sales of automobiles. Ostensibly, the corporate tax fell on GM's profits, while the excise tax fell on the buyers of new cars. But GM probably raised the selling prices for its cars to obtain funds to make its corporate tax payments. Similarly, firms do not 'pay' social security taxes – they collect the funds to pay these taxes by paying their employees lower wage and salary rates.

The large variety of taxes befuddles many taxpayers: if they were aware that 20, or 30, or even 40 percent of their income was taxed, they might be more cautious about proposals for increases in government expenditure. And if all of their taxes were collected by a straightforward income tax or consumption tax or value-added tax, they would have greater incentive to calculate the pay-offs from tax avoidance or evasion.

Economic impacts of corporate tax rate

The legal form of these taxes should be distinguished from their economic impact. Corporate tax and sales tax fall directly on consumers if the demand for the product is sufficiently strong. Consider the impact of a possible increase in the US corporate income tax rate by about 10 percent or 4 percentage points – say, to a rate of 40 percent. Most firms would probably raise their selling prices to offset higher corporate income tax payments, so that the after-tax returns earned by their shareholders would remain pretty much the same in the long run if not immediately. Similarly, the resource-depletion allowance, which allowed oil companies to reduce their tax payments, almost certainly meant a lower price for gasoline; when the allowance was reduced in 1975, the gasoline price went up modestly so that the oil-producing companies would have more or less the same after-tax rate of return (Table 15.2).

But taxes are only part of the story. Governments tax to spend. And while taxes raise costs to firms, some government expenditure may lower those costs. Public expenditure can reduce the need for private expenditure and hence the costs of individual firms. Thus government expenditure on roads and airports reduces

Table 15.2   Corporate income tax rates

	2000	2006
United States	39.4	39.3
Japan	40.9	39.5
Germany	52.0	38.9
France	37.8	35.0
Great Britain	30.0	30.0
Canada	44.6	36.1

Source: Tax Foundation.

transportation costs for manufacturing firms. Expenditure on fire departments reduces the need to purchase similar protection privately, while expenditure on education reduces the need for firms to train their own employees.

Consider the impact of an increase in the tax rate on corporate profits on the selling prices of automobiles produced in the United States. Assume that an automobile sells for $20,000, that the profits-to-sales ratio for US auto firms is 10 percent, and that the corporate tax rate is 36 percent. The profits of $2000 would be taxed, and the tax payment would be $720. If the tax rate were increased to 40 percent, the tax payment would increase to $800. Because these firms will raise their selling prices to pass the increase in the tax bite forward to consumers, then the pre-tax profits-to-sales ratio must rise to 14 percent to cover the increase in the firms' corporate tax payments; the firms' selling prices will increase by less than one-half of 1 percent. If, instead, the profits-to-sales ratio is 20 percent, then the increase in the selling prices will be about 1 percent.

Note that the impact of changes in the corporate tax rate on the final selling price varies with the profits-to-sales ratio – the higher this ratio, the larger the impact of the increase in the tax rate. Profits-to-sales ratios vary by industry; within the United States, the average for many industries is in the range of 2–6 percent. For firms with a 4 percent ratio, the impact of the introduction of a 50 percent tax – from a tax rate of zero – would raise the selling price (again assuming all of the tax is passed forward to the consumer and that previously there had been no corporate income tax) by 4 percent.

Changing the corporate income tax rate will have a modest effect on the competitive position of firms in different industries, although the impact will be larger, the higher the profits-to-sales ratio.

Assume another extreme example – the corporate income tax rate is completely eliminated. Eventually, after a period of adjustment, firms would reduce the prices at which they sold their products, so their after-tax profits would be the same as the after-tax rate of return before the tax was eliminated. One consequence would be that reduction in selling prices in industries with high profits-to-sales ratios would be larger than the price reductions in the industries in which these ratios are low; as a result, the first group of industries would probably expand their sales relative to the second. A second consequence is that the ability of the most profitable firms in an industry to cut prices would be enhanced relative to the ability of the less profitable firms, and so the failure rate of these less profitable firms would increase.

The impact of changes in the corporate tax rate on the prices of goods thus depends on how much of the tax is passed on in the form of higher prices and on whether there is any cost-reducing impact of associated government expenditures. Most economists believe that a substantial part of the corporate tax is shifted forward to consumers, except perhaps for a brief interval after the tax rate is changed.

Corporate tax rates are likely to have a significant impact on international trade only if the tax rates are much higher in some countries than in others. The differences in corporate tax rates among industrial countries are generally smaller than 10 percentage points. For most industries, differences in tax rates can explain only a small part of the differences in selling prices among countries, except for a few industries in which the profits-to-sales ratios are very high. Much of the pattern of international trade and investment reflects differences in real costs: bananas can be produced in Ecuador at a lower cost than in Chicago because nature has been more generous with the requisite climate and soil in Ecuador. But steel can be produced at a lower cost in Chicago, since the iron ore is near the northern end of Lake Michigan and the coal is near the southern end. The differentials in real costs attributable to the uneven beneficence of nature and variations in capital accumulation are much more significant in explaining national differentials in costs of production than differences in national tax rates.

An increase in corporate tax rate in a country, like an increase in wages, may affect its international competitive position in the short run; its economic position in the long run will be unaffected, for the value of its currency will change to offset the price-raising impact of higher taxes on the demand for domestic products. Assume that the corporate tax rate is increased from 30 percent to 40 percent, and that the profit-to-sales ratio averages 10 percent. Then the average firm will increase the selling price for its goods by 1 percentage point – say from 100 to 101 – for the firm to have the same after-tax profits. Firms with high profit-to-sales ratios will increase their prices somewhat more; firms with low profit-to-sales ratios will increase their prices somewhat less.

Customers will respond to the increase in the average selling price by reducing their demand; the country's currency will depreciate. Depreciation by itself will tend to enhance competitiveness, and thus offset the impact of the higher domestic prices. The competitive position of some firms may improve and that of other firms may worsen, but the overall impact on the country is not likely to be economically significant. True, if national cost structures become more nearly similar then differences among national tax systems will become increasingly important. The reduction of any barrier to mobility of goods and capital would make the differences in national tax systems more significant: the search for low-tax jurisdictions would be more intense. Increased attention would be given harmonization of tax rates to minimize shifts in productive activities among jurisdictions. Inevitably, international arrangements would be established to prevent competitive tax practices.

Taxes on foreign income

Tax collectors have a voracious appetite. They continually hunt for new sources of revenue. They tax firms and individuals on a wide range of their domestic activities. In some countries, they tax firms and individuals on their foreign income. The US Government taxes the US income of foreign firms and foreign citizens, much as if they were domestic residents. The US branches and subsidiaries of foreign firms calculate their tax liability to Uncle Sam using the US definition of income and the US tax rates. The US Government also taxes the foreign income of US firms and US citizens, much as if they were domestic residents. The income of the foreign subsidiaries of US firms becomes an effective US tax liability only when the subsidiaries pay a dividend to their US parents. (The incomes of the foreign branches of US firms become an effective US tax liability when the incomes are earned – which means that there is an incentive to organize the foreign activity as a subsidiary when it becomes profitable.) These firms and individuals have paid taxes to the governments of the countries in which they earned this income; the US taxpayers then receive a credit against their US tax liability for foreign income taxes paid, as long as the foreign tax rate is not above the US tax rate. Because of this credit foreign tax payments reduce domestic tax liabilities on a dollar-for-dollar basis. Many foreign governments follow the same approach; occasionally governments, especially in the developing countries, may give tax concessions so that foreign investors are spared paying domestic taxes for 5 or 10 years; these concessions are known as 'tax holidays.' These tax holidays are significant only if the US firm can find some way to shield the foreign income from the US tax authority.

The US Treasury participates in bilateral tax treaties with many foreign governments, which provide that the total tax payments to both governments will not be higher than if the higher of the two tax rates is applied. No government attempts to tax the foreign income of nonresidents, except insofar as they buy domestically produced products and pay the tax that is embedded in the prices of these products.

The opportunity to delay the tax payments on foreign income, known as tax deferral, is like an interest-free loan from the US Treasury to the firms that have earned profits in foreign countries. In effect, the right to delay this tax payment means that the effective tax rate that US firms pay on their foreign incomes is lower than the posted corporate tax rate. At an interest rate of 10 percent, a tax liability of $100 has a present value of $50 if the payment to the US Treasury can be delayed for 7 years. The combination of tax deferrals and tax havens like Zug provide firms with attractive and flexible opportunities to reduce their tax payments. Thus, the profitable foreign subsidiaries of a US firm might be tiered – organized as the subsidiaries of a Swiss or Bahamian subsidiary. Profits in high-tax countries could be diverted to subsidiaries based in tax havens, and the funds could in turn be invested in another subsidiary which is rapidly growing and needs additional funds. Transfer pricing can be used to divert profits to the tax havens; the taxes on these profits are then deferred.

A perennial issue is how to tax domestic residents with foreign income relative to domestic residents with domestic income. The equity approach is that domestic taxpayers should be taxed on the same basis, regardless of the source or type of their income. Domestic income and foreign income, earned income and unearned income, interest income on state and local securities and corporate dividends would all be taxed at the same effective rate.

It is hard to disagree with the general equity principle. But practical problems arise when the taxable foreign income must be defined – is it foreign income before taxes are paid to the foreign tax collector, or is it after-tax income? If it is foreign income after taxes, what recognition should be given to foreign income taxes paid – should the US taxpayer receive a credit for these tax payments? An alternative to providing a credit for foreign taxes paid is to consider these tax payments as a deduction or a cost in computing domestic tax liability: foreign tax payments of a dollar would reduce domestic tax liability by about 50 cents. In this case, the total taxes paid to the two tax authorities would be higher than if the credit approach were used. Foreign investment would be discouraged, and for two reasons. First, income on foreign investments would be taxed more heavily than income on domestic investments and, second, income earned by US firms in various foreign countries would be taxed more heavily than if the same income were earned by firms resident in this country. Thus the foreign affiliates of US firms would be at a tax disadvantage relative to their host-country competitors – and relative to firms headquartered in countries that follow a relaxed approach to the taxation of foreign income of their domestic firms.

From the US point of view, it might seem desirable to discourage foreign investment, since the income accrues to the United States – both to the owners of the investment and to the US tax authorities – only after taxes have been paid abroad. In some cases the after-tax return to the United States might be larger than if the same funds had been invested in the United States; in most cases, however, the after-tax return on the foreign investments is likely to be below the before-tax return on domestic investment. But there may be a wash, since the same argument is likely to hold with respect to the US investments of foreign firms.

The US firms that invest overseas are not impressed with this logic; their own interests are served by maximizing their after-tax income. From their point of view, when you've seen one tax collector, you've seen them all. Given that they must pay a given amount of tax, they are largely indifferent to whether they pay taxes to Uncle Sam or to his foreign colleagues. These firms engage in a marketing campaign and stress the favorable effect of their foreign investments on the US investment income and US foreign policy.

There is an inevitable conflict in the design of international tax policy, depending on whose interest is to be served. The cosmopolitan or world economic welfare is served if investment funds are allocated between domestic and foreign alternatives on the basis of their pre-tax rates of return; the implication is that taxes on foreign income should be the same as those on domestic income. The national economic welfare is served only if the rates of return to the economy on foreign investment, after payment of foreign taxes, exceed the pre-tax return on domestic investment. From the firm's point of view, it should be sufficient that it pays taxes to the countries in which it operates; there should be no residual tax liability to US authorities. From the point of view of US taxpayers, the taxes on foreign income should be the same as on domestic income; if foreign tax rates are lower than US rates, then an additional tax is due to the US Treasury.

Why don't the trains run on time?

It might have been Yogi Berra who said 'A three cent stamp doesn't cost three cents anymore.' The cost of the stamp for delivering first-class mail increased from three cents in 1950 to 42 cents in 2008. The US price level increased by a factor of five during this same period, so the 'real cost' of first-class mail doubled. Actually, the real cost increased even more, for the quality of mail service has declined – there are fewer mail deliveries each day, there are fewer post offices, and often the mail deliveries take longer, and there is more lost mail.

Consider some of the other elements in the decline in the effectiveness of government management. The quality of government-produced services has decreased. In Britain, individuals have opted out of the socialized medical system and bought private services either to reduce waiting time or to acquire medical services that they believe to be of higher quality. Within the United States, the concern about the decline in the level of public education has led to an increase in expenditure on private education, especially in cities and at the elementary and secondary school level. Stores, universities, colleges, churches, and businesses have developed their own police forces – which frequently include many part-timers whose primary employment is with a public police force.

A second element is the decline in the quality of the public infrastructure. Libraries are closed because governments cannot pay for both books and salaries. There are more potholes in the roads and the quality of roads and sewers declines because government is caught between its limited ability to tax and the demands of government employees, almost always organized into unions, for higher salaries. For a long time safety on public transportation in the major US cities declined. The paradox is that the quality of government-provided services declined even as salaries in the public sector increased. The increase in salaries in the government sector has been even more rapid than in the private sector. There appears to be a cost–push element in public-sector wages, because the employees are organized into unions. The unions favor similarity of salaries for individuals, and salaries tend to vary with the seniority and experience of individual workers rather than with their productivity. So it follows logically that those workers with the highest productivity are likely to be attracted to the higher salaries available in the private sector.

The governments with the largest expenditure tend to finance part of their expenditure by relying on the printing press: the tax base isn't sufficiently large. And, for a while at least, they tend to borrow internationally as well as domestically. Thus, when the United States has a large fiscal deficit and the US dollar tends to be weak in the currency market, the high interest rates mean that US dollar securities are attractive to foreign investors.

Fiscal deficits are associated with inflation, which leads to overvalued currencies. Overvalued currencies require exchange controls – barriers or tariffs or other controls that separate the domestic market for goods and services from the world market. Such controls enable the governments (and their friends) to buy foreign exchange on more favorable terms than the 'run-of-the-mill' business firms and individuals. Many countries have used these controls – Britain, the United States, France, Italy, Japan, and many developing countries. But these measures are effective only to the extent that earners of foreign exchange are not tempted to jump off the fence and sell their export earnings at the higher price available in the free market. Hence at times a pegged exchange rate can become like a tax on the earnings of foreign exchange.

One link between the underground economy and international money flows is the movement of 'suitcase money.' Individuals move money to low-tax jurisdictions; this shifting of money out of the country makes it much more difficult for the tax collector to prove that individuals have under-reported their incomes. Or they move currency in suitcases to circumvent domestic exchange controls: they want to get the funds into some other jurisdiction. There are other links – one is that the underground economies flourish in countries with high tax rates, because these countries have high levels of government expenditures. But the authorities find it easier to increase expenditures than tax revenues. So they borrow. Both taxing and borrowing take money from the public – although taxing is more directly coercive than borrowing.

Privatization

One remarkable change that began in the 1980s has been the privatization of government-owned airlines and telephone systems and numerous other government-provided services. Governments have also outsourced the suppliers of a variety of services as a way to reduce costs; these services include garbage collection, the management of prisons, and the operation of libraries.

Initiatives toward privatization can be viewed in terms of developments in particular industries (such as airlines, telecommunications, and banking) or in terms of particular countries (Britain, Mexico, Argentina, Japan, and the United States). (Privatization in Russia, China, Hungary, and other countries that are on the trip to the market from a command economy are discussed in Chapter 23.)

Probably one of the most extensive approaches toward privatization in a traditional industrial country has occurred in Britain. British Airlines was privatized. So was the phone system, gas distribution company, electric power production and distribution, railroads, steel mills, and water supply companies. Prime Minister Thatcher did much more than undo the legacy that the Conservative government had inherited from the Labour governments of the 1940s and the 1950s, which had nationalized steel and coal, the health system, and much of the housing stock. Clearly one of the motivations was ideological – Mrs Thatcher's view was that the government should provide law and order and arrangements for the enforcement of contracts for consenting adults. A second motivation was financial. If government-owned firms could be sold to the private sector, then the government would no longer have to subsidize operating losses (although in some cases the governments might subsidize operating losses for a set number of years). Nor would the government have to provide the cash to finance new investments. And there would be a one-time increase in government revenues when these firms were sold to private investors.

Because of the government's interest in securing a large (if not a maximum) gain from the sale of these firms, they had to be 'prepped' – converted into profitable enterprises. In some cases, thousands of employees were induced to leave, perhaps by taking early retirement. The motivation was that the higher the anticipated profits associated with a firm about to be privatized, the higher the price the potential buyers would pay for it, and the greater the windfall to the government selling the firm.

Argentina began its privatization effort in the early 1990s, and privatized a large number of firms, including airlines and the national oil company. Mexico privatized more than 500 firms – but not the national oil company.

Privatization was far less extensive in the United States than in other countries, in part because the government sector was smaller. Conrail, which had been assembled as an East Coast freight-hauling railroad from the carcasses of some bankrupt railroads, was privatized. Tennessee Valley Authority (TVA) and the various government-owned power-producing firms in the Northwest remain in the public sector. Amtrak continues to be government-owned; the commuter railroads and the bus systems in many cities are still in the public sector. The Japanese privatized Nippon Telephone and Telegraph and parts of their railroads.

That so many different governments privatized firms in so many different industries at more or less the same time cannot be a coincidence. Each government benefited fiscally, both from the reduction in the drain on the government's budget to finance operating losses and the one-shot proceeds from the sale. In many countries there was recognition that government-owned firms could not compete in the global market. Consider airlines. The US airline industry has eight national firms and a much larger number of regional firms. These compete extensively across the continental United States – and they have paid attention to reducing and controlling costs. This focus on costs has been valuable in competing against government-owned foreign airlines that have traditionally been under lesser pressure to reduce costs. Or consider telecommunications, which is essentially a global industry: firms were privatized to reduce the losses that government firms would incur.

Is there a pendulum, a wave of nationalization, and then a wave of privatization?

16
Banking on the Wire

Q: Why are Swiss bankers rich?
A: They compete against Swiss bankers.

The financial crisis and global banking

Lehman Brothers kaput. Bear Stearns induced to marry JPMorgan Chase. Merrill Lynch acquired – precipitously – by Bank of America. Morgan Stanley raised new capital by selling a 20 percent ownership interest to Mitsubishi. (And it was only 10 years ago that the Japanese banks were in financial turmoil after the implosion of property values and stock values in Tokyo.) Goldman Sachs and Morgan Stanley have become bank holding companies so they will have easier access to the Federal Reserve.

The American, British, Irish, Swiss, Belgian, Dutch, and Icelandic Governments have invested money in some of their troubled banks that have experienced sharply depleted capital as a result of massive loan losses. Initially some of these banks were able to sell new shares to investors, especially to sovereign wealth funds headquartered in the Persian Gulf and Southeast Asia. But as the reported losses increased, private investors became increasingly reluctant to provide more capital for the banks.

The policy choice for the authorities in each country was that the banks would sell assets and shrink their balance sheets to match their depleted capital if the governments did not somehow provide more capital to the banks. Governments can provide this capital in several different ways – through the purchase of preferred shares without the right to convert these shares into common stock, through the purchases of preferred shares with the right to convert these shares to preferred stock, through the purchase of common stock, and through the purchase of 'toxic assets' from the troubled banks, perhaps at prices above their market prices.

The US Government initially provided capital through the purchase of preferred shares, and then subsequently rearranged the transaction. The British Government 'nationalized' Northern Rock, in effect becoming the sole owner; the shareholders at the time were dispossessed, although at some stage there may be some compensation payment. One of the unanswered questions is how large the government

236

ownership interest might become before the term 'nationalization' is appropriate. Another question involves the scope of government involvement in the management of these banks, both in terms of policy decisions and administrative decisions.

At some stage – in 4, 5, or 10 years – the governments will sell their ownership interests to private investors. In the meantime, a deposit in an American, British, Irish, or Swiss bank is comparable to ownership of a short-term security issued by the governments of one of these countries. The ownership of the deposit in one of these banks and the ownership of a short-term government security are not quite identical, since there is the risk that a government might allow one of these banks to fail, with losses to the owners of deposits.

Many investors would think that risk is low, and that in the near future governments are not going to allow the banks to fail with losses to the depositors.

The major question is whether implicit government ownership of the banks – implicit because of the uncertain but likely guarantee of deposits – will affect competition among banks headquartered in different countries.

Competition in banking

A revolution is hitting the commercial banking industry. The technology of money payments is changing; the transfer of pieces of paper – currency and checks – is being replaced by transmission of electronic impulses among the payor, payees, and their banks. As a result, the geographic scope of banking markets is expanding, and formally protected regional markets are increasingly subject to competition from banks headquartered in foreign countries. The effectiveness of national cartels in limiting competition among banks is declining. In the 1960s, US banks expanded rapidly abroad; in the late 1970s and 1980s, foreign banks and especially banks headquartered in Japan became extremely aggressive in the US markets for deposits and loans.

The use of credit cards and of debit cards continues to expand. You use these cards when you're at the gas station, convenience stores, and fast food outlets. You may have arranged for the direct payment of your telephone bills and your utility bills.

Consider that you now have an Automatic Teller Machine (ATM) card that lets you obtain cash and make deposits at the local supermarket or at the airport or at almost any bank. Now you no longer need to choose a bank because it has a branch office near where you live or where you work. You can use your card to obtain cash from many tens of thousands of ATMs, including when you're in a foreign country in the local currency. Few readers of the first edition of this book in the early 1970s had an ATM card, whereas now most readers do.

Initially, banking was local – depositors wanted to know the person to whom they were entrusting their money and the bankers wanted to know their borrowers; both wanted to be sure that their money was safe. Some countries developed national banks that dealt with customers from coast to coast, but in the United States the major banks were local and regional.

Traditionally, the banks in each country were protected from foreign competitors by the high costs that a foreign bank would encounter in establishing a branch on the turf of a foreign bank. Regulation, informal as well as formal, also limited the expansion of foreign banks into domestic markets.

Banking traditionally has been highly regulated, initially to protect depositors against loss that they would incur if the banks closed because of large loan losses or theft by the managers. Central banks were established as lenders of last resort, as overseers of the activities of their domestic banks so they wouldn't need to be 'bailed out' by their governments. Commercial banks were required to hold deposits or reserves at the central bank. Ceilings were placed on the interest rates that banks could pay on different types of deposits; the rationale was that if the interest rates that banks could pay on their deposits were limited, they would be less likely to acquire loans that seemed exceptionally risky. Banks were required to hold certain types of assets and prohibited from owning other types of assets. Bank loans to any one customer were limited to a small fraction of the capital of the banks. Banks were required to buy deposit insurance to reduce the likelihood of runs. Moreover, the total loans that a bank might make was limited to a given multiple of its capital.

Measures adopted to limit failure constrained competition among banks. Regulation helped the less efficient banks to be more profitable than they otherwise would have been in a more competitive environment. Regulation has constrained the growth of the more efficient banks and their ability to increase their market share.

Branching and acquisitions

Competition among banks based in different countries takes several forms. More than 50 US banks once had branches in London, primarily to sell US dollar deposits and to buy US dollar loans; these banks also sold deposits and bought loans denominated in the German mark, the Swiss franc, and a few other foreign currencies. Several of the London branches of US banks have a significant amount of business in the British pound in competition with British banks. Indeed, if regulations were changed so that US dollar transactions in London were forbidden or if the sale of US dollar deposits in London became financially unattractive, most of the US banks would close their London branches. Similarly, if US banks were prohibited from selling US dollar deposits and making US dollar loans outside the United States, they would close many of their branches in other offshore financial centers. Three US banks retain large numbers of overseas branches; a few more have branches in London because of its position as a major financial center.

Bank expansion and consolidation has been extensive since the early 1980s, more so than at any previous time. Banks headquartered in Britain, Switzerland, Canada, Germany, Switzerland, and Japan opened offices in New York, Chicago, and San Francisco and began to acquire US banks. Lloyd's Bank, at one time one of the large British banks, bought Western Bank & Trust in California. European American Bank, owned by a consortium of six banks headquartered in different European countries, acquired Franklin National Bank; subsequently European American was acquired by ABN-AMRO, the leading Dutch bank. ABN-AMRO was extremely aggressive in expanding its banking activities in the Midwest and became one of the ten largest banks in the United States. Barclays, another of the large British banks, wanted to buy ABN-AMRO; however a group comprised of the Royal Bank of Scotland, Fortis (a joint Belgian–Dutch firm), and Banco Santander, one of the leading Spanish banks, acquired ABN-AMRO. National Westminster Bank bought National Bank of North America in New York; subsequently Royal Bank of Scotland acquired NatWest. Hong Kong & Shanghai Bank (now HSBC) had acquired Marine Midland and then Republic National in New York and Household Finance as well as Midland Bank in Britain. The branch system of Bankers Trust in New York was sold to the Bank of Montreal, Bank Leumi (Israel), and Barclays. Mitsubishi Bank bought the Bank of California. Bank of Montreal acquired Harris Bank and Trust in Chicago. Toronto-Dominion Bank has acquired Commerce Bank.

US banks have also purchased shares in foreign banks. And when the establishment of branch offices or the purchase of shares in banks abroad has been prohibited or constrained, foreign customers have been invited to do business in the bank's home office or in a convenient regional office. Canadian nationalism has constrained US banks from competing aggressively by limiting their share of the Canadian market for deposits, but Canadian individuals and firms who desire less costly banking services than those available in Montreal and Toronto and Vancouver have been welcome in New York and in Chicago.

Entry into foreign markets by branching or acquisition enables aggressive banks to circumvent the regulations that limit their growth in their domestic markets. Many commercial banks have sought to grow rapidly, in some cases they believe their profits increase with size and in others they may be on an ego trip – they want to be a very large bank. Every central bank, however, manages its monetary policy to directly limit the growth of commercial bank liabilities denominated in its currency – and hence the growth in commercial bank assets – to limit increases in the domestic price level. The upper limit to monetary expansion may be 6, 10, or 20 percent a year, but each central bank has a limit. An individual bank can grow more rapidly than banks as a group only if it can increase its share of the domestic market or its share of a foreign market; if it succeeds, the market shares of some other banks must decline. Aggressive banks expand into new or ancillary businesses that produce fee income – ownership of mutual funds, travel, leasing, and computer services. Banks trade government bonds and currencies. Some banks invest in stocks. An aggressive bank is likely to expand abroad, for the costs of obtaining customers in a market which it has not previously entered are likely to be smaller than the costs of increasing its share of the domestic market.

Changes in the technology of payments

Changes in the technology of money payments are affecting the number of banks and structure of the banking industry, just as the shift from propeller craft to jets altered the structure of the airline industry. Expanding into foreign markets is becoming easier as changes in the technology of money payments processes reduce the costs of economic distance between the head office of a bank and their customers and their potential customers in foreign countries. As more and more payments are made electronically, the market area in which an individual bank can compete becomes larger. To the extent banks in some countries are more efficient or have other competitive advantages – perhaps because they can obtain capital at a lower cost – they are likely to increase their share of the world market for bank deposits and bank loans.

Remember that a commercial bank produces demand deposits and time deposits; the bank 'sells' deposits in exchange for cash or for a deposit in another bank. (The question 'What do banks produce?' was discussed in Chapter 6.) The cash received from the sale of deposits enables the bank to buy loans, mortgages, bonds, and securities, each of which brings interest income. Banks also have numerous other activities for which they receive fees: they rent safe-deposit boxes, sell bonds and stocks, and manage trusts. But the bread-and-butter activity for most banks – and much of the jam – involves selling demand and time deposits and buying loans.

Banks deal with two primary groups of customers, depositors and borrowers. (The term 'depositors' is a synonym for 'investors.') These roles overlap – virtually every borrower is also a depositor. Business firms tend to be predominantly borrowers and households tend to be primarily depositors. Banks are intermediaries between the household depositors who want a safe, secure, and convenient place to store some of their financial wealth, and borrowers, who want to expand their current production or consumption more rapidly than they can on the basis of their current wealth and income. The spread or markup between the interest rates that banks pay depositors and the interest rates they charge borrowers covers their costs and is the major source of their income.

The profits in banking

Profits in banking depend primarily on three factors: marketing skills in selling deposits, investment skills in buying loans and other types of assets, and skills in managing the enterprise. Since selling deposits by paying higher interest rates – that is, through price competition – is usually limited by the authorities – or, in many countries, by a gentlemen's arrangement among the banks – banks often compete by offering toasters, TV sets, and pretty checks as bonuses when they sell deposits. The skill of a bank in selling deposits determines how rapidly it can grow.

Investment skills involve matching the yields on loans, mortgages, and other securities with the risks of each of these securities – both the credit risk that the borrowers might default and the risk that the price of the security may change. Within each economy, riskier loans and securities offer higher returns. Banks – at least the successful ones – seek those securities that offer the highest return for the risk – or, alternatively, the lowest risk for the return. The banks that are best able to determine which securities are underpriced relative to their risks earn the highest profits. The more profitable banks can increase the interest rates they pay on deposits, and hence their deposits are likely to increase at an above-average rate.

In many ways, commercial banks are like other financial intermediaries, including mutual savings banks, savings and loan associations, and life insurance companies. Each firm in these industries sells its liabilities to the public and uses the money obtained to buy loans, securities, and other income-earning assets. Households want to store wealth, and the liabilities of each type of institution store financial wealth. A life insurance policy, a pension, and a passbook deposit are the symbolic forms of wealth; the wealth is the claim on the firm that has issued these liabilities. The loss of the policy or passbook (unlike the loss of currency) does not lead to any loss in wealth, for the institution will issue a replacement policy or passbook.

Commercial banks differ from other financial intermediaries in one important way, however: their demand deposits or checking account liabilities are used in payments and hence are money. Money – by definition – is transferred to pay for the purchase of goods and services and securities. Banks participate in the operation of the payments mechanism, which provides for the transfer of money. Checks are messages from depositors to their banks to transfer ownership of part of the bank deposit to whoever's name follows the phrase 'Pay to the order of.' A check is a symbolic form of money, but not the money itself; the money is the bank deposit.

Banks pay higher interest rates on time or savings deposits than they do on demand deposits. Selling demand deposits might appear more profitable than selling time deposits, since interest rates are lower. But banks incur substantially higher costs in managing their demand deposits, for they must process billions of checks and shift money from the payers' to the payees' banks; these costs are so high that the sale of demand deposits is only marginally more profitable than the sale of time deposits.

The market area of a bank

In the early nineteenth century, the major product of banks was currency notes – engraved pretty pieces of paper that were promises to pay the bearer in 'lawful money,' which often meant gold or currency notes produced by the central bank. Each bank had its distinctive notes; the countryside was full of competing bits of paper. Industrial states chartered banks to finance the building of roads, canals, and railroads; once a bank had received a charter, the banker would lend money to the entrepreneurs that promised to make these investments. Money payments involved the transfer of bank notes in hand-to-hand circulation. The market area for each bank was limited to its immediate vicinity, because individuals lacked confidence in the value of notes issued by banks in distant locations, and hence they were reluctant to accept these notes. If a bank failed, the value of the notes that it had issued would decline and in some cases become worthless. Firms and individuals in Chicago were reluctant to accept notes issued by banks in New York, because they were wary about the credit standing of banks 700 miles away. Banks in New York were even more reluctant to accept notes issued by Chicago banks. Bank notes frequently sold below their face value in distant cities; thus a $1 note issued by a New York bank might sell for 95 cents in the Chicago area, while $1 bank notes issued by banks in Chicago might sell for 90 cents in New York. Since the transport costs of money were relatively high, the price of the notes varied inversely with the distance from the home office of the bank that produced them. The discount below the face value reflected the risk that buyers were taking on both the legitimacy of the note and the financial standing of the bank that issued it.

The geographic scope of the market area of each bank was limited by the costs that potential borrowers and lenders incurred in dealing with the bank: the time and inconvenience of dealing with a bank located in a distant city were higher than those in dealing with a nearby bank. Some banks, especially in the smaller cities and country towns, had a neighborhood monopoly because no other bank was within a convenient walking – or riding – distance.

The use of checks for payments and the expansion of bank branches

The market area of individual banks expanded when checks began to replace bank notes as a means of payment in the latter part of the nineteenth century. Checks had several advantages – one piece of paper could be used for large payments and for payments of odd amounts. The money-transfer process was less risky; the theft of checks, unlike the theft of notes, involved little risk, for payment on the check could be stopped. Since checks could safely be sent through the mail, the transport costs for checks were much lower than for bank notes. Hence the use of checks facilitated transactions between buyers and sellers who were hundreds of miles apart. The increased use of checks coincided with the development of comprehensive railroad systems and improvements in the postal systems. The decline in transport costs associated with the expansion of these systems enlarged the size of the market area for goods, and firms and individuals had more occasions to pay firms that were much further away.

By bringing depositors and borrowers from various locales into the expanding market area of a large number of more distant banks, the change in the technology of payments reduced the monopoly position of each local neighborhood bank. The size of the market was limited by the speed and efficiency of the check transfer process and by the costs of acquiring information about banks headquartered in distant cities. Borrowers still found personal contact with their bankers necessary, for loans had to be negotiated in person, and bankers found it convenient to stay in their offices to meet borrowers; the would-be borrowers had to convince the bankers that they were creditworthy. But even then, the loan negotiations could occur elsewhere – in the borrower's office or on a golf course.

Banks began to develop branches as checks replaced notes. Large banks are more efficient than small banks because there are economies of scale in the basic banking functions – selling deposits, buying loans and other securities, and operating the payments mechanism. Processing the flow of checks within one institution is less costly than moving the checks among different institutions. Branching enables banks to marry offices located in residential areas and suburban areas that primarily serve depositors with their offices in central city areas, which primarily serve business borrowers. As firms became larger they wanted to borrow larger amounts of money and the banks increased in size so they could provide larger loans. In the growing industrial centers, business firms wanted to borrow much more money than banks in the vicinity of their offices could lend on the basis of local deposits. Banks located near these firms found that the business demand for loans exceeded their lending capacity. Since banks in the residential areas received more money in deposits from households than they could readily lend in these local areas, a mechanism was needed so that the money received from the sale of the deposits in residential neighborhoods could be available for loans in central business areas. Banks in residential areas could lend money to banks in business areas, or banks from each area might merge to internalize the transfer of funds within one firm. The growth of branch banks suggests that internalization was less costly.

The move to electronic banking means that checks – and paper – are no longer used in the money-transfer process. With the electronic transfer of funds, when Joe Doe wishes to pay his electric utility bill or his taxes, he signals his bank by instructions on his personal computer, which is connected to the bank's computers. Doe will call his bank, enter his social security number, his bank account number, his Personal Identification Number (PIN) to prevent the misuse of his account by someone else (the coded number serves the same function as the signature on a check), the account number of the electric utility that is to be paid, and the amount of the payment. A synthesized voice will repeat this information to Doe. The signal will then go to the computer in Doe's bank and from there to the computer in the utility's bank.

This system already is in place. The banks have ATMs that distribute cash and accept deposits; a plastic card and a four or six digit code enables depositors to obtain cash in the evenings and on weekends and at other times when the bank is closed. When the bank is open, the ATMs are like an express line at the supermarket; customers with simple transactions process their transactions quickly. Cash can readily be drawn against overdraft limits on Mastercard and Visa and American Express cards. These consoles are now usually located at the doorstep of the bank – and increasingly they are in supermarkets and convenience stores and at airports and in shopping centers.

The electronic banking system has several advantages. Postage costs are avoided. The transfer process is instantaneous: there is no delay between sending and receiving funds. The monthly or weekly balancing of checkbooks is redundant; Doe can determine the amount of money in his account whenever he dials a particular number. And there is no equivalent of a bad check; if Doe wants to pay Roe

$100 and has only $50 in his account, the computer balks. The printing, transfer, and verification of billions of pieces of paper have become outmoded.

Wire transfers mean that many traditional credit cards will be replaced by debit cards. When John Doe fills up his car at the corner gas station or checks out of his motel room, his use of the debit card sends a signal to the bank, and payment will be made immediately, regardless of the time of day or the day of the week. Bankers may work from 9 to 3, but computers work around the clock.

Individuals who make relatively few payments will continue to use checks. And notes and coins will still be used for small payments. But those who make a large number of payments will find the electronic system less costly and more convenient.

Electronic banking will further enlarge the market area for deposits beyond national boundaries. The distance between the customer and the bank will be irrelevant. The neighborhood becomes the world. Banks headquartered in New York will advertise in Frankfurt for euro deposits and loans, while banks headquartered in Frankfurt will compete for New York deposits and loans. Banks will be able to attract foreign customers without the cost of establishing offices abroad. Canadians will be able to bank as easily in Chicago and in New York as in Toronto.

Competition among international banks

Banking has been an international industry for centuries. The Rothschilds and the Fuggers were extended families with banking offices in several different countries; however, they were essentially investors rather than producers of money. In the latter part of the nineteenth century, British banks established branches in their colonies to help finance the overseas trade and investments of firms headquartered in London and in Liverpool; these branches primarily were set up in the outposts of the empire that were poorly served by domestic banks. Relatively few branches of British banks were established in the United States, for British firms could use US banks. Similarly, US banks, when they began to go overseas in the early years of the twentieth century, followed US firms initially to Argentina, Brazil, and other areas not adequately served by domestic banks.

In recent years, the motive for overseas expansion has shifted. Initially, a handful of New York, Chicago, and San Francisco banks followed US firms to Europe, competing for the foreign business of these firms in the hope of gaining more of their US business. The expansion of the overseas branch networks of the three largest US banks – Citibank, Bank of America, and Chase Manhattan (now JP MorganChase) – was especially rapid. The sudden increase in the number of US banks with branches abroad was partly a defensive response by the first US banks that went overseas; the Chicago banks moved abroad to protect their established relationships with firms headquartered in the Midwest from the competitive threat posed by the New York banks that were operating abroad. In 1960 about eight US banks had 130 foreign branches. By 1980, 126 US banks had nearly 1000 foreign branches. In the 1990s, some US banks closed their foreign branches, especially in the smaller financial centers.

Over the same period, more than 50 foreign banks set up branches in the United States, usually in New York. These banks wanted to participate directly in the largest financial market in the world; their direct interest was retaining the US business of their domestic customers – and to attract US customers.

US banks operating abroad and foreign banks operating in the United States share a common problem: they lack the deposits that are needed to make loans. They can borrow these funds from their home offices, they can borrow in the interbank money market, and they can borrow from the offshore market. And they do all three. Once they have the deposits, they can buy loans. In the loan market, both borrowers and banks are mobile; major US banks, once limited by legislation against branching in other states, set up loan production offices in major cities across the country – little more than a suite in a prestigious hotel.

Many countries have been reluctant to admit foreign banks, because they wanted to protect the domestic banks from the challenges of foreign competitors. Thus, Norway and Denmark traditionally did not permit foreign banks to establish branches in their country. At one time Peru and Chile closed the local branches of foreign banks, and Venezuela applied discriminatory legislation to the local branches of foreign banks. For years, US banks found it impossible to establish branches in Mexico. (Mexican policy was reversed when Mexican banks incurred large loan losses and became severely undercapitalized.) Even when a US bank establishes a branch abroad, the price is often a commitment that the bank will not compete actively for domestic business. As a result, most of the Tokyo branches of US banks have been only modestly profitable.

Such attempts by governments to protect their domestic banks from having to compete with the local branches of foreign banks will become increasingly irrelevant. The move to electronic banking will reduce the importance of national boundaries as a limit to the size of the market and will diminish the need to establish foreign branches. With electronic banking, instructions to make payments will be handled over the wire. Thus, banks outside Switzerland, for example, can deal in Swiss francs on the same terms as banks inside Switzerland – perhaps on even more favorable terms.

Money havens will follow the tax havens. The computers may be in the Cayman Islands or in Bermuda, or some other offshore banking center; the terminals attached to this computer will be next to the phone. When face-to-face contact between the bank and the customer are necessary, the bank will send a representative to the customer's office. As the size of the market increases, more and more banks will be subject to more intense competitive challenges from foreign banks.

Competitive edge

The speed of the shift to electronic banking on an international scale is unpredictable. Assume, however, that the system is in place next Monday morning. Some banks will compete vigorously to maintain or enhance their share of the world market for deposits and loans, and several will succeed in increasing market share. Others will lose market share. Whether an individual bank is in the first group will depend partly on how efficient and competitive it has been in its domestic market.

In this new international market, US banks will have three advantages: size, efficiency, and identification with a currency that has been at the top of the currency hit parade for an extended period – but not since the advent of the third millennium. Not only is size important in making large loans, but size confers a competitive marketing advantage, for depositors often equate safety with size. (The cliché is 'too big to fail.') In the credit crunch of 1974, and again in 1982, the competitive positions of the largest US banks improved relative to those of their smaller competitors; investors reasoned that the Federal Reserve might permit the 20th largest US bank to fail, but it was quite unlikely that the Fed would permit any of the 10 largest US banks to close with losses to their depositors. And the largest US banks are generally bigger than most of their foreign competitors, with the exception of banks headquartered in Japan.

Changes in the ranking of banks in the size hit parade frequently result from mergers. Banks in Europe – and, to a lesser extent, Japan – have merged in response to the competitive threat posed by the very large US banks. In Britain, Barclays (the largest bank) merged with Martin's Bank, while Westminster and National Provincial combined into National Westminster. Lloyd's has merged with the Trustee Savings Bank. In Canada, the Royal Bank and the Bank of Montreal merged. In Belgium, Banque Lambert, the fourth in size, merged with Banque de Bruxelles, the second largest. In the Netherlands, the number 2 and number 3 banks have merged. Yet, by international standards, the largest banks in many European countries are still relatively small. The entire Belgian banking system is smaller than Citibank. If European banks want to be as large as one of the three or four leading US banks, they will almost certainly have to merge across national borders. But national differences in ownership and regulatory structures make such mergers difficult – although they should become easier as banking regulation is made at the regional level in Brussels.

US banks are probably more efficient than those in most foreign countries – a result of the greater competition in the banking markets in the United States. More banks compete for deposits and for loans in most markets, except those in the smaller cities and towns. There are nearly 10,000 banks in the United States, more than in the rest of the world combined. The large number of US banks reflects the nineteenth-century populist fear of centralized money trusts, which led to prohibitions against branching across state lines, branching across county lines in Indiana, and for many years branching across the street in Chicago. US banks are both more numerous and larger because the US economy is such a large part of the global economy. There are more financial assets in the United States per capita than in any other country. Demand deposits in Chicago exceed those in all of France.

Since for many years restrictions on branching constrained US banks from expanding geographically and setting up branches in other states, other means were used to attract customers. The contrast between the relatively uninhibited growth of US business, both nationally and internationally, and the sharp restrictions on the domestic expansion of US banks has forced them to become innovative and adaptive. Many of the US banks headquartered in one of the Eastern cities attract deposits from and make loans to firms headquartered on the West coast. Similarly, the market for bank loans and deposits in New York includes banks headquartered in Charlotte, North Carolina, and San Francisco. Banks headquartered in New York City participate in the Chicago market. Competition has prevailed, despite the earlier regulations against interstate banking; the result is that US banks in the major cities have been more fully subject to competitive pressures than banks headquartered in most foreign countries.

One measure of bank efficiency is provided by the spread between the average price the banks pay on their deposit liabilities and the average price they receive on their loans – that is, by the markup between the interest rates the banks pay on deposits and the interest rates they receive on loans. Within a country, competition ensures that spreads among banks are similar; significant differences in markups are not sustainable, otherwise, the banks with larger spreads would lose deposits to more efficient banks that pay higher interest rates on deposits. Among countries, however, spreads tend to differ: they tend to be larger – in some cases, substantially larger – in continental Europe than in the United States. The differences among countries are sustainable only as long as the national market is protected from external competition; gradually, banks in the countries with the higher markups will lose their share of the market.

In this new worldwide market, banks based in countries where larger spreads prevail will be under great competitive pressure. If they offer to pay higher interest rates to depositors while their spreads remain unchanged, their minimal lending rate will be so high that the least risky domestic borrowers will seek funds at foreign banks, which will be charging lower interest rates. If, instead, they set rates on loans competitive with those charged by foreign banks, then their deposit rates will be below those paid by banks that operate with smaller spreads. They may try to reduce their spreads, but they must pay lower wages or induce their employees to work harder, or find some other approach to become more efficient.

Some banks will discriminate by charging a different set of interest rates to those customers who have more attractive opportunities abroad. But such price shading can be only a partial response to the problems raised by the higher costs of European banks. In the final analysis, either costs will be cut or the less-efficient banks will lose market share.

The second advantage of US banks in the new international market is that their domestic currency – the US dollar – is likely to remain a preferred currency brand name. Indeed, the share of world banking business denominated in the US dollar may increase relative to the share denominated in most foreign currencies. This currency preference provides US banks with a competitive advantage, for if depositors prefer dollar-denominated deposits, many will also prefer that these deposits be issued by US banks. With their lower costs, US banks are likely to end up with a larger share of the world market for deposits.

Banking is generally viewed as a 'sensitive' industry, because banks both produce financial wealth and operate the money payments mechanism. Governments are wary of allowing a substantial part of the banking services demanded by their residents to be supplied by foreign banks. If banks in a country are largely foreign-owned, or even if the larger customers of the banks have ready access to foreign banks, then the effectiveness of national regulation and of national monetary policies may seem threatened. Efforts will be made to limit the access of foreign banks to domestic borrowers and lenders, measures that will counter the thrust toward an open international economy.

Financial crises, banking, and globalization 100.0

Thirty years ago there were eight money center US banks; five were headquartered in New York City, two in Chicago, and one in San Francisco. Now there are four money center US banks; two are headquartered in New York, one in Charlotte, North Carolina, and one in San Francisco. Bank of America, once headquartered in San Francisco, now has its home office in Charlotte, a result of its acquisition by what had been the NCNB, or the North Carolina National Bank. Thirty years ago, there were four major British clearing banks headquartered in London – now two are headquartered in London and one in Edinburgh. Thirty years ago, there were three major Swiss banking groups, now there are two. Thirty years ago, there were two major Dutch banks – now most of the banking services provided to the Dutch are from foreign-owned firms – or at least firms headquartered abroad.

Several factors explain the process of consolidation. Some banks have merged because they believe that mergers offer economies of scale and scope. Others have merged to become as large as their competitors. In other cases, banks that have incurred large losses have found it necessary to sell themselves to a better-capitalized firm.

As technology leads to increases in the market areas of individual banks and as firms merge, will there be a pattern in terms of ownership, with a relatively large proportion of the banks headquartered in three or four different countries. Banks use more or less the same technology to process payments, so the likelihood that one might have a lower-cost platform seems low. Similarly, banks are likely to pay the prevailing salaries; a bank would have no incentive to pay salaries higher than those paid by its competitors, and it would not be likely to attract talented labor if it paid below-market salaries. Some countries might continue to have national banks because protective measures handicap the entry of banks headquartered in foreign countries.

Banks headquartered in some countries may have an advantage in that they are more lightly regulated by their national authorities. And banks headquartered in some countries may have a lower cost of capital, perhaps because the shareholders believe that they are less risky.

Basle I and Basle II were international agreements promoted within the framework of the Bank for International Settlements (hence the name) that represented attempts at greater uniformity among the industrial countries in the capital requirements that each applied to banks. A capital requirement generally is expressed as an upper limit in the ratio of the assets of a bank to its capital or its reported net worth. Banks obtain the money to extend loans from deposits and from capital; deposits are a low-cost source of funds and capital is a high-cost source. The higher the capital requirement, the higher the costs of a bank, and hence the less competitive the bank might be. Basle I was designed to ensure that the bank regulators in each of the participating countries would apply the same capital requirements. Basle II carried the process a step further, and was an effort to ensure that capital requirements for more risky assets would be higher than for less risky assets.

These efforts at harmonization of capital requirements generally are introduced as a way to enhance the safety of the banks. Their indirect result is like that of a cartel, since they restrain competition in that a bank that might want to operate with a lower capital requirement is prevented from doing so.

The financial panic of October 2008 led the Government of Ireland to guarantee all of the deposits of the Irish banks. That in turn meant that non-Irish banks would be at a competitive disadvantage relative to Irish banks, and the Governments of Germany and Britain and then the United States followed with similar guarantees. In effect, the credit risks associated with the banks headquartered in these countries has been 'parked' at least as long as the guarantees remain in force.

At some stage, governments will seek to diminish the scope of their guarantees, perhaps by reducing those attached to very large deposits.

17

The Reverend Thomas Malthus, the OPEC Cartel, and the Price of Energy from 1800 to 2100

The Reverend Thomas Malthus of Jesus College, Cambridge, was one of the foremost economists of the early nineteenth century. His key idea was that since population increases at a geometric rate (1, 2, 4, 8, 16) while food production increases at an arithmetic rate (1, 2, 3, 4, 5), the eventual result will be famine – too many mouths, not enough food.

Malthus's logic was irrefutable. His conclusion inevitably followed from his assumption that the rate of population growth was higher than the rate of growth in the food supply. The data of the last 200 years challenge both of his assumptions. Populations do not grow at a geometric rate; rather, they grow rapidly initially as a result of improvements in public health and then the growth rate slows dramatically as families decide a higher standard of living is preferable to a larger number of children. Moreover, the supply of food has increased twice as rapidly as population; when Malthus wrote *An Essay on Population*, the world population was less than 1 billion; now it is 6 billion. Per capita income is 60–70 times greater than it was 200 years ago. (Individuals in the industrial countries are heavier and taller – and there has been a massive increase in the number of obese individuals, a powerful indication that food has become much cheaper.) Moreover, food production would have increased even more rapidly if the US Government and governments in Europe had not limited output to keep prices from declining. Famines have occurred, but they have been local and almost always due to limitations on distribution of food rather than to global shortages.

Now the 'term' Malthusian is applied to those concerned with the exhaustion of natural resources, including nonreproducible raw materials such as petroleum, lead, copper, and zinc – but especially petroleum. The 'irrefutable fact' is that the supply of each of these natural resources is fixed and hence the consumption of each resource this year and next means that the amounts that will be available for consumption in future years is smaller. (Increasingly, the production of many raw materials including gold, copper, and aluminum uses 'scrap' recovered from automobile graveyards and similar depositories.) The Neo-Malthusians – at least some of them – are like those who have identified a particular day when the world will end; they have concluded that the last barrel of oil will be extracted from the deepest well on February 2, 2029 and that the 850 million automobiles then on the world's highways and streets will run out of gas at more or less the same time. Their logic also is irrefutable – but the question is whether their assumptions are consistent with the model and the data.

When the world economy booms, the Neo-Malthusians prosper because commodity prices then are at their cyclical highs relative to their long-run trend and relative to the prices of industrial products and consumer goods. The Club of Rome carries the Malthusian torch; the Club was established in 1972 when the prices of raw materials were soaring during an industrial boom. The gestation period for most raw materials is longer than for manufactured goods. Three to five years are needed from the dates when a decision is made to increase production of some agricultural commodities such as rubber, tea, and coffee until the new crops first appear. Eight or ten years may elapse from the date of discovery of a new oil field until the crude petroleum is produced. The gestation period for lumber is longer, but the market response to an increase in the demand for lumber and in its price is to cut more trees before their optimum time. Increasing the output of minerals – copper, lead, tin, or zinc – may take even longer because new mines must be opened.

As economic expansions continue and morph into booms, the demand for raw materials increases more rapidly than the supply because of the longer gestation periods, and the prices of the raw materials increase relative to the prices of manufactured goods. Central banks may be sluggish in raising interest rates because the increase in the inflation rate is likely to be modest until the higher prices of raw materials lead to significant increases in the prices of manufactured goods and foodstuffs. When the boom ends, commodity prices decline sharply because of the reduction in demand; moreover the investments in new productive capacity that were initiated several years earlier may have led to increases in output.

Commodity prices vary much more extensively than the prices of manufactured goods because as economic growth slows manufacturing firms reduce production for a week or two to reduce supply to minimize the downward pressure on prices. When the demand for primary products declines, only a very few producers – those that are the single largest producers – believe that their self-interest would be enhanced by reducing output and sales; they believe that the loss in revenues from the reduced volume of production will be smaller than the loss that would otherwise occur because of the more rapid decline in price.

At times the producers of a particular commodity seek to develop an arrangement for an orderly reduction of production (often these arrangements are cartels), but it is difficult to induce the smaller producers to follow the lead of the larger firms – and hence governments adopt policies to ensure that each firm adopts measures to limit production.

The apparent paradox is that over the last 200 years the prices of many primary products have declined after adjusting for increases in consumer price levels. The real or inflation-adjusted prices of cereals – wheat, corn, or rice – are much lower now than they were when Malthus was an active theorist. Similarly, the real or inflation-adjusted prices of many manufactured goods have declined in the last 100 years and in some cases sharply. One powerful example is computers; the folklore is that the price of a unit of computing power has declined by 30 percent a year. Ten years ago a laptop computer cost $2000; now the basic laptop sells for $400 – and it is more powerful than the basic laptop of 10 years ago. You can still buy a $2000 laptop, but it is much superior in terms of power and reliability than the one you could have purchased for the same price 5 years ago. Or consider automobiles, which are less expensive in nominal dollars (unless the overall inflation rate is increasing) and real dollars than they were 5 and 10 years ago. (If the real prices of both foods and manufactured products have declined, the real prices of something else must have increased – the something else is services including haircuts, health care, and restaurant meals.)

That the inflation-adjusted prices of most primary products have declined even though these commodities are obtained from less accessible sources reflects that the increase in productivity in extracting resources has more than offset the increase in costs associated with sourcing from less accessible areas.

The concern about impending shortages and 'running out' is applied much more often to petroleum than to any other commodity, perhaps because the market value of petroleum production is so much higher than the market value of the production of these other commodities. Moreover, the surge in the price of petroleum is evident episodically when individuals fill the gas tanks of their automobiles or pay for a delivery of fuel oil. The surge in the price of petroleum from $25 a barrel in 2002 to nearly $150 a barrel in the early summer of 2008 is cited to support the view of eventual exhaustion; industry experts bemoan that few new oil fields are being discovered. The rapid increase in China's demand for energy as its growing middle class buys automobiles is cited as another reason why demand will increase more rapidly than supply; projections indicate that the automobile fleet in China eventually will become as large as the combined fleets in all of the industrial countries.

The term 'peak demand' has been applied to the eventual decline in oil supply; the peak identifies the year when annual production from an oil field is at a maximum before output begins to decline as a result of declining pressure in the underground strata that contains the oil. In the past the rapid increase in production from newly discovered oil fields has more than offset the decline in production from these older fields. Some analysts have concluded that eventually the declines in the production from older fields will exceed the increases in production from newer fields. The logic is impeccable on the basis of the assumption that the supply of new fields is less than infinite – which seems reasonable.

Since the early 1970s there have been four spikes in the price of crude petroleum; three of the four have followed from a political event that led to a decline in global supply. The first shock was in the autumn of 1973, following the Yom Kippur War; Saudi Arabia embargoed exports of petroleum to the United States and the Netherlands because Saudis viewed both countries as supporters of Israel. The oil price increased from $2.50 to $12.00 a barrel in response to a surge in demand from those who were concerned about an impending shortage. The global supply of oil did not decline significantly; rather, the United States increased its imports from other oil producers, and the Saudis diverted their exports to markets formerly served by these other producers. A self-fulfilling prophecy – at least for a while.

Table 17.1   The nominal and real price of oil, 1950–2008

Year	Nominal price (dollars/barrel)	Price level (1990 = 100)	Real price (1950 = 100)
1950	1.71	12.1	1.71
1960	1.50	16.7	1.09
1970	1.30	25.7	0.61
1975	10.60	38.7	3.31
1980	28.67	60.6	5.71
1985	29.69	83.0	4.32
1990	22.05	100.0	2.31
1995	17.20	116.2	1.55
2000	24.30	118.8	1.80
2005	53.40	121.2	3.85
2006	64.30	122.9	4.57
2007	71.10	128.0	4.86
2008	97.00	127.8	6.63

Source: International Financial Statistics.

The second oil shock occurred at the end of the 1970s after the Shah of Iran was deposed; the Ayatollahs reduced oil production. Then in 1979 Saddam Hussein of Iraq invaded Iran, and oil exports of both countries declined by five to six million barrels a day. The oil price increased to $40 a barrel.

The third oil shock occurred in 1989 when Saddam Hussein invaded Kuwait; oil exports from Kuwait declined sharply, and after the invasion of Iraq, its oil exports fell.

The peak of the fourth oil shock was in the early summer of 2008 when the price reached nearly $150 a barrel. Prices began to increase in April 2002 when the US-led coalition invaded Iraq with the intent to overthrow Saddam Hussein; the price reached $100 a barrel toward the end of 2007 in part because of a surge in demand in many developing countries and in part because political factors limited production in Iraq, Nigeria, and Venezuela. Moreover, once the price began to increase speculators – hedge funds, commodity funds, investment banks, pension funds – bought oil futures contracts in anticipation that the price would increase further, which induced more rapid increases in the price.

Amusingly, Saddam Hussein was a significant factor in three of the major price spikes in oil. Saddam is no longer around, but there will be other despots whose imperial ambitions may lead to sharp increases in the oil price. In the meantime, the likelihood is high that there will be a significant increase in oil production from Iraq, perhaps commensurate with its extremely large oil fields.

A horse race – money in the bank vs. oil in the ground

One of the major questions is how rapidly the price of oil might increase if Malthus is proven correct. Assume you won a $10 million lottery prize. Would you be better off investing the money and earning the real rate of interest than you would be if you used the money to buy $10 million of petroleum that you would store in an easily accessible well – or in an empty underground salt cavern?

Each oil-producing firm and each oil-producing country faces this question. Will its financial wealth increase more rapidly if it produces one more barrel of oil and deposits the sales proceeds 'in the bank' and allows its wealth to compound at the interest rate or instead will its wealth increase more rapidly if the oil is kept in the ground because of the anticipation that the market price of oil will increase – and at a rate higher than the interest rate?

If the market price of oil increased at the nominal interest rate (or if the real price of oil increased at the real interest rate), then the increase in the value of your money in the bank would not differ from the increase in the value of your oil in the ground. Some other factors might lead you to prefer one choice or the other – these are important but second-order considerations. A country with massive oil reserves relative to the needs of its current population might decide to produce more oil than is needed to pay for current consumption and put some of the proceeds in the bank, even if the general belief is that the rate of return on money in the bank is lower than the rate of increase in the oil price; the rationale is that there is some likelihood – less than half, and perhaps not more than one-quarter – that the rate of return on oil in the ground would be lower. Having both oil in the ground and some money in the bank is like having a diversified portfolio.

The primary reason for not producing enough oil to put some money in the bank is the belief that the rate of increase in the market price of oil would be significantly higher than the interest rate.

Those firms and investors who believe that the rate of increase in the price of oil would be significantly higher than the interest rate might borrow a lot of money that they would then use to buy oil (or oil reserves); they would profit from the excess of the rate of increase in the price of oil over the interest rate on the borrowed money. And if others mimic their investment strategy, the current price of oil would increase until the 'excess return' declines to a trivial amount.

The answer about the most rewarding policy depends on when the question is asked and the length of the holding period before the oil in ground is sold at the market price. Assume that the question was asked in 1950. The nominal price of oil declined between 1950 and 1970, so that in retrospect the more profitable decision in 1950 would have been to produce more oil and put the money in the bank.

Assume the question was asked in 1970 when the oil price was $2.50 a barrel; then the more rewarding financial choice would have been to hold the oil in the ground. Assume instead that the question was asked in 1980 when oil sold at $40 a barrel; then the more rewarding choice would have been to sell the oil and invest the proceeds at the market interest rate.

The data suggest that the longer the holding period, the more likely that the real rate of return on money in the bank will be higher than the rate of return on oil in the ground.

If the rate of return on oil in the ground always were higher than the interest rate and other holding costs, it would behoove individuals and firms to buy oil and store it, either above or below ground. Below ground storage costs are lower; simply buy someone's proven oil reserves.

One implication of this 'storage model' is that as the demand for oil increases relative to the supply, the price will increase both in nominal and in real terms at a pace that matches the nominal and the real interest rate. Thus the current price of oil already reflects the anticipated increase in the demand for oil relative to the supply. Anyone who believes that the price will increase more rapidly than the interest rate should be hoarding oil for sale at a future date.

For most of the last 100 years, the real price of petroleum has declined even though this 'storage model' suggests that the real price should have increased at a pace at least as high as the real interest rate. The less rapid increase in the real price reflects that the new discoveries have led to an unanticipated increase in supply. The term 'new supply' is comprehensive, and includes reduction in demand as a result of increased efficiency in the use of petroleum. More than 50 percent of the new cars in Europe are diesel-powered, which are 25 percent more fuel efficient than gasoline-powered vehicles. The US car fleet is likely to become increasingly diesel, hybrid, and electric.

If Malthus is right, then the oil price would increase at a rate not much higher than the real interest rate. If there is a surge in demand or a shortfall in supply because of a war, then the nominal and the real price of oil may rise sharply. Thereafter the price will return to the long-run trajectory suggested by the costs of storage.

OPEC and Malthus

OPEC – the Organization of Petroleum Exporting Countries – was established in the early 1960s by the governments of six countries, including several in the Middle East and Venezuela and Indonesia – to increase their revenues from the production of oil. OPEC is a trade union of the energy departments of 12 countries. The governments in these countries established national oil companies to take over the ownership and management of the production and sales of petroleum from the multinational firms including Exxon, BP, and Shell. Before OPEC the volume of oil production in each country was determined by the multinational firms that had obtained the rights from the host-country governments to search for oil in designated areas, often after submitting the winning bid in an auction that involved both an 'entry fee' that was paid to the national governments and a royalty based on the amount of oil produced. These firms had several advantages – they had access to the funds that would be invested in the search of oil and they had the experience and knowledge of how best to search for oil and how to market petroleum products.

The OPEC members have met frequently to discuss the amounts of oil that each member will produce in the effort to 'stabilize' prices. When demand has slackened and prices declined, each member has an interest in a reduction in global supply to forestall further price declines. But each also has interest in ensuring that the decline in production occurs in the other countries since none wants to limit its revenues.

The shift in the ownership of the oil fields in Venezuela, Indonesia, Iran, and other developing countries from privately owned multinational companies to government-owned firms has had three major impacts. OPEC has segmented the national markets in each OPEC member from the global market, where oil is traded freely; one price is that of Brent crude and another is that of West Texas intermediate. The price of petroleum in most of the oil-producing countries is lower than the world price, in large part because the governments are afraid that raising the domestic prices of gasoline and other petroleum products will erode their domestic political support. (The quip is that in some countries 'gasoline is cheaper than water.'). The low price means that consumption growth is not constrained as in the oil-importing countries. The second is that a significant share – often more than half – of the fiscal revenues of the governments in many of the oil-producing countries comes from the sale of oil; if the price declines, fiscal revenues decline. When the price declines sharply, these revenues plummet.

Moreover, the government-owned firms have been less interested in economic efficiency and in minimizing their costs than the privately owned firms would have been; they have relatively more employees than privately owned firms would have had, in part to build and maintain domestic political support.

The combination of below-market selling prices, the allocation of significant revenues to the government, and the lack of attention to economic efficiency means that the government-owned oil firms have less money to invest in discovery and exploration than privately owned multinational firms would have had. Moreover, the government-owned firms have not had access to the newest technologies for developing new oil fields and extracting larger amounts of oil from previously developed fields.

The governments in the OPEC members with relatively large populations are in a unique bind – they need more receipts from the sale of oil as their populations increase, which means they will have to increase production or raise taxes.

One indirect effect of the displacement of the multinationals by government-owned firms is that productive capacity in some of the OPEC countries has increased less rapidly than it would have done if production had been managed by one of the multinational oil firms such as BP or Total or Chevron. Because of OPEC-inspired limits on production, the price of oil in the global market has been higher than it otherwise would have been. The Law of Unintended Consequences has been at work – the higher prices that have followed from restrictions on production by OPEC members have led to less rapid growth in consumption and encouraged the development of alternative energy sources – OPEC has delayed the Malthusian crunch.

Globalization 100.0 and the real price of energy

The critics of the Neo-Malthusian viewpoint suggest that, as the demand for petroleum increases relative to the supply, the price will increase, which will encourage more efficient use of petroleum and stimulate the development of alternative energy sources. During the Second World War there was a sudden shortage of natural rubber, since one of the major sources in the Malaysian peninsula was occupied by enemy forces – and synthetic rubbers were developed that had attributes superior to those of natural rubber. The view of the critics is that long before the world's automobile fleet runs out of gas most of the cars will be powered by electricity produced from nuclear energy or coal or water power; petroleum will be used primarily as a lubricant and in aircraft and trucks because of its very high power to weight ratio.

Moreover, new technologies are being developed that will lead to a 'second life' for some of the older oil fields; some firms will be able to extract much more oil from these fields. The tar sands in Alberta and in Venezuela contain enormous amounts of oil which could be profitably brought to market if the world price of crude oil remained above $50 a barrel in 2008 prices.

The pace of annual increases in the real price of crude petroleum as the supplies become exhausted is likely to be gradual, much less than the annual increases that occurred with the spikes in the price of crude petroleum from the early 1970s. The national economies adjusted to these surges, although recessions followed, in part because the economic booms that occurred at the same time that the price increased sharply (and led to the increase in demand) soon were followed by more restrictive monetary policies to reduce the inflation rate.

As the real price of crude petroleum increases, the demand for energy will increase less rapidly, in part because higher prices will encourage investments that will lead to greater efficiencies in its consumption. Moreover, marginal oil fields will be brought back into production. The spike in the price of petroleum products in the 2005–8 period stimulated the surge in the demand for hybrid engines, which provide much higher gasoline mileage. Increasingly, most automobiles used for commuting and shopping and similar tasks near the residence of home owners will rely on electricity. And a larger share of electricity – although still a small share – will be produced from renewable sources, especially hydro, solar, and wind.

The masters of the OPEC cartel face a dilemma. The more they restrict production in the short run, the higher the price, and hence the less rapidly will demand increase and the larger the share of energy that will come from sources other than petroleum. In addition, a larger share of the petroleum will come from non-OPEC sources; OPEC's share of the world energy market eventually might decline, even though some of the OPEC members would remain among the low-cost suppliers.

At some stage the US Government and the governments in other oil-importing countries may conclude that a substantial part of the variability of their own economies has resulted from the instability in some of the oil-exporting countries. Iraq has been involved in three of the oil price spikes. Nigeria is riven by strife and banditry. Venezuela and Iran have strong antimarket biases. Russia has a strong anti-Western posture. Each of the surges in the oil price has been followed by a recession.

The governments in the oil-importing countries might adopt measures to ensure that prices remain sufficiently high to encourage continued conservation and to provide a profitable environment for producers of electricity from nuclear, coal, and renewable sources. They would only be able to adopt such a policy if measures are adopted to protect their domestic energy market from the global energy market, perhaps by an import tariff or an import quota or some combination of both. The rationale would be that their economies are better off with a high price of energy that is stable than with a price that is lower on average but much more variable. The OPEC countries might then find that they are the residual suppliers of energy to the global market. The larger the share of renewable sources on the supply side, the more distant the Malthusian day of reckoning.

How likely is it that the Malthusian scenario will evolve and that the oil price will increase to $300 a barrel or $500 a barrel in response to the increase in demand relative to supply? A massive political shock could again lead to a significant decline in production, and a sharp increase in price – but such shocks are largely orthogonal to the peak demand story. One group of those who subscribe to the peak demand view assert that production peaked in 2007 at 86 million barrels a day; a competing view is that supply will increase to 120 million barrels a day by 2030 – by about 2 percent a year. The slower the increase in supply, the more rapid the increase in price – but the price increases will be gradual in the absence of political shocks that sharply reduce supply.

Assume that oil production remains at 86 million barrels a year while world GDP grows at 3 percent a year. The inference from the storage model is that the price would increase by 3 or 4 percent a year in real terms; the increase in the real price would encourage both conservation and increased reliance on alternative sources of energy. The more rapid the increase in the real price, the greater the reward for conservation – which will dampen the growth in demand. Moreover, the more rapid the increase in the real price, the higher the rate of return on the production of energy from coal and natural gas and from nonfossil fuels.

Assume that the International Fair Trade Court (okay, this court does not yet exist) concludes that the OPEC cartel is anticompetitive and forbids the member countries from agreeing to limit production. Assume that some of the government-owned national oil companies are privatized, and that the newly privately managed firms seek to become viable competitors in the world market for energy. What would be different in this counterfactual or hypothetical world? The unambiguous result is that oil production would be larger, and the world price of energy would be lower.

The OPEC members face a dilemma. The combination of their inefficiencies in managing their reserves and their drain on profits diverts money from exploration and hence the current price of oil is higher. Further, their efforts to reduce output have the same impact on price. The higher current oil price leads to a less rapid growth in demand and encourages development of alternative energy sources – the extraction of oil from Alberta tar sands, sugar-based ethanol in Brazil, corn-based ethanol in Iowa and Illinois, cleaner coal, and greater reliance on nuclear energy for the production of electricity. Add wind-powered generators, and so on.

Eventually OPEC will become a residual supplier to the global market, even as it retains its low-cost advantage. The importing countries will protect their higher-cost domestic sources of supply because they are viewed as much more reliable. And in that scenario some of the OPEC members would find that they have substantial excess capacity. The likelihood of a Malthusian future is low.

18

The World Market for Bonds and Stocks

Consider two questions:

Q: How many stock markets are there in the world?

Q: Which countries have provided investors with the highest rates of return on stocks over an extended period?

The impacts of globalization

One way to answer these questions is to rely on anecdotes, and particularly the stories of the market participants. An alternative approach is to rely on economic intuition. A third is to scan the data. The answers to both questions are more ambiguous than they seem. Consider the answer to the second question at the end of 1989. Investors who owned Japanese shares had a much higher rate of return than investors who owned shares of firms headquartered in other industrial countries over the previous 10 years, the previous 20 years, and even the previous 30 years. The high rates of return on Japanese stocks reflected primarily the sharp increase in prices of stocks traded in Tokyo; Americans and other non-Japanese that owned these stocks had an even higher rate of return because the yen had appreciated by an average annual rate of 4–5 percent a year between 1970 and 1989.

The comparison of the rates of return on stocks and the bonds denominated in different currencies requires that the rates of return on the various national currencies be compared in terms of a *common currency* – which might be the US dollar, or the euro, or the Japanese yen. The need for a common currency benchmark leaves unsettled a major question – should the rates of return be compared after investors have hedged their exposure to risk of changes in currency values, or should they be compared on an unhedged basis – that is, after adjusting for changes in values of individual currencies? In the second case, the return to investors involves a change in currency values between the dates the foreign bonds or stocks are acquired and the dates these securities are sold.

The globalization theme suggests that the various stock exchanges in the world are little more than geographic extensions of an integrated world market for bonds and for stocks. One analogy is that there is a world market for gasoline, even though prices are not identical at the gas pumps in various countries. Differences in prices for a more or less identical product reflect transport costs, taxes, and the scope of competition in each local market. The analogy suggests that the world market for stocks is not very different from the world markets for photographic film or for automobiles, or for petroleum. The implication of the globalization theme is that the rates of return on stocks traded in each national market should not be significantly different once an adjustment is made for the differences in the risks of the securities traded.

The world markets for bond and stock – segmented or integrated?

One answer to the question of the number of stock markets in the world is to add up the stock exchanges in various countries – thus there are 10 or 12 stock exchanges in the United States, including the New York Stock Exchange, the Boston Stock Exchange, the Philadelphia Exchange, the Midwest Exchange in Chicago, and the Pacific Stock Exchange in San Francisco as well as smaller exchanges in cities in the mountain states. In Canada, stocks are traded on exchanges in Toronto, Montreal, Calgary, and Vancouver. Tokyo has its stock exchange, and so does Osaka. There are five stock exchanges in Germany. Each country has at least one stock exchange, and several large countries have more than one.

In addition, in virtually every country stocks are bought and sold in over-the-counter (OTC) transactions. Indeed, initially stocks were bought and sold in informal markets; then someone had the idea that trading would be facilitated if stocks were traded in an organized exchange with formal rules – when trading would start and end each day, the minimum size of the price movement like a penny or a half-quarter, the standard number of shares traded, and so forth. Firms would pay a small fee to have their shares listed on the exchange – but the belief was that this fee would be modest relative to the increase in the prices for the firms' shares.

That there are 10 or 12 stock exchange in the United States reflects the country's regional history – the smaller firms often were first listed on the stock exchange in the major city in each region. Firms headquartered in Northern California were listed on the San Francisco exchange, those headquartered in Southern California on the exchange in Los Angeles. Listing on the regional exchange was less costly than listing on the national exchange in New York. The reduction in the significance of regional stock exchanges partly reflects that as firms in individual industries have grown, they have consolidated and become national and multinational, the number of firms that were listed on the various regional exchanges declined, and several of these exchanges have merged while others have gone out of business. Moreover, since the managers always want their shares to trade at the highest possible prices, they may have the shares listed on other exchanges or even shift the exchange on which their shares are traded. (Their rationale is that the higher the price at which the shares trade, the easier it is for the firm to raise additional capital. Moreover, as share prices increase, existing shareholders experience capital gains and become richer.)

The significance of regional exchanges within a country can be evaluated by comparing the market value of the stocks listed on the various exchanges in each country. Investors could still trade national firms on the regional exchanges. The exchanges in Chicago and on the West Coast have one major advantage relative to the exchanges in New York – namely, that they are open later.

One world stock market?

The implication is that there is only one significant stock exchange in each country whenever more than 85 or 90 percent of stocks, as represented by market value, are traded on that exchange. The logical extension of this proposition that there is only one stock market in each country is that there is only one stock market in the world. The distinction is between the term 'stock exchange' and the term 'stock market': the stock market is more inclusive and includes the various countries. The rationale for the view that there is one global stock market is that a significant number of investors and large financial firms compare the anticipated returns on foreign bonds and foreign stocks with the anticipated returns on domestic bonds and stocks.

Investors in London have more or less the same knowledge and information as investors in New York, especially about the very large firms like British Petroleum and British Airways. Of course, not every London investor has the same information about the New York market; some investors prefer to buy stocks of the firms that are close to home. Many professional investors – the mutual funds, pension funds, and investment banks – cover the major stock exchanges in different countries in the search for bargains. If as few as 10 or 15 percent of the investors resident in a country compared foreign securities with domestic securities, the markets would be effectively integrated. Many of these firms and investors are resident in large countries including the United States, Britain, Germany, and Japan and seek to diversify the securities in their portfolios to reduce their risk. Some of these firms and investors resident in small countries – Switzerland, the Netherlands, Sweden, Saudi Arabia, Hong Kong, and Singapore – have 'outgrown' their countries and invest abroad because there are so few opportunities to diversify at home.

Obviously most investors do not compare the anticipated returns and risks on foreign securities with those on domestic securities. The key question is whether enough investors compare the risk and the return on foreign securities with those on domestic securities so the markets can be considered integrated. The answer varies, depending on currency pairs and the dates the comparison is made. For example, the US and the Canadian bond and stock markets have been integrated for an extended period. The Swiss and the German and the Dutch markets have similarly been integrated.

Segmentation or integration?

The question is whether the national markets are segmented or integrated, or – perhaps more appropriately – the extent to which the markets are integrated and the extent to which they are segmented. Just as firms headquartered in Illinois,

Texas, and California arranged to have their shares listed on the stock exchanges in New York, so firms headquartered in Britain, Germany, and Japan have had their shares listed on the New York Stock Exchange.

The argument that the national financial markets are segmented has two major components. The first is that most of the profits of most of the firms traded on the stock exchanges in each country are based on their domestic sales. The second is that most of the investors in most of the countries hold a very large share of their wealth in domestic securities, and a very small share in foreign stocks and bonds.

The debate has the characteristics of 'the glass is half full – the glass is half empty' conundrum. Moreover, the thrust of declines in the cost of communication and control is that the markets are becoming less segmented even if they are not yet fully integrated. And there are the asymmetries between markets in the large countries and markets in the small countries – changes in the prices of stocks and bonds in large countries are likely to have a larger impact on prices of stocks and bonds in small countries, whereas changes in these security prices in small countries are far less likely to have a significant impact on prices in large countries.

Consider now the nature of linkages among financial markets in different countries. Why do stock prices rise? One story is in terms of investor optimism about the future; the cliché that a 'rising tide lifts all ships' might be applied to the impacts of changes in US stock prices on stock prices in every other country, quite independent of underlying economic conditions. Or this cliché might be applied to the impact of buoyant economic conditions in the United States on economic conditions in Canada, Mexico, Japan, and the other countries that are large trading partners of the United States. Both stories might be relevant.

Anecdotes are helpful. In October 1987 stock prices declined precipitously in most industrial countries except Japan. The bubble in stock prices in Japan impacted the financial markets in Taipei and Seoul, but not the US and the European markets. The bubble in US stocks associated with the dot.com boom in the late 1990s was associated with significant impacts on foreign markets. Stock prices in the United States, Europe, and Japan declined sharply in the October 2008 panic.

A cousin to the question of whether the stock markets in the various countries and the bond markets in various countries are integrated is whether the stock and bond markets within each country are integrated. In effect, the question is whether the border between different types of financial instruments within a country are higher or lower than the borders between the same types of instruments across countries.

The cliché that a 'rising tide lifts all ships' can be applied to both stocks and bonds within a country. Periods of economic optimism are associated with increases in both bond and stock prices. As bond prices rise, interest rates decline (this is the same statement, not a statement about cause and effect) and some investors in search of higher returns buy stocks. A more scientific version of the relationship is that when interest rates decline, the anticipated returns associated with the cash flows of stocks are discounted at a lower interest rate, which means that stock prices increase.

Within a country, many investors specialize in buying bonds and others specialize in buying stocks. But there are a few investors who choose between stocks and bonds on the basis of the anticipated returns on each type of security.

In a world of perfect foresight, the rates of return on the bonds denominated in the different national currencies should be similar after adjusting for the realized changes in exchange rates. As long as the perfect-foresight assumption is made, then the interest rates on bonds denominated in the currencies of the countries with the higher inflation rates will be higher. And the difference in interest rates would reflect both the differences in inflation rates and the anticipated and realized changes in currency values.

Box 18.1   Investing the Lottery Prize in Bonds

Assume you won the lottery, with the caveat that you are to search for bargains among the bonds available in different countries and denominated in different currencies.

Assume that you have won the $10 million lottery prize and that you have decided to invest in long-term bonds, so it's a horse race between bonds denominated in the US dollar, bonds denominated in the Japanese yen, bonds denominated in the German mark, and bonds denominated in any of 10 or 15 other currencies. First note that the US bond market is much the largest in the world.

Consider interest rate relationship in the absence of international trade in bonds in a zero inflation world. Interest rates will be high in those countries identified with high rates of economic growth and high rates of investment relative to their savings rates.

Now relax the assumption that prohibits trade in bonds. Investors will move funds to buy bonds in those countries where interest rates are higher, with the result that interest rates will not differ significantly as long as inflation rates remain similar.

Now relax the assumption that inflation rates are similar. Interest rates will increase in those countries with the higher inflation rates, and their currencies will depreciate in the foreign exchange market.

The world of perfect-foresight assumptions is a useful benchmark. But the real world is characterized by frequent unanticipated shocks – oil shocks, inflation shocks, crop failures, financial bubbles, and banking crises. One basic proposition is that investors want to be compensated for holding risky securities or for holding securities denominated in currencies deemed riskier.

The intuition is that the rates of return on the bonds denominated in most foreign currencies will be higher than the rates of return on bonds denominated in the US dollar after the purchase of the foreign exchange on the date the race begins and the purchase of US dollars on the date the race ends. The story is that investors want to be compensated for incurring cross-border risks, especially the risk of changes in currency values.

Because the interest rates on securities denominated in the currencies of countries experiencing high rates of inflation are likely to be higher to compensate investors for the decline in the purchasing power due to the increase in the consumer price level, the comparison of the returns on bonds denominated in different currencies must necessarily occur only after adjustment for the realized changes in currency values.

The horse race is between the rate of return from holding US dollar bonds and the rate of return from holding bonds denominated in the foreign currency, after first having purchased the foreign currency in the foreign exchange market. The outcome of the horse race is sensitive to the date the race begins and the length of the race – the length of the holding period. There is a foreign exchange transaction at the beginning of the horse race, and one at the end. The outcome, incidentally, is not sensitive to whether your benchmark currency is the Japanese yen, or the euro, or the Swiss franc, since in each case you would begin by buying a foreign currency before buying the bond denominated in the foreign currency and then buying the initial currency at the end of the holding period. Note that to keep the experiment simple the interest income is reinvested in the foreign country. And similarly, to keep the experiment simple also assume that you buy the least risky government bond in each country.

Throughout the 1950s and 1960s the interest rates on bonds denominated in the Swiss franc were below those on securities denominated in the US dollar. Then, in the late 1970s, the interest rates on US dollar bonds increased above interest rates on bonds denominated in the German mark, the Dutch guilder, and the Japanese yen as these foreign currencies were appreciating. As long as these currencies were appreciating, the total return on these foreign bonds was generally higher than the return on US dollar bonds.

During short periods, say 5 years and less, there may be significant differences in the rates of return on bonds denominated in different currencies because of very large changes in currency values. The longer the period, the smaller the differences in the rates of return. Still, the differences remain, in part because investors believe that the bonds denominated in some currencies are riskier than bonds denominated in other currencies, in part – and only in part – because of changes in currency values.

The horse race in stocks

Again you've won the lottery, and this time the investment choice involves the market basket of the representative stocks available in the United States, Britain, Germany, Japan, and Switzerland. If you buy foreign stocks, you must first buy foreign currency, and then at the end of the horse race or holding period, the total value of your investment in foreign stocks must be sold in the currency market. You need to decide whether the comparison of the rates of return should be after currency exposure associated with owning foreign stocks has been hedged. (This question is more complicated than it might seem. Many British firms – British Petroleum, British Airlines, Shell, and Unilever – have large US dollar revenues and profits; indeed their US dollar revenues may be larger than their British pound revenues. An American that buys one of these stocks is acquiring part of a US dollar revenue stream that has been priced in the London Stock Market.)

In the late 1990s the market value of US stocks was greater than the combined market values of all other national stock markets. The ratio of market valuation of stocks to GDP in the United States is higher than in most foreign countries for four reasons – the corporate sector is a larger part of the economy, the US corporate sector is a large part of some foreign countries' economy because of the role of US multinationals, the earnings of US firms have been higher as a share of GDP, and stock prices have been higher in relation to earnings – the price/earnings (P/E) ratio of US firms is higher than the comparable ratios for firms in most other countries.

The return on stocks in each country is the sum of the dividend payments and the change in the price of the stock between the beginning and end of the period. The market valuation data are readily available but the dividend data are not available for the stocks in each country; for most countries, dividends appear small in relation to the price of stocks.

There have been many examples of sprinters in the horse race that faltered in the home stretch. In the 1980s, stock prices in Japan increased by a factor of six, while US stock prices were increasing by a factor of three. There was lots of chatter about the stellar performance of the Japanese economy, and the pace of research and development of Japanese firms, the high savings rate, and the concern of Japanese investors for the long run rather than quarterly changes in corporate earnings. By the early 1990s, it became clear that the sharp increase in Japanese stock prices in the late 1980s had been a 'bubble' – in 2008, Japanese stock prices were more or less where they had been in 1984.

The intuition is that the rate of return on the stocks in individual countries should reflect their rates of economic growth. Thus stocks of the firms headquartered in rapid-growth countries like Hong Kong and South Korea should have high rates of return because the earnings of these firms will grow as rapidly as their GDPs, and investors will pay higher prices for these stocks. A second element in the economic intuition is that since many investors consider stocks and bonds to be substitutes for each other, then the countries with high interest rates will tend to have low stock prices. However, the rate of growth of stock prices should tend to be high because the anticipated rate of growth of GDP, and hence corporate profits, should be high.

Consider Hong Kong, a phenomenal example of rapid growth. Hong Kong's per capita GDP is not much below per capita GDP in the United States. In 1960 and

1970, per capita GDP in Hong Kong was way below that in the United States. Moreover, Hong Kong's population has increased much more rapidly than the US population. So the GDP growth argument suggests that returns from holding Hong Kong stocks should have been considerably higher than the returns from holding US stocks.

There is a third story, which is that the return on the stocks available in a particular country will increase as foreign investors in their search for bargains become intrigued with these stocks and add these stocks to their portfolios.

The returns on US stocks generally were higher than the returns on the stocks available in most of the foreign countries. In the mid-1990s and in the late 1990s, year-to-year increases in US stock prices were exceptional – the American version of the events in Japan during the previous decade, although not anywhere near as extreme. But then US stock prices dived in 2001 – the decline between 2001 and 2003 was 40 percent. Stock prices declined again in 2008, and at the end of the year were not very significantly different from values 10 years earlier.

Because stock prices are much more variable than bond prices, the outcome of the race will be much more sensitive to the choice of the date when the race starts and when the race ends. Once again there were lots of explanations – there was a new US economy, investors had a long-term orientation and were far less concerned with short-term blips in corporate earnings, there were billions of new cash in retirement plans that had to go someplace, and the managers of firms were paying much greater attention to reducing costs and increasing profits.

These explanations may prove to be much more stolid than the explanations offered 10 years ago for the boom in Japanese stock prices. And then, again.

19

MBSs, ABSs, CMOs, CDOs, Zeros, Swaps, Options, and Credit Default Swaps – The Revolution in Finance

The new world of finance

One of the swear words attached to the financial crisis is 'derivatives' – a term applied to a wide array of new financial instruments often identified by their acronyms – asset-backed securities (ABSs), mortgage-backed securities (MBSs), collateralized mortgage obligations (CMOs), collateralized debt obligations (CDOs), private mortgage insurance (PMI), and credit default swaps (CDSs). These instruments are designed by financial engineers, who often have been trained as applied mathematicians; these 'quants' develop the features of these instruments and often have been involved in their pricing.

Those who attach responsibility for the crisis to these new instruments often start with the statement that 'There are $26 trillion of derivatives outstanding and no one knows where they are.' (If no one knows where they are, how could they be counted?) And the related charge is that these new instruments have allowed the investment banks and the commercial banks and the insurance companies to take on much more leverage.

One of the simplest financial instruments is an option, which is the right to buy (or sell) a particular asset before a specified date at a stipulated price. John Doe is interested in purchasing an office building that is offered for sale at $1 million; John pays $10,000 to the seller for the exclusive right to buy the property at that price within the next 30 days. The payment to the seller is the premium.

Orange County, California, one of the richest in the United States, sits on the Pacific coast, and abuts Los Angeles to the north and San Diego to the south. The county is one of the politically most conservative in the United States – strong voter sentiment for large military expenditures (an armada of retired naval officers lives there), a balanced budget, sending illegal immigrants home, limiting tax increases, and reducing the size of the government.

In December 1994 Orange County went bankrupt as a result of efforts by its chief financial officer to increase the rate of return on the county's portfolio by several sophisticated transactions. One was the use of leverage: borrowing short-term funds and using the borrowed monies to buy longer-term securities that carried higher interest rates (which meant that Orange County increased its interest income by the excess of interest rates on long-term securities over the interest rates on the borrowed short-term money funds). Another was the purchase of esoteric financial instruments that had been invented only a few years earlier.

The losses incurred by Orange County amounted to $1.6 billion. Since there are about 4 million people in the county, the losses per capita amounted to $400. Not small change. There may or may not be a relationship between the wealth of Orange County, its voting preferences, and the losses. A cynic might say that this was an expensive way for a conservative citadel to learn that 'there's no such thing as a free lunch.' It may take longer to learn this lesson in a rich county than in a poor one. In previous years, when interest rates on US dollar securities had been declining, Orange County had increased the return on its portfolio from the use of leverage. The decline in long-term interest rates meant that the prices of long-term bonds were rising, so Orange County benefited from both the capital gains and the excess of interest rates on long-term securities over the interest rates paid on the borrowed short-term funds. The year 1994 was not especially comfortable for investors, for interest rates increased quite rapidly – which meant that the prices of long-term bonds declined sharply, so much so that the capital losses from the decline in their prices was much greater than the excess of long-term over short-term interest rates.

It's probable that the additional returns that Orange County realized from this strategy in the 1993 and earlier years had been larger than the losses incurred in 1994. So the strategy had been profitable over an extended period. But the additional income from these earlier years had been spent, and wasn't available to forestall the move into a bankruptcy court.

Orange County had good company in taking a bath in the new world of finance. Gibson Greeting Cards incurred losses of $20 million on its purchases of some esoteric securities from Bankers Trust in New York; Gibson was not pleased by the loss and claimed it was led astray by the sophisticated Wall Street city slickers. Gibson filed a lawsuit claiming it was the victim; there was an out-of-court settlement. Procter & Gamble (some might say aptly named) was reported to have lost $120 million following the guidance of the same city slickers. Piper Jaffray of Minneapolis was one of the small city slickers and its investment managers lost millions of the hard-earned money of the widows and orphans of the Twin Cities in what was supposed to be a conservatively managed money market fund. Baring Brothers, one of the oldest investment banks in London, reported a loss of $1.4 billion as a result of transactions by a rogue trader in Singapore who had been dealing in option contracts; because of this large loss, the firm was forced out of business.

In August and September 1998 various hedge funds – supposedly the most sophisticated investors around – reported their recent investment results. Quantum Fund reported losses of $2 billion on its various Russian-related investments. Long Term Capital Management (LTCM) in Greenwich, Connecticut – the whiz kids of finance with the most sophisticated computer models around – reported that it had lost about $2 billion of the $4 billion that it had had under management during August 1998; the firm indicated that it was going to investors for additional funds and would reduce its management fees. Several weeks later the Federal Reserve arranged a $3 billion bailout by the lenders to LTCM to delay or forestall the liquidation of its highly leveraged positions. Nomura Securities, the largest investment bank in Japan, reported losses of more than $1 billion; a significant part of these losses were from activities in Russia and the emerging markets. Other investment banks and commercial banks with groups that mimic the trading activities of the hedge funds also reported large losses on their trading activities.

Securitization and the subprime mess

The practice of securitization first developed in the 1980s, but then it soared during the housing boom in the first decade of the twenty-first century. An investment bank would acquire one thousand home mortgages with somewhat similar attributes such as maturity. These mortgages would be placed in a trust, and the investment bank would issue shares that were claims on the trust; these shares would then be sold. The buyers of these shares in the mortgage-related securities wanted the higher interest income attached to mortgages; they also believed that these shares could be readily traded and hence were much more liquid than any of the mortgages that had been bundled. Moreover, owning the shares that were claims on the trust provided a low-cost way to diversify the credit or default risk attached to individual mortgages – it was inevitable that some borrowers would default, but exceedingly difficult to identify these borrowers. The likelihood that many of those that had obtained mortgage loans would default at more or less the same time was low.

The bubble in US residential real estate between 2001 and 2007 was facilitated by the development of ABS and a subgroup of MBS, otherwise known as CMOs. CMOs were sliced into four or five tranches differentiated by their riskiness and the tranches were repacked as collateralized debt obligations (CDOs) that were differentiated on the basis of whether they were the first claimant of interest income or the last claimant, after the claims of the other tranches had been satisfied. Then a diverse group of CDOs were acquired and provided the basis for issuing CDOs-squared.

Each of these CDOs was a free-standing legal entity; the bank or investment that created the security had made a trivially small capital investment in the 'institution.' The investment banks collected fees each time they packaged mortgages into CMOs; they collected more fees each time they sliced the CMOs to yield the CDOs, and they collected even more fees when they organized a fund to buy the CDOs.

An investment bank might develop its own in-house hedge fund to buy some of the CMOs and the CDOs that it had brought to the market. This fund would borrow a significant amount of money and buy the CMOs and the CDOs that the firm had brought to the market. Because of the leverage, the hedge fund was able to provide returns of 11–12 percent.

The credit rating agencies were involved in establishing the sensitivity of each of these securities to default. (The credit rating agencies are paid by the issuers of the securities.) One of the amazing bits of alchemy was that the blessing of a rating agency seemingly could convert the riskiest of the tranches into a low-risk security, which was easy to sell because the promised return was high while the perceived risk was low.

US home prices peaked at the end of 2006. Previously home owners that had been unable to make their monthly mortgage payments could sell their homes, and perhaps receive enough cash to repay their mortgage loan. When home prices began to decline, this option was no longer available, and hundreds of thousands began to default. Suddenly the market value of the CMOs and the CDOs that included these mortgages began to decline. At the same time, valuing these securities became much more difficult, since the prospect was that the foreclosure rate would increase.

Credit default swaps (CDS) were another new financial instrument. Think of insurance. Individuals that wanted to buy a home and lacked the traditional 20 percent of the purchase price as a down payment could buy Private Mortgage Insurance (PMI). They would pay a premium to an insurance company, which in effect would guarantee the lenders against loss if the borrowers defaulted. CDSs were the wholesale counterpart of PMI – a firm might buy some MBS that offered high interest rates, and then buy a CDS to protect itself against a loss. The sellers of the CDS were attracted by the premium income that they would receive from the buyers of the swaps.

When the housing bubble imploded, the investment banks incurred two different types of losses. They owned numerous mortgages that were in the packaging pipeline, and they had not hedged the credit risk attached to these mortgages. Moreover, they had retained the most risky tranches of the CDOs, either because they were attracted to the higher income, or because investors were not interested in these mortgages. The losses on their holdings of these mortgages were the major factor that accounted for the sharp decline in their capital.

What are hedge funds?

The losses incurred by the hedge funds were so large that the name seems a bit of a misnomer. These funds generally combine the capital of their owner-managers with those of various large and wealthy private and institutional investors who seek above-average returns; the hedge funds then borrow additional money, often in the ratio of $9 or $10 of borrowed funds for each $1 of their own and investor capital. The managers of the hedge funds then invest in a wide variety of different financial instruments, often with borrowed money. For example, if the hedge funds were to buy a commodity futures contract on the Chicago Mercantile Exchange, then they might be able to develop a $1 million position on the basis of a $50,000 cash investment. And $40,000 or $45,000 of this cash investment might have been borrowed; $10,000 or $5000 of this investment would reflect the capital of the fund obtained from the manager-owners and their investors.

The leverage of the funds – at least some of the funds – was large. Long Term Capital is reported to have had positions of $200 billion on its capital of $4 billion – leverage of 50 to 1.

The name 'hedge fund' comes from the idea that the risks attached to the different assets in their portfolios are somewhat offsetting – in effect, the funds have diversified portfolios. For example, a hedge fund might go long Italian Government bonds and short German Government bonds in the belief that in the move to the euro, the interest rates on these two bonds should converge: the interest rate on the Italian bonds would decline sharply and the interest rate on the German bonds would increase modestly. Often the funds would seek profits from very small price movements – still, the product of a small number (a very small price movement) and a large number (the size of their position in these securities) can be a large number. In some cases, however, these funds were attracted by the high yields available on the stocks and bonds available in the emerging-market countries.

A few hedge funds went broke prior to 1998. But many reported annual rates of return of 30 or 40 percent. So the owner-managers became very rich in a short period of time. And the high returns attracted many others who wanted a piece of the money machine. Obviously Bankers Trust, Piper Jaffray, and LTCM didn't set out to lose their clients' money – and, more importantly, their own. Indeed, they almost certainly anticipated that their clients would profit from these transactions, so that their own incomes and reputations would be enhanced.

Sophisticated financial instruments are rather like the automated luggage system of the new airports in Denver and Hong Kong – if it's very new and very large, it's a good bet that initially it won't work quite the promised way.

Where do financial revolutions come from?

The 1980s was most exceptional in terms of changes in financial arrangements, and particularly in the rapid increase in the number of new instruments – zero coupon bonds, futures contracts in foreign exchange, options on futures contracts in foreign exchange, collateralized mortgage obligations, foreign exchange swaps, interest rate swaps – the list goes on and on. The comprehensive buzzword was *derivatives* – the meaning was clear, the new set of instruments were derived from, or based on, traditional bonds, stocks, and foreign exchange.

One factor behind the explosion in the growth of financial instruments was the sharp changes in the prices of stocks, bonds, and currencies in response to the acceleration of inflation rates in the 1970s and then the decline in these rates throughout the 1980s as a result of the contractive monetary policy adopted at the end of 1979. The large changes in the prices of these assets meant that the risk attached to the ownership of these assets increased sharply. So banks and other financial institutions and individuals wanted the high rates of return attached to these securities, but also wanted some way to reduce their exposure to the risk of large loss should the price of the securities decline. The risk was inherent in the system as long as interest rates were changing sharply; if some investors were successful in reducing their exposure to these price risks, then either their exposures would be offset by the mirror-image exposures of another group of investors, or these risks would be transferred to others more willing to carry them. The second factor was the continuing decline in the costs of information, attributable to remarkable developments in communications and personal computers, which meant that the costs of evaluating these risks and trading them also declined sharply. The third was the surge in business-school graduate specialists in finance, who became skilled in relating the prices of these instruments to their risks.

Debt, stock prices, and junk bonds

Moreover, the financial environment was changing sharply. There was an explosion in the growth of debt in the 1980s; US Treasury securities outstanding increased from $800 billion at the end of 1979 to $2900 billion at the end of 1989. The debt of most national governments increased at comparable rates; the major exception was the British Government, which successfully reduced its debt, thanks in large part to receipts from privatizing a number of large government-owned firms such as British Airways and British Telecom. Household debt and corporate debt also increased rapidly in the United States, the increase in corporate debt resulting from the financing associated with massive leveraged buyouts. The privatization initiatives in many countries, and particularly in emerging-market countries like Mexico and Argentina, resulted in a sharp increase in the number of stocks that could be traded.

There was a surge in stock prices, led in part by the increases in New York and in Tokyo; the Dow Jones index of equity prices increased by a factor of three in the 1980s, while the counterpart Nikkei 225 increased by a factor of more than six. (It's only a coincidence that the percentage increase in the Dow more or less matched the percentage increase in the US Treasury's debt.) Because the decade was identified with declines in actual and anticipated inflation rates, the prices of bonds generally were increasing – although bond prices in the United States declined sharply in 1987. The price of commercial real estate in many large cities in the United States and abroad surged, which led to construction booms in London, New York, Tokyo, and Toronto; in some of these cities the supply of usable office space doubled. There was an explosive growth of 'junk bonds' – so called because they had not been rated by the credit-rating agencies that customarily ranked the riskiness of individual bond issues. The king of junk bonds was Michael Milken who both 'invented' and developed the market for trading them; his success in selling these bonds boosted his firm Drexel Burnham close to the front rank of investment banks. Milken claimed that the returns on these bonds were extremely high relative to the risk, and so the investors in these bonds would earn an 'excess return.' The end – and there always is an end – was that the junk bond market collapsed and the owners of these securities incurred large losses, which appear to have more than offset the higher interest rates they had earned in earlier years. Drexel went bankrupt and Milken was indicted by the US Government on various different charges and spent several years in jail.

Financial engineering

'Financial engineering' was one of the buzzwords of the 1990s. The firms in the financial services industry – the brokerage firms, the investment banks, the banks, even the life insurance companies – make a lot of money when they have new products to sell. Initially the profit rates for those that first developed the new products were high, before the followers and imitators entered the market to increase market share by driving down returns. Milken became a billionaire as a result of his success with junk bonds.

One of the terms under the financial engineering banner was 'securitization,' which involved a bank or some other firm taking a large number of somewhat similar types of securities – home mortgages, car loans, student loans, credit-card debt – and bundling them, which then became the basis for issuing a new security which might be attractive to particular investors because of somewhat higher anticipated rate of return. A pension fund might be interested in acquiring credit-card debt or car loans because the interest rates would be higher than on traditional securities; the pension fund would not have the facilities to manage the monthly collection of interest on these loans. So the bank that initially made the student loans or the auto loans would become an originator and a bundler, and it would invest its own monies as it arranged these loans into bundles that would be attractive to institutions that were willing to hold these securities for the long term. Even after the bundles were sold, the bank might continue to service the loans – it would collect the monthly interest payments and forward the money to the pension funds. Securitization was made possible by the sharp reductions in the costs of collecting and organizing information and data. As a result, relatively more money would flow into housing loans, auto loans, and other types of loans that could be easily packaged.

The mirror of bundling numerous $10,000 and $20,000 loans into a large loan was that a traditional security such as a $100,000 US Treasury bond could be unbundled into a number of different securities. The traditional long-term bond issued by the US Treasury pays interest twice a year; the owner of the bond would be repaid the principal in 30 years. The security has 60 coupons; each coupon is like a dated check from the US Treasury, and provides for the payment of interest on a stipulated date, for example January 15 and July 15 during each of the next 30 years. The investors would frequently put their bonds in a safe deposit box at a bank and then visit the bank every 6 months to clip the interest coupon that represented the interest payment that was currently due; this coupon would then be deposited in the bank as if it were a check from the US Treasury.

Investment banks such as Goldman Sachs and Merrill Lynch would buy these bonds and then 'strip them' – they would sell each of the interest payment coupons as a separate security. Similarly, the 'corpus' of the bond – the body that stipulates the terms for the repayment of the principal – would also be sold as a separate security. So the 30-year bond would become 61 different securities – the first interest coupon, the second interest coupon, the third interest coupon, all the way to the 60th interest coupon; the corpus of the bond would be the 61st security. Each of these securities would be sold separately, although individual investors might buy several of them. The investment banks anticipated that the total revenues from selling the 61 separate securities (zeros) would be higher than the revenues from selling the bond with the attached coupons – and higher than the price they paid when they bought the bonds; otherwise why go through the activity of stripping the coupons?

The income to the investors that bought the zeros came from the difference between the low initial price they paid for them and the face value of the zero on the date that each interest coupon could be deposited.

Investors were attracted to zero coupon securities for one of several different reasons. Zeros provide an easy way to match the date when a payment will be made with a particular security. For example, a grandparent of a newly born child might buy a zero that would mature in 18 years, when the child might be expected to enter college. Or a couple in the 50-year-old age cohort might buy a coupon that would mature in 20 years, soon after the date of their planned retirement. Moreover, zeros were convenient; there was no need to go to the safe deposit vault to clip the interest coupon because the effective interest rate was built in to the general increase in the price of the bond on its journey to maturity. In addition, zeros provide a marvelous way for the investor to implicitly reinvest the interest income, which was especially attractive in a period when interest rates were high and expected to decline. Finally, for a while, the income attached to ownership of a zero was treated as a capital gain, and hence the tax payment would be delayed until the security was sold; subsequently, the Internal Revenue Service ruled that each year's capital gain would be taxable even if the gain had not been realized.

Various corporations realized they could issue zero coupon bonds at somewhat lower interest rates than traditional bonds; zeros provided an easy way to raise funds without an immediate cash outlay. When the bonds matured, someone else would have to worry about the source of the cash to pay the bondholders. Caveat emptor.

Index funds

One of the perennial questions is whether 'stock pickers' can beat the market – whether over an extended period individuals and firms can choose a portfolio of stocks that will have a higher rate of return than 'the market.' Much of the finance industry is based on the view that there is a positive rate of return to picking stocks – thousands of analysts earn their living from seeking to outperform the market, and a few earn a very good living. The cynics would say that their high incomes reflect that they have generated plenty of commission income for their firms and that the number of yachts owned by the clients of these firms should be compared with the number of yachts owned by the managers of the firms.

Some of the studies show that 50 percent or so of the mutual funds fail to achieve the average rate of return on the market as a whole. As a result of the combination of the skepticism about the skills of stock pickers and the low cost of computation, a new section of the financial services industry has developed that enables individuals to buy 'a share of the market.' These index funds mimic the market, they choose the stocks to buy based on the ratio of the market value of an individual firm like Exxon or General Electric (GE) to the market value of all stocks as a group. A big advantage of the index-fund approach is that transactions costs are much lower than those for the average mutual fund, in part because there is relatively little trading compared with the run-of-the-mill mutual fund. Research and administrative costs also are lower.

The index-fund approach has been extended to different segments of the market. For example, a mutual fund might take the index approach to the 30 stocks included in the Dow Jones or the 100 largest firms or to the firms in a particular industry on a national or a global basis.

Swaps

Foreign currency swaps and interest rate swaps also were among the major new financial instruments developed in the 1980s. Consider first a foreign currency swap.

Assume Lufthansa has bought a Boeing 747, with the part of the purchase price financed by the US Export-Import Bank (ExImbank); the loan terms entail semi-annual payments of principal and interest for the next 8 years. So Lufthansa may conclude that it has a foreign exchange exposure in the US dollar. And the airline may take the view that it is in the business of moving individuals in slender aluminum tubes rather than in speculating in foreign exchange and so it may seek to reduce its foreign exchange exposure.

At the same time a number of US airlines have bought jets from the European consortium, Airbus; part of the purchase price was financed by borrowing from government-owned export credit agencies in Germany and in France – their counterparts of the US Export-Import Bank. The payment terms are likely to be similar, with the difference that the US airlines have to make semiannual payments in the euro. These US airlines almost certainly wish to hedge their foreign exchange exposures.

The foreign exchange swap enables Lufthansa and the US airlines to offset their foreign currency exposures. Lufthansa enters into a foreign exchange swap with Deutsche Bank, or J.P. Morgan, or another of the top 30 commercial banks; Lufthansa is guaranteed the exchange rates at which the bank will convert the euro into US dollar for each of the two yearly payment dates over the next 8 years. United Airlines enters into a mirror-image swap with the same bank; the bank guarantees the exchange rate at which United can obtain the euro for dollars on the two annual payment dates for each of the next 8 years. So each firm hedges its foreign exchange exposure with the bank, and the bank enters into two swaps that have mirror-image features. Provided the bank has done its homework correctly, the bank has incurred no foreign exchange exposure.

Swaps tend to have somewhat standard features. Payments tend to be twice a year. Maturities tend to be 8 years. The swaps are quoted in nominal values, but the principal amounts are never swapped – only the effective interest payments. The banks as middlemen love the income that is the difference between the prices at which they buy and sell the payments in different currencies. The banks acquire two risks – there is the credit risk that one of the parties to the swap may go bankrupt and not be able to deliver the foreign exchange. (There is an asymmetry, in that the bankrupt firm may fulfill the swap if the swap is 'in the money' because the currency that it has agreed to purchase has risen in price above the price implicit in the swap contract.) And because of the inability of the firm to complete the contract, the bank may have a foreign exchange exposure.

Interest rate swaps share the same feature – the parties to the swap contract to exchange a set of future payments. Consider a typical saving and loan (S&L) association in the United States, which holds a number of fixed-interest rate 20- and 30-year mortgages; the interest rates on these mortgages cannot be changed during the life of the contract. In contrast, the interest rates on the deposit liabilities of these S&Ls change frequently. So the S&L has an interest-rate risk; this S&L would enter into a swap contract to pay a fixed interest rate and to receive a floating interest rate as a way to reduce its exposure to interest-rate risk. The success of the S&L depends on the success of the banks as middlemen in finding a firm that would like to receive a floating interest rate and pay a fixed interest rate – the mirror-image of the payments and receipts of the S&L.

Some long-term lenders such as the World Bank are in this position. So each of these firms enters into a swap with a bank as a middleman. Both the foreign exchange swaps and the interest-rate swaps tend to reduce the risk of the participating firms.

Derivatives and options

One of the new products that had been developed extensively is the *option*; option contracts are readily available on bonds, stocks, and futures contracts in foreign exchange. Consider an option that John Doe buys when he is interested in buying a large house at the corner of Fifth Avenue and Main Street; the price of $300,000 is agreeable but he needs several weeks to tie up some loose ends before he fully commits to the purchase. So he pays the owner of the property $2500 for a 30-day option to buy the house at the $300,000 price. This option contract has three features – a money payment (the premium) from the buyer of the option to the seller (or writer) of the option, an expiration date (30 days), and the price that the owner of the option will pay the owner of the property if the option is exercised (the strike price).

Call options on foreign exchange are one example of these new instruments. Assume that ABC Manufacturing believes that the euro is going to appreciate. ABC can buy the euro in the spot exchange market or it can buy the euro in the forward exchange market; if, instead, the euro should depreciate, then ABC will lose money. So ABC buys a call option on the euro. ABC pays First National Bank a premium of $300 for the right to buy 50,000 euros within 3 months at the price of US $1.25 per euro. In this case, if the euro should depreciate, then ABC loses only the premium paid for the option. If, instead, the euro appreciates above the strike price, then ABC exercises the option and receives the euros at the strike price.

The seller of the call option often owns the euro and is motivated by the premium received from ABC. Or the seller of the call option might believe that the euro will depreciate, so there is little likelihood that it will be obliged to deliver the euro: the seller again is motivated by the premium income. (In the former case, the seller is writing a 'covered option' and in the second, the seller is writing a 'naked option.')

Assume, instead, that ABC owns securities denominated in the euro and is concerned that the euro might depreciate. To limit its losses, ABC could buy a put option on the euro. ABC pays a premium to the seller of the put option; if the euro should depreciate, then ABC delivers the euro to the seller of the put option at the strike price so its loss from the depreciation of the euro is limited. The seller of the put option is motivated by the premium income. In some cases, the seller of the put option may have a short position in the euro; in this case, the seller is hedged because the gain from the decline in the value of its short position will offset the loss from taking delivery of the euro. In other cases, the seller may believe that the euro is unlikely to depreciate, and so the seller writes a 'naked option.'

Call options and put options on the euro are available with different maturity dates and different strike prices. At times, the strike price may be below the market price of the option, and so the option is said to be 'in the money.' But there is no immediate profit, because the difference between the strike price and the market price is smaller than the premium charged for the option. If the strike price differs significantly from the market price, the option is 'out of the money.' The more distant the maturity date, the larger the premium for a given strike price.

Options are available on a large number of currencies, government bonds, the shares of individual firms, the shares of a portfolio of firms, Treasury bills, Eurodollar deposits, gold, silver, and a variety of other commodities. Banks and other firms trade options because they provide a substantial and additional source of income. Individual firms and investors like options because they provide a way to shuffle risks – especially the risks of large changes in the prices of securities and commodities – on to others who are more willing to carry these risks – for a price. Competition among the firms that sell options is expected to keep these prices reasonably low. Investors can also buy options based on the market as a whole; if the option is exercised, then the investor receives a share in an index fund that owns a portfolio of stocks.

'The collapsing house of cards?'

One of the observations about hedge funds in the 1990s was that as a group they were reporting phenomenally high returns. Since the 'no free lunch' cliché applies to financial markets, the general inference was that these funds must be taking exceptional risks. The exceptional returns to the owners of the funds and their investors reflected the large leverage of the funds. Every time a new financial instrument is developed there is concern that the system is becoming riskier, and the metaphor of the 'collapsing house of cards' is again brought out of the closet; earlier the metaphor of the 'inverted pyramid' had been applied to the Eurodollar market. The fear was that one or two of the cards at the bottom of the pyramid would buckle, and the cards above them would tumble even though these cards had individually been well positioned.

One aspect of the answer depends on whether the risks that are inherent in a market system are being concentrated in a smaller number of firms and individuals and whether the risk in the portfolios of these firms and individuals is increasing or decreasing. Innovations allow individuals and firms to reduce their risks, often by allowing them to hedge their exposure to risk at much lower cost. Yet financial innovations also enable some firms and individuals to acquire more risk, particularly by writing naked options for premium income. If the changes in the prices of the underlying securities differ sharply from the anticipated price changes, then they will incur large losses, and some (or even many) may go bankrupt. One of three largest Swiss banks, the Union Bank of Switzerland, is said to have lost more than $1 billion from mispricing options and as a result of the erosion of its capital position was forced to seek a merger with another of the large Swiss banks.

If a large market participant incurs losses and becomes bankrupt, then losses will be incurred by the firms and individuals on the other side of its contracts. It is possible that some of these firms and individuals might be forced into bankruptcy because the contracts are not fulfilled. The more likely case, however, is that the counterparties will be able to absorb the losses. For years hedge funds earned exceptional returns because they were earning the risk premium inherent in the higher yields on riskier assets. As the funds prospered, they increased in size and number, and so they had to take on larger positions in particular trades. One analogy is provided by the market in junk bonds: for years, investors in junk bonds earned exceptional returns because few of the firms that issued these bonds tanked. Yet during the recession a large number of the firms that had issued these bonds failed, and the owners of junk bonds incurred losses that were substantial relative to the high levels of interest income in the earlier fat years. Milken's fortune remained largely intact.

Another analogy is provided by the firms that sell insurance against losses due to floods. Floods tend to be infrequent in many areas, so that for many years – indeed, until the floods occur – the premium income of these funds will be very large relative to the money paid out in the settlement of claims to those who incurred losses as a result of the floods. When the floods occur, however, watch out.

When the funds are profitable, their capital tends to increase; since they are highly leveraged, their purchases tend to raise asset prices. Moreover, there is something of a herd instinct in their behavior, so they may purchase the same or similar securities at the same time. When the funds incur losses on particular contracts, they may be subject to margin calls, and they may either then have to sell part or all of their positions, or else provide their counterpart with additional capital. The usual response to a margin call is to sell the most liquid assets or positions first, as a way to minimize the adverse price movement associated with these sales. If the capital of the large hedge funds should shrink because of adverse price movements and they sell assets to raise cash, the probability is high that they will sell their most liquid assets – which will cause the prices of these assets to decline.

There is a fundamental proposition in finance that, in the long run, the rate of return on securities cannot exceed the rate of return on real assets. The rate of return on financial assets is the sum of the dividends, capital gains, and interest that investors earn on their holdings of stocks and bonds and deposits and other financial instruments, and through their ownership of shares in mutual funds and pension funds relative to the value of their investments at the beginning of the year. The rate of return on real assets can be viewed as the profits and interest payments of firms relative to their productive assets. The logic behind the statement is that the cash secured by investors as dividends, realized capital gains, and interest must come from someplace; those who pay out this cash must earn the money from profitable investments. So the real rate of return is based on the underlying productivity of the economy, and can be viewed as the rate of growth of national income – actually, the rate of growth of national income adjusted for the increase in the labor force.

A large part of the income to investors in particular years comes from capital gains – the increase in the price of stocks and bonds and real property. The general basis for these gains is that the buyers of these stocks and bonds and real property seek either the future cash income attached to these assets, or the gains to be made from selling these assets to someone else who seeks the cash income from the future gains. In some cases, firms provide cash to the stockholders by buying back shares, either as a substitute for dividends (the capital gains are taxable at a lower rate) or as a complement to dividends. In the end, the investors want cash or paper that can be readily converted to cash.

Our fundamental proposition seems inconsistent with the data for the 1980s and the 1990s – at least, the data for most countries – for the rates of return on stocks and bonds and real property appear to have averaged 15 or 20 percent or more, while the real rates of growth were in range of 3–6 percent. Part of this discrepancy is that the rates of return on stocks and bonds and real property are in monetary terms while the rates of return on the real assets include an adjustment for inflation; comparability suggests that the rates of return on stocks and bonds and real property be adjusted downward by the inflation rate – or, alternatively, that the rate of return on real assets be adjusted upward by this rate.

Even after this adjustment, however, the rates of return on stocks and bonds and real property would be significantly higher than the rate of economic growth.

Part – perhaps a substantial part – of this discrepancy can be explained by the fact that in the inflationary 1970s the rates of return on stocks and bonds (but not on real property) were substantially below the real rates of economic growth, as a result of the decline in the prices of these assets. So the high rates of return on stocks and bonds in the 1980s and the 1990s partially reflects a form of 'catching up.'

It's possible that the high rates of return on stocks in the United States and some other countries reflect 'irrational exuberance' and that investors were buying stocks because they expected that stock prices would continue to increase at 20 percent a year forever. This approach to investing in stocks was evident in Japan in the late 1980s; for the 1990s as a whole, the rate on stock prices and real property has been negative while the real rates of return have been modestly positive.

The financial services industry blossomed in the 1980s and the 1990s because high rates of return on stocks and bonds and real property led to buoyant trading activity. The incomes of these firms surged as a result of the combination of commissions associated with their brokerage function, their own trading profits, and the capital gains associated with owning inventories of stocks and bonds in an environment of rising asset prices. Investors have been willing – perhaps reluctantly willing – to share some of their gains with investment banks, brokerage firms, and hedge funds. During this extended period of rising asset prices, hedge funds have had exceptional returns because the prices of risky assets have increased relative to the price of less risky assets and the capital structure of these funds and their high leverage suggests that they will have more long than short positions.

When the period of secular increases in the rate of return on securities relative to the return on real assets ends – and it's a safe bet that it will end – the returns to the firms in the financial services industry will decline, and perhaps sharply. In this new environment asset prices will decline more often, even though on average the prices of stocks and real property may increase more frequently than they decline. It will then be fun to develop a scorecard on the hedge funds to determine whether they have earned exceptional returns, or whether instead their great success in the 1980s and the 1990s reflected simply the combination of high leverage and a rising asset-price environment.

20
Why Are Multinational Firms Mostly American?

A note to the reader: The title of this chapter, taken from the first edition, may seem dated in view of the rapid pace of acquisitions of American enterprises by firms headquartered in various foreign countries – especially in Japan and to a lesser extent in Britain. Sony acquired Columbia Records and then Columbia Pictures. Matsushita bought MCA-Universal, another of Hollywood's major studios. Bridgestone Tire acquired Firestone Tire. These were the types of transactions that made the front pages of the major newspapers. In the latter part of the 1980s, there were usually more than a thousand of these acquisitions each year; and 30–40 percent of the acquisitions were by firms headquartered in Japan. US firms were continuing to expand their foreign investments, but the rate of growth of these investments was swamped by the investments of foreign firms in the United States. One striking feature was that a very large part of these new foreign investments in the United States involved the acquisition of established US firms; when US firms have gone abroad, in contrast, they often have built new factories on 'greenfields.'

So it may seem strange keeping the chapter title from the first edition. Read on. In the late 1960s one of Europe's best selling books was *Le Défi Américain* – the American Challenge. The author was Jean-Jacques Servan-Schreiber (JJ-SS), publisher of *L'Express* (the French imitation of *Time*), *L'Expansion* (the French version of *Fortune*), and for a while the French counterpart of the *Harvard Business Review*. Servan-Schreiber was energetic, if not original. By 1981, *Le Défi Américain* was obsolete; JJ-SS came forth with *Le Defi Mondial*, next, *Le Défi Intergalatic*.

The central thesis of *Le Défi Américain* was dramatic. After the United States and the Soviet Union, the third economic power in the world was US business firms in Europe. As evidence, JJ-SS cited the increasingly important position of the subsidiaries of US firms in European industry, especially in such technologically advanced fields as computers and electronics.

The striking feature of these US firms was that they then were far ahead of their British, French, and German competitors in integrating their production and marketing across European borders. International Harvester's (now Navistar) French plant produced transmissions for tractors, while its German plant produced the engines; each of these plants exported its product to the other.

IBM-Europe produced its computers using components made in various plants across the Continent; indeed, its production line in Europe was seven countries long.

Servan-Schreiber advocated numerous changes to help Europe meet the US challenge. European business should become more like American business – more graduate business schools like Harvard, more professional managements like that of Exxon, greater decentralization of corporate decision-making as at ITT, and more expenditures on R&D as at IBM.

One of the not-so-best selling books in London in 1902 was *The American Invaders*, by F. A. McKenzie, a Scot worried by the American threat to British industry. Americans, he wrote, were 'succeeding in Europe because of advantages in education, their willingness to accept new ideas, and their freedom from hampering tradition.' In part, the supremacy of US firms was reflected in US exports, in part by the growth of the European subsidiaries of US firms. McKenzie noted the dominance of US firms in the new industries: 'applications of electricity to traction, the typewriter, the automobile, and the machine tool.'

Servan-Schreiber never acknowledged McKenzie or *The American Invaders*. If he had, he would have had to explain why 65 years and two world wars after 1902, US firms owned only 5 percent of corporate assets in Europe and accounted for 10 percent of European imports. And he would also have had to explain why the ratio of US foreign investment to US GDP in the early 1970s was significantly below the ratio in 1913.

McKenzie was somewhat premature in predicting American dominance of European industry. So was Servan-Schreiber. While a few US firms had set up branches in Europe as early as 1850 and direct foreign investment (DFI) increased at the end of the nineteenth century, direct US foreign investment was modest until the 1920s, and largely confined to firms engaged in mining and producing crude petroleum; these firms had integrated 'upstream' to source for the US market. In the 1920s US investment in manufacturing abroad jumped sharply, and especially in Europe. From the 1930s through most of the 1950s, foreign investments were modest because of the Great Depression and the Second World War; indeed, in the 1930s many US firms sold the European subsidiaries that they had acquired in the previous decade. But beginning in the late 1950s, direct US foreign investment soared; US firms purchased many foreign firms and set up their new plants abroad.

Direct foreign investment

By 1970 a substantial part of total manufacturing in Canada was foreign-owned, especially by US firms; indeed, in some Canadian industries more than three-quarters of the local plants were foreign-owned. US firms in the 'new' industries continue to invest abroad extensively, much as they did in McKenzie's day; the major difference is that the new industries were pharmaceuticals and computers rather than the application of electricity to traction. But US firms are well established abroad in traditional industries, such as hotel-keeping and food processing, automobiles, soaps, and toothpaste. The numbers of Hilton Hotels and Holiday

Inns and McDonald's and Wendy's outside the United States are growing rapidly. (Holiday Inn is now owned by a British firm.)

Altogether, DFI for firms headquartered in all countries totaled about $75 billion in 1960, of which slightly more than half was undertaken by US firms and 10 percent by British firms. Forty percent of US foreign investment was in manufacturing, 10 percent in petroleum, and nearly 10 percent in mining. Foreign investments by German and Japanese firms were small until the late 1980s, when they began to increase rapidly (one cost of being on the losing side in a war is that the foreign subsidiaries of domestic firms almost always are expropriated – and that was expensive for shareholders of German firms). From 1973 to 1978 the value of US direct investments abroad increased by two-thirds; during the same period, foreign investments in United States doubled. US direct foreign investment continued to grow in the 1980s at about the same rate as in the 1970s; in contrast, foreign investment in the United States surged, and especially in the second half of the decade. Much of the investment in the United States was undertaken by firms headquartered in Japan and Britain and, to a lesser extent, in Germany, Switzerland, and the Netherlands.

Firms based in a small number of countries – the United States, Britain, the Netherlands, Switzerland, Sweden, and Japan – account for most of the DFI. Foreign investment is extensive in some industries (aluminum, petroleum) and minimal in others (textiles). Dutch firms (Unilever, Shell, and Phillips) are large investors abroad, while Belgian firms are not. Swedish firms are big foreign investors, while Danish and Norwegian firms are not.

In the late 1970s foreign firms began to increase their investments in the United States at a rapid rate: they were prepared to compete in the US firms' backyards. British Petroleum acquired Sinclair Oil and then began to buy Standard of Ohio and eventually acquired Amoco. Imperial Chemicals, the leading British chemical firm, acquired Atlas Chemical, which then ranked about 20th in the United States in sales; BASF (a German chemical company) acquired Wyandotte Chemical. The chemical industry is truly international, in that a very large share of the investment of US firms is in foreign countries; similarly a very large share of the investment of European firms is in other countries. (Curiously, the foreign investments of Japanese firms in the chemical industry are relatively small compared with the foreign investments by Japanese firms in other industries.) Panasonic, one of the top three Japanese electronics firms, bought the Quasar Division of Motorola while Sony bought Warwick Electronics. A subsidiary of Nestle, a Swiss firm, successfully bid for Libby, McNeill & Libby, a Chicago-based food processor. Grand Union, one of the largest food retailers in the United States, was acquired by a French–British firm. The Imperial Group in London bought Howard Johnson's – and then sold it. Volkswagen set up an assembly plant in Pennsylvania to turn out 200,000 cars a year. Toyota, Nissan, Honda, Mitsubishi, and Mazda established plants to produce autos in the United States. Three of the major drug suppliers in the United States – Ciba-Geigy, Hoffmann-La Roche, and Sandoz – are Swiss. Petrofina, the Belgian petroleum firm, is beginning to refine and distribute in the United States. The European penetration of the US market has gone so far that the Good Humor Company is part of the Liverpool-based Thomas Lipton tea empire.

DFIs in the United States now are larger than US direct foreign investments, despite the head start that US firms developed between 1920 and 1980. US foreign investment surged in the late 1950s and the 1960s in response to market forces, and especially to the anticipation of more rapid growth in Europe because of the bounce-back after the Second World War and because of the optimistic expectations associated with the development of the Common Market. Many US firms were sometimes viewed as playing 'follow-the-leader' in their industries; if this observation is correct, then the motivation for the foreign investment by the 'leader' would have to be explained. The 'follow-the-leader' strategy is likely to be expensive if the market opportunities are inappropriate.

Then in the late 1960s the growing overvaluation of the US dollar induced US firms to invest more abroad to source for their export markets; initially, these firms had supplied foreign markets from US plants. But as US costs increased the US plants lost their competitive edge – in the US as well as in the foreign market – and firms needed to produce abroad to protect their market share. Then some US firms began to invest abroad to protect their market share in the US market because production costs in the United States were increasing rapidly; thus US electronics firms set up manufacturing and assembly plants in the Far East to protect their position in the US market from the competitive thrust of Japanese firms.

The depreciation of the US dollar relative to European currencies and the Japanese yen in the 1970s reduced the incentive for US firms to invest abroad. German and Japanese firms then began to invest more extensively in the United States; Volkswagen, which had previously supplied the US market by exporting from Germany, decided to establish a US assembly line. Just as US firms had increased their foreign investment as the US dollar became overvalued, so German, Japanese, and other foreign firms increased their US investments as the US dollar became increasingly undervalued. Foreign investment in the United States began to grow three times as rapidly as US investment abroad. The foreigners were coming.

The new imperialism

The relation between foreign investments and the national interests of host countries and of source countries came under critical attack as nationalist pressures increased. By the late 1960s, when Servan-Schreiber's book was published, ownership of domestic factories and resources by foreign firms – especially by US firms – had become a sensitive political issue in many countries. Was Canada worse off because such a large part of manufacturing facilities in Canada were owned by US firms? Many Canadians, including a nontrivial number of Canadian economists, thought so. Canadian and other host countries feared that the activities of the giant multinational firms, especially those based in the United States, were a new form of imperialism, more insidious than the gunboats of the late nineteenth century. Nationalists in many countries – primarily in developing countries, but also in France and Canada – complained about a loss of sovereignty to the large international companies. Nationalist pressures were especially directed against firms engaged in extracting resources in developing countries. Peru expropriated International Petroleum, the local subsidiary of Exxon and also some of the local properties of W. R. Grace. Bolivia took over the local operations of Gulf Oil. In Chile, the Christian Democratic Government of Eduardo Frei purchased 50 percent of Anaconda Mines; subsequently, the Marxist Government of Salvador Allende nationalized the rest of Anaconda as well as the mines of most other foreign companies. Mexico and many other developing countries restricted foreign ownership to participation in joint ventures with Mexican partners. Hugo Chavez in Venezuela has been complicating life for the foreign multinationals and especially those headquartered in the United States.

From time to time the countries in which firms that have been investing abroad are headquartered are also concerned about foreign investment, especially about its possibly harmful effects on the balance of payments, on unemployment, and on tax revenues. The labor unions in the United States – and many of their friends in the US Congress – believed that Mexican entry into the North Atlantic Free Trade Agreement (NAFTA) would mean that US firms would increase their investments in Mexico, both to source for the Mexican market and to source for the US market.

Patterns of market penetration

What needs to be explained is why the pattern of DFI changed so sharply, beginning in the late 1970s but especially the latter half of the 1980s. In 1988 or 1989, Servan-Schreiber might have written *Le Défi Japonais* – or maybe *Le Défi Chinois*. However, the Japanese threat evaporated, because foreign investments of Japanese firms in the 1990s declined almost abruptly as they had surged. In the mid-1990s the foreign investors of a handful of firms headquartered in South Korea surged in response to market forces rather than in response to a plan.

Why a firm acquires productive facilities in one or several foreign countries cannot be answered without first considering its unique qualities. A firm consists of a set of individuals engaged in production and in marketing; their diverse activities are coordinated by central management. The managers buy certain inputs to produce a variety of outputs. Most of the productive activities within the firm could be purchased, in modular fashion, from other firms. The managers might hire one company to develop new products, a second to produce them, and a third to market them. The choice of whether to conduct an activity within the firm or to acquire the product of the same activity 'in the market' is usually made on the basis of cost; competition forces the firm to choose the low-cost alternative. Some magazines – for example, *Playboy* and *Penthouse* – are primarily cut-and-paste jobs; a small editorial staff buys most of the stories and photos from freelancers. *Time* and *Newsweek*, in contrast, once maintained much larger staffs who write virtually all of the stories. US truck firms are rather like *Playboy*, in that they assemble components manufactured by other firms; US auto firms, in contrast, tend to produce most of the basic components of autos. (Traditionally, there have been sharp differences among the US automobile firms, in that Chrysler did more outsourcing than General Motors, although more recently General Motors has increased its outsourcing.)

Each type of firm has certain advantages – managerial and financial skills, marketing and engineering know-how, and customer loyalties. Firms are identifiable as collections of production skills, marketing skills, financial skills, or organizational skills; these tags denote their advantages relative to their competitors. Each firm continually seeks to exploit its advantages in the most efficient way. Since its competitors constantly try to erode its advantages, the firm must continually strive to maintain its market position by developing new advantages and by exploiting its established advantages in new markets, including those in foreign countries.

When a firm considers expansion into foreign markets, it must focus on the most efficient way of exploiting its advantages: it might export from its domestic plants, produce in the foreign market, or sell its knowledge and other advantages to firms with productive facilities in these foreign countries. If the firm decides to produce abroad, it must consider whether to enter into a partnership with a host-country firm in a joint venture. The choice will depend on a variety of economic – and, perhaps, political considerations.

Initially, the firm may supply the foreign market by exporting the output of its domestic plants. Then, after the foreign sales have become sufficiently large the firm may establish a plant abroad to produce for the foreign customers. Or the firm may acquire an established firm headquartered in the foreign country. At first, the production in the foreign country may involve only the assembly of imported components, so as to save on transport costs and tariffs. The drug companies, for example, repackage drugs from large containers into smaller bottles; the auto companies assemble cars and trucks from kits and then from imported components.

As the size of the foreign market expands, a larger share of the inputs to the product may be locally produced, although the parent may continue to supply senior management, technical knowledge, and some financial assistance. Increases in the scale of output in the host-country plant are likely to be associated with declines in unit production costs; the output of this subsidiary may supplement, and perhaps ultimately supplant, exports from the home-country plants.

At some point, the costs of production in the foreign subsidiary may fall below those of domestic plants, and the firm may begin to supply part or all of the domestic market from foreign subsidiaries. Ford imports the Escort for the US market from its Mexican subsidiary. Some US electronics firms produce part or all of the components for particular products in Taiwan, South Korea, Singapore, and Malaysia; these components are then shipped to the United States for assembly into the final product.

Integration of manufacturing

The extensive integration of manufacturing activities in different countries is a recent innovation. Initially the market for many products was local or regional, and most of the local needs were satisfied from nearby production. Imports were minimal. Every town had its butcher, baker, and candlestick-maker, as well as its cobbler, tailor, cigar maker, and brewery. The potential for cost reductions associated with large-scale production was small. And even where savings in production costs were possible, the extra costs of controlling a large-scale production operation with activities in widely separated locations might dominate the savings from large-scale production.

The change in the last 150 years is that technological developments have both greatly increased the savings associated with large-scale production and reduced the costs of coordinating distant activities. Thus bauxite mined in Jamaica is shipped to eastern Venezuela for refining to take advantage of extremely low-cost electricity produced on the Rio Caroni. At one time some US electronics companies sent partially assembled radio receivers to South Korea by air freight for further processing by skilled, relatively inexpensive labor. The combination of increasingly sophisticated products – higher unit values – and sharp declines in costs of transportation and communications has reduced the pressure on firms to locate productive activity near either the market or the source of raw materials; instead, production can be shifted to those sites where unit production costs will be the lowest. As in banking, these changes in technology have increased the size of the market; regional markets are grouped into national markets, and national markets into the international market.

Expansion of national markets has encouraged firms to integrate their activities in different countries. In some countries, a firm may both produce and market, in others it may only market, and in still others it may only produce. It is useful to distinguish between the share of the world's market for a product held by US firms, British firms, and Swiss firms, and the share of total production in each country undertaken by domestic and by foreign firms. The factors which explain where particular goods are produced are likely to differ from those which explain shares of a particular national market held by domestic and by foreign firms. Servan-Schreiber focused on output shares, which is what US industry in Europe is all about. Whereas US firms produce largely in Europe to satisfy the European market, European firms traditionally have sourced for the US market by exporting from their domestic plants. General Motors and Ford have major subsidiaries in Britain and Germany, which were acquired in the 1920s. In the 1980s the larger Japanese auto firms – Toyota, Nissan, Honda, and Mitsubishi – established plants in the United States.

Why do firms invest abroad?

The prospect of profits motivates most business investment decisions. There are a few exceptions: some decisions are made for vanity or the flag. General Leonard Wood established Sears, Roebuck stores in Mexico, and elsewhere in Central America because he wanted to plant the US flag south of the Border. Air France maintains some money-losing routes for the glory of the country. A few firms may invest abroad because the corporation president likes those twice-a-year trips to Madrid or Florence. The list of ad hoc explanations for these noneconomic investment decisions is long, and some individual investments may indeed be explained by one or several factors. Most of these noneconomic investments are, however, likely to be a small part of the firm's activities; otherwise they would be too large a drag on the firm's ability to maintain its market share relative to aggressive competitors.

Since the patterns of foreign investment do not appear to be random among countries, there almost certainly must be a systematic explanation for most – but not necessarily all – foreign investments.

Compensating advantages and superiority theorems

US firms competing in the European market are usually at a disadvantage in relation to their host-country competitors, since they incur costs their host-country competitors do not. Similarly Japanese firms producing in the United States generally incur higher production costs than their US competitors – unless they've sited their plants in areas with relatively low wage rates and tax rates relative to their established US competitors. The activities of the European subsidiaries of US firms must thus be managed from New York, Los Angeles, or Des Moines if they are to be integrated with those of the US parent. The salaries and expenses of US managers in Europe may be several times higher than those of comparable European managers; the US managers receive housing allowances, travel allowances, and educational allowances. Because of this cost disadvantage, firms with foreign subsidiaries must possess some offsetting advantages if their profit rates are to be comparable to those of their host-country competitors.

Similar statements might be made about European and Japanese firms which have bought subsidiaries in the United States. These firms believe that it is more profitable to satisfy the US market by producing in the United States than by exporting. The implication is unless they have a compensating advantage, their profits will be below those of their US competitors.

Three possible and nonexclusive advantages are attributed to source-country firms – firms that establish productive facilities abroad. According to Servan-Schreiber, the US advantage is the product, and a combination of managerial know-how and a flexible business model. US businessmen may be exceptionally competitive. The problem with superiority theories is that they imply that Mother Nature has favorites in the distribution of talent. If Americans were superior managers, the low-cost response for European firms would be to hire more American managers. Some do, and the success of the US management consulting firms in Europe – the McKinseys, Booz Allens, and Boston Consulting Groups – is a substitute for hiring American managers. Other objections to the superiority hypothesis include its failure to provide insights about why foreign investment is so large in some industries and so small in others – and its failure to explain why the Dutch and Swiss invest extensively abroad, unless the Dutch and Swiss are also superior. Moreover if this view is correct, it implies that the superiority of

US businessmen declined sharply in the 1980s while the superiority of Japanese businessmen increased. And the would-be superiority of the Japanese firms must more or less have stopped in the early 1990s.

Indeed, this 'theory' is no more than a tautology – all it says is that the managers of firms based in some countries are superior, and the evidence of their superiority is that they invest abroad.

A second explanation is that source-country firms have an advantage in the form of a patent or technical know-how, or marketing skills, or other firm-specific advantages. In a few industries, these advantages may derive from large US Government programs in defense and space; however, this argument is irrelevant for the foreign investment activities of Ford and General Motors, Playboy Clubs, Holiday Inns, Coca-Cola, money center banks, firms in food-producing industries, and the like. Of course, the advantages might reflect the fact that relatively high US wages compel US firms to give greater attention to reducing their costs by developing labor-saving processes, while intense competition forces US firms to develop new products for both old and newly created needs. So US firms tend to develop 'advantages' more rapidly than firms in other countries. Once these new products and processes have been developed to satisfy the US domestic market, these firms then seek to exploit these advantages to satisfy demands in foreign markets. This explanation is directed to the market-share question.

Presumably, the factors which explain why US firms develop these advantages might also explain why firms headquartered in the Netherlands, Switzerland, and Sweden also develop advantages which they used to increase their sales abroad. The question of what source country firms headquartered in different countries have in common becomes a question of the identification of the shared characteristics of the firms that develop advantages that have value in foreign countries.

The shortcoming of explanations of international ownership based on firm-specific advantages is their incompleteness about why firms in some countries develop more of these advantages than firms in other countries. Moreover, US firms, Swiss firms, and Dutch firms could sell their patents, know-how, and product advantages to foreign firms rather than incur the costs of managing subsidiaries located abroad. Indeed, many US firms do exactly that by licensing their advantages. Coca-Cola sells franchises and its concentrate to foreign bottling companies. Most McDonald's outlets in foreign countries are licensed. If the sales prices for advantages were sufficiently high, few US firms would ever incur the cost of establishing subsidiaries abroad.

The reluctance to sell the firm-specific advantages to host-country firms must be explained. One suggestion is that firms fear that such sales might facilitate the growth of foreign firms which would later become their competitors. An alternative suggestion is that firms may find it difficult to sell the advantages, perhaps because they are ill-defined, especially if R&D leads to continuing changes in the advantages or if they involve marketing know-how. Thus each time the 'know-how' changes, a new negotiation between producer and buyer might be necessary.

The more general reason for their reluctance to sell their advantages is that these firms believe their income will be higher if they exploit their advantages through wholly owned subsidiaries rather than if they sell them.

A third explanation is that firms invest abroad when maintaining the rate of growth of sales within their traditional industries in the domestic market becomes increasingly difficult or expensive. One reason might be that domestic demand for their products is growing more slowly, perhaps because the domestic market has become saturated. The intuition is that the firm's sales grow rapidly in the areas approximate to the garage or shop or store where the firm was established initially; then in response to the rapid increase in the market share in these nearby areas, the firm begins to increase sales in more distant geographic areas. The motivation is that it is easier or less costly to achieve a given increase in sales if the market share is small than if the market share is large. The firm realizes that if the growth rate of sales slows, the firm is likely to age; both its employees and the plant equipment are likely on average to become older. The logic is that when the firm is expanding its sales at a rapid rate, the new employees will be relatively young and there will be substantial investment in new plant and equipment. As the growth rate slows, then the labor force is likely to become older, and the unit labor costs may increase because the increase in wage rates will exceed the increase in productivity. Similarly as the growth rate slows, the rate of investment in plant and equipment is likely to decline, and the average age of the productive facilities will increase; other firms in the same industry that have been able to maintain more rapid growth rates will invest in plant and equipment that may incorporate the newest technologies.

In this situation, the firm might expand into other industries in the domestic market – that is, the firm might cross the borders between industries. Alternatively, the firm might cross national borders and expand abroad with its traditional products. And, of course, the firm might do both. For many firms, crossing national borders may be easier than crossing industry borders at home, given their expertise in producing and marketing particular products.

The proposition that the firm wishes to maintain its growth rate to prevent or limit aging may explain why the firm continues to hunt for new markets as its share of the established markets increases; eventually some of these new markets will be in foreign countries. This view might explain why firms seek foreign markets, but not why they produce abroad – it might explain market shares, but it does not explain output shares.

The shortcoming of this group of explanations is that they tell a story about why the firm may wish to expand and why it may wish to expand its sales in foreign countries, but they don't identify the advantage of the source-country firms that enable them to compensate for the costs of economic distance. And these approaches don't provide a handle for explaining the distinction between source countries and host countries, and why the United States appears to be becoming a host country after having been a dominant source country.

A fourth explanation of the country pattern of DFI – the capital market view – is that US firms and those based in other source countries have an advantage in the world capital market. The advantage is that these firms can borrow at interest rates below those that most of their foreign competitors must pay. An even more important form of advantage is that shares of these firms headquartered in countries tied with low interest rates sell at higher prices than the shares of firms in the host countries – the countries identified with higher interest rates. These firms benefit from a country-specific advantage in the form of a lower cost of capital.

Interest rates on US dollar bonds have been lower than those on comparable securities denominated in nearly every other currency for most of the last half century, and especially during those periods when US firms invested abroad extensively. Since the US dollar is their domestic currency, US firms generally have been able to borrow on more advantageous terms than their foreign competitors. Canadian and European firms have come to New York to issue US dollar bonds, not because they want to spend the funds in the United States but because interest rates on US dollar securities were sufficiently below their domestic interest rates to justify incurring the risk of loss from depreciation of their currencies relative to the US dollar.

One consequence of the general preference of investors for US dollar securities was that US firms were willing to pay a higher price for an advantage – such as a technological innovation – than non-US firms. And given an opportunity to increase its income by undertaking a new project, a US firm would generally pay a higher price for the same anticipated income stream than a non-US firm. The other side of the coin is that if a US firm buys a French firm, even though the earnings of the French subsidiary remain unchanged, investors would be willing to pay more for the shares of the US firm because of their preferences for US dollar-denominated securities.

This view suggests that the advantages of US firms are inherent in investor preferences for securities denominated in the US dollar, just as the advantages of Swiss firms are inherent in investor preferences for securities denominated in the Swiss franc. US firms are identified with US dollar equities, just as Swiss firms are identified with Swiss franc equities, and Dutch firms at one time with guilder equities. A firm cannot change the currency denomination of its equities without changing its national identity. And firms almost never change their nationalities. (Some British firms that were primarily involved in Malaysia shifted their domicile from London to Kuala Lumpur after Malaysia became independent, and one or two firms headquartered in Hong Kong moved their main offices elsewhere in anticipation of the British departure from Hong Kong in 1997.) As long as interest rates on US dollar securities are low relative to those on comparable securities denominated in other currencies, US firms will have a country-specific advantage.

The implication of this capital market explanation is that the source countries for foreign investment are those with relatively low interest rates. Casual observation suggests that the countries other than the United States which have been large exporters of DFI – Switzerland, the Netherlands, and Britain – have traditionally been low-interest rate countries. The Netherlands was the low-interest rate country in the eighteenth century, when the Dutch empire was expanding abroad and Dutch trading firms were setting up overseas offices. In the nineteenth century, Britain was the low-interest rate country, and British firms followed the expansion of the empire. Even though both empires have shrunk markedly, the large international businesses such as Unilever and Shell in the Netherlands and in Britain have continued to flourish.

The capital market view also explains the pattern of ownership in different countries – whether individual countries will be source or host countries. As long as the US dollar is the preferred currency, US firms will establish foreign branches and buy up foreign firms. Foreign ownership of plants in the United States and foreign takeovers of US firms may increase, but the capital market explanation suggests that the growth of US investment abroad will be substantially larger: more importantly, the output shares of US firms will increase.

The test of any theory is its ability to explain observed events. One of the most demanding phenomena to explain is the surge in investment in the United States by Japanese and European firms in the late 1970s and again in the second half of the 1980s. How capable are these theories of explaining the takeovers of Howard Johnson's and A & P and Marshall Field & Co. by firms headquartered abroad? The Servan-Schreiber view would be that – all of a sudden – the Europeans and the Japanese developed superior abilities to combine technical and managerial skills. In contrast, if the theories that emphasize firm-specific advantages are correct, the implication is that Japanese and European must have surged ahead of US firms in developing such advantages – yet the relevance of these advantages to the foreign takeovers of firms is questionable.

Some newspaper stories have suggested that foreign firms invested extensively in the United States because they wanted to participate in the largest consumer market in the world; however, many participate in the US market by exporting their domestic production. Some firms are said to have invested in the United States as political insurance; they feared that military events in Europe or moves toward governmental ownership would handicap their survivability. Yet the advantage of these foreign firms relative to US firms in the US market remains unexplained.

Few theories do a good job of explaining why the incentives of US firms to invest abroad declined in the 1980s and why the incentives for German and Japanese firms to invest abroad increased. The change in the low-cost location of investment is explained by the changes in exchange rates, which have been larger than the changes in relative costs of production. During the same period that the German mark and the Japanese yen appreciated, interest rates on assets denominated in these currencies fell; and so firms headquartered in both countries had less of a disadvantage – and more of an advantage – than firms based in the United States.

US firms on the hit parade of multinationals

Several factors explain why US firms still seem to dominate the lists of multinationals, despite the surges in the foreign investments of Japanese and German firms in the 1970s and the 1980s: dominance on the list of multinationals might be measured by total sales or aggregate assets. One is that the domestic US market for most goods is large, more than twice as large as the Japanese market, and more than three times as large as the German market. So US firms become relatively larger by producing just for the domestic market. At some stage, however, the domestic market tends to become saturated, and the opportunity to maintain the rate of growth of sales in the domestic market diminishes, so if firms are to maintain their growth rates, then they must begin to sell abroad. Partly because the levels of per capita income in the United States have been higher than in most other industrial countries, this limit tends to be encountered in the United States before it is met abroad – even though the foreign countries are smaller. For example, the rate of growth of auto sales in the United States slowed in the late 1950s and the 1960s because most families already had a car; the similar limit in Japan was encountered only in the 1980s.

Partly because US wages in many industries were higher than in the same industries in other countries, production costs in United States were generally higher for much of the period from the 1920s to the 1970s. US firms were obliged to invest and produce abroad if they were to be competitive in foreign markets. The result of the real depreciation of the US dollar relative to the German mark and the Japanese yen in the late 1970s and the late 1980s is that the locational advantage changed in favor of the United States. Firms headquartered in Europe and Japan realized that they had to establish US factories to be able to continue to supply the US market on a profitable basis; both Mercedes and BMW, for example, established automobile factories in the southeastern part of the United States. (Some Japanese firms have invested in the United States because of a fear that their access to the US market might be constrained by import barriers.)

A third reason for the US dominance is that US firms have generally had an advantage in the international capital market throughout most of the period since the end of the First World War, with the exception of the late 1970s and the 1980s; the cost of capital for US firms was below the cost of capital for firms in most foreign countries, with the exception of Switzerland, the Netherlands, and (in the 1980s) Germany and Japan. This cost of capital advantage reflects the fact that the US dollar has been the currency at the top of the hit parade for most of the twentieth century, with the exception of the brief period when the US inflation rate seemed out of control and then when a tough antiinflationary policy was adopted to move the United States back to price level stability.

Paradoxically, US firms seem dominant in the industries associated with rapid technological change such as biogenetics and computer hardware and software. At the same time, US firms have a major market share in fast foods and soft drinks – industries identified with economies of scale and marketing skills.

One question that follows is why foreign firms are so eager to invest in the United States, even though they frequently first enter the United States by acquiring established US firms, and often pay premium prices for these firms. One reason is that the US market is the largest and generally the most open in the world, so that a foreign firm entering the US market is less likely to elicit a direct challenge from domestic competitors than if the firm enters some other foreign market with the same level of foreign sales. A related reason is that the lessons developed in the US market are like a postgraduate course in marketing and strategic development; the lessons that German firms learn in the US market will be useful in competing with US firms in the German and other European markets.

The costs of direct foreign investment

One of the paradoxes of recent decades is that both home-country and host-country governments have questioned the economic advantages attached to the activities of multinational firms. That these firms have grown and expanded suggests efficiencies greater than those of the smaller domestic firms they have replaced. The benefits of these efficiencies must be distributed among their employees in the form of higher wages and salaries, or among their customers in the form of lower prices, or among their shareholders as higher profits and dividends. And if wages and profits are higher, then the tax collectors will gain, since the tax base will be higher. All four groups may gain. And the source country or the host country may gain as a result of their activities, or both may gain; it is implausible that both home and host countries could be worse off at the same time.

The source countries have several major criticisms of multinationals. One involves runaway jobs; unions often find that the multinational firms circumvent their national monopoly over the supply of labor. Foreign investment affects the distribution of jobs among countries, just as changes in trade patterns do. Belatedly – 50 years belatedly – the unions are becoming interested in the international labor situation. Hence, the choice for the unions in the source country is whether to merge with unions in the host countries or to develop some other fraternal relationship with them.

A second criticism involves taxes: the foreign income of the multinational firms headquartered in the United States is taxed initially by the foreign government, and in most cases there is little left over for the US tax collector. The United States has double-taxation agreements with many other countries; these agreements provide that the income is taxable first in the country in which it is earned, and that the combined tax rate of the foreign host and the US Government cannot exceed the higher of the two national rates. Assume the British tax rate is 40 percent and the US rate is 50 percent. If a US firm invests at home, each dollar of profit generates 50 cents for the US tax collector. If the firm invests in Britain, each dollar of profit generates 40 cents for the British tax collector and only 10 cents for the US tax collector.

A third concern involves the adverse balance-of-payments consequences of multinationals' activities. Foreign investments mean that exports decline and imports increase more rapidly than might otherwise occur. While the payment of dividends may counter the loss of exports, the offset may be partial rather than complete.

These criticisms of multinationals imply that the source-country firms face a choice between producing at home or producing abroad, when the effective choice for some firms may be producing abroad or not producing at all. The shift in the production of many electronic products to Southeast Asia occurred because production costs there were much lower than in the United States; if US firms had not joined German, Dutch, and Japanese firms in this move, they would have lost both their export markets and the domestic market. The loss of US jobs, the shortfall in US tax revenues, and the adverse impact on the US balance of payments would have been even sharper. Even if US firms retained a domestic market, at least for a while, without shifting to offshore production, their long-run competitive position would have been weaker.

There are other criticisms. During the dollar crises, the multinationals moved funds to avoid losses from changes in exchange rates; some may have also sought to profit from these changes. Some critics even suggest that the dollar crises resulted from the behavior of these firms, and not from the mismanagement of the system. An even more sensitive issue involves the alleged political involvement of multinationals in the host countries. Multinationals may contribute to political parties, much as host-country firms do. ITT tried to forestall the election of Allende in Chile; many foreign firms retain representatives in Washington. Again, the firms say they act to protect their interests. The criticism is that the interests of the multinational firms may not be identical with US national interests nor with the interests of the host countries – but then the interests of US firms may not be identical with those of the US Government.

Host-country governments – or at least the US Government – may be embarrassed and inconvenienced by disclosure of the political activities of multinationals. But the managers of the firms are paid to protect the firm's interests, and they have on occasion found that the methods of decision-making and persuasion that are typical, or at least not uncommon, in the host country would not be generally accepted at a New England town meeting.

Host-country attitudes toward multinational firms are ambivalent.

Many countries compete to attract foreign firms, for they bring employment, on-the-job training, and tax revenues. In many products, these firms provide access to world markets. Yet foreign investment has been much criticized within the host countries. Some of these criticisms are vague and reflect simple-minded xenophobia; foreign investment is equated with imperialism. Having nationals work for foreigners or having foreigners own domestic resources is said to demean the nation. Other criticisms are more specific: the foreign firm exploits the nation's patrimony of nonreproducible petroleum, copper, bauxite, or tin, or reduces employment, or evades taxes, or stifles domestic entrepreneurship. The host-country government may feel that foreign-owned firms diminish its sovereignty and may resent these firms' involvement in the domestic political process.

Appraisal of these criticisms requires a benchmark – a view of what would have happened to growth, income, employment, and corporate development in the host country had foreign investment not taken place.

One of the major concerns of small countries is that they might become technological backwaters; these countries fear that because their own science and technology and industries do not offer attractive careers, highly educated and trained nationals will migrate to the larger countries. (People in Kansas feel the same way.) Multinational companies often centralize their R&D activities in a relatively few locations, which is why government officials sometimes conclude that the multinational firms impede the development of a viable local scientific community. The presumption is that in the absence of the multinational company, domestic firms would undertake R&D comparable to that done abroad by the foreign firm. Perhaps. But it is equally possible that the domestic firms might import their R&D because the costs of imports would be less than domestic production costs.

Host-country governments worry that multinational firms diminish their sovereignty. Occasionally the head office of a multinational firm may, in response to pressures from its own government, direct the subsidiary to cease exporting to certain markets or to shift funds to the home office. Host countries fear that the power and influence of the state may not be used directly against a foreign firm, perhaps because it enjoys the backing of its more powerful government. The host-country government would like to be able to rely on foreign as well as on domestic firms to increase exports or boost employment, or to take other measures that may not be in the firm's interests. Foreign firms may be less amenable to such measures than domestic firms would be. Perhaps. But foreign firms know they can be asked – or forced – to leave the country; for this reason, they may be less able than domestic firms to withstand government pressures.

To the extent that multinational firms offer access to the world market, they are likely to be the 'pawns' of competing national governments. For example, when Canada adopted a set of measures to induce US auto companies to produce more cars in Canada, US employment and US tax revenues declined. When Malaysia adopted a set of measures to attract foreign electronics firms, Singapore and Taiwan began to worry, much more than the United States and Japan did.

Foreign firms are sometimes accused of making excessively high profits, especially in the extraction of nonreproducible resources. Host-country governments know that mines or wells will eventually be exhausted, so they want to maximize national gains from these resources. Typically, the host-country governments have auctioned concessions to exploit the resources; they may receive a lump-sum payment or a contingent payment based on profits. If a concession proves attractive and profitable, then a host country may seek to revise the contract in its own favor. But the game is asymmetrical; if the firm fails to discover oil or the concession proves unprofitable, the company never gets a refund. In some cases, of course, the arguments for reopening the contract may be strong; perhaps the state issued the concession under duress, or a minister may have been bribed and have thus betrayed the interests of his government. Since most resource-owning countries manage to attract foreign firms to exploit their resources, the threat of contact renegotiation cannot be too severe. And, increasingly, the firms may recognize the likelihood of expropriation as they determine how much – or how little – to bid.

In manufacturing, the profits earned by a foreign company reflect its efficiency. High profits mean that the firm can satisfy the market demands more efficiently than its domestic competitors. High profits also mean higher taxes to the host-country government. And greater efficiency allows the firm to use fewer domestic resources, which are thus available for other uses. Most governments, of course, would like to get the taxes and the efficiency, but at a lower cost in terms of profits to foreign firms.

The arguments are inconclusive. At various times (like nearly every other year), the Canadians have set up study groups to determine whether Canadian interests have been served by the presence of multinationals. There is a supply of anecdotes about their misbehavior; the critics have a point or two, if not a case. The virulence of the criticism is more evidence of the increasing nationalist sentiment so evident in national monetary policies. Various governments have set up foreign investment review boards to screen desirable foreign investments from less desirable proposals. The United Nations has developed a code of conduct for multinational firms, a sort of Miss Manners' guide to 'correct' behavior. Why the code should apply only to multinational firms is unclear; fairness suggests that all domestic firms should also follow the code.

Whither the conflict?

The conflict between governments and multinationals is likely to become more intense. Problems arise because the firms are dynamic organizations and respond to developments in technology and markets, while political organizations – states – remain largely static. Firms grow and consolidate and expand their activities around the world in response to changing profit opportunities, while states are locked into a more or less fixed set of boundaries. Reductions in the costs of transportation and communication increase the mobility of business firms, but this increased mobility may be viewed as a threat by the host-country governments.

In many industries the growth and expansion of multinationals has increased competition and reduced the monopoly power of the dominant domestic firms. The US automobile industry is much more competitive because of the eagerness of foreign firms to export to the US market, and the German automobile industry is more competitive because of the presence of General Motors and Ford. Sony and Panasonic have greatly increased competition, so there is now an international electronics industry. In drugs, chemicals, and numerous other industries, trade and investment have substantially increased the number of participants. Evidence of unusually attractive profits induces other firms to enter the market. Inevitably, pressures to regulate the multinational corporations – and to regulate the capacity of states to regulate these corporations – will develop. Because the issues are complex and the interests of various states and corporations highly diverse, ambitious efforts at a regulatory code are not likely to succeed.

Three changes are possible. The first is an agreement among governments to limit their reach into the foreign activities of firms which they identify as 'their corporate citizens' – or into the extraterritorial span of national control. This change would be directed primarily at the United States. The second, a set of rules governing the entrance of foreign firms into manufacturing, would be much like the rules governing the access of foreign goods to the domestic markets. These rules might specify when access should be unimpaired and when the firm might be required to join with a local partner. The third is a set of rules about compensation for foreign firms when their property is expropriated or when they are otherwise deprived of the full value of their advantages.

Yet the likelihood of meaningful rules is small, at least in the near future. And the reason is that governments in both the source and host countries appear to find more political support in what is effectively an ad hoc approach to regulation – in other words, the economic issues interest them less than the domestic votes.

21
Japan – The First Superstate

In 1970 Herman Kahn, physicist and nuclear war theorist, predicted that Japan would become the 'First Superstate' – that its GDP would double between 1970 and 1975, and again between 1975 and 1980 – a fourfold expansion in a decade. Between 1970 and 2000, annual growth rates would average 9 percent a year, so that by the year 2000 GDP in Japan would be nearly 16 times the 1970 level. The news was heartening to the Japanese and frightening to most other countries because continued rapid growth would lead to declines in the world prices of the goods that the Japanese produced – and to comparable declines in the prices of similar goods produced in other industrial countries.

The Japanese challenge

No country presented more of a challenge to international trade and monetary arrangements in the 1970s and 1980s than Japan. Yet a prediction in 1950 or in 1960 that Japanese firms would present a major threat to US and German firms in a relatively few years would have seemed absurd. Japan had been bombed extensively in the last several years of the Second World War, its factories ravaged. Japan had lost its colonies in Manchuria, Korea, and Formosa – the island now known as Taiwan. Japan's only abundant raw material was coal; Japan imported much of its energy and its food and paid for these imports by exporting low value-added manufactured goods. It seemed as if Japan would remain forever on the international dole – if there had been any willing donors.

Within a generation, Japanese exports were growing more rapidly than those of any other country. Japanese firms dominated world markets for steel, ships, autos, electronic products, and photo optics. By the early 1970s the Japanese firms in many industries were threats to their foreign competitors, more insidious than during the Second World War, for the Japanese seemed to winning even as they played by the rules of the system. Then Toyota and Nissan and other Japanese auto firms began to establish assembly facilities and later production facilities in the United States and Europe. Then Toyota and Nissan began to produce the Lexus and the Infinity which were superb upscale models and a challenge to Mercedes and Jaguar and other European producers of luxury automobiles.

Early in the 1960s the Japanese Government had adopted a 10-year 'Doubling National Income' plan. With a population growth rate of 1 percent a year, per capita incomes would double in a decade if productivity gains – annual increases in output per person employed per year – averaged 7 percent. The growth performance exceeded the targets of the plan, in contrast to most other countries where economic performance almost always lagged behind the targets. In the 1960s per capita income in Japan was increasing by 10 percent a year, and by 1967 per capita income was twice as high as in 1960 – a remarkable accomplishment.

Kahn's prediction was based on the extrapolation of the growth rates of the 1960s through the next 30 years. In the 1960s, economic growth in Japan averaged 12 percent a year; in contrast, the US growth rate was 3 percent, and the rates in Germany and France were in the range of 6–7 percent. If a country with a lower level of GDP grows more rapidly than countries with higher levels of GDP, then eventually the GDP in the rapid-growth country will surpass the GDPs in the slow-growth countries, no matter how large its initial disadvantage.

Secrets of the miracle

In the early 1980s, a new industry appeared – books which offered the 'secrets' of the Japanese economic miracle. The story in *Japan as Number One*, by Ezra F. Vogel, is one of tradition, high levels of literacy, social cohesion, and a Puritan or Confucian work ethic. *The Art of Japanese Management*, by Richard T. Pascale and Anthony G. Althos, and *Theory Z*, by William Ouchi, emphasized the skill of industrial managers in developing a consensus among workers before introducing change. *The East Asia Edge* highlighted the 'Four Tigers' – South Korea, Hong Kong, Taiwan, and Singapore – who were achieving gains in economic well-being about as rapidly as Japan. *Shogun*, by James Clavell, had its own story, at least by implication; business firms in various industries competed extensively for market share, just as several centuries earlier feudal war lords had competed for power and turf, fame and attention.

Some explanations highlighted 'Japan, Inc.,' which asserted that the economic success of Japan was a result of its industrial policy which involved cooperative planning between business and government leaders about developing new products and exporting manufactures to foreign markets. The story was that the heads of the large firms in each industry met with the senior officials of the Ministry of Finance (MOF) and of the Ministry of International Trade and Industry (MITI) in the 'special situations' room in the basement of the Imperial Palace to decide how to conqueror world markets. Probably each of these explanations had some validity – and the question is to determine their relative importance.

Increases in GDP result from increases both in the number of hours worked and in labor output or productivity per hour. Increases in the volume of capital equipment and technological improvements increase productivity: the workers are smarter and have more powerful machines to work with.

In most industrial societies, the labor supply increased rapidly during the 1960s as members of the post–Second World War baby boom graduated from school and entered the labor force. But in each of these economies the work week was becoming shorter, vacations were becoming longer, there were more holidays with pay, and the retirement age was lowered. These changes were normal economic responses to growing material affluence, which led to a decline in the number of hours of work per year for each member of the labor force. Increasing absenteeism and more voluntary unemployment also led to a reduction in the effective labor supply. The differences among countries in their growth rates largely reflected differences in productivity. Somehow the Japanese did something better – while they may have worked harder, they could not have worked progressively harder year after year for several decades or else they should have been able to run the mile in two and a half minutes.

The arithmetic of economic growth should be distinguished from the economics of growth. What was needed was a story that explained why Japanese firms invested so much more than firms in other industrial countries, and whether the high productivity in Japan resulted from the high rates of household saving and of business investment. The personal savings rate – three times as high as in the United States – was explained by the much lower level of government retirement benefits than in the counterpart US program and those in other industrial countries – hence individuals saved much more to provide for their old age. Moreover because the real rate of interest earned by savers – the money interest rate adjusted for the inflation rate – was low and even negative in many years, individuals needed to save a high proportion of their income to achieve an increase in the purchasing power of their cumulative savings.

Then the willingness of Japanese firms to invest had to be explained. One story centered on the Japan, Inc. concept – that the business and government leaders planned the penetration and takeover of foreign markets. The usual story was that the Japan, Inc. model facilitated business investment especially in new products that offered higher value-added. Moreover, the Japanese took advantage of low tariffs abroad, but foreign firms found it difficult to sell in Japan because of both formal and informal import barriers. There were continued suggestions that the Japanese Government provided subsidies to those domestic firms that were developing new products – but documenting this view proved difficult. And the officials in the MOF had rigged the credit system through ceilings on interest rates; indeed because real interest rates were negative, business borrowers were implicitly subsidized by household savers.

The idea that government planners might enhance the growth rate was heretical for the fans of the market system and free trade; it was an article of faith that government intervention in the economy would lead to a lower growth rate because the regulations would distort the efficient use of resources. There was a lot of empirical support for this view. Similarly the idea that a country could gain if it maintained tariffs and other barriers to imports was unsettling because the free trade argument that dates back to Adam Smith's *The Wealth of Nations* in 1776 claimed that such barriers retard growth.

The slowdown in the growth rate

Soon after Kahn's book appeared, the Japanese economy began to falter, beginning with a sharp recession in 1971. Then the Japanese consumer price level increased by 30 percent a year during the first oil shock in 1973–74. In 1974, Japan was hit by the world recession and the foreign demand for Japanese goods declined. The cyclical behavior of the Japanese economy mimicked the swings of the world business cycle, but in an exaggerated fashion. When world business was booming, the Japanese economy purred. But when the world economy burped, the indigestion in Japan was severe. Despite these burps, the Japanese economic growth rate in the 1970s was higher than in other industrial economies although the excess of the Japanese growth rate over the US growth rate was significantly lower than in the previous several decades.

The slowdown in the Japanese growth rate was almost certainly inevitable. Those who had projected a continuation of rapid growth had failed to recognize a truism – 'No element in the system can grow more rapidly than the system' for an extended period. Rapid growth in Japanese income requires a corresponding rapid growth in Japanese imports, because Japan lacks raw materials and also imports many of its foods. The growth in imports must be financed by an approximately equal rapid growth of exports. If Japanese exports grow at 8 percent a year while world exports grow at 4 percent a year, then Japanese exports would eventually become larger than world exports – and that would be a neat trick.

The second factor that is usually overlooked is the contrast between Japanese economic growth in the 1950s and the 1960s and the country's growth rate before the Second World War. From the late nineteenth century until the beginning of what in Tokyo was sometimes euphemistically called 'The Great Pacific Confusion,' economic growth in Japan averaged between 4 and 4.5 percent a year. The increase in the growth rate in the several decades before 1900 resulted from a commitment to industrialize, undertaken to prevent or withstand the rapacious Western powers who coveted spheres of influence and turf in Japan comparable to the ones they had achieved in China. This economic growth rate, which consisted of productivity gains of about 3 percent a year and increases in the labor force of about 1 percent a year, was modestly higher than the growth rates of most other countries during the early stages of their industrialization.

Per capita income in Japan did not change significantly during the Second World War – at least not until the last year or two of the war. Per capita income declined sharply immediately after the war because Japan was cut off from raw materials and bereft of foreign markets. The handicaps in exporting meant that Japan could not earn the foreign currencies that it needed to buy raw materials, and without these materials firms could not produce for export. It was Catch-22 all over again.

In the late 1940s and early 1950s, economic growth in Japan began to increase rapidly, more so than at any time in the previous 60 years. Most of this growth was 'making up arrears' and recovering from the calamitous economic consequences of the war. By replacing the railway switches, the 'system was put back to work';

small investments in a few strategic locations led to a large increase in output. Productivity was phenomenal. However, not until the mid-1950s did per capita income in Japan reach 1940 levels. In contrast per capita income in the United States had more than doubled during the same 15 years.

Assume, in the absence of war, that Japanese income had continued to grow at the historic rate of 4 percent a year from 1940 onward. Then per capita income would have doubled from 1940 to 1958 and doubled again from 1958 to 1976. However, in the mid-1950s, per capita income was one-half of what it would have been if the economy had continued to grow at the 4 percent rate. The rapid growth in the 1960s meant that Japan actually achieved the income levels it would have otherwise attained in the early 1970s had there been no war.

Thus far, the story is one of arithmetic. A number of stories might explain why the growth rate was so much higher after the war. One is that once the labor force, the savings rate, and competitive spirit were organized to achieve an 8 percent growth rate, that momentum alone would lead to a continuation of this rate. The increase in the growth rate in the early postwar years could be viewed as a counterpart to the increase in the growth rate in the late nineteenth century, when the campaign to industrialize was first undertaken.

The competing scenario is that there was a large amount of latent excess capacity in the years immediately following the Second World War, but that the growth of the economy was handicapped by severe bottlenecks that resulted from wartime damage both to the plant and equipment and to traditional trade relationships. Rapid growth resulted from relaxing these bottlenecks and restoring trade relationships so that Japan could benefit from increases in imports of basic raw materials. Repairing damage to the railway lines would enable the whole transport system to carry much more freight. As the idle capacity became utilized, continuing the growth momentum would become progressively more difficult. Similarly, the skills of the labor force may have been less than fully utilized if many individuals were working at jobs below their potential as gauged by their education. Once the skills of the labor force were fully utilized, the growth rate would inevitably decline.

Japan, Inc.

All economies face the same questions – what goods and service should be produced, in what volumes, and by what techniques? In some economies, decisions about what to produce and how to produce are made in a highly decentralized way by the managers in tens of thousands of firms in response to their views about consumer demands and industrial demands. In other countries a few government officials – perhaps at a planning agency or the finance ministry – make these same decisions; if they err, some goods will be in short supply and others will pile up in the stores. In both cases there is always the concern that if many firms invest in the plant and equipment designed to produce similar goods, excess productive capacity will develop, and competitive forces will lead a few firms desperate for cash to reduce prices below total costs, anticipated profits will not be realized, and some firms will incur substantial losses and be forced out of business.

Adam Smith observed that businessmen rarely meet without deciding how to 'carve up' markets – they want to avoid the type of competition that might lead to declines in the prices of the goods they sell. In the United States, legislation limits various practices that might lead to a decline in competition. A few other countries have similar pro-competitive legislation. The concern is that as a consequence of the more stringent US antitrust policies, foreign firms have an advantage – they can be confident that their investments will be profitable and that the supplies of goods produced will not be so large as to depress prices sharply, because they can meet and discuss the measures to limit production. In contrast, managers of US firms are subject to greater uncertainty about whether contemplated investments will prove profitable and they are more reluctant to make the investments in new plant and equipment.

An unfair competitive advantage?

In the 1960s and the 1970s the Japanese success in increasing their share of the world markets for textiles, steel, TVs, and many other products led to the view that their firms had an unfair competitive advantage. Partly the criticism centered on trade imbalances, and in particular Japanese trade surpluses. Japanese imports were largely raw materials, and most of these products were noncompetitive with anything produced in Japan – although some of its imports of rice and beef were competitive with domestic production of these goods. In contrast, Japanese exports to the United States and other industrial countries were manufactured goods, and almost always competitive with goods produced in those countries. The ratios of Japanese imports of manufactured products to domestic consumption of these same manufactures was much below the comparable ratios in every other industrial country, which led to the charge that Japan had both formal and hidden import barriers. Moreover many Japanese imports of manufactured goods were luxury items like BMWs, Mercedes, and French crystal – goods which had few Japanese counterparts. There was also continuing concern that the Japanese were subsidizing exports or otherwise 'dumping them' – selling these goods in the United States and in other foreign markets at prices significantly below the sums of the prices of these same goods in Tokyo, Kobe, and Osaka, and the transport costs for these goods from Japan to the United States. Or perhaps the Japanese had an unfair advantage in the way their business system was organized.

The Japan, Inc. metaphor developed while the country's growth rate was much higher than in other industrial countries. The view was that businessmen and government officials met to formalize market-sharing arrangements. The MOF controlled the supply of credit, and hence was in a powerful position to secure the cooperation of both the commercial banks and the individual firms that needed to borrow to expand their productive capacity. The MITI controlled import licenses and was in a strong position to influence the investment decisions of individual firms. If corporate managers slighted the guidance from the government agencies, MITI would stall on requests for import licenses. The Japan, Inc. story was that businessmen responded readily to government initiatives, suggestions, and requests – to ensure that they could obtain credit and import licenses.

An alternative model of competition within Japan is a twentieth-century version of struggles among feudal warlords for power, authority, and prestige. According to this view, the descendants of these warlords, the *zaibatsu* or *keiretsu* – the Sumitomos, the Mitsubishis, the Mitsuis – are families of related firms in many different industries. Each family is centered on a bank and includes a trading firm, a steel firm, a shipping line, a petrochemical complex, a subset of textile firms, and so on. Each family of firms engages in extensive mutual support, favoring other members of the group when buying inputs – the officials in Mitsubishi bank and the Mitsubishi trading firm usually would buy Mitsubishi autos. Similarly the officials in Mitsubishi Bank would be more generous to related firms when extending credits. Moreover there are interlocking share ownerships, which sharply reduce the likelihood of hostile takeovers. Finally each firm within its industry is extremely conscious of its market position – whether it is the number 1 or the number 5 in terms of market share. Each firm accepts its market position, and is very reluctant to see any decline in its position because its prestige – and hence the prestige of the group – would diminish. The data indicate that very few large firms go out of business, and mergers in most industries have been very infrequent.

The second model differs sharply from the Japan, Inc. view and suggests that rapid growth resulted from extensive competition among firms in the same industry, which was more pervasive than in other countries.

The roles of the capitalists and the bankers

Consider the number of firms in each of the major industries in Japan, which almost always is much larger than the number in each of these industries in the United States and in Europe. There are eight or nine major automobile firms in Japan, whereas there are two large US automobile firms and four large firms and a few boutiques in Europe. The Japanese motorcycle industry includes Honda, Suzuki, Kawasaki, and Yamaha; Harley-Davidson is the only significant US producer of motorcycles. Kenwood, Matsushita, Sony, Toshiba, Hitachi, Sanyo, Sharp, AIWA, Yamaha, Denon, Nakamichi, Onkyo, and Luxman compete for market share in consumer electronics. Industry by industry, there are many more firms in Japan than in the United States and in Western Europe, even though the Japanese economy is less than half the size of the US economy. Economic growth has not been associated with a sharp reduction in the number of firms in Japan.

To maintain its market share, each firm in Japan must obtain the funds necessary to finance new investment in plant and equipment. If a firm incurs losses, it can obtain financial support from others in the same family. Moreover the workers know that their employment security is intimately linked with the success of their firm so they accept smaller-than-average wage increases and smaller-than-average semiannual bonuses if the firm has not had a good year. If their firm were to go bankrupt, the future of the employees would be bleak because the lifetime employment system means that the likelihood that they could obtain a comparable position in some firm was low.

The implication of these two factors – the emphasis on maintaining market share and lifetime employment – is that the roles of capitalists and bankers and workers in Japan are reversed from those in other market economies. In the United States, Britain, and Germany, the workers have the first claim on the revenues of the firm; if the firm's wage rates and labor bill are too high relative to its revenues, there needs to be enough money left over to repay the bankers and other lenders and to finance its new investments, otherwise the firm fails – becomes bankrupt. (Recently pilots and other employees of many US airlines have agreed to large reductions in their wage rates, often after the firm has gone bankrupt.) In Japan, by contrast, the firm first makes the investments necessary to maintain its market share and then it pays interest to the bankers; the funds left over are divided among the workers, usually on the basis of their ages – the older workers receive higher wages than their younger counterparts, even when they perform similar tasks. As a result, within most industries there are substantial differences in the wages paid to individual workers with the same labor skills. Moreover, part of the wage payment consists of a semiannual bonus whose size is varied as revenues change: if revenues are modest, then the bonus will be small.

The stability of market shares of individual firms in particular industries might seem consistent with the planning model or with the competitive model. If the planning model were the better explanation, it might be inferred that government would have attempted to rationalize the business system by encouraging mergers. Such mergers have occurred – but only to a modest extent – and often among banks to 'save' other banks that have been crippled by large loan losses. To the extent that the planning model is relevant, the Japanese growth rate has been reduced and the impact of Japanese competition in world markets has been dampened.

The mother of all asset price bubbles

One of the surprises in the 1980s, and especially in the last several years of the decade, was the rapid climb of Japanese firms in their ranking on various world financial hit parades. Seven or eight of the ten largest banks in the world were Japanese, at least as measured by assets or deposits – but not by profits. The market value of firms headquartered in Japan increased sharply relative to the market values of firms headquartered in every other country; indeed, at the end of the decade the market value of Japanese firms was more than twice the market value of US firms. Since Japanese GDP was then half of US GDP, the ratio of the market value of Japanese firms to Japanese GNP was four times the same US ratio. The value of real estate in Japan increased to twice the value of US real estate – and Japan is about the size of California, and much of the country is mountainous. Newspapers were full of stories of the membership prices at various new golf courses – in some cases the prices were in the range of $200,000–$300,000. Japanese investors were massive buyers of real estate in the United States and Europe, especially of trophy properties – the Rockefeller Center, the Pebble Beach Golf Course on the Monterey Peninsula in California. Japanese hotel groups and individual Japanese were large buyers of real estate in Hawaii; one new hotel was so costly that the average daily room rate was projected at $800 a day. Japanese firms went on a massive acquisition binge in the United States and Europe.

The Japanese appeared to have all the money: it seemed as if Herman Kahn's forecast was coming true. The Japanese were beginning to count the months and years before the forecast implicit in the title *Japan as Number One* would come to pass.

From the beginning of January 1990, Japanese stock prices began to decline; by mid-1992 equity prices were 40 percent of their peak December 1989 values. Real estate prices began to decline, although at a slow rate. The buyer of the Pebble Beach Golf Course – who had paid $760 million – sold the course for $480 million to another Japanese. Japanese real estate and construction firms began to go bankrupt. Many of the real estate loans held by the Japanese banks became non-performing, because the rental incomes were much lower than the interest payments. The loss in personal wealth from the decline in stock prices and in real estate prices was phenomenally large. For the previous 40 years investment in real estate was a sure way to make money, because real estate prices always increased. As a result of the decline in real estate prices, individual investors began to reduce their spending. Because so many office buildings were less than fully occupied, the banks were reluctant to lend for new construction, with the result that spending on new buildings declined sharply.

The Japanese economy moved into a recession; for most of the period from the early 1990s until 2007, the growth rate in Japan was below the US growth rate. Because of the sluggish growth in consumer demand, business firms were reluctant to invest. Suddenly Kahn's forecast looked less brilliant. In part, the slowdown in the economy was an inevitable result of the implosion of asset values and the resulting decline in household wealth. Moreover, the government's sluggish response in recapitalizing the banks in a formal way compounded the problem; banks have not been aggressive lenders because they were increasingly concerned that their outstanding loans were too large relative to their capital.

The key question was whether Japan would recover its former growth momentum, or whether instead the Japanese economy would limp. The story told by those who believe that the sun is setting on Japan is that the country's population is aging at a rapid rate. Each female in Japan has only 1.8 children, in part because of the very cramped living accommodations in the urban areas and in part because young women have tasted the freedom associated with their own incomes and are reluctant to become homemakers. The absolute size of the population will begin to decline about 2015. As the population ages, consumption expenditure will decline because older populations buy fewer durable goods and less clothing, and even entertainment. Their savings tend to increase, at least until their final illness.

The paradox is that concern about the adequacy of funds for retirement led to an increase in household savings. Sluggish growth in demand and the economy meant that interest rates declined far below those in other industrial countries; indeed, the last time interest rates had been at this low level was in the Great Depression of the 1930s. Because a large part of the income of the retired Japanese comes from the interest on their savings accounts, the decline in the interest rates meant that their incomes declined, and their consumption spending fell. The consequence was that the private virtue of a high savings rate had become a public vice because spending levels had declined below the levels necessary to keep the economy fully employed and growing at a rate higher than 2 percent a year.

Lousy demographics or the negative wealth effects?

Japanese demographics – the rapid aging of the population – might explain the sharp slowdown in the country's rate of economic growth. As an increasingly large share of the population saves more in anticipation of retirement, domestic savings seem inordinately high relative to the domestic investment opportunities.

A second explanation for sluggish economic growth is the decline in household wealth associated with the sharp declines in stock prices and real estate prices, and the indirect effects of these declines on the capital of Japanese banks. The loan losses of these banks were three to four times larger than their capital; some estimates indicated that these loan losses were between 15 and 20 percent of Japanese GNP. Even though these banks were 'underwater' in any strict 'mark-to-market' test, there was little indication that the banks might be closed with loss to depositors; everyone acted as if they had full confidence that the government would bail out the banks, or at least the depositors. The banks appeared reluctant to extend loans, which led to the observation that there was a credit crunch.

The guarantee that the banks could not fail meant that they had been informally recapitalized by the government; the government had become the silent, major stockholder. But there was a stalemate: the government appeared unable to get sufficient agreement among the banks to move to a formal recapitalization – which would have meant that the banks would have to recognize these losses. One problem was that the best managed banks – those with the smallest losses relative to their capital – did not want to be seen in the same group with the banks that had much higher ratios of loan losses to capital. But there almost certainly are other explanations for the sluggishness in the move from informal to formal recapitalization.

And yet there is a paradox – despite the shortcomings of the Japanese economic performance as shown by the relatively high rate of unemployment (for Japan), the sluggish rate of growth, and the decline in industrial production, there was relatively little urgency in developing new government policies. Washington had a varied menu of measures that the Japanese Government should adopt, including tax cuts, increases in government spending, and reduction of government regulation of firms in the financial services. In part, the lack of urgency in the development of such policies may have resulted from the lack of evidence about hardship in the streets.

The external impacts of the Japanese business cycle

The rapid increase in the size of the Japanese economy has had an increasingly disruptive impact on its major trading partners – and especially on the US economy. In the 1950s and 1960s, during the pegged-rate exchange system period, Japan had a stable balance-of-payments cycle: three years of progressively larger payments deficits attributable to an acceleration in the rate of economic growth were followed by a year of tight money, slow growth, and a payments surplus. As the business expansion in Japan developed momentum, imports increased rapidly while the export growth slowed. These payments deficits were financed by increases in the amounts borrowed from US and European banks. As the ability to borrow decreased, the Bank of Japan was forced to contract the expansion of domestic credit, and the growth in Japanese demand and income became sluggish. Import demand dropped sharply and exports soared because firms were much more eager to sell abroad once domestic growth slackened.

The Japanese payments balance responded quickly and a large payments surplus developed; the funds from the payments surplus were used to repay the loans incurred in the several earlier years. Because export sales often were 20–30 percent of domestic sales, a small reduction in domestic demand led to a much larger percentage increase in exports. The story was straightforward: once Japanese firms had the productive capacity in place, goods would be produced; if these goods could not be sold at home, they would be sold abroad at the prices necessary to clear the market. Better to sell at discount – or even at distress prices – abroad than to engage in price competition in the domestic market, or not to produce at all.

Thus whenever the rate of growth of domestic demand in Japan faltered, the United States and many other industrial countries experienced an increase in their imports from Japan. The growth of Japanese exports was countercyclical to the growth of Japanese domestic income. The ability to divert productivity capacity from domestic to foreign markets enabled Japan to cushion the swings in its business cycle. Japan was exporting an expansive impact to its trading partners when its own economy was booming because of the surge in its imports, and it was exporting a contractive impact when its own growth slowed because of the decline in its demand for imports.

In the 1950s and 1960s, the international monetary system could readily adjust to the payments deficits that resulted whenever the Japanese wanted to have payments surpluses because Japan still was a reasonably small country. Many of its exports were directed to the United States, which was the national market most open – or least closed – to Japanese goods. Moreover, marketing in the large open US economy was substantially easier than trying to sell the same volume of goods in smaller countries whose combined GDPs were comparable to the US GDP. Individual firms and groups of firms in the United States complained about unfair competition: they asserted that the prices of these goods in the US markets were substantially below the prices of comparable goods in Japan. The Japanese had two responses – that they were not dumping, but even if they were dumping, cutting prices was the only way they could increase their US sales. The US response was to lean on Japan to follow 'orderly marketing procedures.'

The export of imbalances

The response of the Japanese economy to the move toward a more expansive monetary policy since the implosion of the bubble in the early 1990s has been very different from the response in the 1950s and most of the 1960s. In the earlier period, the economy resumed its rapid growth rate after the Bank of Japan shifted from a contractive monetary policy. However, in the late 1960s the increase in effective domestic demand was weaker when the Bank of Japan moved to a more expansive monetary stance. Because domestic demand in Japan was not growing nearly as rapidly as productive capacity Japan continued to realize large payments surpluses as exports boomed. In effect the Japanese were selling Toyotas and Sonys abroad and using some of the funds from their export earnings to buy US Treasury Bills.

In both 1969 and 1970, Japan's current account surpluses were in the range of 4–5 percent of its GDP; in 1972, this ratio approached 10 percent. Since there is a counterpart deficit for every surplus, the inability of the Japanese to manage domestic demand meant that its trading partners – principally the United States – had very large payments deficits.

For the US consumers, increased availability of goods from Japan was a tremendous advantage in two different ways. The variety of goods available in the US market was much larger and for an extended period, the quality of many of the goods available to the US consumers improved sharply. US producers responded by improving the quality and variety of their own products – the quality improvement was especially evident in automobiles produced by US firms. But for US producers of goods competitive with imports from Japan, the story was less hopeful: the increase in imports from Japan meant a decline in market share, output and employment, and profits – and a large number of US firms went out of business.

The large Japanese trade surplus in 1970 and 1971 was a major factor in the breakdown of the Bretton Woods system of adjustable currency parities. Even in the absence of more rapid inflation in the United States than abroad, the Japanese surpluses would have threatened the stability of the system. The revaluation of the Japanese yen in response to the excessively large Japanese payments surplus would have reduced its trade surplus somewhat; the tentative 'somewhat' reflects the fact that Japanese imports are not especially price-sensitive to decreases in their effective prices to Japanese consumers because such a large part of these imports are industrial raw materials and energy. Moreover, Japanese exports are not especially price-sensitive because Japanese firms are reluctant to reduce production and sales, even when net selling prices decline because their commitments to lifetime employment means that a large proportion of their costs are fixed. However if a small revaluation would not have been effective, then a larger revaluation might have succeeded. Japan was reluctant to revalue the yen: any decline in exports relative to imports would have led to an increase in the unemployment rate. A large part of the Camp David initiative in August 1971 was directed at inducing Japan to revalue the yen or to permit the yen to float.

In 1973, as the world economy boomed and prices of raw materials imports increased, Japan's trade surplus declined. Japan's oil import bill increased by $15 billion a year. Japan had a modest payments deficit in 1974. When the world recession hit in 1975, domestic demand in Japan grew sluggishly, and once again Japanese producers shipped more abroad. Comparisons across countries indicated a much greater cyclical variation in the Japanese payments balance than in those in other countries. The story was that when the growth in Japanese GDP was rapid, Japan's exports would grow slowly, and when Japanese GDP increased slowly Japanese exports would grow rapidly. Variations in the growth of domestic income were the major factors in explaining the changes in the growth of Japanese exports and in the Japanese trade surplus.

With the move to floating exchange rates in the early 1970s, the textbooks predicted that Japan would always be in payments balance. But the senior officials in the MOF and the Bank of Japan had not read the textbooks; from time to time the Bank of Japan was a large buyer of US dollars to limit the appreciation of the yen. Paradoxically, these Japanese payments surpluses were much larger than had ever been experienced when the yen was pegged; when the rules of the Bretton Woods system were abandoned, the system was left without rules. If the Bank of Japan had not bought large amounts of US dollars, the yen would have appreciated sharply, and Japanese exporters would have been obliged to cut export prices dramatically or else forgo sales. The problem was the same as under the pegged-rate system if domestic income was growing sluggishly, then excess productivity capacity would have to be geared to export sales.

In the mid-1980s, Japanese investors concluded that US dollar securities were attractive, largely because the interest rates were 3–4 percentage points higher than the interest rates on comparable Japanese securities. One result of large imports of US dollar securities by various Japanese investors was that the Japanese yen depreciated extensively; another was that Japan again developed very large trade surpluses and very large current account surpluses, whose counterpart was large US trade and current account deficits.

The world's largest creditor country

During the 1980s Japanese foreign investments began to increase at a rapid rate; by the late 1980s Japan had become the world's largest creditor country (which meant that the excess of Japanese-owned foreign assets over foreign-owned assets in Japan was much larger than the comparable ratios for other countries), displacing the United States from the position it had achieved in the 1940s. The counterpart of the Japanese purchases of US and other foreign assets was that Japan developed a persistently large trade surplus. About half of the total Japanese trade surplus was a result of its bilateral trade surplus with the United States. Moreover,

Japan had trade surpluses with many of its neighboring countries including China that were large exporters to the United States; many of their exports contained large Japanese components. Thus the multilateral Japanese trade surplus with the United States was larger than the bilateral trade surplus.

The counterpart of Japan's move to the world's largest creditor country was that the United States became the world's largest debtor country. Now Japan receives increasingly large interest receipts and profits on its foreign investments, which are used to buy more foreign securities and assets. The paradoxical result is that the stronger yen handicaps the ability of firms producing in Japan to export on a profitable basis – which increases their incentive to invest abroad.

The global recession of 2008 and 2009 led to a dramatic decline in the foreign demand for Japanese exports – and Japan imported a recession that initially appeared more severe than the ones in the United States and Europe. Export-led growth policies are like the proverbial two-edged sword; the downside is that the decline in the demand in the importing countries has a larger impact on those that had geared their own growth to the growth of exports.

In a mercantilist world, the Japanese trade and payments surpluses might represent the success of economic policy. But the proposition is not convincing: the excessively large surpluses represent the failure of policy. The managers of Japan, Inc. have failed to design a system which is able to cope with cyclical imbalances without placing great strain on its international trading relationships. The likelihood that Japan will bear out Herman Kahn's prediction is low.

22
China – The 800-Pound Gorilla

China is big history

In the last several decades there has been a remarkable expansion in the product line of Chinese restaurants in America and Europe. The traditional Cantonese cuisine that dominated menus in the 1950s and the 1960s has given way to cooking in the Mandarin, Szechwan, and Hunan styles. The differences in cuisine reflect the immense size of China, and regional differences in basic foodstuffs – the Cantonese chefs work around rice dishes; seafood is an important component of the menus. Mandarin cooking is northern with wheat as the basic starch. Meats were important in the cuisines of Hunan and of Szechwan; and because the meats were not always fresh, hot spices were added to distract from the taste of the basic ingredients. The north–south wheat–rice distinction more or less parallels the Yangtze River, which bisects China; 500 million people live north of this river and 800 million south of it.

China is a big country, physically larger than the United States. And like the United States, Brazil, Russia, and Australia, the other large continental economies, China has an abundance of raw materials and for a long time it produced the basic foods for its population – almost twice the combined populations of Europe and North America.

China also has a 'big history,' which starts in the third millennium before the beginning of the Christian era. Its early industrial achievements included the development of bronze, porcelain, moveable type, and paper. China had a well-organized governmental bureaucracy when most of Europe consisted of tribes warring to expand their turf. Marco Polo, the Venetian-based adventurer, traveled to China in the thirteenth century and reported on its superior achievements. Until the seventeenth century or perhaps even the eighteenth century, per capita incomes in China were higher than those in Europe.

China missed the Industrial Revolution for more than a hundred years, and fell far behind a rapidly developing West. European power was directed at China in the middle of the nineteenth century; Britain developed a coastal enclave in Hong Kong while Portugal colonized Macao. During the first half of the twentieth century the struggle for power dominated domestic politics: an imperial family dynasty that had ruled for three centuries was challenged by republicans that wanted a representative government, who then were challenged by the communists in the 1930s. In the late 1930s Japan occupied the seaboard provinces in a prelude to its more ambitious adventures throughout Southeast Asia.

The hermit kingdom and its sequel

The communists consolidated their power in 1949; the remnants of the Republican government moved to what is now Taiwan, along with several millions who feared for their futures under a communist regime. China became a 'hermit kingdom' for the next 30 years under Chairman Mao's rule; in the early 1950s Mao promoted backyard steel mills in the misnamed 'The Great Leap Forward' that proved to be an economic disaster. Then he sent tens of millions of the urban middle class – the teachers and the professors and the doctors and the engineers – to the farms to feed the pigs in what was euphemistically called the 'Cultural Revolution.' There was a strong effort to obliterate individualism; everyone wore the same tufted blue cotton suit that came in two sizes. Contact with the West was extremely limited. There were more extensive contacts with the Soviet Union, but then the inherent conflicts between the national interests of the two countries came to dominate superficial ideological affinity. Economic growth during the period of Mao's leadership was less than 1 percent a year, one of the lowest rates in the world.

Industrial China in the Mao period centered on state-owned enterprises that were organized like medieval manors; a large factory would own the housing for its workers, and provide medical care, vacations, even much of their food. Several of the major army groups had their own business units, which included hotels and manufacturing plants. Various government ministries and the central bank had their own universities; one university owned a factory that produced the university's desks, chairs, and other classroom furniture.

China's economic policies changed dramatically after Mao's death. Deng Xiao Ping, Mao's successor after a brief struggle for power, opened the door for the move toward greater reliance on the market and more foreign trade. Foreign firms were encouraged to invest in China; usually they were required to participate in joint ventures with state-owned Chinese firms. Some of the state-owned firms were privatized. Individual Chinese had much greater opportunity to study and visit abroad, and the overseas Chinese including those in Taiwan were encouraged to visit and invest in China.

Since the early 1980s the rate of economic growth in China has averaged 10 percent – a remarkable achievement. Despite this rapid growth, per capita GDP in China is about $2000 because the level initially was so low. (The US dollar equivalent of per capita GDP in China varies with changes in the price of the US dollar in terms of the Chinese yuan; as the yuan price of the US dollar has declined, the US dollar equivalent of China's GDP has increased.) China's GDP is about one-fourth that of the United States. Growth has been much more rapid in the seacoast provinces where much of the new industrial investment is located;

per capita incomes of the 250 million people that live in these provinces is four to five times the average for the rest of the country. The rapid growth-provinces include Guangdong, which is up the Pearl River estuary from Hong Kong, and Fujian, which is opposite Taiwan, and both Shanghai and Beijing.

If the growth rate for the next 20 years continues at the rate of the last 20 years, then in 2025 China's GDP will be not much below that of the United States, even though per capita incomes would still be one-fourth those in the United States. China's GDP is higher than that of every other Asian country. If the 10 percent growth rate continues for the next 50 years, then per capita incomes in China in the middle decades of the twenty-first century will approach that in the United States, and China will be a dominant global economic power.

Long-term projections of the impacts of differences in national growth are interesting arithmetic exercises, but they tend to be wide of the mark because countries encounter domestic and external constraints that eventually limit growth. The 1980s projections that Japan would surpass the United States as the dominant economic power demonstrates the risk – and the potential embarrassment – in making long-term growth projections. In 1965 some analysts projected that if Japan continued to grow at 8 or 10 percent a year when the rest of the world was growing at an annual rate in the range of 2–3 percent, then eventually per capita GDP in Japan would exceed per capita GDP in the United States. That prediction has not yet been proven correct. Nevertheless Japan achieved growth rates sufficiently high so that the United States had more trade frictions with Japan than with any other country; indeed, US trade frictions with Japan were more extensive than with all European countries as a group. These trade frictions centered on both the exceedingly large Japanese trade surplus and the surge in the Japanese market share in particular industrial products. Japanese growth has faltered since the implosion of the bubbles in its real estate and stock markets at the beginning of the 1990s.

Still, 20 and 30 years are a blink in Chinese history; the dates are less important than whether the trend can persist. If the growth rate were to decline to 5 percent, then eventually China's GDP would exceed that of the United States; similarly at a much later date, its per capita GDP would exceed that of the United States.

Limits to Chinese growth

Japan and South Korea also realized high rates of economic growth as they industrialized. The China story is similar; unskilled labor has moved from the farms and villages to the cities and to the factories where it produced – initially – toys, textiles, baseball caps, apparel, bicycles, sports equipment, hammers, screwdrivers, electric drills, auto parts, and luggage. The productivity of each worker in industry and in construction was three or four times higher than on the farms; hence the redeployment of 4 or 5 million workers each year from the farms and the villages to the factories and the cities led to a significant increase in the growth rate, even though the productivity of the factory workers was very low. The departure of the workers from the farms had no measurable impact in reducing agricultural output, since there had been too many workers on the land. Per capita incomes on the farms increased, partly from the reduction in the number of farmers, and partly from the increase in demand for food in the cities, which led to higher prices.

Many of the items produced in the factories – the toys, textiles, and apparel – were exported, and the foreign currencies that were earned were used to buy machine tools and essential imports and foodstuffs for those who lived in the cities.

Perhaps 200 million individuals have moved from the farms to industry and construction; another 350 million workers are still on the farms. Many countries can feed their populations when no more than 10 percent of the workers are on the farms. Assume that China develops to the point where 65 million farmers – 10 percent of the labor force – can supply most of the foodstuffs necessary to feed the urban masses. Some foods would be imported, and payment for these imports would take the form of exports of manufactured goods.

The improvement in agricultural productivity means that employment opportunities would have to develop for nearly 200 million more workers in nonfarming activities – manufacturing and services and during the transition, construction.

Manufacturing might then account for 40–50 percent of the labor force – the 50 percent figure suggests that employment in manufacturing in China would then total 325 million. By comparison, employment in US manufacturing is 20 million – at the global level, employment in manufacturing now totals 80–100 million.

For the last 20 years, the increase in employment in manufacturing in China has led to a shift away from manufacturing in the United States and other traditional industrial countries. That shift has been reflected in the increase in the China's trade surplus and the counterpart increases in the trade deficits of China's trading partners.

At some stage, China will encounter a limit to the expansion of its trade surplus – indeed that limit may already have been reached.

China's ability to increase its production of manufactures will depend on both supply and demand factors. One of the important supply factors is the ability to finance the construction of manufacturing plant and associated infrastructure. The savings rate in China has been extremely high, between 35 and 45 percent, and has facilitated high levels of investment in industry, infrastructure, and both rural and urban housing. (The stadiums and airport terminals and other facilities developed for the 2008 Olympics were remarkable testimony of the government's ability to obtain funds for investment in infrastructure.) The entrepreneurial tradition in China is strong, despite several decades of communist planning. Government restrictions have been modest – and often they have been ignored when they seemed burdensome. The Chinese leadership has been dominated by individuals trained as engineers, and the government has provided the infrastructure for growth – power and transport – and these facilities have been developed at a rapid rate, although there have been occasional shortages of electricity.

One of the brilliant decisions – in retrospect – of the Chinese planners was to invite the multinational firms from Japan, Taiwan, South Korea, the United States, and Europe to manufacture in China, primarily for the global markets – although many of these firms established factories in China because they were interested in the large domestic market. The caricature is that the multinational firms shipped high value-added components that had been produced in the United States or Japan or Taiwan or South Korea to China for final assembly by young ladies whose major 'machine tools' were several screwdrivers; the products were then exported to global markets in the established supply chains of the multinationals. Many of the goods that China exports have low Chinese value-added. China has had a trade deficit with its Asian neighbors as a result of these imports. Part of the Chinese trade surplus with the United States and other industrial countries in reality is a surplus with the countries that produce these high value-added components. Because of the low level of wages, production costs in China were lower than in the industrial countries and in most other Asian countries, and these firms began to fill their supply chains with goods produced in China. Chinese exports increased at a very rapid rate; the lack of foreign currencies – which had constrained growth in both Japan and South Korea – did not limit Chinese growth.

The success of China's exports is evident in the increase in its international reserve assets, which reached $2000 billion at the end of 2007. It is as if each Chinese man, woman, and child had invested $1500 in US Treasury securities, a phenomenal development in a country with a low per capita GDP. The accumulation of these reserve assets has resulted from China's trade surplus which has become the largest in the world; its trade surplus with the United States is larger than that of any other country.

The increase in China's holdings of international reserve assets reflects the success of the export-led growth policy. Rapid productivity gains in manufacturing have led to significant declines in unit production costs and contributed to the growth in exports. The accumulation of international reserve assets is an unintended result of the policy of maintaining a low value for the currency as a way to promote exports.

Some of the factors that led to the slowing of the growth rates in Japan and South Korea eventually will lead to a slowing of China's growth. At some stage the supply of excess labor on the farms will become depleted – that process took one generation in both Japan and South Korea, but it might take two or even three in China. A second constraint is that as China's exports increase relative to world exports, it will become more difficult to maintain the growth rate of exports. A third is that achieving a rapid growth rate is much easier when the gap in per capita incomes is large than when it is smaller; as per capita GDP increases, wage costs and unit production costs will increase. A fourth is that the savings may prove too high relative to its domestic investment opportunities with the result that demand growth will be sluggish; in this case savings is a private virtue but a public vice in the sense that demand growth is too slow.

Chinese growth has already presented problems for the United States and its other trading partners. Formal and informal barriers to imports are extensive;

China – like Japan and South Korea – is reluctant to import products if comparable goods are produced by state-owned enterprises or by other firms in China. The joint venture arrangements with the multinational firms have been renegotiated after they have proved successful and the new terms are more favorable to the Chinese partner. The exceedingly large trade surplus is evidence that China is much more eager to export than it is to import. There is a modest tradition of respect for intellectual property rights.

The limits to Chinese growth are more likely to occur on the demand side than on the supply side. The question is whether demand will increase and particularly whether domestic demand will increase more rapidly to compensate for the slowdown in the growth of foreign demand.

Export-led growth, the trade surplus, and the asset price bubble

China has mimicked the export-led polices adopted by Japan and South Korea. The thrust of these policies was to maintain a low value for the currency and for wages so that exports would grow at a rapid rate. The money earned from exports can be used to buy capital equipment and technology and raw materials so the growth rate would remain high.

One regulatory practice imported from Japan and South Korea was to regulate the financial system to maintain low interest rates for both household savers and business borrowers, much below the rate of economic growth and often in the same ball park as the inflation rate. The real rate of return to household savers often was not significantly above zero, which meant the households had to maintain a high savings rate to achieve their wealth goals. Firms – both privately owned firms and state-owned firms – had a strong incentive to borrow at what in effect were very low real interest rates so they could invest.

The Japanese and the South Korean experiences suggest that these financial regulatory practices had two direct impacts. One was that the firms wanted to borrow much more from the banks than the banks were willing to lend, because the anticipated profit rate was so much higher than the interest rate on the borrowed money. Investment spending was much higher as a share of GDP than in Western industrial countries and latent excess capacity developed.

The second was that the household saving rate was high because the real rate of return on saving was so low. Two China-specific factors contributed to the high saving rate. One was that the move from the command economy toward a market economy in the 1990s meant that individuals were personally responsible for paying for their medical care, the education of their children, and their own retirement. The other was that the one child–one family policy meant that each member of the labor force would be somewhat responsible for the economic welfare of two retired parents.

The high savings rate and the high investment rate complemented each other; it would not have been possible to have a high investment rate without a high saving rate. The result was that China began to develop excess capacity in many basic industries.

The overseas Chinese economies

One of the great economic success stories of the last 50 years is that of the 150 million overseas Chinese – the 25 million in Taiwan, the 7 million in Hong Kong, and the 4 million in Singapore, and the millions in Malaysia, Indonesia, Thailand, and Vietnam as well as in the United States and Canada.

Several 'Chinese countries' have trade surpluses. Hong Kong has a trade surplus and so does Taiwan. Singapore has a very large trade surplus. If these countries continue to grow and if they continue to have trade surpluses, it's a safe bet that the US trade deficit with China will increase, with the associated job losses in US manufacturing. The trade surpluses of these countries reflect their savings rates are high relative to their domestic investment opportunities and some of the savings are used to purchase foreign securities and real assets.

The national income of the 150 million overseas Chinese is much larger than China's national income. Hong Kong, Taiwan (or, as it sometimes called China Taipei), and Singapore are largely Chinese. The business communities in many other countries in Southeast Asia – Vietnam, Malaysia, the Philippines, Thailand, and Indonesia – are largely Chinese (and would be even more extensively Chinese if the governments in Kuala Lumpur and Jakarta had not adopted affirmative action-type policies to favor the Malays in their business activities). Within the United States the Chinese have been remarkably successful in terms of academic achievement and business success, especially in small family businesses.

Hong Kong, Singapore, Taiwan, and South Korea are grouped as the 'Little Tigers,' a response to their sustained rates of economic growth of 6–8 percent for about 30 years. Singapore and Hong Kong are small island economies, whose only natural resource are their remarkable harbors. Both are extensively involved in transit trade as well as manufacturing (although most of the manufacturing in Hong Kong has moved across the Chinese border to the various sites along the Pearl River estuary). Singapore's imports are 50 percent larger than its national income – a large part of imports are processed or assembled, or refined or somehow modified and then reexported.

The role of the Hong Kong Government toward managing its economy differs from the approach taken by the Government of Singapore. Hong Kong has been about as freewheeling an economy as possible; the economic role of government has been small, and limited primarily to providing law and order, building an efficient infrastructure, expanding educational facilities, and developing public housing. Until the handover of sovereignty to China in mid-1997 the Hong Kong Government was a benevolent dictatorship; the citizens had little, if any, say in their choice of leaders or in the policies of the government. In contrast, the Government of Singapore was involved in extensive economic planning; individuals were forced to save a very large share of their incomes partly in government funds. Extensive efforts were undertaken to attract foreign firms and to upgrade the technological skills of the labor force. The government was not tolerant of criticism and dissent: a facade of democratic institutions was maintained but the dominant political party had total control.

Much can be made of the differences in the political arrangements in Hong Kong and Singapore. Yet despite their differences both have been remarkable success stories – which suggests that the political arrangements may not be very important as long as their economic and political environments are stable.

Taiwan also has been an amazing economic success story, despite the lack of natural resources and large defense expenditures. In 1949, per capita income in Taiwan was about $100 a year (although the number is uncertain because of the large immigration from the mainland); currently the level is about $10,000. Taiwan ranks 10th–15th on the world list of GDPs, a remarkable accomplishment in terms of its inherited handicaps and an unfriendly neighborhood. The economy consists of tens of thousands of very small firms and relatively few large firms comparable to those in Japan and South Korea. Taiwan's holdings of international reserve assets are larger than those of any country in Europe and exceeded only by those of Japan – and on a per capita basis, Taiwan's foreign exchange reserves are almost three times those of Japan.

South Korea obviously is not Chinese, but the link to the various Chinese economies is through the Confucian value system. The economic success of South Korea is even more remarkable than that of Taiwan. When the Korean War ended in 1954 much of the country was in shambles; most of what is now South Korea had been overrun twice by the armies from North Korea. Prior to the war and the division of the country in 1945, most of the country's industry had been in the North. Since the war the country has maintained a large army: its defense expenditures account for nearly 10 percent of GDP. Partly because South Korea is larger than the other three 'Tigers' combined and partly because of the strong sense of national identity, South Korea has tried to develop its economy on the basis of its domestic firms. South Korea has been unfriendly to foreign investment in general and to Japanese firms in particular, although it has imported and adapted technologies that had been developed abroad. A very large share of productive activity occurs in the 30 large chaebols – family-based holding companies that may own controlling interests in 40 or 50 different operating companies in a wide range of industries.

What are the common factors that might explain the economic success of the 'Tigers'? Each country has a high savings rate. Each country has made a large investment in upgrading its educational system and labor skills; literacy rates are high. Each country has had a very strong export orientation. The role of government in productive decisions is modest, although the governments have a strong investment orientation. And each more or less started with a 'clean slate' – there was a trivial industrial structure.

China has several of the factors associated with the economic success of the 'Tigers.' The savings rate in China is high, above those in most of the tigers. China – at least China of the 1980s and the 1990s – has a strong orientation toward increasing exports and participating in the world economy, much like the 'Tigers.' Indeed, the ratio of imports to GDP is extremely high for a large country with a rich and varied resource base, and more or less self-sufficiency in agriculture.

What are the differences between China and the four 'Tigers' and how might these differences affect China's economic growth over the next 10–20 years?

One is size; China has more than 15 times the population of the four tigers combined. Large countries are more difficult to manage than small countries. Regionalism has been a pervasive problem in Chinese history; from time to time the central government has found that the disparate regions want to go their own ways. As in so many other countries, the wealthy regions are reluctant to share resources with the poorer ones. There are elements of informal provincial trade barriers; the only automobile models that can be used as taxis in Shanghai are those produced in the local area.

Competition among the regions for the steel mills and the automobile plants and other high-visibility investment projects has been extensive. The result has been a rapid growth of productive capacity. A nontrivial part of this capacity has been used to create more capacity, which in turn has been used to create even more capacity. At some stage, the expansion of productive capacity will slow and probably dramatically; there will then be massive excess capacity in many industries. One impact of the surge in excess capacity will be downward pressures on prices, another will be a surge in unemployment, a third will be a sharp increase in exports, and a fourth will be massive loan losses by the banks that lent much of the money to create the capacity.

A second is geography; the 'Tigers' are close to the sea and have relatively easy access to foreign markets. Much of China is far from the sea; the implication is that industrial development in the inland areas will be more difficult and hence growth potential is lower because of the higher costs of developing the infrastructure.

A third is that China is resource-rich. China can feed itself despite its extremely large population. And China has most of the resources necessary for its industrial development, which means that it has less need to export to earn the foreign exchange to import these materials than any of the 'Tigers.'

A fourth is recent history and ancient history. China has international political ambitions that none of the 'Tigers' has. Much attention is given in Beijing to recovering the 'lost province' of Taiwan. China wants to become an even more important regional power, with stewardship over the overseas Chinese. Their ambitions may extend to becoming a global power, with the implication that military expenditure may increase as a share of national income.

A fifth is recent industrial history. The 'Tigers' started with a clean slate. In contrast, China has an industrial base that has been inherited from its 30 years under Mao. There are more than 100,000 medium and large state-owned firms that together employ more than 110 million people. Most of these firms are highly inefficient with employment levels that are extremely large relative to their levels of output – some estimate that redundant labor may total 50 million people. Many of these firms are in debt to the state-owned banks, which have made many loans that will never be repaid – the estimate is that the accumulated loan losses of these banks may be $500 billion.

One challenge to China is to provide good jobs for those now effectively unemployed and for the tens of millions who will become unemployed as agriculture in China becomes more efficient.

The savings–investment paradox

The inference from China's large trade surplus and the increase in its holdings of international reserve assets to an extremely high value is that domestic savings in China are significantly larger than the sum of domestic investment and the government's fiscal deficit, so part of the savings flows abroad. Domestic supply capability is significantly higher than domestic demand. This problem is common to a number of countries in the neighborhood (except South Korea) that have high savings rates. China's potential supply capabilities will be even greater because there are tens of millions of workers who are underemployed on the farms and an abundance of savings that could be profitably invested.

The excess savings in Japan and other nearby countries became apparent only when their per capita incomes were much higher than that in China. The high savings rate in China reflects the absence of social institutions that provide money to cope with retirement or medical or other emergencies; the savings rate might decline if new institutions were developed to provide money to the retired elderly, like the 'safety nets' in most other industrial countries, and to provide money to cope with costly medical situations. The excess saving might also decline if there were an increase in the domestic investment rate, although this rate is more likely to decline as excess productive capacity becomes more evident in many industries.

One lesson from the sharp decline in the growth rate in 2009 is that the large trade surplus meant that employment in manufactures was dependent on foreign demand – and when the recession led to a decline in foreign demand, 20 million individuals became unemployed. During a recession, countries with large trade deficits may seek to adopt measures to limit imports and promote exports as a way to reduce unemployment in the production of tradable goods. Since China has had the largest trade surplus, it is vulnerable to these developments.

China has reacted to the decline in the foreign demand for its manufactures with an economic stimulus program largely designed to enhance its infrastructure. Productivity in these new economic activities is likely to be much lower than in manufactures. The growth rate will decline and perhaps sharply.

One limit to the continuation of a rate of economic growth of 6 or 8 percent a year is external; China will find it increasingly difficult to grow its exports at these rates because its share of foreign markets for textiles, footwear, toys and sports equipment, and apparel already is very large. Continued rapid growth of exports is necessary to obtain the foreign exchange to pay for imports – and the need for imports might increase as domestic supplies of various raw materials become depleted, or need to grow commensurate with the growth of the economy.

There are also several possible domestic limits to factors that might lead to a sharp decline in the growth rate. Many of the state-owned industrial firms may wither, unable to recover costs by making attractive products and unable to retain their most productive employees. Tens of thousands of these firms may remain active even though their losses are subsidized by loans from the state-owned banks that will never be repaid. At some point these banks must be recapitalized, or a new set of banks must be established to provide credit for profitable and productive enterprises.

China appeared largely immune to the Asian financial crisis of the late 1990s, although its growth rate declined from 8 percent to 6 percent. The irony of China's development prospects from the economic viewpoint is that its savings rate may be too high to provide the growth in demand necessary to provide the jobs for those in industry. As in Japan, an increase in economic uncertainties may lead to an increase in saving. So the economic conditions for the continuation of a rapid rate of growth include broadening the mix of exports to include a larger share of high-value-added products, the continued dismantling of the tens of thousands of inefficient enterprises, the development of an efficient banking system, and a modest reduction in the savings rate. Even if these conditions are satisfied, political developments may constrain growth. Regionalism is an ever-present source of friction because of the sharp differences in per capita income. Growth is likely to require some decentralization of decision-making, and the monopoly of power held by the Communist Party will be challenged.

The economic growth rates in both Japan and South Korea slowed dramatically once the supply of excess labor on the farms had been exhausted; less than 5 percent of their populations now are employed in agriculture. Farmers account for nearly 50 percent of the labor force in China, and there are several hundred million individuals that could move to the factories – assuming that the demand for the goods produced in the factories continues to expand. Currently 120–140 million individuals work in the factories.

The global recession that developed at the end of 2008 led to a sharp reduction in the foreign demand for Chinese goods. Slightly before this shock occurred, the investment spending that had been undertaken in anticipation of the Olympic Games had been completed. Millions employed in the production of tradable goods lost their jobs. The decline in their income will have two dramatic impacts – one is that investment spending will decline, because excess productive capacity has surged. The other is that household saving may increase because there is more uncertainty about economic and financial futures.

23
From Marxist Command Economies to Market Capitalism

The implosion of an empire

One of the remarkable changes since the fifth edition of this book has been the collapse of the 'Evil Empire.' The Berlin Wall is now in pieces in hundreds of museums, and Eastern Europe has moved west and has been rechristened Central Europe. The USSR – the Union of Soviet Socialist Republics – is no long a union, no longer soviet, and far from socialist. What had been the Soviet Union is now Russia and 12 or so independent republics, some less independent than others and few republican. Poland and its neighbors have moved from coerced dependence on Moscow to becoming parts of the global market economy. The Baltic Countries – Estonia, Latvia, and Lithuania – have regained the independence they lost in 1939. Ukraine, which had been part of Russia for more than 100 years before the Russian revolution, is now an independent country – one continually at odds with Russia over the price of natural gas, the charges for the use of the pipelines, and access to naval bases on the Black Sea.

The separation between the First World and the Second was the 'Iron Curtain,' which went from the Baltic Sea to the Adriatic. Berlin – West Berlin – was an island republic within East Germany, surrounded by barbed wire and guard towers.

For nearly 50 years the metaphor for American–Soviet relations was two spiders in a bottle – each had the ability to inflict extreme harm on the other. The Soviets had a large army, poised to march to the West from its bases in Poland and other satellite countries, and the Americans had a massive air force with nuclear weapons.

The demise of the Iron Curtain probably occurred because the Russians concluded – after oil prices had declined sharply in the second half of the 1980s – that the costs of maintaining an empire in Eastern Europe were too high relative to the benefits. The end of empire led to a massive restructuring in patterns of trade, production, and finance, both for Russia and for the countries on its western borders from Estonia in the north to Bulgaria in the south.

During the Soviet period most of the international trade of the countries in the bloc was with other countries in the bloc; trade with the 'outside world' was minimal, and then largely to deal with exceptional shortages. During this period a group of central planners in Moscow decided which goods would be produced in which countries in the bloc, and how these goods would be allocated among the countries within the bloc. The Russians produced most of the heavy equipment, but the Bulgarians produced most of the fork lift trucks for the bloc. When production declined below target, often because of weather, and the wheat harvests were poor, food was imported from one of the market economies.

When the Iron Curtain came down, each of the countries faced more or less the same decision – what was its niche in the global market economy – what could it export to the West, and what should it expect to import, and what should be done with factories that never had to be concerned with marketing because they had a captive market.

What is a transition economy?

A: A country on the move from a command economy to a market economy.

Q: Which countries are considered transition economies?

A: The big ones are Russia, Ukraine, and Poland; there are 20 smaller ones, including what had been East Germany, the three Baltic countries of Lithuania, Latvia, and Estonia, the Czech Republic and Slovakia, Hungary, Rumania, Belarus, Armenia, Georgia, Albania, and Tajikistan.

Q: What is the best way to move from a command economy to a market economy?

A: Who knows?

The ruble was a heavy currency

During the Soviet period the ruble, the zloty, and the lek were not included in the hit parade of currencies, since they could not be freely traded. An individual in Warsaw who might have won the lottery or otherwise had a large amount of cash could not use the money to buy the US dollar, the German mark, or the Swiss franc – at least not legally.

When state-owned enterprises in Russia exported to the West, they were paid in US dollars, which they then transferred to a bank in Moscow. The bank in Moscow then placed these dollar funds with a captive bank – the Moscow Narodny Bank in London or the Banque Commerciale pour L'Europe du Nord in Paris or Wozchod Commercial Bank AG in Frankfurt.

The Russians fantasized that the ruble was at the top of the currency hit parade – the financial market counterpart to their claims of inventing the sewing machine, the typewriter, and baseball. Still, the ruble needed a price in terms of one of the Western currencies, and since there was no way that the Americans would peg the US dollar to the ruble, the Russians pegged the ruble to the US dollar in 1937 at 4 rubles to the US dollar. In 1950 they set a parity for the ruble in terms of gold at the rate of 140 rubles per ounce of gold. (Note the arithmetic – since the US dollar price of an ounce of gold was $35, the effective price of the US dollar in terms of the ruble was not changed.) From the point of view of the apparatchiks in Moscow, the ruble was now on the same footing as the dollar, since both had parities in terms of gold. But the new parity was meaningless, since the amount of gold produced had nothing to do with the relationship between the costs of production (often by political prisoners) and the price at which gold could be sold to the central bank.

In 1961 the Soviet Union underwent a currency reform, and a new heavy ruble was established in exchange for ten old rubles. (The currency reform was a tax on those who had acquired large amounts of the old ruble notes, since there was a limit on the amount of old ruble notes that could be exchanged for new ruble notes.) The Russians set a new parity for the ruble in terms of gold at 32 rubles per ounce of gold, which was about 10 percent less than the US dollar price – as if it mattered.

At the end of 1992, soon after the break-up of the Soviet Union, Russia joined the International Monetary Fund (IMF); the exchange rate was then 472 rubles to the US dollar. Throughout the 1990s the ruble depreciated, in large part because the country was experiencing hyperinflation – the old tax base had disappeared before a new one could be installed. The government went to the central bank to get some of the money to pay its bills, and the money supply increased at a rapid rate.

The paradox was that there was a shortage of money despite the rapid expansion of the money supply. The demand for money and credit was increasing more rapidly than supply, and the supply was increasing to finance government expenditure. Firms in the government sector were starved for credit and resorted to barter. Workers were sometimes paid with the goods produced in the factories which could not be sold because of the shortage of credit.

In the early 1990s President Yeltsin decided to privatize as much of the economy as possible in the effort to decentralize power and get the 'country moving again.' These government businesses were sold for relatively low prices, in part because many seemed unprofitable and in part because the buyers were in cahoots with the functionaries that were the sellers. Corruption had become endemic during the Marxist period when the enemy was the state and it became more brazen afterward.

The command economy and the market economy

Consider several of the differences between a command economy and a market economy.

In a command economy the means of production – the factories and airlines, the banks and retail stores, the houses and apartments – are owned by the state; in the market economy the factories are owned by companies and individuals – and individuals own the companies.

In a command economy the price of each good and service is set by the planners in the central government and is only tangentially related to the costs of production of each good and service; in the market economy the price of each good and service is closely related to its costs of production.

In a command economy the funds necessary to finance the costs of government are collected in the prices of goods (essentially a sales tax); in the market economy, direct taxes on personal income and corporate income provide a significant part of fiscal revenues, but many governments also rely on value added taxes and sales taxes.

In a command economy the major task of the factory manager is to produce the volume of goods necessary to satisfy the targets set by the central planners; in the market economy the major task of the factory manager is to design the goods that the consumers are eager to buy.

In a command economy everyone had a job and there was full employment; in the market economy there have been high levels of unemployment because some individuals wanted to take more out of the pot in the form of wages than they were contributing to the pot in the form of productivity. In effect they weren't earning their keep – which meant that they had discovered a free lunch or a partial free lunch.

In a market economy each worker receives the value of his or her marginal product – at least, that is what the textbooks say.

In the command economy engineers are at the top of the decision-making hierarchies; in the market economy the marketing specialists and the finance MBAs are at the top of the hierarchies.

In a command economy of what had been the Soviet Union there was a strong belief in economies of scale, and that unit production costs would be minimized if the total amount of each good that was to be produced in accord with the plan were made in one factory. One state-owned factory would produce all of the large trucks, another all of the machine tools, a third, all of the shoes, and so on. The factories that produced certain inputs would at times be at a considerable distance, and even in different countries, from the factories that used these inputs.

In the command economy there are no commercial disputes because there is no private property; in the market economy there is a need for a system of courts – and of lawyers and independent judges – to resolve disputes between producers and consumers and among different producers.

In a command economy and in the market economy those who get to the top have sharp elbows.

With the fall of the Berlin Wall and the collapse of the Soviet Union, Russia, Ukraine, Poland, the Czech Republic, Hungary and others have all faced the same problems of getting from there to here – of moving to a market economy, and with minimum decline of GDP and minimum hardship for pensioners and others who had a secure standard of living – if at a very low level – because of the safety net in the command economy. These countries needed a new tax system. Their industrial structures were high cost and obsolete by global standards. The aircraft used by the airlines were inefficient in their use of fuel. A system of courts was necessary. Institutions had to be developed to finance imports and exports.

Some of the countries have been much more successful than others in making the transition to a market economy. One way to rank these countries is in terms of the changes in GDP and per capita GDP on the transition road. Another way to rank them is in terms of how pensioners have fared. The Czech Republic ranks high on the scorecard of the countries that have made a successful transition. So do the Baltic Republics – Estonia, Latvia, and Lithuania. In contrast, Russia and Ukraine have had many more problems in the transition, and many of the remarkable democratic reforms that had occurred in Russia when Yeltsin was Prime Minister in the 1990s have eroded under his successor, Prime Minister Putin.

During the command economy period, per capita incomes differed sharply among these countries. Per capita incomes were higher, the closer a country was to Paris, London, and Rome. Standards of living in most of these countries probably were significantly higher – in comparison with similar standards in Western Europe – than the data on per capita incomes suggest. There were two arguments, which were partially offsetting. GDP estimates would have been higher if the various goods and services had been valued at Western prices. The currencies were partially overvalued prior to the move to the market economy.

The history of what had been the Democratic Republic of Germany – more popularly known as East Germany – differs sharply from every other command economy because Germany was reunified in 1990 (the first German unification occurred in the 1870s) and the Bonn Government spent $100 billion a year – roughly $5000 per individual – to increase the living standards of the 17 million people who lived in what had been the East. The West German Government believed that this massive subsidy was needed to induce the East Germans to remain in their home towns; otherwise millions of East Germans would have moved to Hamburg and Frankfurt and Munich, or a new counterpart to the Berlin Wall would be needed to prevent them from moving west. The increase in per capita incomes in what had been East Germany primarily resulted from subsidies rather than from increases in productivity; the unemployment rate in what had been East Germany has remained much higher than in what had been West Germany.

The transition economies have received financial transfers, including loans from the World Bank and the European Bank for Reconstruction and Development (EBRD), the International Monetary Fund (IMF), as well as investments by firms headquartered in Germany, France, the United States, Japan, and South Korea. German firms invested extensively in the Czech Republic: Skoda, the Czech auto firm, was acquired by Volkswagen. General Electric (GE) purchased the large electric-lightbulb factory in Hungary. Various Western petroleum companies invested in Russia. The financial transfers from the West Germans to the East Germans are several hundred times larger than the transfers to the more than 20 countries that have made the same journey.

One of the key questions is why some countries have made a more successful transition than others. A related observation is that the score on the transition appears related to geographic location – the further west the country, the more successful the transition. The basic problems include development of market institutions, privatization, fiscal reform and macro stabilization, and industrial efficiency.

Where do market institutions come from?

A pervasive observation is that the desire of individuals to trade is universal. There are street markets in virtually every country in the world. Such markets were extensive in the command economies, even when they were illegal. The move from street markets to a market economy is not linear – a market economy has a lot of institutional arrangements that are more or less taken for granted; street markets cannot be readily extrapolated into a market economy.

A market economy has accountants who compute the profits of individual firms and their tax liabilities; the accountants provide information to the share-owners about the profits of individual firms that are a check on the statements of the managers. Moreover, the accountants compute the tax liabilities of both firms and individuals. There are few, if any, accountants in a command economy, since there is little need for estimation of profits or of tax liabilities. The cash associated with the sales of the output of individual firms goes to the bank accounts of the state rather than to the bank accounts of the firms so the firms lack the cash to upgrade their factories or even to keep them in good repair.

A market economy has lawyers who facilitate the resolution of commercial disputes. Disputes are inevitable when property is privately owned. Mechanisms – especially low-cost mechanisms – are needed to resolve these disputes. Moreover, a market economy has judges and courts that are deemed impartial. These lawyers and judges and the set of laws cannot be readily obtained from a mail order catalog.

A market economy has banks with loan officers who help allocate household savings. Training individuals to estimate the profitability of individual borrowers and the likelihood that they will honor their commitments to repay the borrowed money is complex. There's a bit of a chicken and an egg problem here: borrowers can't develop their credit reputations until they have received loans, but their ability to develop a reputation for repaying on time can be determined only after they have received loans.

The common feature of accountants, lawyers and judges, and loan officers is that they involve *trust*. Trust was in short supply in command economies, which relied on coercion to implement the decisions made at the center. Decision-making in a command economy was not transparent; the consequence of the centralized approach to decision-making was that the citizens developed a cynical approach to the state.

Industrial restructuring

Tourists in Moscow have the opportunity to view the world's largest bell and the world's largest cannon when they visit the Kremlin. The bell was never used because it developed a large crack during the casting process. Fortunately, the cannon was never fired because the barrel almost certainly would have exploded because of the large charge designed to propel the shell. The Russians appear to have a fixation with size; large is often deemed better. The Russians have the largest aircraft and the largest airline.

It is as if there is a strong belief in the economies of scale and ignorance about the diseconomies of scale. Large is large, very large is very large, but very large often is not efficient. Efficiency may seem irrelevant in a Marxist world of monopoly producers, but efficiency become central in a competitive world.

One of the major problems of the former command economies involved restructuring their industry so that individual firms could be competitive in a global economy. The central planners in Moscow had a strong belief in the economies of scale – each type of good would be produced in only one factory. Many of the factories would be in or near one of the major Russian cities, and a few of the factories would be in the satellite countries. Each factory had relatively little competition, at least within the Eastern bloc – whatever was produced would be sold. And if some goods couldn't find buyers, that was the problem of the planners, not of the factory managers. The attention to marketing, quality control, and consumer satisfaction was minimal; firms sold into what were captive markets.

The shift from the command economy to the market economy was wrenching, especially for Poland and its neighbors that wanted to reorient themselves to the West. The problem was especially severe for the factories.

The firms that produced raw materials and primary products found the adjustment much easier, since these goods were commodities and almost always homogeneous. Russian nickel and Canadian nickel were perfect substitutes and sold on the basis of price. Similarly Russian aluminum was more or less identical with the same metal produced in the West.

They might rely on Western firms to help reduce costs. A few of the former command economies may be able to make their way in the world by exporting raw materials, much like some of the countries in the Middle East, Africa, and Latin America. Several earn and will continue to earn lots of foreign currencies from tourism; several will earn foreign exchange from the remittances from nationals who are guest workers abroad. Hundreds of thousands of Poles and Lithuanians have moved to Britain and Ireland in search of higher incomes. The key question involves the efficiency of industry – the steel mills, auto and truck factories, textile and apparel factories, food producing factories, factories that produce machine tools, lightbulbs, and toothpaste. The managers of these plants are caught in the classic 'Catch-22' situation. To update the plants, they need huge investment capital. Even though the savings rates in these economies are not low, the countries lack the institutional mechanisms to allocate these savings among the firms with the greatest productive potential.

The costs of the manufacturing firms in these former command economies are so high and the industrial plant so obsolete – by Western standards – that the efficient solution often is to abandon the enterprise. The problem is the lack of employment opportunities for the workers who will be displaced; the labor force in many of these factories was large relative to the value of output because there was no tradition of minimizing costs. The quality of the products from many of these factories has been low by the standards of Western goods, and the workers in the factories have not had the experience that their incomes will depend on the quality of the goods they produce.

Macro stabilization and the price level

Most of the former command economies experienced hyperinflation – increases in their price levels of more than 50 percent a month for a year or two – in the transition to a market economy. In contrast, each of these countries generally had a low inflation rate during the years of the command economy, because the prices of most goods and many services were set by the authorities rather than by the market – hence 'queuing time' cleared the markets. Those with the sharpest elbows, the greatest patience, and close friends in high places got the goods while the others allowed their money holdings to accumulate. There were black markets in both domestic goods and imported goods, and the prices in these markets were not included when the inflation rate was measured.

Part of the increase in money holdings consisted of the increase in savings deposits in state banks and the rest of the increase was in holdings of currency notes. Some individuals increased their holdings of US dollars and German marks even though the purchases of foreign currencies were illegal. Changes in relative prices were inevitable as these countries moved to a market economy. The alignment of the prices of particular goods and services changed to match the alignment of prices of the same goods and services in the world economy. The prices of petroleum and various petroleum products rose to the world price level, or else various investors bought oil in the East to sell in the West. Similarly goods which are cheap in the West – manufactures such as automobiles and various electronic goods – would be imported. Tariffs and other trade barriers could drive wedges between the prices in the West and the prices in the transition economies – and these wedges might be 30 or 40 percent.

The change in relative prices inevitable in the integration into the world economy should be distinguished from the increase in general price levels which resulted from the combination of a self-fulfilling prophecy and the problems of developing a tax system appropriate for a market economy – and collecting the taxes necessary to pay for government expenditures. During the command economy period, government expenditures varied from 60 to 80 percent of GDP; the ratio was higher in those countries in which agricultural production occurred on state-owned farms. Because these high taxes became embedded in the prices of goods, the prices of these goods were extremely high compared with the prices of similar goods in Western economies. Footwear, clothing, and household goods had much higher prices than their Western counterparts, but a large component of the high price was the indirect tax.

The cliché in the West was that the workers in the East had to work 15–20 times as long to buy a pair of shoes. The major reason shoes were so expensive was that shoes were heavily taxed – the difference between the price of the shoes and the cost of their production was used to finance subsidies for housing, medical and health care services, the military, and the general costs of government. With the move to the market economy, the decline in the price of shoes meant that the major source of tax revenues declined. No one would have continued to buy these shoes given that shoes produced in the market economies could be imported. So the governments needed to increase taxes and at the same time, they needed to reduce subsidies to those factories and other enterprises whose revenues were below their costs.

These countries need to develop a new tax system. Because spending by the government sector remained high as a share of GDP, tax rates had to be high. The taxes could be direct or indirect. There is little tradition of paying taxes: individuals were reluctant to pay taxes because government waste was evident. But the governments were reluctant to reduce waste quickly because that meant they had to reduce the 'hidden unemployment' on the factory floor.

Privatization

In command economies the means of production are owned by the state. The problem was to transfer titles of ownership of factories, airlines, banks, homes and apartments, land, local bus systems, corner grocery stores, gas stations, butchers, bakers, and the candlestick-makers.

Consider the basic alternative approaches toward privatization. One is to give the factories and shops to the workers, another is to give the assets to the citizens at large, and a third is to sell the assets for the highest possible or the second highest possible price. These approaches can be combined – 10 or 20 percent of the shares might be given to the employees, 30 or 40 percent might be given to the citizens, and the remaining shares might be sold to the highest bidders. These ratios might differ by firm and the size of the business unit.

In the West, governments that have privatized have often first reorganized the productive enterprises into a few independent government-owned firms that were given ownership titles to particular assets – factories, airlines, mines, and oil wells. Various measures were then undertaken to reduce the costs of these firms, often by inducing employees to take early retirement. Then shares in the firms were either sold to the public or distributed to the public or both; often the shares were sold in an auction, usually to the highest bidders. Once the firms had become profitable, buyers could easily be found; there were few serious potential buyers for firms that were not profitable because the potential buyers were reluctant to incur the turmoil associated with reducing employment until profits were achieved.

Consider the range of possible buyers. One is the public at large; since all the factories had been owned in common, shares in these factories might be distributed to the public much like an income tax refund, except that each citizen would get the same number of shares.

(Of course there are problems – would children qualify? What about citizens that are living in foreign countries?) This broad-scale distribution would not work well for apartments, but then individuals might be given the apartments that they were living in and perhaps even the small shops where they worked. Or, alternatively, the plants might be given to the employees; the employees would then have to decide on each one's share of the total ownership. Or the shares might be sold to citizens at large.

The difficulty in selling the shares is that relatively few individuals would have had the cash to buy them. Moreover, a nontrivial number with the cash may have acquired it in ways that 'bent the rules' under the old system. Because cash was so limited the amount offered for these firms would generally be low relative to the intrinsic value of the enterprise. The shares in a particular enterprise might be sold in stages – 20 percent in the first year, and then 20 or 30 percent in each of the next several years. If shares were to be sold, will foreigners be allowed to bid for the shares – if not, will foreigners be allowed to buy the shares in the secondary market?

There is an asymmetry in the privatization process. The demand would be relatively strong for those productive activities that would be immediately profitable to the new owners and weak for those activities not likely to be profitable.

President Yeltsin decided that the quickest way to promote democracy in Russia was to privatize industry at a very rapid rate; Russia would become a much more plural society. One reason for the eagerness to privatize was that the government was in desperate need for cash, because the tax base had eroded rapidly in the move from the command economy to the market economy. Those with the cash often had developed new private banks. The rapid sale of some of the government properties – especially in the resource extraction industries – led to the rapid rise of the oligarchs.

The debacle in Russian finance

A major shock occurred in Russia in the summer of 1998; the government's fiscal deficit then was nearly 10 percent of its GDP. Various types of wage and payments arrears had developed because tax collections increased too slowly and the government could not reduce its expenditure. The interest rates on the ruble debt, which had been 30 percent in April, increased to 60 and 90 percent; at these levels the surge in interest payments meant that the government debt would double in less than a year. There was a race between the ability of the Russian Government to reduce its fiscal deficit before the increase in interest payments was so large that the government would be forced to default. The sharp increase in interest rates on ruble debt partly reflected that the ruble might be devalued, and partly that the Russian Government would default on its debt. The Russian Government was caught between a rock and a hard place. Tax rates were extremely high because tax collections were so low. No one – well, hardly anyone – could afford to pay all the taxes they were supposed to pay.

The Russians tried to reduce the crunch in two ways. The first was that the ruble debt was swapped into US dollar debt, which reduced the amount of the ruble debt to be financed. The second was that the IMF provided loan commitments of more than $20 billion; the actual cash would be available as the Russians succeeded in reducing their fiscal deficit.

The Russian Government both defaulted and devalued, and the ruble lost more than half of its value. The paradox was that individual Russians had stashed US$50–$100 billion outside their own country – including tens of billions in the form of holdings of US dollar currency notes and German mark currency notes. The flow of funds from Moscow was several times larger than the flow of foreign loans to Moscow. The Russians – at least the Russians with access to cash – had relatively little trust in their own banks and their own government.

Prime Minister Putin's Seven Fat Years

The 'election' of Vladimir Putin to succeed Boris Yeltsin as President of Russia was a 1999 event. The price of oil then was in the range of $20–$30 a barrel. The oil price increased at an accelerating rate and reached nearly $100 a barrel at the end of 2007 and continued to increase through the first half of 2008. The price of natural gas increased almost as rapidly. The prices of nickel and other minerals also increased sharply. The receipts of the Russian Government also increased sharply. Moscow became a boom town, and one of the most expensive cities in the world.

Putin brought financial stability to Russia after the turmoil of the 1990s, so much so that *Time* magazine named him its 'Man of the Year.' The Putin Government recovered some of the properties from the oligarchs who had acquired them in the early 1990s, and it restricted press freedoms.

Private property remained, but without the protection of the rule of law. Foreign oil companies that were involved in joint ventures with Russian partners were 'squeezed' as long as the oil price was increasing.

The fiscal problems of the Russian Government were 'solved' by the surge in oil revenues from 2002 to 2008; Russia repaid its debts and its holdings of international reserve assets climbed to more than $600 billion. The Russian Government became much more bellicose toward some of the newly independent countries that formerly had been part of the Soviet Union. The Russians and the Ukrainians seemed to be continually squabbling over the payment for natural gas.

The sharp decline in the prices of crude petroleum and other raw materials in the global recession had a devastating impact on the value of the ruble in the currency market and on the revenues of the Russian Government. Some of the oligarchs also encountered financial headwinds, since they had borrowed a great deal of money from the Russian banks during the period when commodity prices were increasing and then effectively defaulted on their loans when the prices declined. The banks – and the Russian Government – acquired some of their properties.

If prices of crude petroleum and other minerals are high, the Russian economy will develop like an oversized principality on the Persian Gulf. The value of the ruble in the currency market will be high, and most of the country's manufactured goods and some of its services will be imported. Russia will only become a competitive producer of manufactured goods if the price of oil and other primary products is low, and then the fiscal problems of the government will be intense.

24
Fitting the Pieces Together Once Again

Someday, perhaps, the international money problem will disappear. Perhaps the nation-state will be phased out as the basic political unit; without nation-states, there won't be national monies. Or independent countries may merge their currencies into a common international currency. Sort of Globalization 100.0, the end of the sequence of the discoveries of globalization.

The impacts of the 2007 financial crisis

One impact of a financial crisis is a move to greater nationalism as political leaders seek to reduce distress and provide increased employment for their voters and supporters. The Great Depression of the 1930s was associated with an extremely sharp decline in international trade, in part because of the much lower level of economic activity and in part because of the sharp increase in import barriers.

The political turmoil in Europe in the 1930s often has been attributed to the macroeconomic dislocations and the 'beggar-thy-neighbor' policies of individual countries as they manipulated currency values to enhance domestic employment. This view led to the ambitious initiatives of the 1940s to develop new international economic institutions that would forestall a repetition of the inward-looking policies of the 1930s. The International Monetary Fund (IMF) was designed to provide an orderly framework for changes in currency values, while the World Bank, more formally the International Bank for Reconstruction and Development (IBRD), would facilitate the economic recovery in Western Europe. The proposed International Trade Organization (ITO) was stillborn, although its preamble, the General Agreement on Trade and Tariffs (GATT), provided a framework for the negotiation of tariff reductions and for the resolution of trade disputes. The establishment of the World Trade Organization (WTO) in 1995 can be viewed as the delayed birth of the ITO.

Forty-four countries participated in the negotiations that led to the establishment of the Fund, the Bank, and the GATT; the United States and Britain took much of the lead in developing these treaties. Japan and Germany, two of the countries that have since become very important in international trade and finance, were not present because they were opponents of the United States and Great Britain in the Second World War. Some of the other European countries were represented by governments-in-exile. The US role was dominant, in part because of its relatively large economic size.

The enhancement of living standards in the six decades since the end of the Second World War has been remarkable and unprecedented, and a result in large part of the ability of many countries to industrialize. Their exports of manufactures have increased at a rapid rate, and in large part because foreign markets have been open.

A major question is how much of the global prosperity in the second half of the twentieth century can be attributed to the Fund, the Bank, and the GATT. The GATT, with its attention to reducing trade barriers, has been extremely important because economic growth has been associated with openness. The waves of financial crises that began in the early 1980s are a knock on the Fund, which almost appears to have abandoned its initial raison d'être of enhancing international financial stability. The succession of senior managers at the Fund has been much too complacent about origins and consequences of systematic and persistent imbalances.

Once the global economy moves past the crisis that began in 2007 there almost certainly will be new initiatives toward developing institutions that will reduce the likelihood of new waves of bubbles and crises.

A common international currency?

One perennial reform proposal is for a common international currency. Consider the negotiations that would lead to that development. How many countries would be involved – now more than 150 countries are members of the IMF. Virtually every one of the newly independent countries has opted for its own currency, and some have gradually moved to monetary policies directed at their domestic objectives. Many other countries, long independent, have also oriented their monetary policies to domestic objectives.

The nation-state appears unlikely to disappear in the foreseeable future as the basic unit for organizing political activity – for supplying law and order, and deciding on income distribution and economic priorities. Nor is there any indication of a broad-based movement toward the merger of national monies, except in the context of the European Union (EU). There is a lot of chatter in Asian capitals about a common currency – but thus far only chatter. No other group of nations seems close to planning seriously for a common money. Trade patterns of these countries suggest that the adoption of a common currency will be much more difficult than the adoption of the euro.

A merger of national monies makes economic sense only if the economic structures of the participating countries are similar – if their business cycles have similar phasing, if their labor forces grow at a similar rate and are similar in terms of skills, and if their preferences for price stability and full employment are also similar. The adoption of a common currency in Europe followed 40 years of measures to integrate the European economies by abolishing barriers to trade among the member countries – and even then much of the motivation was political, aiming to use economic harmonization as a way to enhance sufficient political cohesion so that there would not be another disastrous war within Europe.

Vested interests within many countries would strongly oppose the merger of currencies since the control over the rate of growth of a national money is closely linked with the exercise of sovereignty. Management of the rate of growth of the money supply is one of the most effective measures available to government leaders as they seek increased support from their constituents.

National monetary policies are responsive to domestic political forces – the employment level and the inflation rate and interest rates have important impacts on election outcomes. The price levels tend to increase more rapidly in some countries than in others, and often the countries with higher inflation rates develop payments deficits. Eventually adjustments are needed to restore payments balance – or reduce extensive imbalances. Either currency values change, or some other variables must be adjusted so that the imbalances decline to sustainable values.

Inevitably, the anticipation of changes in currency values leads to complicated management decisions in profit-oriented business firms because the amount and the timing of these changes are uncertain. These changes in currency values can have a more important impact on reported profits – or losses – than traditional production and marketing decisions. If some firms earn profits from these changes then losses will be incurred by others – either the central banks, the commercial banks, or individual investors. The movement of money across borders in anticipation of changes in currency values often has taken the initiative away from the authorities; they may be forced to alter their parities or their monetary policies or their exchange controls on payments. Moreover, the authorities in the countries with the trade or payments deficits and their counterparts in the countries with the surpluses are frequently at odds about who should take the initiative in adopting measures to reduce the imbalance. And they also disagree about the best policies to use, especially whether market forces are superior to bureaucratic decisions.

The collapse of rules

The increasingly domestic focus of national monetary policies led to the breakdown and collapse of the IMF rules about adjustable parities in the early 1970s; several countries in Western Europe concluded that the US Government was too complacent about the increase in the US inflation rate. The IMF rules about changes in parities were a guide to national behavior: they indicated when countries could change their parities and when they could not, and when they could use controls on international payments and when they could not. These rules had been adopted to reduce the likelihood that a country might export its unemployment problem or its inflation problem as it attempted to solve its own problems. Smaller countries wanted to be protected against the likelihood that they might import unemployment or inflation from a large trading partner while the large countries wanted to be protected from the 'free-riding' tendencies of smaller countries.

That the IMF agreement on changes in currency values became obsolete should not be a surprise, for the history of most international financial agreements is that they last for only a decade or two. Then, when the economic circumstances for which the rules were intended change, the rules become passé. (Although the institutions established to manage the rules live on and the employment rosters in these institutions increase.) While it might be possible to design a set of rules sufficiently broad to cope with all possible changes in the international financial environment, such rules would almost certainly be so general that they would have no bite or impact. The purpose of the rules is to increase the confidence that each country can have about the policies of its trading partners. Few countries, however, are likely to accept severe constraints on their freedom of actions – or to abide by the constraints if doing do is expensive to their domestic objectives.

Two events occurred in the 1970s that were not contemplated when the IMF rules were drafted in the 1940s. One was world inflation and the unwillingness of Germany to accept an increase in its inflation rate comparable to the increase that was acceptable in the United States. The second was the decline in the relative economic position of the United States, evidenced by the more rapid growth in Germany and Japan, and subsequently by many countries in Asia and particularly China and India.

New rules or new international monetary institutions?

New sets of rules might be negotiated to deal with several different international financial issues. Rules could be directed to limit the intervention of national central banks in the foreign exchange market. Or rules might be directed to limit the purchases of international reserve assets by individual central banks – which would affect their exchange market interventional activity. Rules might be adopted to limit trade imbalances, and especially the ratios of trade surpluses and trade deficits to GDP. In the absence of new rules, ad hoc approaches will be adopted to cope with changes in currency values or imbalances. Each country is likely to adopt the measures that suit its immediate needs and interests, with minimal regard for the consequences for its trading partners – and for the global system.

Designing the arrangement most likely to work requires foreknowledge of the types of economic problems that are likely to be dominant in the next 5, 10, and 20 years. Unemployment? Inflation? Unemployment and inflation simultaneously, stagflation all over again? Will recessions and booms occur at the same time in the United States and Western Europe, or will they occur at different times? Will nationalism continue to become more powerful, or will the pendulum swing? And will individual countries become more sympathetic toward relying on market forces to resolve imbalances or will they instead move toward greater acceptance of bureaucratic regulations? Will the worldwide move toward more conservative economic policies continue or will governments become more interventionist especially in the aftermath of the global slowdown and recession? The types of rules most likely to be effective in resolving international imbalances vary with the answers to these questions.

One frequently mentioned alternative to new rules is to rely on an international authority: to endow those who manage the international monetary institutions – the IMF and its successors – with the power to make those decisions deemed necessary for greater international financial stability. But this approach seems unlikely in the next 10–15 years, for one counterpart to the increased attention to domestic objectives is most countries' increased reluctance to delegate substantial decision-making power to an international institution. The larger countries – the United States, Germany, France, Italy, Spain, China, Japan, and Britain – might conclude that representatives from smaller countries would have too great a voice in the international institutions. The IMF did not emerge from the Mexican crisis of 1994 or from the Asian crisis of 1997 or from the Russian crisis of 1998 or from the Argentinean crisis of 2001 with glory; the cliché that the Fund is always 'behind the curve' seems applicable. The Fund seemed to ignore the bubbles in real estate markets that preceded the global recession. There would be increasing reluctance to delegate more power to the IMF or a similar institution. Almost inevitably, the important decisions are likely to be made in national capitals. The managers of international institutions are increasingly responsible to committees of representatives from national capitals – the G-3, the G-7, the G-20, the G-44; the international civil servants will police the rules, but they will not make the rules, nor will they determine when the countries should change their policies about supporting their currencies in the foreign exchange market.

Crises – especially over changes in currency values – are inevitable in a world of more than 100 currencies. While the US authorities, the Canadian authorities, the authorities at the European Central Bank (ECB), and many economists continue to favor a world without fixed values for national currencies, many countries, especially the smaller ones, appear committed to a return to some form of an adjustable parity arrangement. The more important foreign trade is to a country's economy, the stronger its commitment to a parity for its currency. The authorities in some countries have concluded that the reliance of market forces to determine currency values was not the panacea that its proponents had promised. The Americans and the Europeans believe that a return to parities for currencies will impose constraints and complicate the attainment of their employment and price-level objectives. The Germans are concerned that once again they will import inflation from their more expansive neighbors, while the Americans are concerned about once again taking on an external constraint on US domestic economic policies; they are also concerned – they should also be concerned – that some countries are free-riders, and maintain extremely low values for their currencies as a way to import jobs.

The paradox is that the period since the breakdown of the Bretton Woods system has been one of exceptional growth in the world economy. But there also have been four waves of financial crises; each has been preceded by a credit bubble. The range of movement in currency values has been exceptionally large, much larger than would have been forecast based on the differences in the national inflation rates.

A second feature is the remarkable change in the US international investment position from the world's largest creditor to the world's largest debtor country, which resulted from the surge in the foreign demand for US dollar securities and US real assets. The annual increases in US net international indebtedness seem too large to be sustained indefinitely, although this indebtedness position could continue for an extended period at lower annual values.

Exchange controls

One of the clichés of international finance is that independent national monetary policies, pegged values for currencies, and free capital movements are not compatible. Parities are sustainable only if capital movements are constrained by controls. The severity of this conundrum depends in part on the width of the support limits.

The alternative to changes in currency values as a way to balance international payments and receipts is direct regulation of international payments through exchange controls. The stylized fact is that these controls tend to be adopted during wars or some other major crisis. One attraction of greater reliance on controls is that domestic political costs may seem smaller. The objection to increased reliance on an exchange-controls approach is that it fragments the international economy, for transactions in different types of securities tend to be subject to different controls, especially if relatively few transactions are controlled. The more comprehensive and uniform the controls over imports and exports of goods as well as securities, the more nearly this approach is equivalent to a change in currency values. The distinction is that bureaucrats rather than market forces determine when the effective value for a currency is changed. But while academicians talk about the attractions of controls as long as they are comprehensive, the bureaucrats and politicians are likely to find compelling reasons for numerous exceptions to comprehensive controls. Eventually, the rules must deal with the issue: what are the acceptable forms of controls, when can they be used, and how do they relate to changes in currency values?

The role of gold

If there is to be a move away from floating exchange rates toward some form of adjustable parity arrangement, the adequacy of international reserve assets will again be of great concern, despite the surge in the US dollar holdings of central banks in Europe, Japan, China, and other developing countries. Central bankers will again ask whether gold should have a monetary role. A closely related issue is whether the US dollar holdings of foreign central banks will be convertible into gold or some other asset. Now, any central bank is free to acquire gold, but at the prevailing price in the private market.

As long as foreign central banks hold more than $6000 billion in US dollar securities, the US Treasury will be reluctant to accept convertibility of the dollar into other international monies because of the fear that there might be a run on the dollar. Either gold will increasingly lose its monetary role or central banks will tend to formalize arrangements to deal in gold at prices nearer the market price. Gold demonetization could occur passively: central banks could continue to sell gold in the private market. Such sales are likely to be minimal until the conviction spreads that gold will be demonetized. Some central banks might even be buyers in the commodity market.

The gradual demonetization of gold would require agreement on a comprehensive arrangement to produce a new international money; otherwise there might again develop a shortage of international reserve assets. The paradox is that the decline in credibility resulting from US gold demonetization may make it more difficult to obtain agreement on alternative means to produce international money. In any negotiations, the Europeans would be preoccupied with the concern that if the United States could effectively demonetize gold they might later 'demonetize' the new international money by refusing to buy it in exchange for the US dollar.

The alternative to gold demonetization – a worldwide increase in the price of gold – seems less impractical and unlikely than it did 20 years ago, even though most economists and editorial writers deplore the use of a 'barbarous relic' as money. While the continued use of gold as money may be barbarous, the continued demand for gold reflects that many nations lack faith in the commitments of their major trading partners, and so they put more value in a commodity money than in a paper money. Their decision may be wise or unwise – but it is their decision. Most of the objections that stalled the inevitable increase in the monetary price in the 1960s are irrelevant because of the sharp increase in the market price of gold. Relatively little attention was given to the implications of a higher gold price (or of gold demonetization) for monetary arrangements. And while taking gold out of the mines of South Africa and Russia to bury it again in the vaults of central banks is stupid, at least those who acquire the gold pay most of the costs. If once again there were a monetary price for gold, more gold would be available to satisfy the monetary demand. The increase in the monetary value of existing gold holdings would enable central banks to move toward the preferred combination of gold, dollars, and Special Drawing Right (SDRs) in their international reserve holdings. An increase in the gold price would not resolve all international monetary problems forever; no price can be fixed forever and, on the international scene, no agreement lasts forever. A US initiative to increase the world gold price has some strong arguments in its favor, however. Many Europeans prefer this solution, and they would bear nearly all the economic costs. There may even be some favorable impacts on the relationship between the US dollar and other currencies, for the ratio of US gold holdings to foreign holdings of US dollar securities would increase.

European preferences are conditioned by the monetary events of the last several decades and especially by their dependence on the United States – and their interpretation of this dependence. The countries in Western Europe want greater control over their own monetary policies, but their attitudes are ambivalent: they want to achieve payments surpluses while ensuring that the United States does not have a deficit. Such attitudes are inconsistent. They want to achieve price stability while maintaining pegged exchange rates, two objectives which are consistent only if the United States also achieves price stability.

Just as no price can be fixed forever, no currency is likely to be at the top of the hit parade forever. The shift from the US dollar into gold and other currencies in 1970 and 1971, a result of US inflation and speculation against the dollar, may suggest that the dollar's tenure as the top currency may be over. Yet the shift from US dollar may have been a short-term phenomenon, largely an anticipation of the appreciation of the German mark. Some diversification in reserve holdings is likely, primarily to supplement rather than replace the dollar. But once the principle of diversification is accepted, the practical problem of identifying the alternatives becomes central.

Political pressure will certainly develop to diminish the dollar's international role. The Europeans would like the euro to be 'an equal' to the dollar, but in the absence of a major US inflation or financial debacle such an outcome seems highly unlikely. Foreign countries do not like the asymmetry of having to revalue or devalue their own currencies relative to the US dollar; in effect, they hope that a revision of the arrangements might protect them from US inflation – they hope for an external constraint on US policy. The move toward a paper gold arrangement is an effort to use political power – the force of numbers – to provide an external constraint on the United States and to reduce the impact of US policies on other countries. The political route is taken because economic forces are still likely to keep the US dollar at the top of the hit parade.

The conflict is not unusual; it is what the international money game is all about. National interests conflict on both major issues and minor issues, and the bureaucrats and politicians know that their own roles require that they achieve gains for their constituents. Each will agree to modify institutional arrangements only if its constituents gain. Conflict is inevitable as long as there are national monies; changes in the rules and structure cannot eliminate it. The various solutions – eliminating gold, raising the gold price, relying on paper substitutes for gold, or letting exchange rates float – do not resolve the conflicts; instead, they shift the arena in which the conflicts occur.

Index

Note: Page numbers in **bold** refer to boxes and tables respectively.